Windows 95

FOR BUSY PEOPLE

Second Edition

Blueprints for Windows 95

On the following pages, we provide blueprints for some of the best ways to use Windows 95:

- Organize Your Busy Person's Desktop
- Make the Most of Multitasking
- Get Help
- Organize Your Home Office
- Go Long or Short with Filenames
- Customize Your Start Menu
- Go Looking for Trouble
- Set Up a Network
- Put It in Print

BLUEPRINT FOR BUSY PEOPLE™

Organize Your Busy Person's Desktop

Put commonly used folders on the desktop for easy access (pages 161-163).

Leave the My Computer window open to provide a quick glimpse at the resources at hand (page 85).

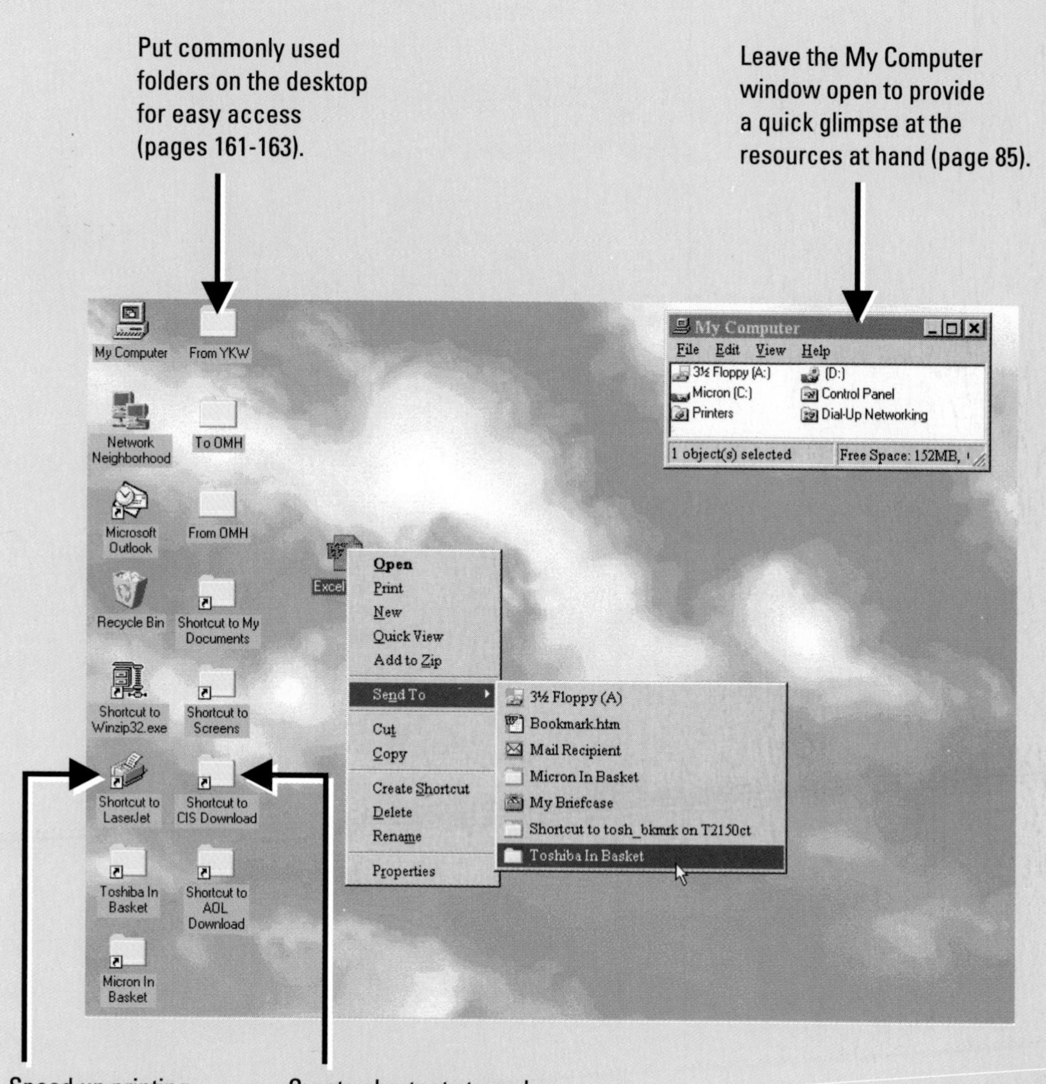

Speed up printing by adding a printer shortcut, then dragging files to it to print (page 210).

Create shortcuts to make working with downloaded files from America Online and CompuServe more efficient (pages 161-163).

BLUEPRINT FOR BUSY PEOPLE™

Make the Most of Multitasking

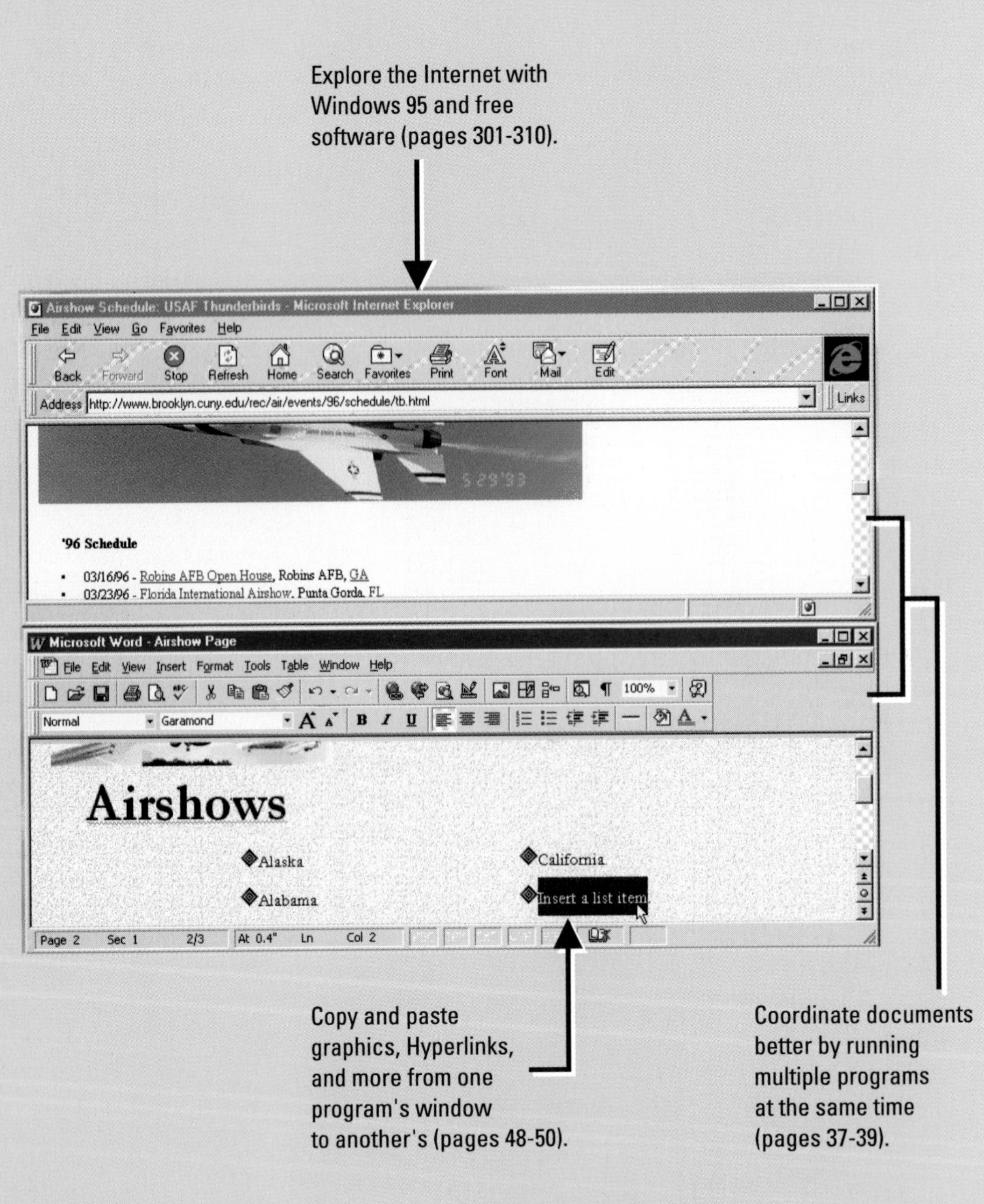

BLUEPRINT FOR BUSY PEOPLE™

Get Help

Get quick answers from the online help feature provided with most Windows programs and Windows 95 itself (pages 57-64).

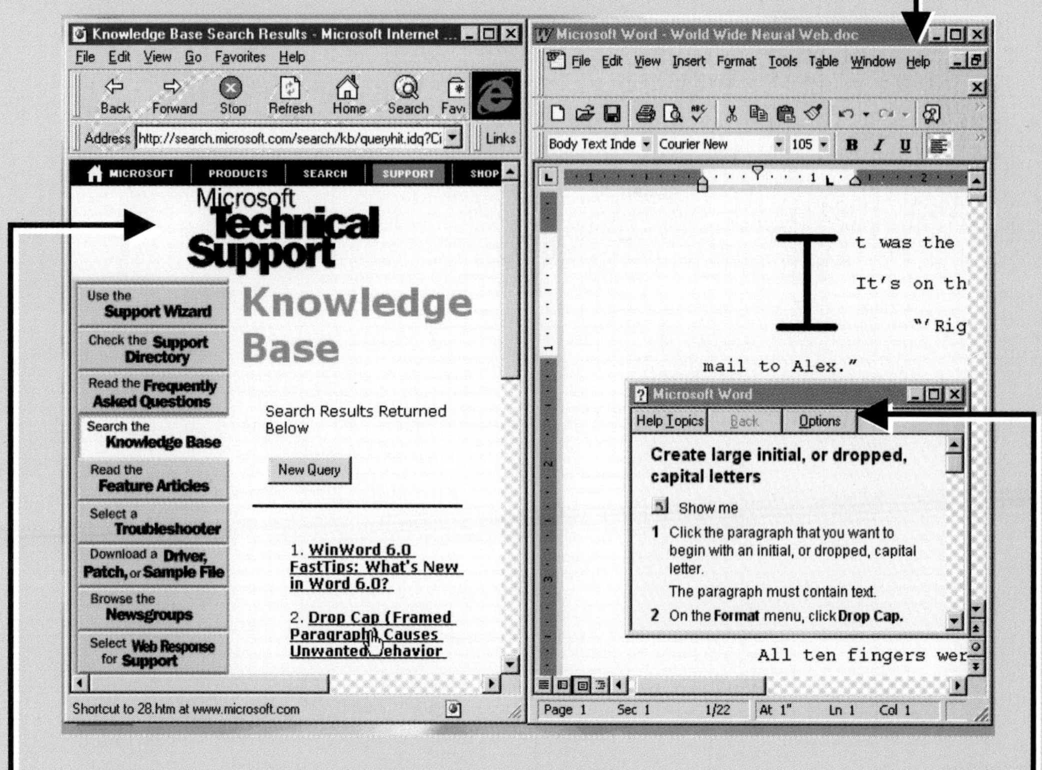

Consult the Internet for help with really tough problems (pages 69-72).

Create a hard copy reference by printing out help topics (page 66).

BLUEPRINT FOR BUSY PEOPLE™

Organize Your Home Office

Keep your personal and professional documents separate by arranging shortcuts to frequently used disks, folders and files in business and family groupings (pages 161-163).

Consider using separate hard disks for business and family documents (pages 83-84).

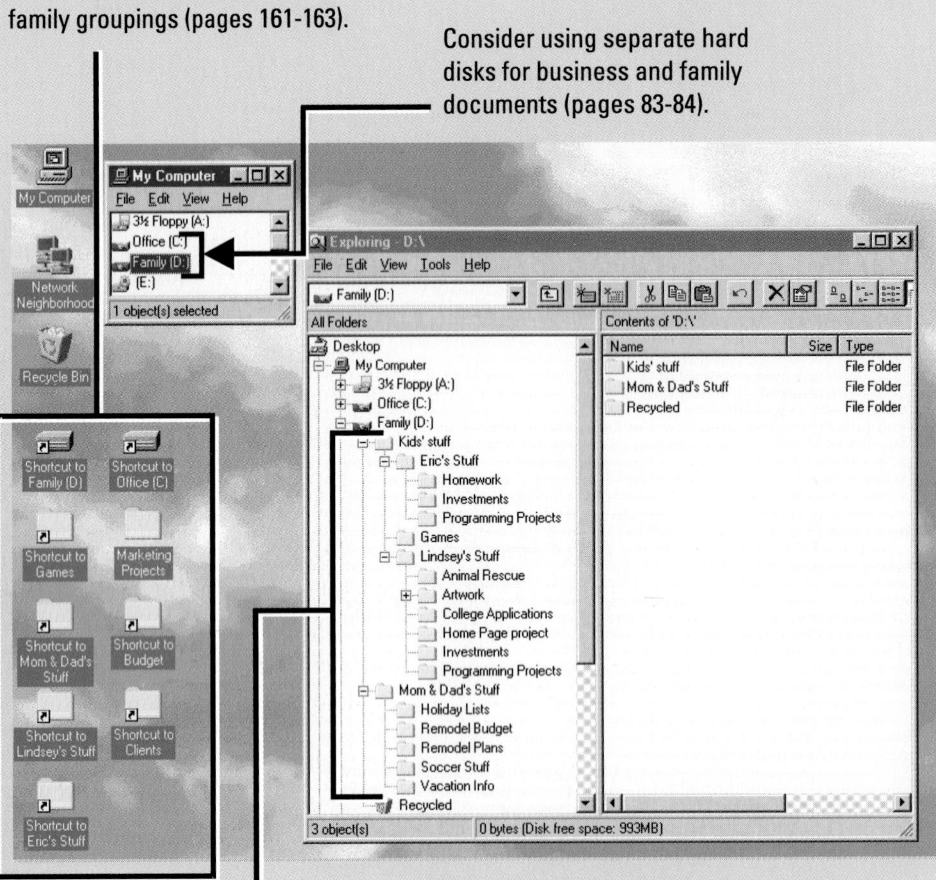

Use folders within folders to reduce clutter and keep things organized (pages 95-102).

Go Long or Short With Filenames

Some filename extensions (like ".txt" in this example) won't display in Windows 95 unless you turn on the right options (pages 109-110).

For greater flexibility and convenience you can display file information in either Windows 95 or MS-DOS (pages 22-24).

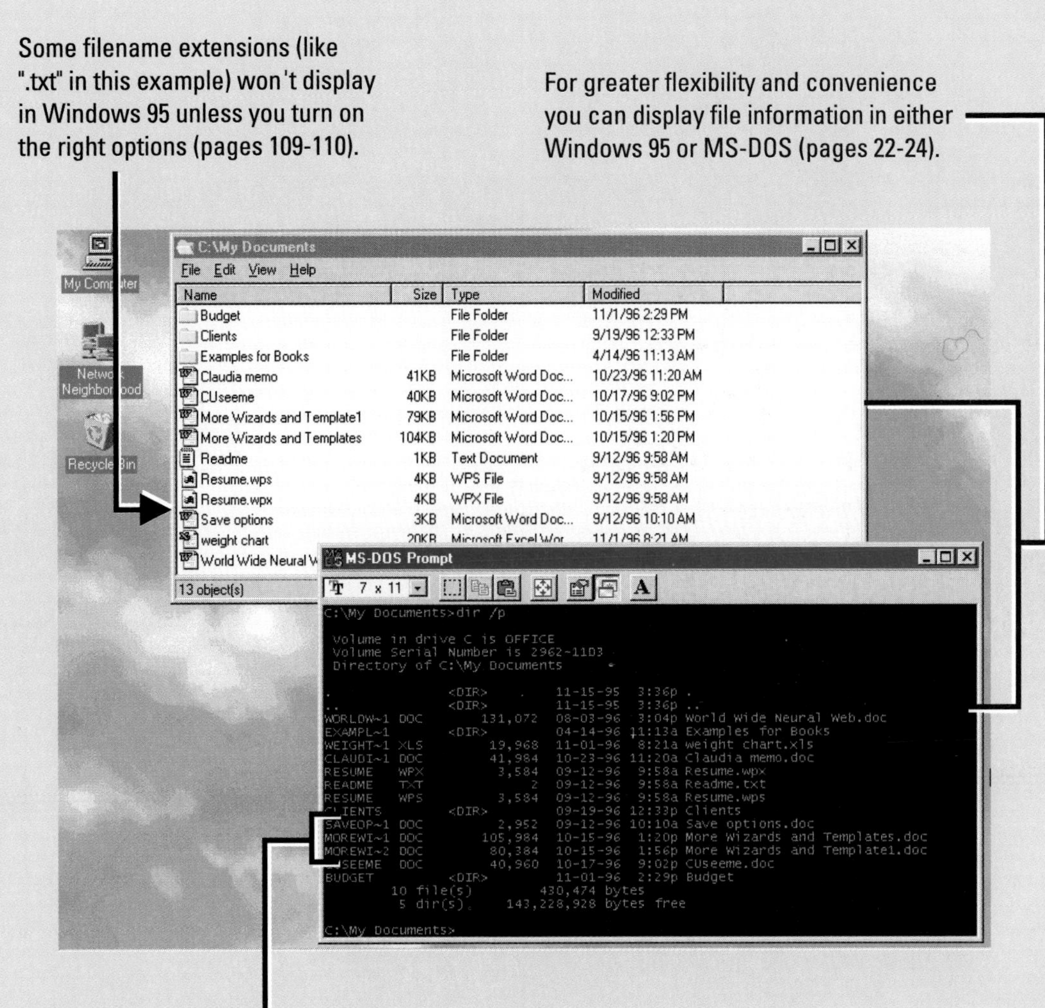

Learn how to cope with the short filename restrictions of MS-DOS and many older programs even when you create long filenames in Windows 95 (pages 107-108).

BLUEPRINT FOR BUSY PEOPLE™

Customize Your Start Menu

Tailor your Start Menu so you can quickly reach your favorite programs without wading through the rest (pages 226-228).

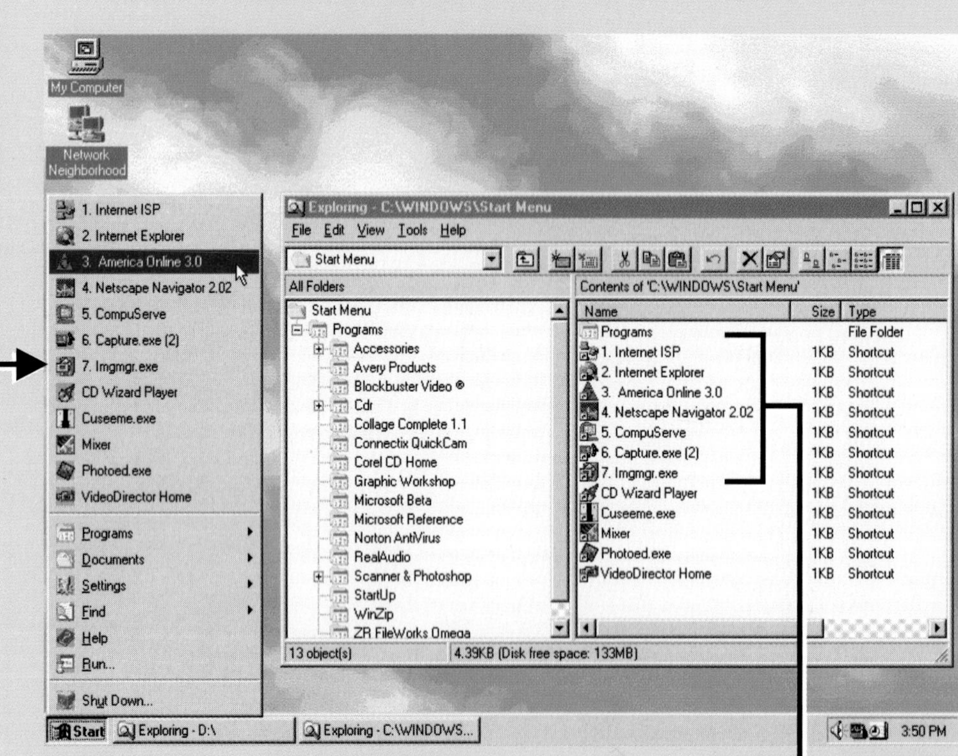

Put frequently used programs in order of preference for easy access (pages 228-229).

BLUEPRINT FOR BUSY PEOPLE™

Go Looking For Trouble

Minimize the risk of infection by purchasing a good virus detection program and keeping it current (page 143).

Avoid any damage from infected files like these word processing documents delivered via e-mail (pages 142-144).

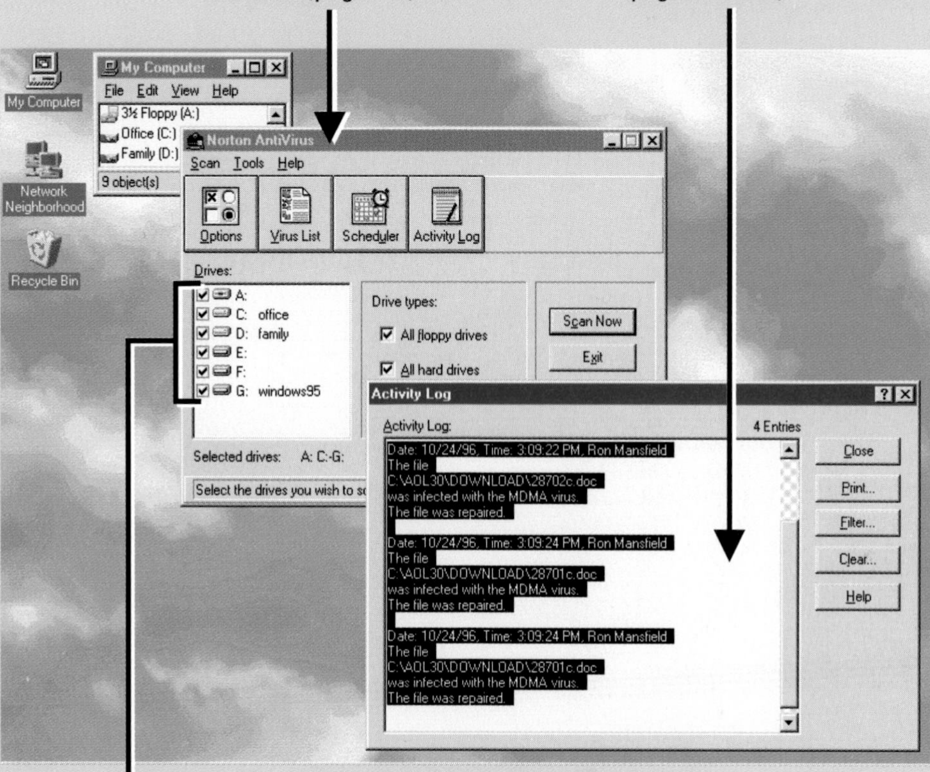

To be safe, be sure to scan all your disks including floppies and CD-ROMs regularly (pages 142-143).

BLUEPRINT
FOR BUSY PEOPLE™

Set Up a Network

Set up your own network with Windows 95's built-in networking features (pages 269-275).

Keep an eye on who is using your files (page 281).

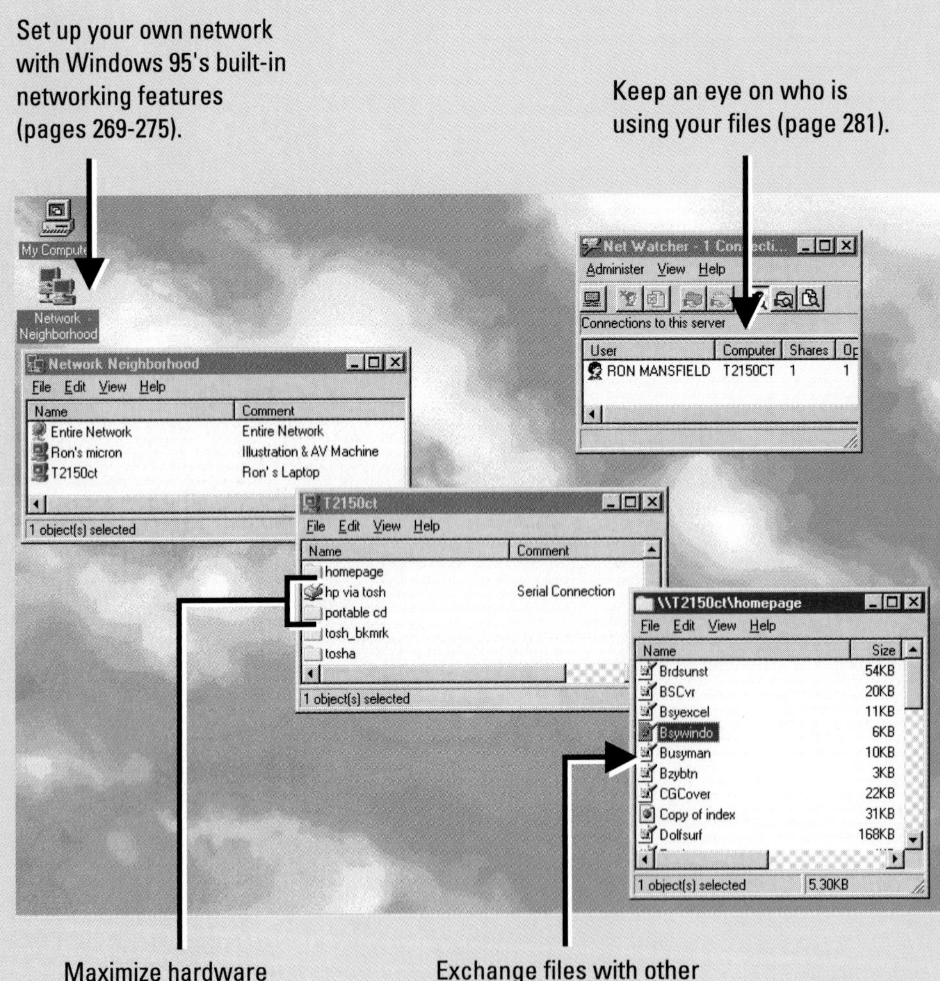

Maximize hardware use by sharing printers and CD-ROM drives (pages 278-280).

Exchange files with other computers in your home or office (pages 275-277).

BLUEPRINT FOR BUSY PEOPLE™

Put It in Print

Add fonts to make your documents more appealing (pages 212-216).

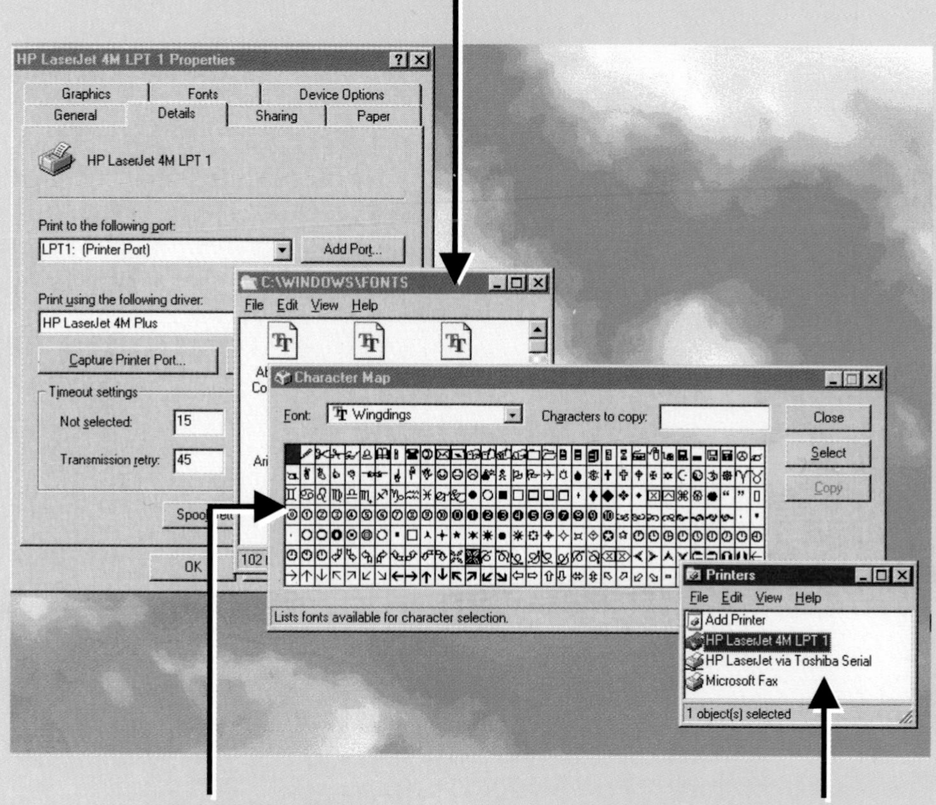

Need special characters and accent marks? Most Windows programs and printers support them (pages 217-218).

Install and configure multiple printers to increase your printing options (pages 197-205).

CAFÉ
MAIL

Windows 95 FOR BUSY PEOPLE

Second Edition

The Book to Use When There's No Time to Lose!

Ron Mansfield

OSBORNE

Osborne/**McGraw-Hill**

Berkeley / New York / St. Louis / San Francisco / Auckland / Bogotá
Hamburg / London / Madrid / Mexico City / Milan / Montreal / New Delhi
Panama City / Paris / São Paulo / Singapore / Sydney / Tokyo / Toronto

A Division of The **McGraw-Hill** *Companies*

Osborne/**McGraw-Hill**
2600 Tenth Street
Berkeley, California 94710
U.S.A.

For information on translations or book distributors outside the U.S.A., or to arrange bulk purchase discounts for sales promotions, premiums, or fundraisers, please contact Osborne/**McGraw-Hill** at the above address.

Windows 95 for Busy People, Second Edition

1234567890 DOC 9987

ISBN 0-07-882324-2

Publisher: Brandon A. Nordin
Editor in Chief: Scott Rogers
Acquisitions Editor: Joanne Cuthbertson
Project Editor: Claire Splan
Associate Project Editor: Heidi Poulin, Cynthia Douglas
Editorial Assistant: Gordon Hurd
Technical Editor: Heidi Steele
Copy Editor: Gary Morris
Proofreader: Pat Mannion
Indexer: Valerie Robbins
Graphic Artist: Lance Ravella
Computer Designers: Roberta Steele, Leslee Bassin, Peter F. Hancik
Quality Control: Joe Scuderi
Series and Cover Designer: Ted Mader Associates
Series Illustrator: Daniel Barbeau

To Bivian Marr, N.P. and Dr. Amy Rosenman, M.D.
Your alertness and loving care saved Nancy's life.

About the Author

Ron Mansfield is a microcomputer consultant and author of many best-selling, critically acclaimed computer books, with over 2,000,000 copies in print. He is a frequent lecturer at national computer seminars and has written hundreds of articles for industry magazines and newsletters. He is also the author of *Excel for Windows 95 for Busy People* and *PowerPoint for Windows 95 for Busy People.*

Contents

ACKNOWLEDGMENTS

Even after having written more than two dozen books, I am *still* amazed at how many people it takes to design, author, edit, and produce a computer text. This revision was no exception. There seemed to be yet another flood of new phone voices, e-mail addresses, and unfamiliar handwriting in the margins. So, with apologies to anyone I've missed, let me first thank Larry Levitsky, whose idea it was to create the *Busy People* series, and Brandon Nordin, who has promised to make the *Busy People* series an even bigger success than it already is.

Then there's Joanne Cuthbertson, who first introduced me to Osborne. Joanne played a key role in developing not only this book, but the entire *Busy People* series. To her credit, she was not trampled in the process, and maintained her sense of humor throughout the publishing equivalent of childbirth. It would have been a lot less fun (and perhaps even impossible) without her. But best of all, she helped me get the job done on time, and the final product looks fantastic.

Speaking of how this book *looks,* perhaps it was the design that first attracted you. Credit for that belongs to Ted Mader Associates, backed up by Osborne's own talented design team, including Roberta Steele. The illustrations and characters wandering through the pages were created by the talented Dan Barbeau. A fun touch, don't you think?

Authors would look mighty foolish without editors to remind us of our lapses and reform our bad habits. Project editor Claire Splan did her best to do both. Heidi Steele, our exceptional technical editor, also helped recreate some of the Windows screen art you see in the book. Our meticulous copy editor, Gary Morris, polished up the language, and proofreader Pat Mannion supplied that crucial last minute once-over. Thank you, one and all.

Once a book has been written, rewritten, and rewritten again, it's off to production, where the sun never sets. Marcela Hancik headed up a team of hard-working typesetters who transposed my prose into the pages you see here. Thanks to Leslee Bassin, Roberta Steele, Lance Ravella, Peter F. Hancik, and quality control guru Joe Scuderi.

Now on to the management at Osborne. Scott Rogers, Editor in Chief *par excellence,* thanks for your continuing support of the series and your marketing savvy (what a way with words!). Katherine Johnson, thanks for backing the concept from the get-go. Anne Ellingsen, thanks for helping us get noticed! And Kendal Andersen—your unique marketing ideas set us apart from the pack.

As always, my hats off to the Osborne/McGraw-Hill sales folk who convince bookstores to make room on their crowded store shelves for my work, and to you bookstore buyers who keep saying yes.

The fun thing about revising editions is you get to include comments from readers and reviewers. Thankfully, the reviews have been great, and the reader mail heart warming. Thanks one and all for the kind words!

Finally, I want to thank *you readers* for purchasing this, and my other books. Many of you have helped spread the word by telling your friends and family about my creations. It's appreciated.

Thanks, again, each and every one of you. I have you all in mind when I write.

INTRODUCTION

When Osborne/McGraw-Hill approached me about their new *Busy People* series, I couldn't wait to get started! The publisher was looking for authors who understand that many readers have only a night or a few lunch hours to learn a new software package. Certainly the digital revolution has empowered us, but it has also accelerated everyone's expectations. How often do people say to you "Fax me that draft," or "E-mail me those statistics," or "Our product release has been moved up due to competitive pressures," or "It took longer than we thought. Can you make up the time at your end?" The goal of this book is to help you meet these challenges—*fast*.

I Know You're in a Hurry, So...

Let's cut to the chase. As 150 million people now use Windows-based software, the *Busy People* series assumes that you already know computer basics. I suggest cruising through Chapters 1 and 2 first, but you'll be fine no matter how much you bounce around. In a remarkably short period of time, you'll be able to

- Start and quit Microsoft Windows 95
- Run programs

- Find, move, copy, rename, organize, protect, back up, and delete your files
- Find lost files
- Install and remove programs
- Deal with printing and font issues
- Personalize the look, feel, and sound of Windows
- Compute on a network
- Use your modem for faxing, exchanging files, dialing the phone, and more
- Create, view, and use multimedia files

Along the way you'll find timesaving tips and techniques, and advice about upgrading your hardware.

Remember, though: just because you *can* do something with Windows doesn't mean that you *should*. Simple is often best, particularly when you are busy. I'll try to remind you of that from time to time.

Windows 95: The New Paradigm

Windows 95 further refines the way you and your computer interact. Most everyday tasks are now easier to accomplish than ever before. For example, the second mouse button has become a powerful weapon. The old Windows Program Manager and File Manager have been replaced (or at least completely rethunk). The desktop tools that replace them are reminiscent of those found on a Macintosh. Speaking of Macs, there's a *Recycle Bin* (Microsoft's court-approved homage to Apple's Trash Can?) that makes it easier to recover accidentally deleted files.

Your computer will probably crash less running Windows 95 than it did with Windows 3.1 and 3.0, or even DOS. Most memory-related obstacles have been removed. Built-in networking features make it easy to reliably share files with co-workers across the room or across the world.

And, MS-DOS as we know it, while not gone, is so well hidden that you'll rarely give it a thought. Yes, you can still run DOS programs and older Windows applications with Windows 95, but busy people like you will probably want to spend most of your time using Windows 95-savvy applications, instead. Why? Well, for one thing you'll be able to use long filenames, like Letter to the President re: ashtrays instead of, say, LTPRESAT.DOC.

Microsoft says it is moving toward a time when we will all think more about our *data* and less about the specific, name-brand *programs* used to create them. The lines are already blurring as we employ tools like Object Linking and Embedding. If you believe the Microsoft public relations blitz, one day you'll forget about Microsoft Word and Excel and PowerPoint and just assemble menus of your favorite data-manipulating commands. Naturally, Microsoft will be selling us these tools, or perhaps building them into Windows 99. There are many miles to go before this becomes a reality, if it ever does. But in this book, I'll point out a few of the signposts for these new directions and try to get you into the habit of thinking about your documents and tasks rather than just about the programs you use.

Windows 95 plug-and-play compatibility makes it easy to upgrade your computer hardware. And portable computer users will like what Microsoft has done to make *their* lives calmer.

A new Windows 95 shortcuts capability makes it easy to reach frequently used files and other necessities. A new Find feature helps you locate and examine the contents of files in a flash.

Most of this is accomplished without sacrificing performance. In fact, many things (like printing) usually happen faster now, thanks to 32-bit support and other Windows 95 advancements.

A Guide to Using This Book

You can use this book as a reference, or read it cover to cover. Here's a quick run-down of the important elements you'll encounter as you go.

Blueprints

Blueprints, which you saw at the very front of the book, are illustrated examples of things you can do with your computer with Windows 95. They are designed to illustrate the response "Gee, I wish I could do that." You can. Read on.

Fast Forwards

Each chapter begins with a section called *Fast Forward.* These sections should always be your first stop if you are a confident user, or impatient, or habitually late. They offer everything you need to get back in stride. Think of these sections as the *Readers Digest* version of each chapter. Each one is, in effect, a book within a book—a quick, illustrated reference guide summarizing the key tasks explained in the chapter, point by point.

The Fast Forwards may leave you hungry, especially if you are new to Windows, so each one also includes page references to guide you to the more complete explanations later in the chapter.

Expert Advice

Don't overlook the *Expert Advice* notes. These short, highlighted paragraphs suggest timesaving tips, techniques, and worthwhile habits and addictions. (Habits and addictions can be a good thing, you know. As Mark Twain once said, "Nothing so needs reforming as other peoples habits.") The Expert Advice topics also give you the big picture and help you plan ahead. For example, the long filenames you can use in Windows 95 are great, but they cause some interesting problems if you share files with users of Windows 3.1. So I've included some suggested file-naming strategies.

Shortcuts

These are custom-designed for the busy person. When there's a way to do something that may not be as fancy as the procedure outlined in the text, but is *faster,* I described it in a highlighted box with a special Shortcut icon (just follow the bouncing necktie guy).

Cautions

Sometimes it's just too easy to plunge ahead, fall down a hole, and spend hours of extra time finding your way back to the place you were before you went astray. The familiar road sign appears in your path from time to time to warn you before you make potentially time-consuming mistakes.

Definitions

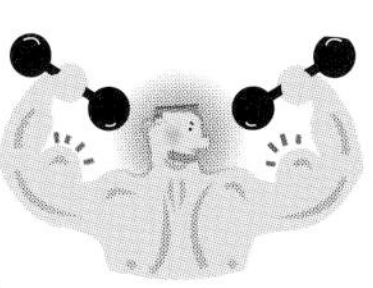

Usually, I'll explain computer jargon in the text wherever the technobabble first occurs. But occasionally you'll see a highlighted paragraph with a really buff guy next to it. Most of these definitions are informal, and they're often a little playful.

STEP BY STEP

Step-by-Steps

The sky blue *Step-by-Step* boxes that pop up throughout the text will walk you through the necessary steps of everyday tasks, using helpful illustrations. In this edition, Step-by-Steps have a new look. Hope you like it.

Upgrade Notes

If you've used earlier versions of Windows, be on the lookout for *Upgrade Notes.* They will alert you to features that are new or changed in Windows 95, and make sure you don't miss any of the latest advances.

Let's Do It!

Ready? Then order that pizza, and let's dig into Windows 95 before Windows 97 arrives!

Incidentally. I'm always happy to hear your reactions to this or any of my other books. You can reach me through the publisher, or on the net (*rmansfield@aol.com).*

PRIORITY!
MEMO:
FIRST CLASS
OVERNIGHT
RUSH!

CHAPTER

1

Starting Windows 95 and Running Programs

INCLUDES

- Starting and quitting Windows 95 and programs
- A quick Windows 95 test drive
- Windows 95 accessories and games
- Running DOS programs from within Windows 95
- Tips for the unlucky and frustrated

Start Windows 95 ➤ pp. 5-7

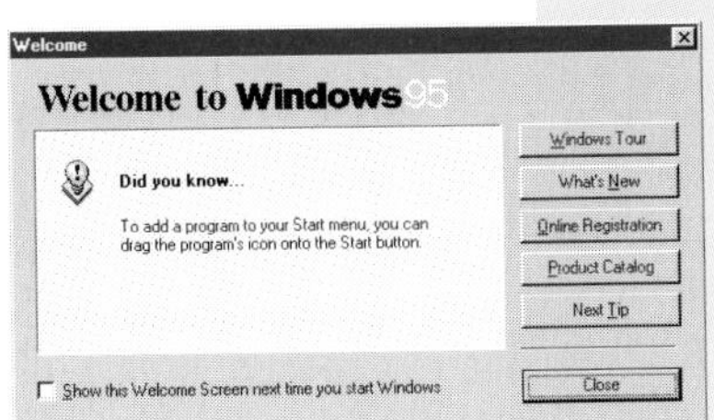

Windows 95 starts automatically when you turn on or boot your computer. If you are asked for a password, enter it (if you know it) and press ENTER or click OK. If you don't know the password, try pressing ESC, or clicking OK without typing anything. Perhaps no one has assigned a password.

Use the Taskbar and Start Menu ➤ pp. 9-13

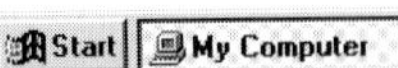

The *Taskbar* at the bottom of your screen includes the Start button. You use this button to reveal a Start menu from which you run programs, change computer settings, and perform other tasks. (If you don't see the Taskbar, slide your mouse pointer to the bottom of the screen. This should make the Taskbar appear.) When you run programs or open windows, their names appear on buttons on the Taskbar.

Start a Program ➤ pp. 13-19

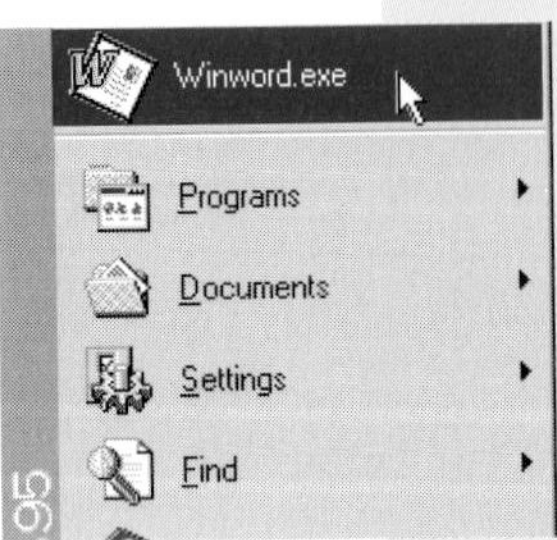

1. Click the Start button on the Taskbar. This will reveal the Start menu.
2. Point at the program or group (some menus will have multiple levels) that you wish to select, and click the mouse button.

(To use the keyboard instead of the mouse, press CTRL-ESC to bring up the Start menu, then use the arrow keys to highlight menu choices, and press ENTER to run the selected program.)

Start a Program via the Run Command ➤ *pp. 17-18*

1. Choose Run from the Start menu.
2. When the Run dialog box appears, type the path to the program you want to run, including the program's filename (**a:\ setup**, for example), or use the Browse button to find the desired program, then choose it.
3. Click OK.

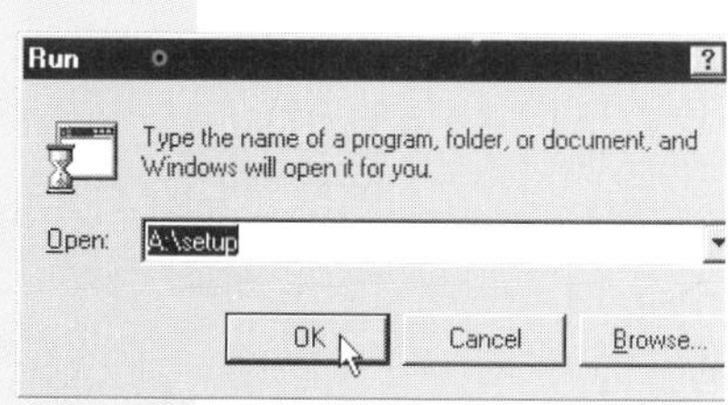

Run a Program by Selecting a Document ➤ *pp. 18-19*

Double-click on a document icon or its shortcut icon, or choose a recently used document from the Documents portion of the Start menu. Any of these actions will run the appropriate program, or reveal the program (bring it to the forefront of your screen) if it is already running.

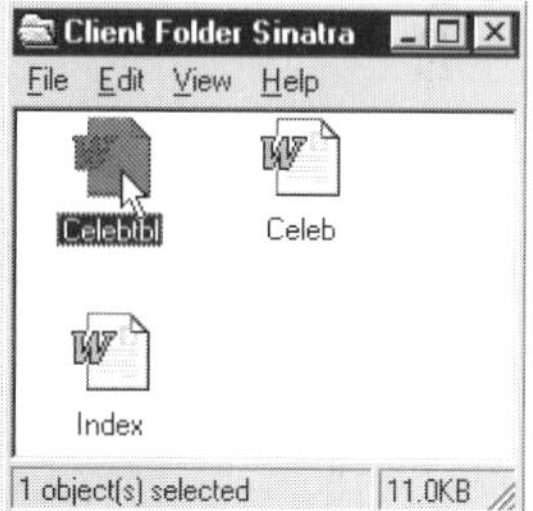

Quit a Program ➤ *pp. 19-20*

You can use any of these methods to quit programs:

- Select the Exit command on the program's File menu.
- Use the keyboard shortcut ALT-F4 or ALT- F, X.
- Close the program's primary or "parent" window.

Windows will shut down all program(s) for you after prompting for any possible saves.

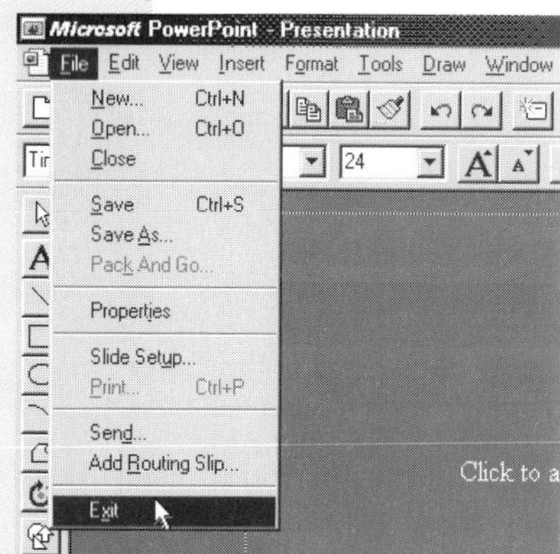

Quit Windows 95 ➤ *pp. 20-22*

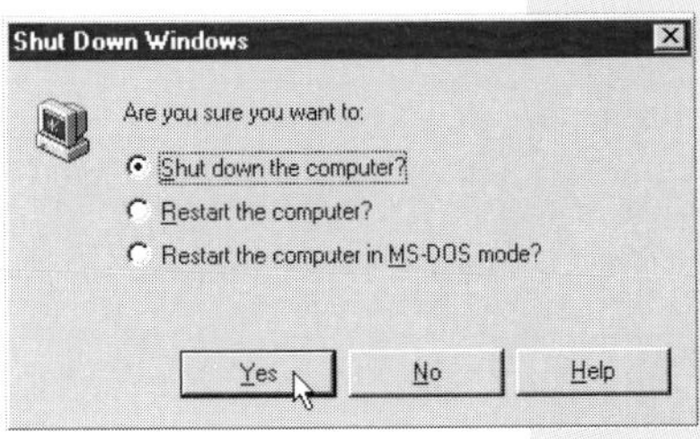

1. Click the Start button.
2. Click the Shut Down option.
3. Choose the desired shutdown option (shut down, restart, etc.).
4. Windows will quit all programs that are running (but not before prompting you to save any unsaved work).
5. Watch the screen and *wait for permission before powering down your computer*!

There are nearly a dozen ways to launch programs such as Microsoft Word or Excel from within Windows 95. In this chapter, we'll review some old and new tricks. It's also possible to run DOS programs from Windows 95. That's covered later in the chapter.

Starting Windows 95

If you have the CD-ROM version of Windows 95, then whenever the disc is inserted in your drive, you'll see an opening screen with six buttons. You might want to click the Windows 95 Tour button and take the resulting tour before you continue reading this chapter.

Unlike earlier Windows versions, Windows 95 starts automatically when you power up or reboot your computer. You no longer need to type **win** at a DOS prompt. Shortly after your computer beeps for the first time, you will see a Windows 95 *splash screen* proclaiming the wonders of Microsoft and showing off the new 95 logo.

Windows 95 Passwords

The developers of Windows 95 have spawned a rash of new password options that might or might not rear their ugly heads when you start Windows 95.

If you did a typical installation of Windows 95 and you are not living or working around computer wonks, you can skip the entire topic of passwords for now. If, however, you are asked for a password when you start Windows 95, you'll need to know whussup. Be advised that you may need a user password, a network password, or a Windows password. Contact your network administrator or Help desk for assistance. Often, you can simply press ESC or click OK to proceed without a password.

Tip of the Day

Anything as mind-boggling as Windows 95 should be learned a little at a time. Windows can help you out in this regard by giving you a new tip or insight

If you don't see the Tips when you start Windows, either Chapter 10 or the online help topic "Welcome screen, viewing" can show you how to activate the Tip feature. (You need only type* welcome *when searching. See Chapter 3 for a discussion of online help.)

each time you start it. This slick feature is called Tip of the Day. Tips of the Day appear on the Welcome screen unless you or someone else has disabled tips. Some are powerful. Others are no-brainers. A few are just plain entertaining. Here's an example:

Did you know...

You can put shortcuts to your printers on your desktop.

Reading Multiple Tips

You can cycle through multiple tips with the Next Tip button, or go to online help (as described in Chapter 3) and search the index for "**tips.**" You can then select and read only those tip topics that interest you.

EXPERT ADVICE

Trust me on this. Get in the habit of reading the tips. You'll laugh. You'll cry. You'll learn amazing new cocktail party trivia. But best of all, you'll become more confident and productive. And remember to practice the techniques you learn.

What's New

If you've been using Windows 3.1 or Windows for Workgroups, try the What's New button on the Welcome screen. It will answer many of the questions commonly asked by upgraders.

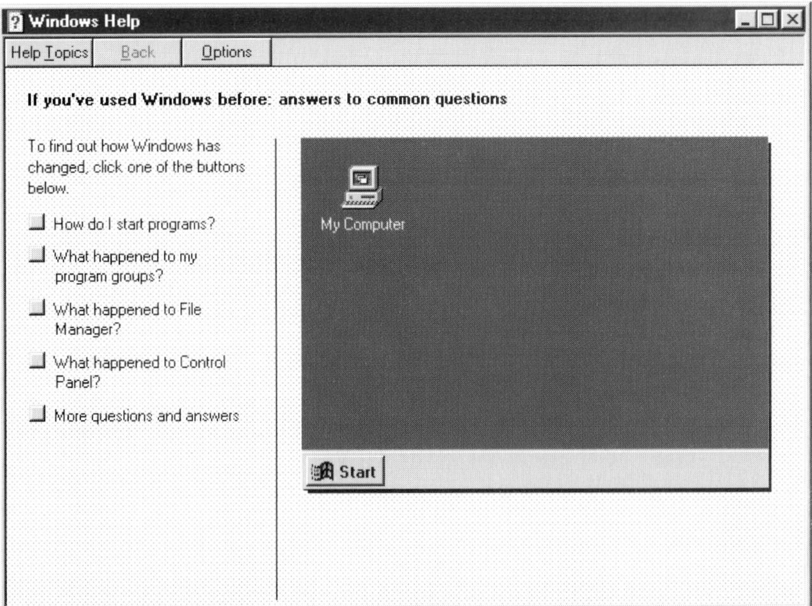

You can also reach this information from the Help window by following these steps:

1. Click the Start button.
2. Click the Help choice in the resulting Start menu.
3. Click on the Index tab.
4. Type **what's new** and press ENTER.
5. Click the topic of interest in the Topics Found dialog box and press ENTER.

Enabling and Disabling the Welcome Screen

Once you've convinced yourself that you know it all, you can disable the tipster by removing the checkmark next to the label "Show this Welcome Screen next time you start Windows". To remove the checkmark, just click on it. To bring it back, click on the item again. (But then you already knew that, right?)

Windows 95 Desktop Tour

The actual appearance of your desktop and the sounds that Windows makes at startup are more or less under your control, as you will see in Chapter 10.

When the disk drive's whirring and buzzing finally dies down, you should see a Windows *desktop* that looks something like the one in Figure 1.1. (And, unless your computer is aurally challenged, you'll probably hear musical notes like a "ta-da," or some rude sound effects at this point.) But forget those bells and whistles for now, busy person, and contemplate the following onscreen desktop gizmos:

- The Taskbar
- The Start button
- The Start menu
- The My Computer icon
- The Microsoft Network icon
- The Inbox icon

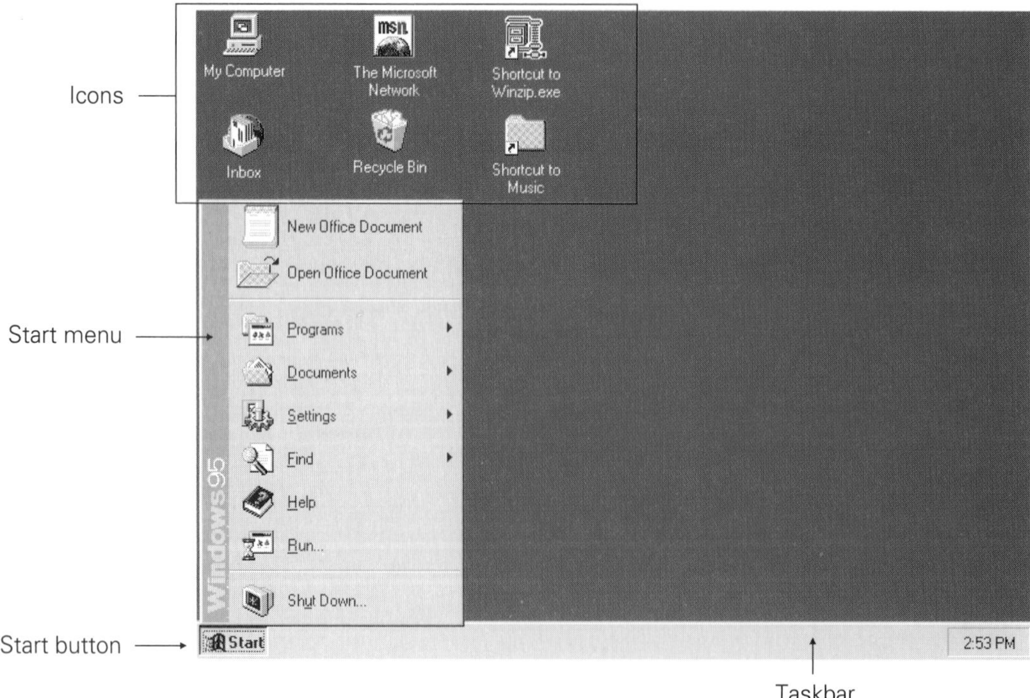

Figure 1.1 A typical Windows 95 desktop

- The Recycle Bin icon
- Shortcut icons

Wonks call these things *graphical objects.* (Your screen might have more or fewer of these than are visible in Figure 1.1.) They are onscreen devices you'll click, drag, and/or double-click on to run programs, organize your disks, and personalize your computer's behavior. Like doors to huge labyrinths, these objects lead you to many a mystery and adventure. For now, let's start by looking at the Taskbar.

DEFINITIONS

wonk: *Any T-shirt-attired, caffeine-addicted person with two or more computers in his or her bedroom. (See also* Jolt Cola.*)*

graphical objects: *Onscreen pictures of things like disk drives and buttons. Frequently you interact with them by pointing with your mouse and clicking.*

Taskbar

The Taskbar resides at the bottom of your screen, as you saw when you activated the Start button earlier in this chapter. Depending upon optional settings (described in Chapter 10), your Taskbar might not be in view. If it isn't, move the mouse pointer to the bottom of your screen to reveal it.

At a minimum, the Taskbar always displays the Start button. If you are currently running programs (such as a word processor or spreadsheet package), or if you have open windows for things like disk drives, you will see additional, labeled buttons for each item. For example, in Figure 1.2 the Taskbar tells you that I am running both Microsoft Word and Excel, and that I have a window opened called My Computer.

Normally you'll also see a clock in the right corner of the Taskbar, and perhaps a speaker icon and other toys. You'll learn to fiddle with these later, but I want to show you something interesting before we continue:

1. Slide the mouse pointer over the Start button, but don't press any mouse buttons.
2. Leave the pointer there for a moment.

3. You should see a *ToolTip* (also called a *ScreenTip*) message.

When you're in doubt about the function or meaning of a graphical object in Windows, slide the mouse pointer over the object and see if Windows displays some information about it. In many Windows programs (such as Word and Excel), sliding the mouse pointer over graphical objects like toolbar buttons tells you the name or function of the objects. And sometimes, instead of getting the name of the object, you'll see other useful information. For example, try sliding the mouse pointer over the digital clock in the lower-right corner of your screen:

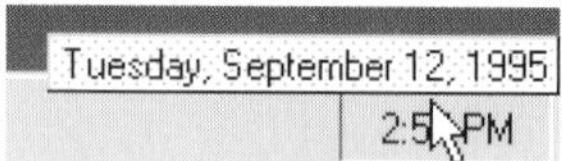

Cool, huh? Alas, not all objects reveal themselves this way.

Chapter 3 discusses a variation on the ToolTip theme, a feature called What's This.

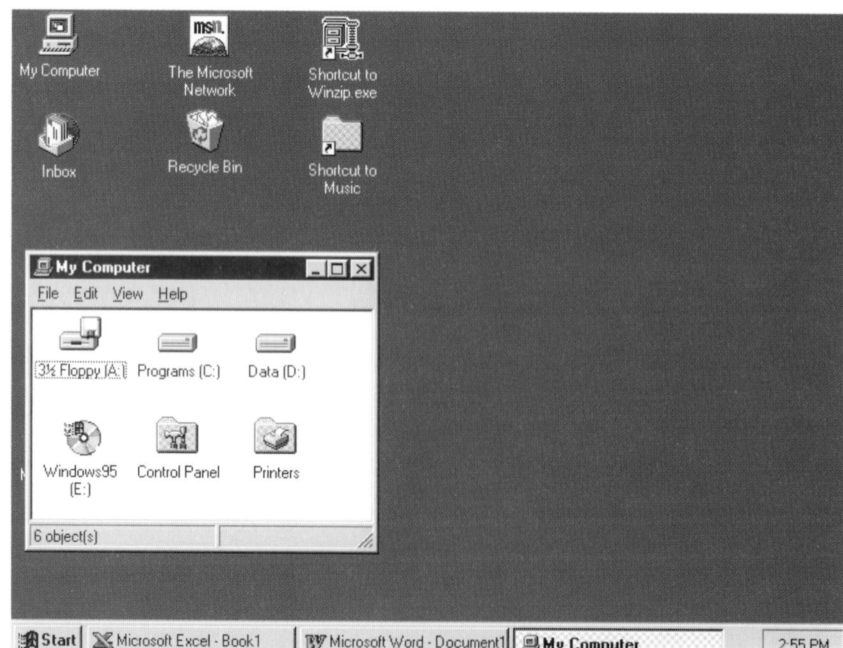

Figure 1.2 The Taskbar shows Word and Excel running, and the My Computer window open

The Start Button and Start Menu

Your menu might display different options. For example, a portable computer might have an Eject PC option.

Okay, let's get back to the Start button. It's located on the Taskbar, and makes it easy for you to run programs. It also lets you quickly change computer settings and even locate documents. Clicking the Start button reveals the Start menu, which contains many choices, some of which generate additional menus with additional choices called *submenus*. A triangular arrow to the right of an item on your Start menu indicates that additional submenus will appear when you point to that menu item. The Start menu contains four options—Programs, Documents, Settings, and Find—that have submenus. Either press CTRL-ESC or follow these steps to bring up your own Start menu.

STEP BY STEP Using the Start Menu

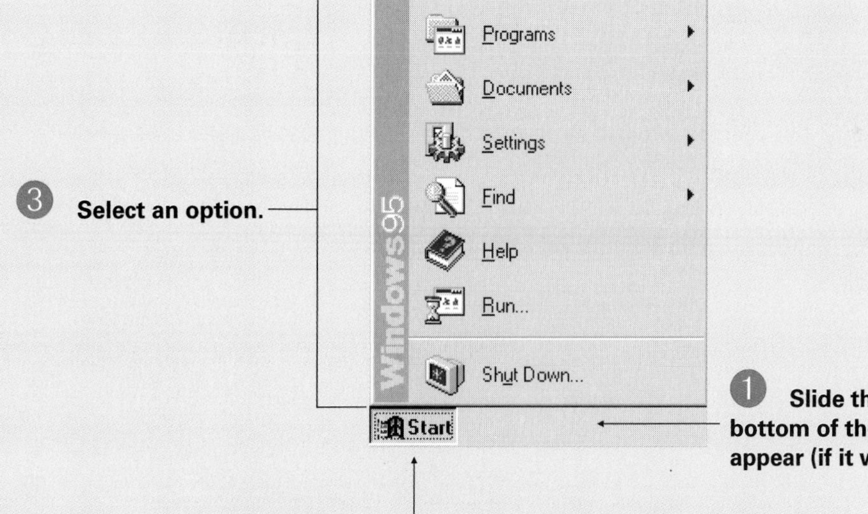

1. Slide the mouse pointer to the bottom of the screen. The Taskbar will appear (if it was previously invisible).
2. Click the Start button. The Start menu appears, displaying a variety of options (similar, but not necessarily identical, to those in the illustration).
3. Select an option.

Start Menu Organization

The Start menu displays a list of programs and other options. Virtually everyone's Start menu is different (at least once you scratch the surface).

Some of the items on the Start menu were placed there by the Windows 95 Setup program when Windows 95 was initially installed. The Windows 95 Setup program creates menu items named after programs (and *groups* of programs) that it finds on your computer at the time of Windows 95 installation. You can change the names of the menu items and their organization, as you will see in Chapter 10, but for now let's look at the automatic naming and organization of Start menu items.

See if you can find the Accessories group on your Start menu. Click the Start button and click Program. You should see it.

Try clicking on the Calculator option with your primary (normally the left) mouse button. Notice how when you run the Calculator program, its window's name appears on the Taskbar. To quit the Calculator, press ALT-F4.

upgrade note

The Start menu and submenus are the Windows 95 replacement for the Program Manager and program groups. Things that were in program groups when you were running earlier versions will be in submenus of the Start menu.

Frequently, Setup programs place new choices in the Programs submenu of the Start menu. Other times, as you purchase and install additional programs, changes occur at the "top level" of your Start menu—that is, rather than putting the choice on the Programs submenu, the installer places them on the Start menu proper.

If you haven't already discovered it, the trick to reaching submenus is revealed in the following steps.

STEP BY STEP Reaching Submenus

③ **Slide the mouse to the *right*, then *up* or *down* for the next choice (Accessories, for instance).**

② **Slide the mouse pointer to highlight the Start menu item of interest (Programs, in this example). Either click or wait a second for the first submenu to appear. There is no need to hold down the mouse button while you slide the mouse.**

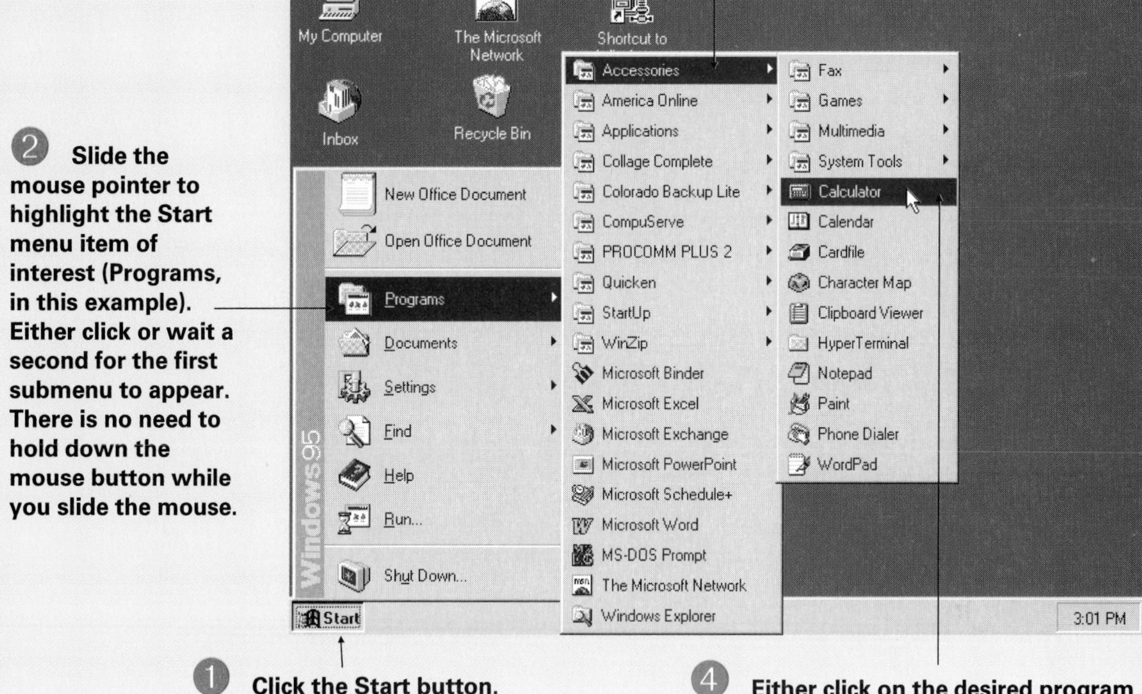

① **Click the Start button.**

④ **Either click on the desired program or choose the next submenu of interest.**

Starting Programs via the Start Menu

If you tried the preceding Calculator accessory example, you've already run a program from a submenu of the Start menu. But since there are variations on this theme, keep reading.

EXPERT ADVICE

If you are a touch typist or keyboard shortcut fanatic, get in the habit of pressing CTRL-ESC or the Microsoft logo key on newer keyboards to pop up the Start menu. Use the arrow keys to select menu items, and tap ENTER to execute your choices.

Not all of the choices on the Start menu necessarily lead to submenus. Some of the choices are programs that you can run directly by just clicking on them in the Start menu. For example, the choice labeled Help runs the Windows 95 help program without displaying any submenus. You can add your own favorite programs to the "top level" of the Start menu to avoid visiting a seemingly endless line of menus for everyday items such as the Calculator or your America Online software. Here's what my normal Start menu looks like:

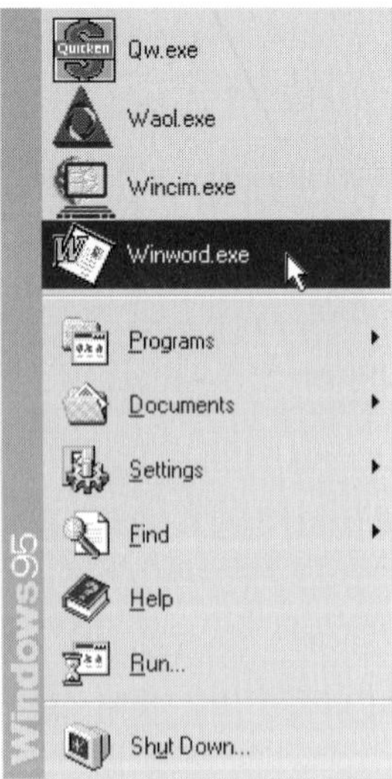

I use Winword (Word for Windows) and those other three programs above it so often that I want to see them each time I bring up the Start menu. So I added them. You will learn how to do the same thing in Chapter 10. Meanwhile, continue with our tour, faithful reader, knowing that soon you too will be in control of *your* own destiny.

The Documents menu can list files stored on far-flung networked drives or floppy disks. If you wish to retrieve and reuse such files, you need to be connected to the appropriate network server, or have the floppy disk handy. If a file that appears on your Documents menu has been renamed, moved, password-protected, or deleted, by you or anyone else, you won't be able to access it.

The Documents Option

The Documents option on the Start menu lists the last 15 documents you used. So if, over the last few days, you've written a couple of memos, contrived a spreadsheet, and used Quicken to balance your checkbook, the files you've created and played with in the process will be listed in the Documents submenu right there for God and everybody to see. Here's what mine looks like at the moment:

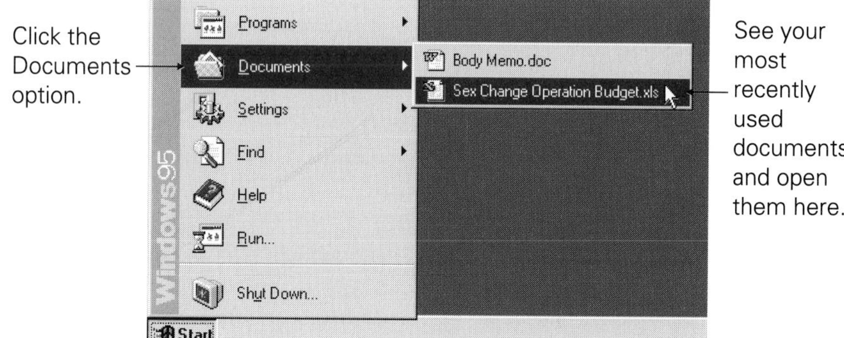

So let's say I want to revise that recently used spreadsheet of mine, or print an extra copy of that urgent memo. Rather than rummaging through my entire computer to find the program used to create the document, and then looking for the document itself, I can simply visit the Documents submenu, choose the document, and blam—it will appear on my screen. (If the program used to create the document isn't already running, Windows 95 will fire it up for me first.)

Curiously, not all recently used documents get listed. For example, Microsoft Word version 6 has the nasty habit of not adding things to the Documents menu, while Word for Windows 95 does just fine. Microsoft explains this by blaming the program used to create your documents.

CAUTION

Anyone who walks up to your computer can see what you've been doing by looking at your Documents submenu. So, if you've saved a memo to your boss with a title such as "Take this job and shove it," clear the Documents submenu. You can do this by changing the Taskbar properties settings as described in Chapter 10.

The Settings Option

The Settings menu consolidates most of the day-to-day computer "maintenance." It looks like this:

So if you wish to change the screen saver, or choose a different printer, or change Taskbar settings (to clear the Documents menu, for example), the Settings menu choice will lead you in the right direction. Chapters 8, 9, and 10 give you detailed information on how to work with the three options on the Settings menu. But feel free to explore the settings choices on your own at this point if you wish.

The Find Option

The Find menu will help you quickly locate documents, programs, and other items of interest, be they on your hard disk or on some network server in another country. The process is described in detail in Chapter 5.

The Help Option

As I mentioned earlier, the Help option on your Start menu runs the Windows 95 Help program, which is described in Chapter 3. Again, feel free to play with online help before turning the page, if you like. It's your computer. For now, here's what the Help window looks like:

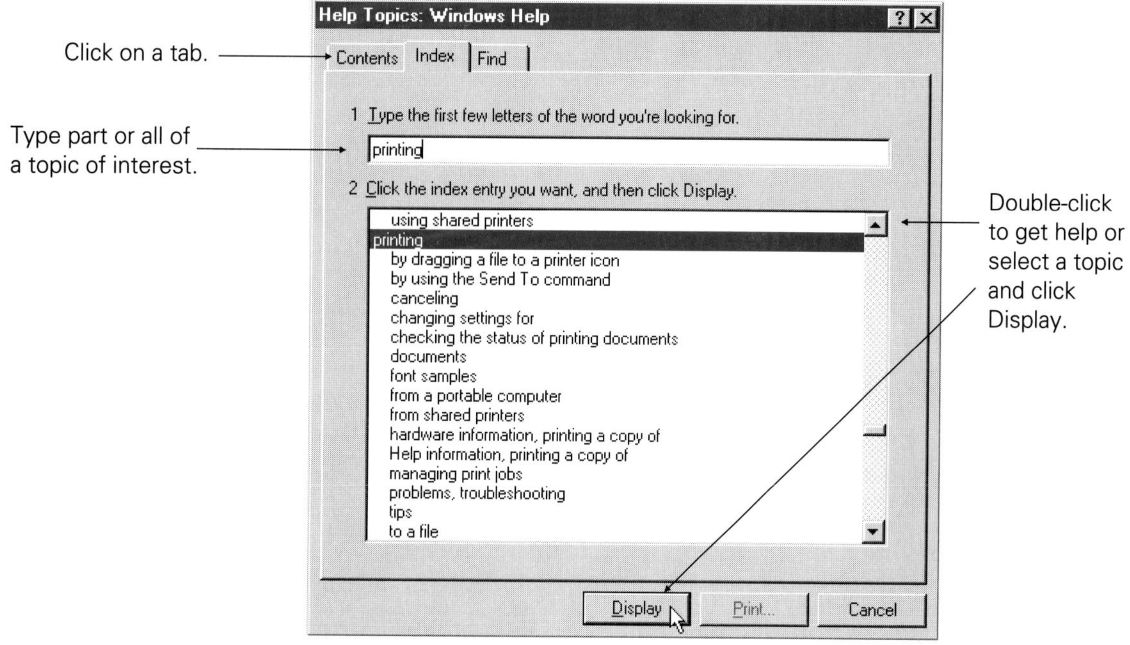

The Start Menu's Run Option

The Run choice on the Start menu lets you run programs by typing their names and paths. Although Windows provides easier (or at least more intuitive) ways to run programs, you'll probably want to use this command when you install new programs, fonts, and other things that come on floppies or CD-ROMs containing Setup or Install programs. For example, here's how a typical new software installation might be done using Microsoft-provided floppies:

1. Choose Run from the Start menu. The Run dialog box appears.
2. Type the drive letter, any necessary path info, and the program name, as you see here:

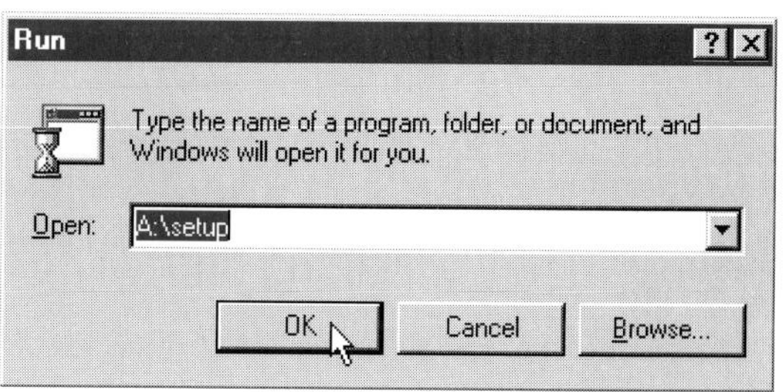

3. Press ENTER or click OK.

Double-Clicking to Start Programs

Double-clicking on either program icons or document icons starts programs if they are not running, or brings programs (and often documents) to the forefront of your screen. Let's look at a few examples of this.

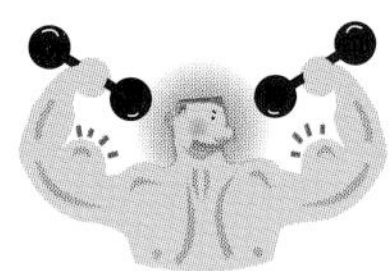

DEFINITION

double-clicking: *The process of clicking the mouse button twice in rapid succession. Chanting "There's no place like home!" while you double-click is optional. (See also* Kansas.*)*

Double-Clicking Program Icons

To run a program, double-click its icon. For example, this illustration shows that I've just started a program called Setup.exe on a CD-ROM in my E drive by double-clicking the Setup.exe icon:

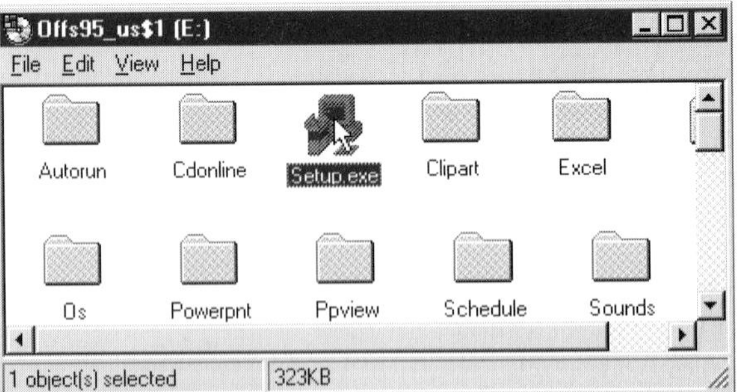

upgrade note

Windows 95 does not automatically display file extensions (like *.exe*), but it will display them if you like. Just follow the procedure discussed in Chapter 4 (see the section "Displaying Filename Extensions").

Double-Clicking Document Icons

Double-clicking the document icon for your checkbook file, a database file, etc., will run the program associated with that document type. For instance, if you double-click an icon for a memo created by Microsoft Word, Windows will either start Microsoft Word or "bring it forward" if it is already running, and then load the memo so that you can edit with Word.

Open With: When Windows Gets Confused

If you never receive document files from other people, if you never remove programs from your computer, or if you never double-click on document icons, you will probably never see the formidable Open With dialog box. It is Windows' way of saying, "Hey, I don't know which program was used to create that document. Which program (of those that we have) shall I use?" You are then presented with a more or less complete list of programs from your hard disk. Chapter 4 tells you what to do when this happens.

EXPERT ADVICE

When you're done working with a program, you ought to quit it. This will help speed up the programs that you are working with, and may also improve system reliability.

Quitting Programs

You can quit programs using any of these methods:

- Choose Exit from the program's File menu.
- Close the program's main window (by clicking in the Close box).
- Use the ALT-F4 key combination.
- Use the ALT-F, X key sequence.
- Choose Shut Down from the Windows Start menu, which will quit Windows and all running programs.

In any case, you will be prompted to save or abandon unsaved changes before each program quits.

Quitting "Locked-Up" Programs

Sometimes programs freeze up and refuse to respond no matter how much keyboard pounding and cursing you employ. When you are certain a program is being unresponsive, hold down three keys at once: CTRL-ALT-DEL. This will bring up a Close Program dialog box listing all of the programs currently running. Select the troublesome program and click the End Task button. In theory, this should quit just the problematic program and leave any others you have running unscathed. Being a cynic, right after I encounter a problem like this, I like to gracefully save any other work I have in progress and restart the computer.

Shutting Down Your Computer and Quitting Windows

Never (never, ever) just switch off your computer without visiting the Start menu, choosing the Shut Down command, and then the "Shut down the computer?" check box.

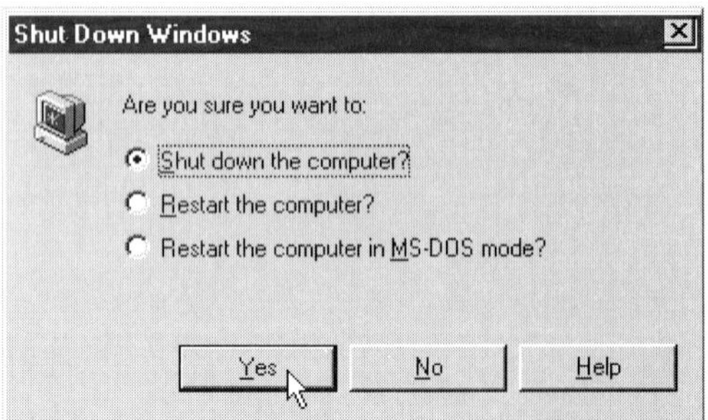

Always (always, always) wait until Windows tells you that it is okay to turn off the power. (It will give you a message saying, "You can now safely turn off your computer.") Windows does some housekeeping when you quit and, if you turn off the power too soon, Gump happens.

CAUTION

Unless you have no other choice (like when your computer completely locks up), turning off the power too soon angers the Reliability Gods, and you will pay!

A Normal Shutdown

In a simple world these are the steps for a typical, graceful shutdown:

1. Either press the ALT-F4 key combination, or choose Shut Down from the Start menu.
2. Click Yes in the resulting dialog box or press the ENTER key.
3. Deal with any shutdown complications (messages about unsaved work, etc.).
4. Stare patiently at the screen that says "Please wait while your computer shuts down." But do *not* power down yet! Instead, wait for the message "You can now safely turn off your computer."
5. Turn off the machine (some computers might even shut themselves off).
6. If you have an external monitor and other power-hungry accessories, shut them off too.

Shutdown Choices

When you choose Shut Down, Windows 95 offers three or four choices, depending on whether your computer is on a network (see the Shut Down Windows dialog box on the preceding page). Normally, you'll want to pick the default choice, "Shut down the computer," and click OK. If you change your mind about shutting down, click the No button to abort the shutdown process.

The other choices, with the possible exception of Restart in MS-DOS mode (covered at the end of this chapter), should be self-explanatory.

Shutdown Complications

Windows might find good reasons not to shut down even if you want to. For example, if you have set up your computer so that others can share your files, you might get a message warning that someone is using your computer. As tempting as it might be to play Terminator at this point and blast those pesky network users into oblivion, remember: they might be using your database or spreadsheet files. And if you power down without asking them to save their work and quit their programs properly, *your* files on *your* computer are the ones they'll be damaging! Sometimes when people are not actually using documents on your computer, Windows will warn you anyway. Once you've determined that users do not have any of your documents open, it's fine to ignore the warning and shut down.

Sometimes Windows 95 will just plain refuse to shut down. This can happen for so many reasons that Microsoft published a seven-page document titled "How to Troubleshoot Windows 95 Shutdown Problems." (Article ID Q145926 in the Microsoft Knowledge Base. See Chapter 3.) There's no choice but to power down when Win 95 locks up.

You might also get messages about unfinished printing jobs when you try to shut down. In a sentence: read the screen carefully at shutdown, and think before you click.

Shutting Down Portables and Other Fancy Machines

Newer portables and some other computers have built-in power control features that will turn off the power automatically when you choose Shut Down. Windows generally detects this capability and switches off the power for you.

Running DOS Programs with DOS Windows

Normally, you'll want to run MS-DOS programs from within Windows 95 in MS-DOS *windows*. You'll be able to switch back and forth between your Windows-savvy and DOS-savvy programs this way. Moreover, you'll often be able to move information from DOS windows to Windows windows and back. Here's what the DOS window looks like in Windows 95:

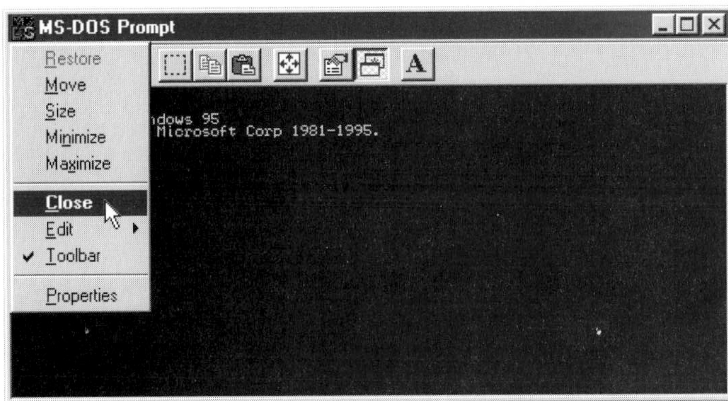

To run a DOS program in Windows 95, follow these steps:

*Forget a DOS prompt, or switch rule or other DOS trivia? Type **help** and press ENTER at the DOS prompt, and then pick the command of interest from the resulting list. (You should be able to use your mouse to select help topics.)*

1. Start your computer and Windows (if they are not already running).
2. Visit the Start menu.
3. Choose Programs.
4. Choose MS-DOS Prompt. A smallish MS-DOS window will open.
5. Type a command (**dir c:**, for example) at the DOS prompt, just like you did in the good ol' days.
6. To close the MS-DOS window, finish whatever you are doing in DOS, then click the Close box.

Chapter 2 will give you more information about sharing data between DOS and Windows 95 windows. It will also show you how to change the size and shape of the DOS window.

Starting Your Computer in DOS Mode, sans Windows 95

The rumors of the death of DOS are exaggerated. It is alive and well, albeit pretty well hidden in Windows 95. You can avoid running the Windows 95 graphical interface and start out right at the DOS prompt in at least three different ways:

- Boot from the Windows 95 Startup floppy.

See the online Windows 95 help topics "Startup Files" and "Startup Trouble-shooting," or consult your Windows 95 manual, for further startup details.

- Choose "Restart the computer in MS-DOS mode" from the Windows 95 Shut Down Windows dialog box.
- When booting, press the F8 function key as soon as you see the message "Starting Windows 95." (Among other things, this gives you the choice of using or ignoring your Autoexec and Config files.)

When you have finished playing DOS wonk, you'll need to reboot your machine to use Windows 95. Typing **win** will not work at the new and improved DOS prompt, but typing **exit** will reboot and run Windows 95.

32-Bit vs. 16-Bit Programs

I'll spare you the details, but I think you should know that Windows is a 32-bit operating system, and it will run both 32-bit and 16-bit software. Given a choice, you almost always want to pick the 32-bit version of a program. 32-bit software was designed for Windows 95. It often runs faster, and in theory ought to make your system more reliable.

Accessory Programs

Windows 95 comes with some small "accessory" programs. You might find many of them useful. They each contain online help, and, while in many cases the programs are not the best choice for everyday work, hey, you paid for them, so let's have a look. They are all found in the Accessories submenu of the Programs menu on the Start menu.

Calculator

I used this Microsoft Calculator accessory religiously until I found a talking calculator shareware product I prefer (included with the CD-ROM for this book). But we are here to explore the *Microsoft* accessories, so let's stay on track. Take a look at Figure 1.3.

This program will display either a scientific calculator or a smaller, simpler, "four-function" calculator with a memory. You can switch from scientific to four-function with the View menu. The calculator will remember the last view

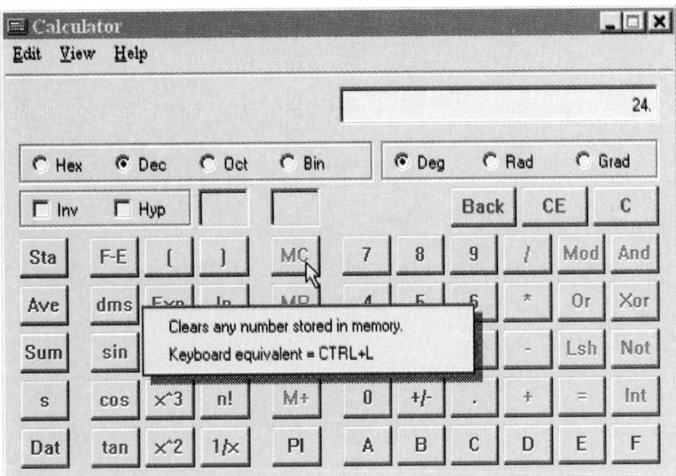

Figure 1.3 The Windows 95 Calculator accessory in Scientific view

you used and come up in that view next time. In either view you enter numbers by typing on your keyboard, and you can enter operators (+, -, etc.) either from the keyboard, or by clicking the onscreen calculator buttons with your mouse. Answers appear in the display and you can copy those results to the clipboard (with the Edit menu's Copy command or the CTRL-C keyboard shortcut), then paste the results into other programs—a word processing document or whatever. To learn more about the calculator, its functions and keyboard shortcuts, use the built-in online help.

WordPad

WordPad is an interesting little word processor. It is one of two shipped with Windows 95. (The other is Notepad, described in a moment.) While WordPad lacks a lot of bells and whistles, if it was the only word processor you had with you on a desert island, you could probably use it to draft that Great American Novel you have inside you. But for everyday, polished work where you need things like page numbers, multiple documents open at the same time, a spelling checker, and so on, Microsoft wants to make sure you purchase a copy of Microsoft Word. So they've left many important features out of WordPad.

You can use WordPad for browsing, printing, and modifying Readme.txt, Autoexec.bat, and similar text files. However, by default, Windows 95 uses Notepad to open and edit text files. You'll need to associate WordPad with text files instead of Notepad if you want to automatically launch WordPad when double-clicking on text files. See Chapter 4 to learn how.

WordPad will open documents created with a number of other word processors, including most versions of Microsoft Word. Be aware, however, that as word processing file formats evolve, older versions of WordPad might not work with the new files. Word 97 files are an example of this problem, at least if you purchased Windows 95 a while ago. Figure 1.4 will give you a glimpse at WordPad. If you think you might like to know more about this program, fire it up (from the Accessories submenu) and check out the online help. Since WordPad supports OLE and related technology, it's a good tool to use when playing with these toys. Just remember—you are busy!

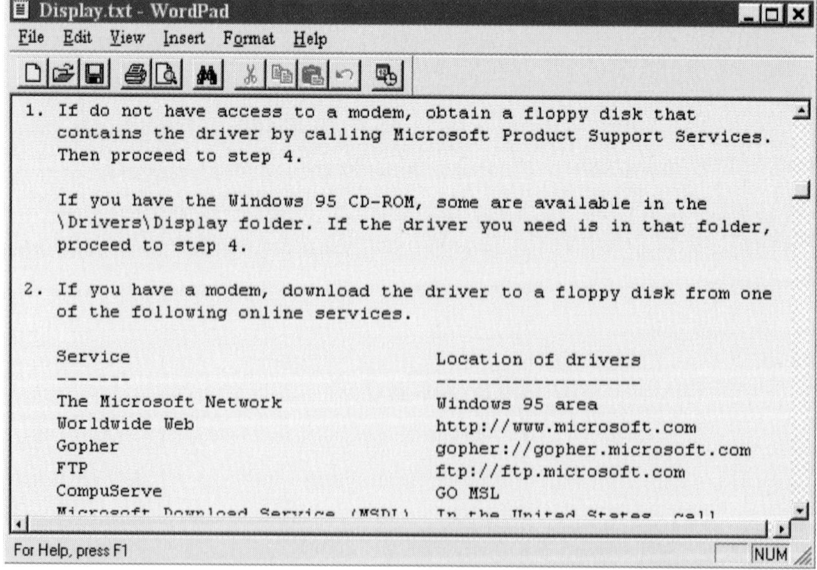

Figure 1.4 The WordPad Calculator accessory displaying a Readme file

Notepad

Notepad is an earlier, further stripped-down word processor that has even fewer features than WordPad. Its primary claim to fame is that it is the program Windows 95 uses by default to open, view, and edit Readme and batch files (Readme.txt, Autoexec.bat, etc.). It is very plain and balks at large documents. Figure 1.5 says it all.

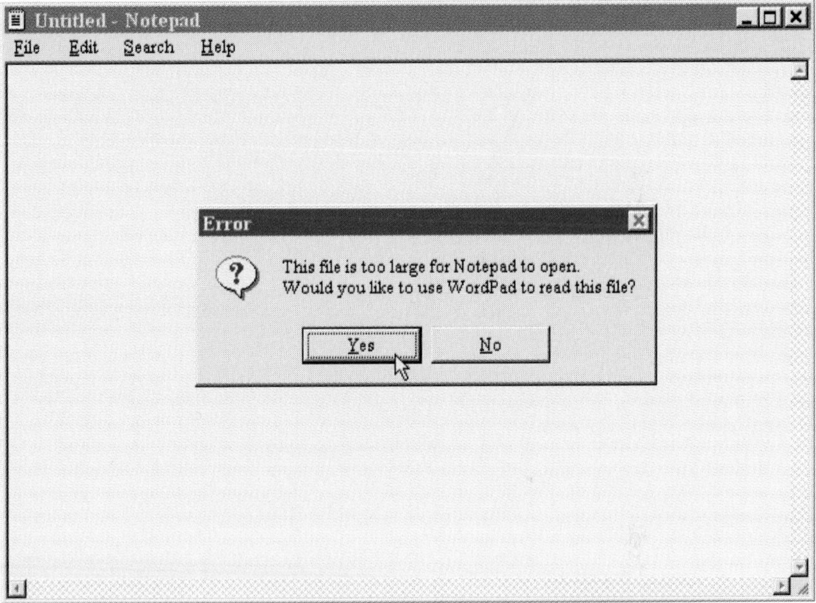

Figure 1.5 Notepad: a no-frills text editor

Paint

Paint is a nice little drawing program used to view, edit, and create bitmap pictures. Unless you change the association, Windows 95 uses Paint to open bitmap graphics files. You can use Paint to display, print, and draw simple graphics; rotate and resize them; change their colors; and more. For example, you can create a rectangle, fill it with a color, change the color of the lines used to draw it, add some text, and so on. Hovering your mouse pointer over the painting tools reveals each one's function.

Finished paintings can either be pasted to your clipboard or saved as bitmap files for use by other programs. Figure 1.6 gives you an idea of Paint's possibilities in the hands of a nonartist.

Figure 1.6 Paint at work

Cardfile

Okay, campers. Hopefully, you bought this book partly to read my (sometimes strong) opinions. In my opinion, and with apologies to Microsoft, Cardfile is not worth your time. It is a very simple electronic Rolodex-like program designed to collect and organize related information—people's phone numbers, notes to yourself, etc. There are so many better products on the market (my current favorite is *Microsoft Outlook,* which comes with Microsoft Office 97) that, if you spend more than ten minutes exploring Cardfile, you've stayed too long.

Games

Sitting in the center seat of a 727? Thumping your desk while listening to music on hold? Consider one of the games provided with Windows 95. I have two favorites. The first gets installed automatically; the other requires a separate installation step, or it can be run directly from your Windows 95 installation CD-ROM. The game that gets installed automatically (unless you've opted for a minimal install) is 3-D Pinball for Windows. Check out Figure 1.7. Really nice graphics. Great sounds, nice action. Addicting. The second game I like is a killer multimedia demo called Hover. Run it from the automatic "splash" screen that should appear when you insert your Windows CD-ROM, or install it on your hard disk and add it to your Start menu. Hover always draws a crowd, so if you are supposed to be working, keep the sound turned down.

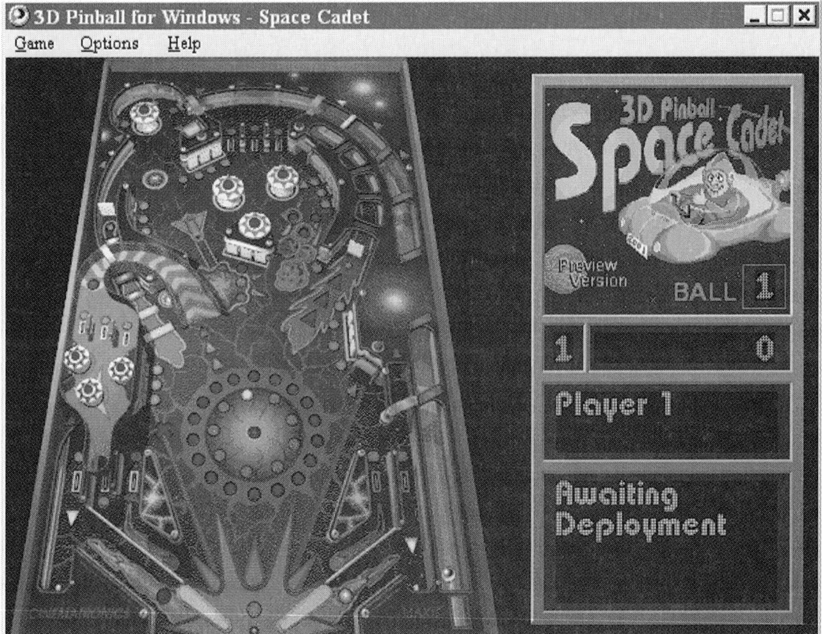

Figure 1.7 3-D Pinball: one of many "free" games shipped with Windows 95

There are other amusements in the Games submenu of the Accessory submenu. They include three card games: FreeCell, Hearts, and Solitaire. Then there is Minesweeper, one of those board games where you uncover squares hoping to not blow yourself up (or get fired for goofing off) in the process. Tic tock.

Well, you're off to a booming start. Time to grab a quick cup of coffee and try using an accessory or two, along with some of the other techniques you've learned, before you move ahead to Chapter 2. Check out some tips of the day. Practice bringing up the Start menu. Double-click on a document to start a program. Experiment. Then it's on to Chapter 2, where you'll learn to manage the windows that are sprouting up all over your screen—and get them working for you!

CHAPTER

2

Managing Windows in Windows 95

INCLUDES

- Windows 95 window parts and their names
- Running multiple programs simultaneously
- Opening and closing document and program windows
- Activating and switching between windows
- Resizing windows
- Moving and arranging windows on your screen
- Moving information between windows

FAST FORWARD

Activate a Window ➤ pp. 40

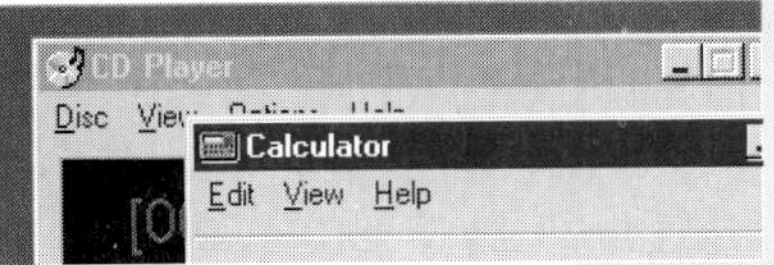

There are two methods for activating windows:

- The names of running programs and certain other open windows appear in buttons on the Taskbar. Click the appropriate button on the Taskbar to switch to the window you want.
- Press ALT-TAB repeatedly to display a revolving graphic selection of currently running programs and open windows. Release the ALT key when you see the item you want to activate.

Make a Window Disappear (and Reappear) ➤ pp. 40-42

1. To remove a window from view without actually closing it, click its Minimize button, which is the first of the three small buttons in the window's upper-right corner. The window will vanish, but its name will appear either as a button on the Taskbar (if it is a program window) or an icon at the bottom of its parent window (if it is a document window).
2. To restore and activate the window, click its button or icon.

Change the Size of a Window ➤ pp. 42-44

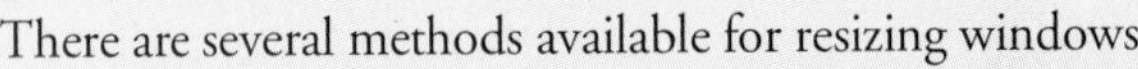

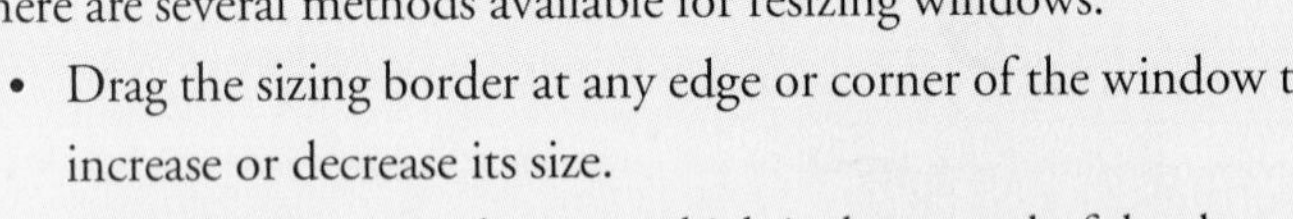

There are several methods available for resizing windows:

- Drag the sizing border at any edge or corner of the window to increase or decrease its size.
- Click the Maximize button, which is the second of the three small buttons in the upper-right corner of the window, to make the window as large as possible.
- Double-click the title bar to toggle window resizing.
- Click with the right mouse button on the window's title bar to see the Resizing menu, and then select the Maximize option.
- Select the Size option from the Resizing menu, then use the arrow keys on the keyboard to make the window incrementally smaller or larger, and then press ENTER.

Move and Arrange Windows ➤ *pp. 44-45*

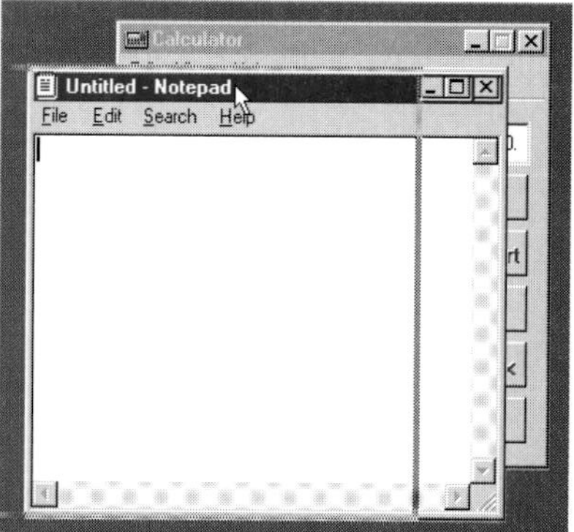

You can organize windows on your screen in virtually any arrangement you like using a variety of techniques:

- Drag windows by their title bars to relocate them on your screen.
- Point to a buttonless place on the Taskbar (that is, anywhere but on a button), and click the second (usually right) mouse button. Choose either Cascade, Tile Horizontally, or Tile Vertically.
- Click with the right mouse button on the window's title bar to see the Resizing menu, select the Move option, then use the arrow keys on the keyboard to move the window to the location you desire, and then press ENTER.
- Use the commands and features that many programs (including Microsoft's Office products) provide to let you quickly arrange document windows (tile them, stack them, and so on).

Close a Window ➤ *pp. 45-46*

You can close a window using one of several methods:

- Click the Close button in the upper-right corner of a window.
- Double-click a title bar icon.
- Click the Close choice in the File menu, which closes document windows, not program windows. (Most but not all windows offer this option.)
- Click with the right mouse button on most title bars to see the Resizing menu, and then select the Close option.

Copy Information from One Window to Another ➤ pp. 47-52

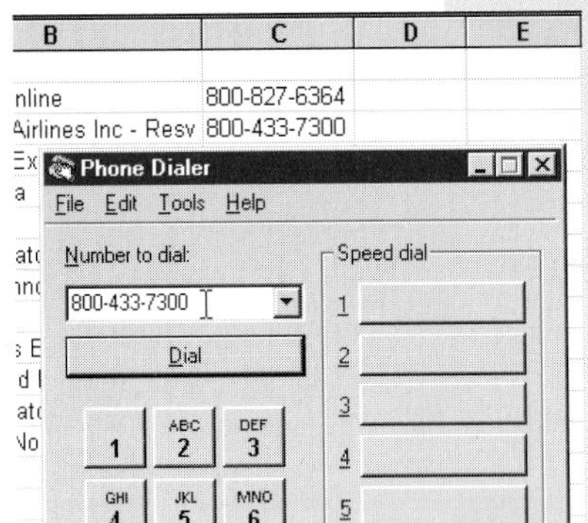

1. Select the information you want to copy.
2. Choose Copy from the Edit menu or press CTRL-C.
3. Switch to the destination window by clicking anywhere within it.
4. Position the insertion point by clicking where you want to place it.
5. Choose Paste from the Edit menu or press CTRL-V.

Move Information from One Window to Another ➤ pp. 47-52

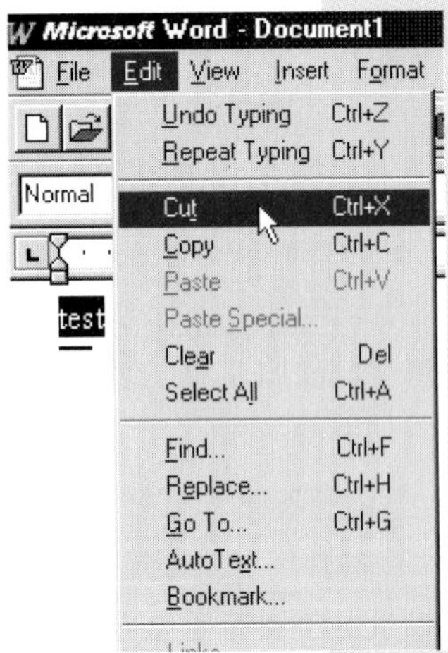

You can move information from one window (let's call it the *source* window) to another (the *destination* window) with these steps:

1. Select the information you want to move or copy from the source window.
2. Choose Cut from the Edit menu or press CTRL-X.
3. Switch to the destination window by clicking in it.
4. Position the insertion point by clicking where you want to place the selected information.
5. Choose Paste from the Edit menu or press CTRL-V.

Some of the ground covered in this chapter will probably be familiar, but please at least skim this material. Most people still struggle with aspects of Windows "window management." I know I do. And Windows 95 adds some new options and wrinkles that can slow down even veteran users (if they don't read this chapter).

Parent and Child Windows

Those rectangles on your screen in which you work are all called *windows.* (Note the lowercase "w".) Frequently, you will see more than one window on your screen at the same time. There are different types of windows for different tasks. You don't need to know the exact names of every window type (unless you are a programmer), but there are two types worth noting: parent and child windows.

Parent windows are usually program windows. They contain menu bars, toolbars, etc. They also frequently contain one or more child, or document, windows. In Figure 2.1, the outermost window with "Microsoft Excel" in its title bar is the Excel parent window. The smaller window containing "Proposed Ticket Price changes" is the child. You will often have more than one child window for a single parent window.

Figure 2.2 shows two document (or child) windows within the Excel window. Look at the title bar of each window and notice the names of the three different windows. Only one document window can be active at a time. In this case it is "3 Foxes Competition Pricing.xls," on the left. The active window is always the one with the bolder (and/or more colorful) title bar.

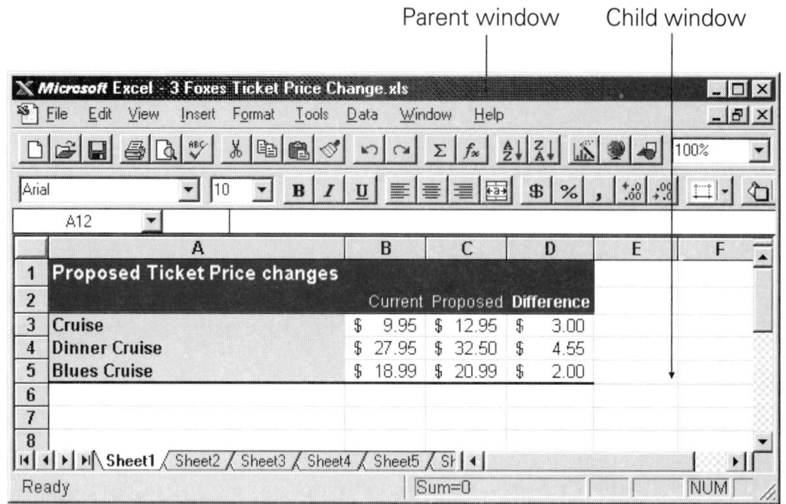

Figure 2.1 A Microsoft Excel "parent" containing a document "child"

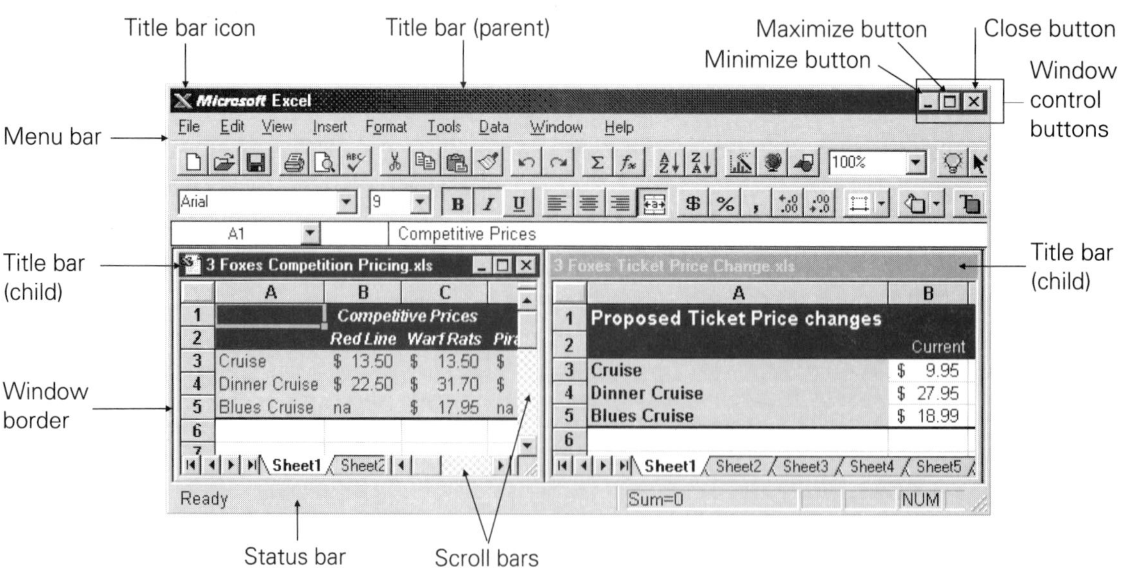

Figure 2.2 A Microsoft Excel window containing two document windows

Running Multiple Programs Simultaneously

One of the key advantages of Windows 95 is its ability to juggle more than one program at once. You can, for instance, use your word processing program and your spreadsheet program while downloading a file from the Internet all at the same time. You do this by simply launching additional programs as you need them without quitting programs you are already running. Now, obviously, the more things you ask your computer to do at the same time, the slower things will get. When you run more programs than will fit in your computer's RAM, Windows 95 shuffles things temporarily off to your hard disk when it needs RAM for a task at hand. That's what all that clattering is about when you try to run too many things at once. So if you frequently need to run more than one program, be sure you have a minimum of 16MB of RAM, and ideally more. Finally, a reminder that the more complex things get, the more likely you are to anger the Reliability Gods. So, it is a good idea to only run programs you are using, and not to forget to quit programs when you are done with them.

EXPERT ADVICE

Keep an eye on the Taskbar. It is the easy place to see what's running.

The Parts of a Window

It's worth knowing the names of the major components of Windows windows. Even though not all windows are identical, they all have in common the parts described in this section. Look again at Figure 2.2.

Title Bar

The title bar contains the name of the program (Microsoft Excel in the case of Figure 2.2). Sometimes it contains other information as well. Document names often can be found in title bars, as in this illustration, where you can see the document name "3 Foxes Ticket Price Change.xls":

Microsoft Excel - 3 Foxes Ticket Price Change.xls

Title Bar Icon

A title bar icon is the little picture associated with the program creating the window. You can see the MS Excel icon on the left side of the title bar in the illustration. The Excel icon is a big X, in case you were wondering.

Menu Bar

The menu bar lists the available menus (lists of choices). Clicking on a menu name reveals the entire menu.

Window Control Buttons

As you saw earlier in this chapter, the three window control buttons in the upper-right corner of most windows are called (from left to right) the Minimize, Maximize (or Restore), and Close buttons.

Scroll Bar

The scroll bars let you see information that can't fit in the window. Clicking in the scroll bar or on scroll arrows, or dragging scroll boxes, changes the information displayed in a window. Watching the position of the scroll box gives you an approximate idea of your relative position. For example, in a ten-page document, if you see the scroll box in the middle of the scroll bar, you can assume that you are near page five in the document. As the box approaches the top of the scroll bar, you are approaching the beginning of the document, and so on. You often can use the navigation keys (PAGE UP, PAGE DOWN, HOME, etc.) to scroll in the active window.

Frame or "Window" Border

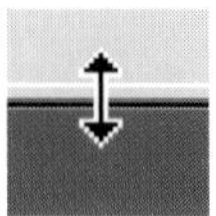

The window border (officially known as the frame border) defines the outer edges of the window. Frequently you can drag borders to change the size and shape of a window. Notice how the mouse pointer changes to a two-headed arrow when you place it on the border.

Most windows have special areas in their corners that allow you to drag in two dimensions at once—for example, diagonally to the upper-right of your screen. When this is possible, diagonal arrows appear when you drag over a corner (as opposed to horizontal or vertical arrows).

Status Bar

The status bar often contains useful information about a window. For instance, here the status bar informs the user that three items have been selected. Get in the habit of checking this area regularly.

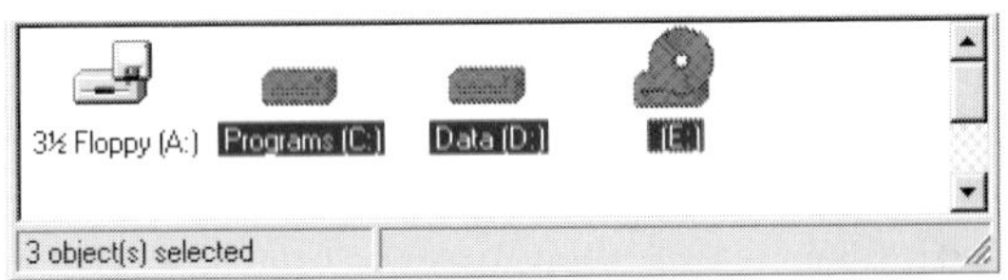

Things You Must Know How to Do

To make your life easier, you need to know how to do at least the following:

- Open new windows
- Activate windows (switch from one to another)
- Minimize windows (set aside without closing)
- Resize windows
- Move windows around on your screen
- Close windows when finished with them
- Scroll in windows
- Move information from one window to another
- Run multiple programs simultaneously

Opening a Window

There are a variety of ways to open windows. You've learned some already. Here's a list of typical ways, so that you can experiment and use the methods that make you most productive:

- Use the Open commands on most File menus.

- Use the keyboard equivalent (often, but not always, ALT-F, O, or CTRL-O).
- Double-click on icons.
- Click on window names in the Taskbar.

Activating a Window

Activating windows is a snap with the Taskbar. The names of running programs and certain other open windows appear as buttons on the Taskbar:

Remember, you can only work in an active window. Color displays show the active window's title bar in a different color than the title bars of inactive windows. On monochrome displays, the active window has a more distinct title bar than the other windows.

Click the appropriate button to switch to the window you want.

One of my favorite keyboard techniques (a holdover from Windows 3.1, I must admit) involves activating windows with the keyboard. To use this method, hold down the ALT key while repeatedly pressing the TAB key. This presents you with a revolving "list" of windows displayed as a series of icons.

When a square surrounds the window you want to activate, simply release the ALT key.

Hiding (Minimizing) a Window

Minimizing is less useful now than it was in the days before the Taskbar, but there might be times when too many open windows obscure a desktop icon you need to reach. Minimizing a window gets it out of the way without closing it. You can minimize either program windows or document windows or both.

Suppose, for instance, that you have your word processing program running and are using it to edit several documents. Suppose that you also have the calculator program running and your America Online program humming along as well, as in Figure 2.3.

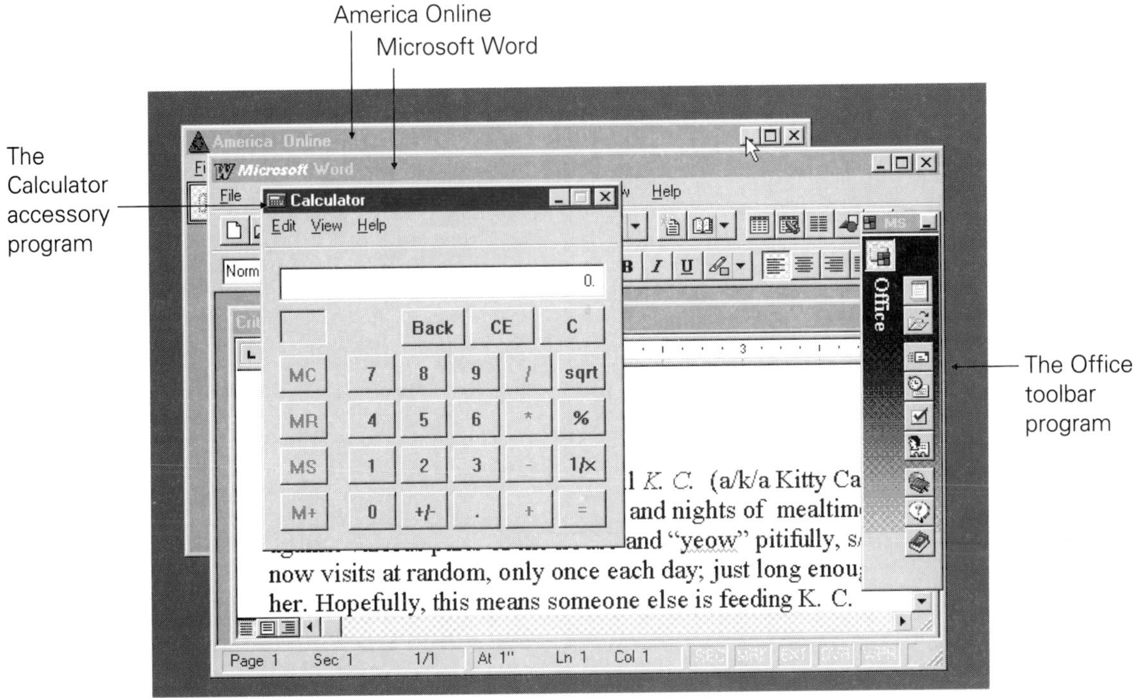

Figure 2.3 Running several programs at once

You need to reach the My Computer icon, but it's covered up; because you don't have the My Computer window open, its name is not on the Taskbar. As is often the case, you have several ways to minimize windows:

- Click the Minimize button in a window's title bar. (This button is third from the right, and looks like an underscore.) The window will vanish, but its name will appear either as a button on the Taskbar (if it is a program window) or an icon at the bottom of its parent window (if it is a document window).
- Click the window's title bar with the second mouse button (usually the right one) to reveal the resizing menu. This menu has a Minimize option that corresponds to the Minimize button: selecting it will shrink the window down to a button on the Taskbar or an icon in its parent window. (You will learn more about the Resizing menu very shortly.)

- To minimize *all* open windows, point to a non-button area of the Taskbar, click with the right mouse button to reveal the Shortcut menu, and then click the Minimize All Windows option.

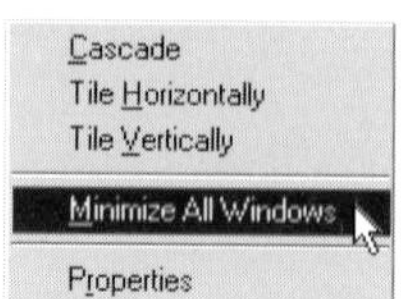

Remember that both document windows and program windows can have Minimize buttons. If you use a document window's Minimize button, the program window remains onscreen. Using the program window's Minimize button minimizes both the program window and any associated document windows.

CAUTION

If you have a dialog box open in a program, the window cannot be minimized. First, answer whatever question you are being asked, then click OK to issue the command, or click the Cancel button to close the dialog box without issuing a command so that you can minimize the window.

Restoring a Minimized Window to Its Regular Size

Restoring a minimized window makes it "reappear." To restore and activate a minimized program window, click its named button on the Taskbar. To restore and activate a document window, click its icon in the parent window.

Resizing a Window

Changing the size and shape of windows is quite useful. You can drag the edges and corners of windows to shrink or expand them to virtually any size you like. There are also a number of tools designed to make resizing easy. Here are the key techniques.

Maximizing a Window

If a parent window does not already fill your screen (or if a child window does not fill the available space in a parent window), you can make it do so by clicking on its Maximize button, which is the middle button in the three-button collection at the upper-right corner of most windows.

Restoring a Maximized Window to Its Smaller Size

If you've maximized a window and then wish to restore it to its smaller size, use the Restore button, which replaces the Maximize button whenever a window is maximized.

The Resizing Menu

Click the title bar with the second mouse button. The resizing menu will appear.

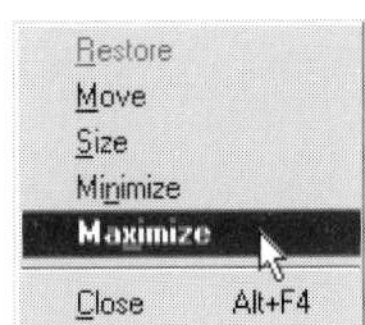

The Maximize option on this menu corresponds to the Maximize button: selecting it will make the window as large as possible. The Size option allows you to resize the window with the keyboard instead of dragging with the mouse. Simply select Size, and then use the UP ARROW, DOWN ARROW, LEFT ARROW, and RIGHT ARROW keys to adjust the size of the window incrementally. Tap the ENTER key to finish.

SHORTCUT

Double-click on a window's title bar to toggle resizing.

Resizing an MS-DOS Window

Use any of these methods to change the size of a DOS Window:

- Press ALT-ENTER to maximize/restore the MS-DOS window.
- Click the Full Screen button (the one containing the four arrowheads).
- Use the Minimize, Maximize, Restore, or Close button (which all work the same way as they do in non-DOS windows).

SHORTCUT

To close the MS-DOS window and restore your Windows desktop after using DOS in the full screen mode, type exit at the DOS prompt.

Moving and Arranging Windows on Your Screen

Moving a window is dirt-simple. Just drag it by its title bar to any location you like. You can organize multiple windows on your screen by dragging and possibly resizing them until you have a useful arrangement. You can also use the Taskbar to arrange windows on your screen.

To automatically resize and rearrange all open windows at once, follow the steps in the box on the next page.

You can use the arrow keys on your keyboard to move a window, just as you can to resize it. First click with the right mouse button on the window's title bar; this opens the Resizing menu. Select the Move option, and then press the arrow keys to move the window to the location you desire. Press ENTER to finish.

Finally, many programs (such as Microsoft Word and Excel) have their own windows management tools, which often can be found on their Windows menus. (These sometimes even give you ways to *split* windows.)

STEP BY STEP Organizing Windows with the Taskbar

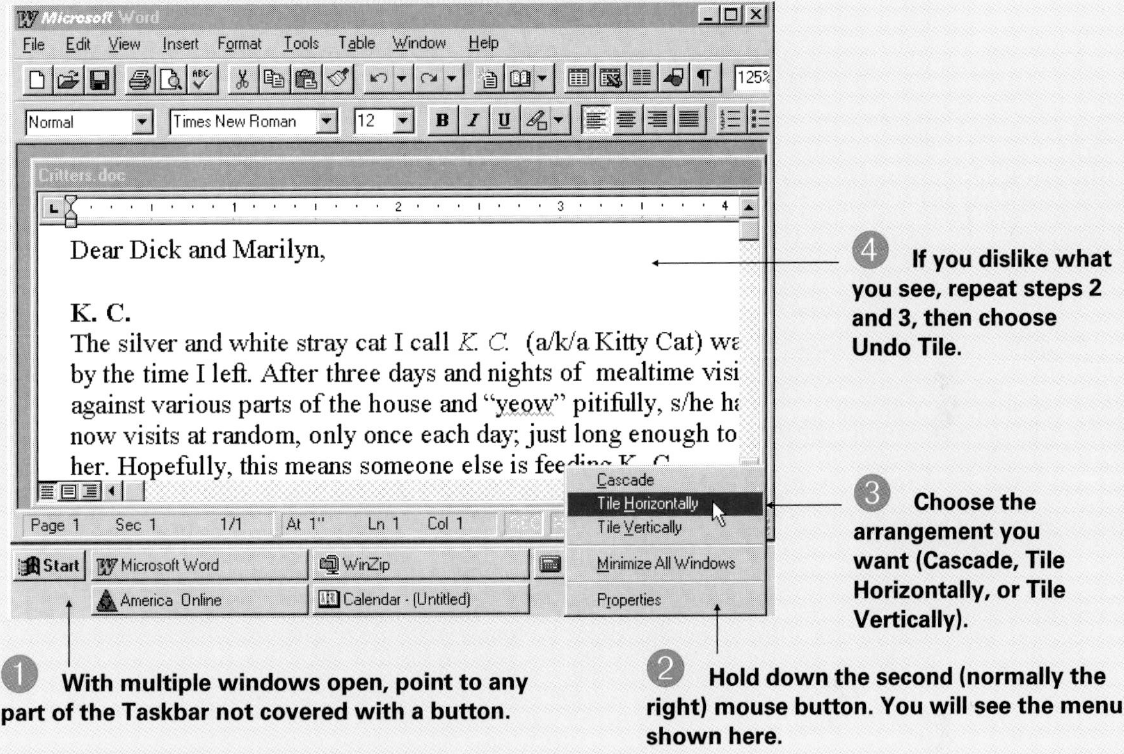

Cascade
Tile Horizontally
Tile Vertically
Minimize All Windows
Properties
1 With multiple windows open, point to any part of the Taskbar not covered with a button.
2 Hold down the second (normally the right) mouse button. You will see the menu shown here.
3 Choose the arrangement you want (Cascade, Tile Horizontally, or Tile Vertically).
4 If you dislike what you see, repeat steps 2 and 3, then choose Undo Tile.

Closing a Window

Closing a window (as opposed to minimizing it) "puts away" whatever it is you were working on. Different window types react differently when closed. Two quick ways to close a window are:

- Clicking on the Close box
- Selecting Close from the Resizing menu

EXPERT ADVICE

It's important to note that the buttons on the Taskbar get smaller as you add more items, and names of programs are often truncated as the buttons shrink. At some point the names may get too short to be meaningful. Close unneeded windows to remove them from the Taskbar. If you must use a crowded Taskbar, drag the top edge of the Taskbar to increase its height, thereby giving you more button room.

If you close a *program* window (such as the Microsoft Word window), the process of closing quits (exits) the program. If you have unsaved changes in files being used by the program whose window you attempt to close, you'll be prompted to either save or discard changes. Closing *document* windows (such as a memo) will not quit the program, but you'll still be prompted about saving changes.

Scrolling

Information in a document often exceeds your available screen space (for example, your text might be longer than the size of the screen in which you're viewing it). Most programs provide a number of tools for scrolling, which allow you to see the parts of your document hidden from view. These tools include:

- Horizontal and vertical scroll arrows
- Horizontal and vertical scroll boxes
- Keyboard commands PAGE UP, PAGE DOWN, etc.

Figure 2.4 shows the onscreen scrolling tools in Windows 95.

Here are some tips to keep in mind when you're scrolling around in your document:

- Clicking on scroll arrows usually moves the document a short distance up, down, left, or right.
- Holding down the mouse button initiates repetitive scrolling, which continues until you release the button.

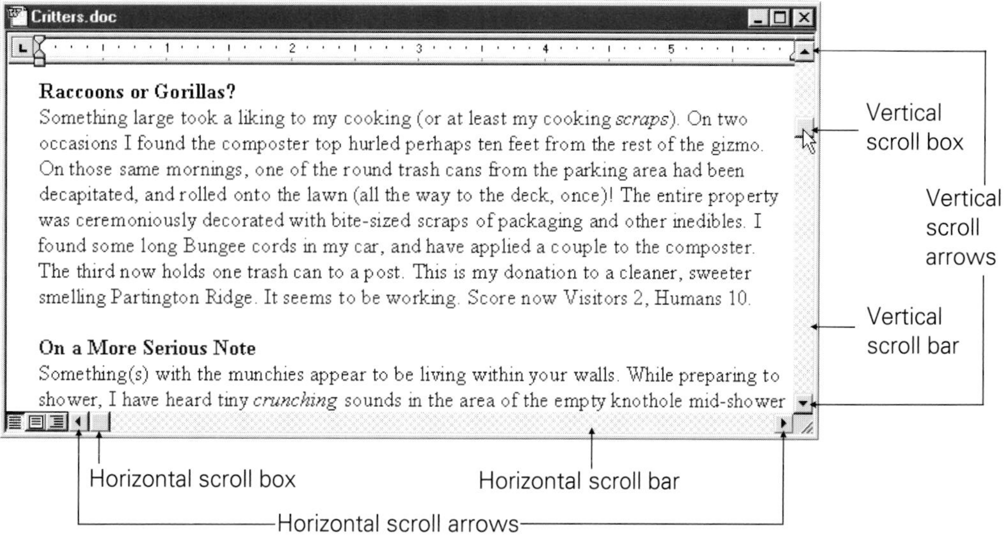

Figure 2.4 Scrolling tools

Microsoft is now marketing a new "Intellimouse" with a small wheel on its top. Rolling the wheel scrolls, if your programs are new enough to be compatible. For example, Word 97 supports it; Word 95 does not.

- Clicking in the area above, below, to the right, or to the left of the scroll boxes scrolls you further than clicking on the arrow itself. (Typically, one click moves you one screen full.)
- You can drag the scroll boxes to take you near the right position in your document. For example, to move to the middle of a long word processing report, drag the scroll box to the approximate middle of the window.

Moving Information from One Window to Another

One of the advantages of a graphical interface like Windows 95 is its willingness to help you pass information from one document to another. For example, you might want to include some spreadsheet numbers in a memo without retyping them, or you might want to add a logo or other graphic to your letterhead.

You can do things like this by using these methods of transporting material from one application to another (or from one document to another):

- Copying and pasting
- Cutting and pasting
- Dragging and dropping
- Creating "Clips" on your desktop
- Linking or Embedding

CAUTION

The ability to exchange information among differing programs has come a long way in the past decade, but we have light years to go. When moving information from one program to another, you may not always get the results you expect. You can make real guacamole out of a perfectly good spreadsheet, report, or database. When experimenting on important files, use copies of the files, not the originals. Test and retest. Know the rules! It's a jungle out there.

Sometimes information exchange is a blissfully simple process. Other times it's as frustrating as herding cats. Because entire books have been written on the subject of information exchange, we'll just touch upon some of the key concepts here and let you experiment. Should you decide to make understanding information exchange technology your life's work, check out online help or consult Ralph Soucie's excellent *Making Microsoft Office Work* (Osborne McGraw-Hill, 1995).

Exchanging Information by Copying or Cutting and Pasting

Copying leaves the information intact in its original location, whereas cutting removes the information from its original place. In the simplest case, you can move information from the source window to the destination window using this general recipe:

1. Click in the source window, if necessary, to make it the active window.

2. Select the desired information (text or spreadsheet cells or database records or whatever). In Figure 2.5, the information being copied is text from a Word document.

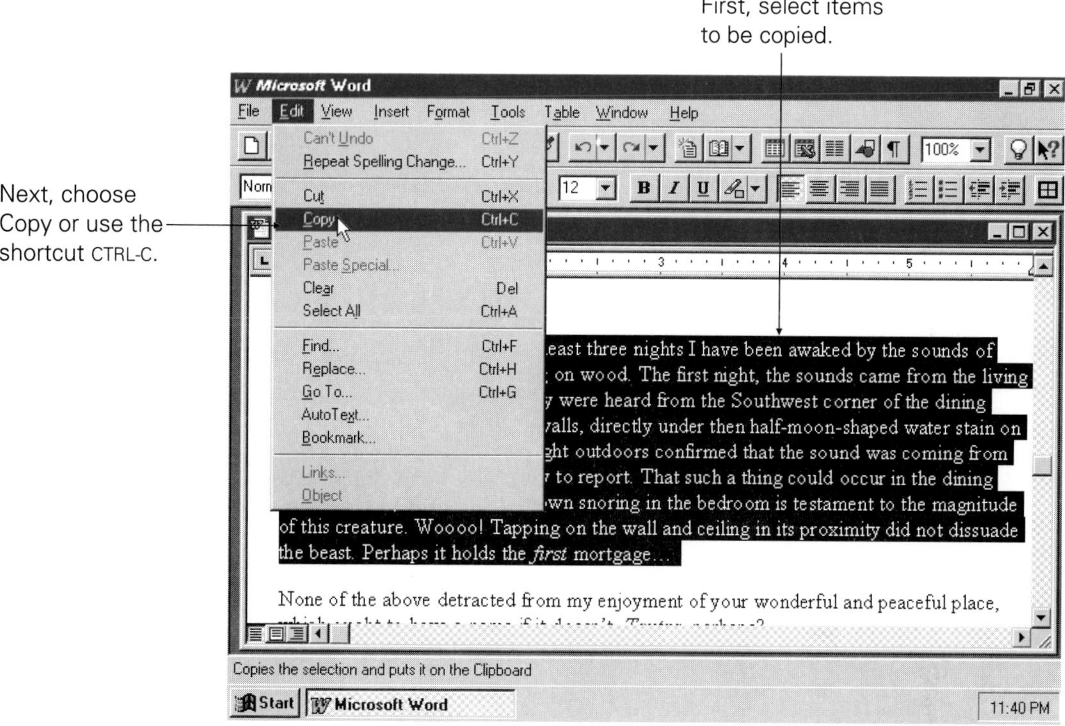

Figure 2.5 Copying text from one window to another

3. Use the Copy or Cut command from the active window's Edit menu to copy the data you've selected. The keyboard shortcuts for Copy and Cut are CTRL-C and CTRL-X, respectively.
4. Activate the destination window by clicking anywhere on or in it.
5. Position the insertion point at the desired location in the destination document by using the mouse to point and click where you want to insert the data. Here the text is going to be pasted into an America Online mail message:

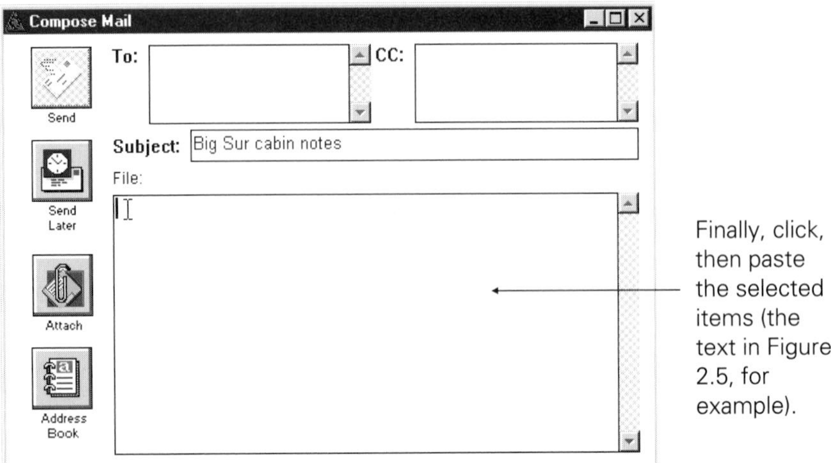

Finally, click, then paste the selected items (the text in Figure 2.5, for example).

The clipboard viewer is now an optional accessory.

6. Choose Paste (CRTL-V) from the destination window's Edit menu.

The data will be placed in the destination document. Its appearance will be affected by a slew of factors described in a moment.

When you copy or cut information, it is saved in an invisible neverland called the *Clipboard*, replacing whatever was there before. Suppose, for instance, you are running Excel and Word. You copy some cells from an Excel worksheet. These copied cell contents replace the prior contents of the Clipboard.

Although you can't easily see the Clipboard in Windows 95 (which probably frustrates you diehard Win 3 and Macintosh users), you can create things called *scraps*, which are an intriguing new item in Windows 95. Chapter 7 covers scraps in greater detail.

You also can use a helpful Windows feature called *drag and drop*, which can move information from place to place within a document or between windows, even if the windows are created by different programs. Chapter 7 covers drag and drop as well.

Copying Information from an MS-DOS Window

When working in a Windows 95 MS-DOS window, you might want to copy text from that window into a Windows program's window. The steps are similar but not identical to those used when copying between Windows windows. Take a look:

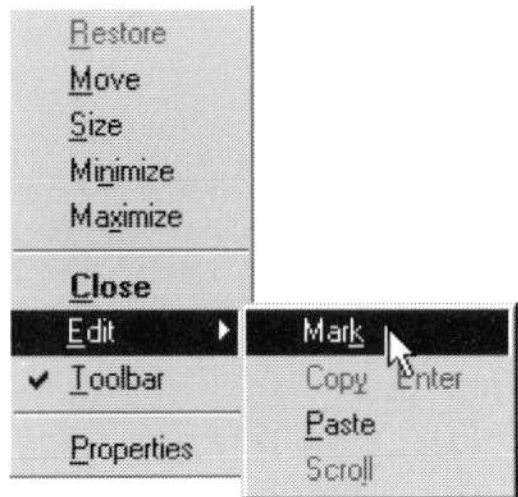

1. Switch to the MS-DOS window.
2. Choose the Mark command from the MS-DOS Edit menu or click the Mark button.
3. Drag to select the desired text.
4. Click the MS-DOS icon and choose Edit, then choose Copy (or click the Copy button).
5. Switch to the Windows program and activate the desired destination window.
6. Move the insertion point to the correct spot.
7. Choose Paste from the Windows program's Edit menu or use the CTRL-V shortcut.

Copying Information to an MS-DOS Window

You also can copy and paste from Windows to some MS-DOS programs, or between two MS-DOS programs if they will let you. (You cannot paste to an MS-DOS program running in full screen mode, however.) Sometimes, though, you can run a program in a maximized DOS window and use the Paste button. (CTRL-V won't work here.)

Not every DOS programmer had these tricks in mind when designing software, so expect some frustration and remember to experiment on *copies* of files instead of the originals if they are mission-critical.

A Word about Autoexec.bat and Config.sys Files

Windows 95 doesn't need Autoexec.bat and Config.sys files itself, but some of your old Microsoft-DOS programs might. If you are having problems with old Microsoft-DOS programs running under Windows 95, explore the possibility of creating Autoexec.bat files (and in very rare cases Config.sys files) for use with your Microsoft-DOS programs under Windows 95. The manufacturer of the old program might be able to help you with this.

At this point you know enough to be dangerous. You can run Windows 95, launch programs, rearrange, resize, hide windows, and more. You could stop now, but please don't. Take a few minutes to practice what you've learned in this chapter. Run two programs simultaneously, then arrange both windows so that you can see them on the screen at the same time. Resize the windows. Copy information from one to the other (cells from a spreadsheet into a word processing document, for example). Try the different closing and resizing techniques described in this chapter until you find the ones you like. When you are ready to move on, the next chapter will show you some powerful timesaving tricks. Keep reading.

CHAPTER

3

Getting Help

INCLUDES

- Getting online help with Windows 95
- Printing help topics
- Creating your own help notes
- Getting help from readme files
- Getting help over the Internet

Start Online Help ➤ p. 57

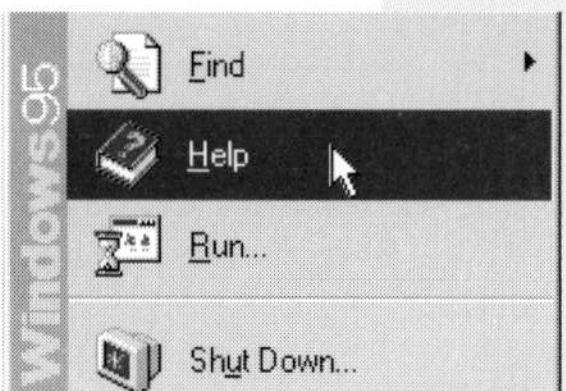

Choose Help from the Start menu or press the F1 function key. Many programs (like Word and Excel) have program-specific Help menus as well.

Use the Help System's Find Tab ➤ pp. 57-59

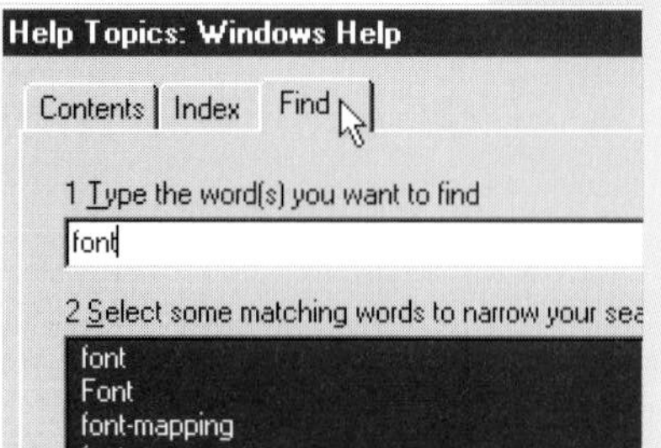

1. Choose Help from the Start menu or press F1.
2. Click the Find tab if necessary to bring it forward.
3. Type word(s) of interest.
4. Double-click a topic in the resulting list.
5. Hit the ESC key to close the Help window.

Use the Help System's Index Tab ➤ pp. 61-62

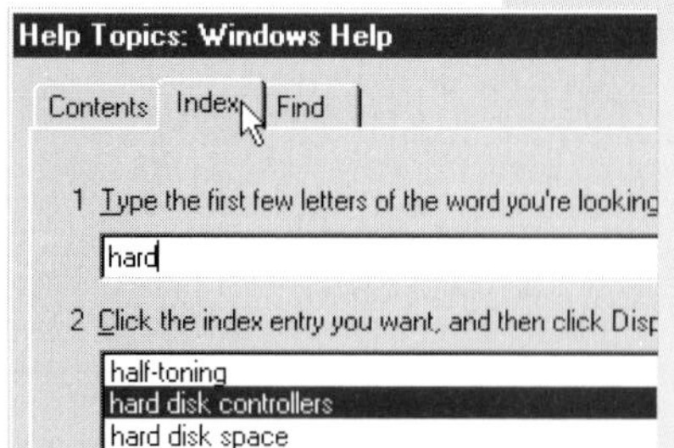

1. Choose Help from the Start menu or press F1.
2. Click the Index tab if necessary to bring it forward.
3. Type word(s) of interest.
4. Double-click a topic in the resulting list.
5. Hit the ESC key to close the Help window.

Use the Help System's Contents Tab ➤ pp. 62-64

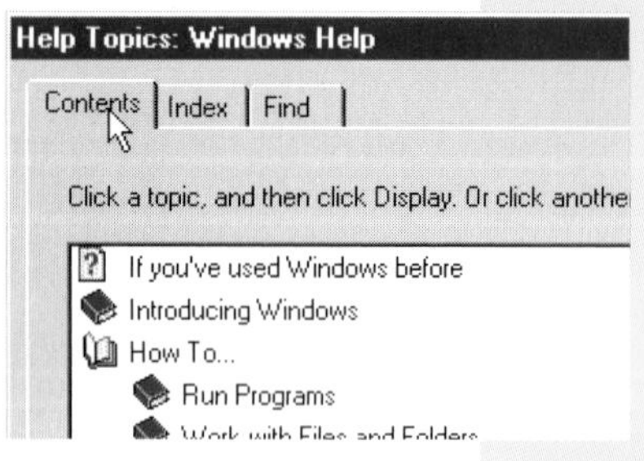

1. Choose Help from the Start menu or press F1.
2. Click the Contents tab if necessary to bring it forward.
3. Double-click book icons representing your topics of interest.
4. Double-click page icons when you see them.
5. Hit the ESC key to close the Help window.

Print Help Topics ➤ *p. 66*

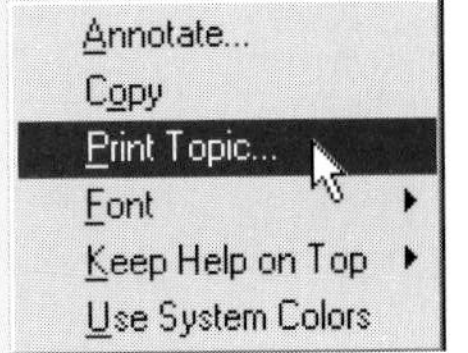

1. Make sure your printer is ready.
2. Bring up a help topic.
3. Click the Options button.
4. Choose Print Topic.
5. Click OK.
6. Press the ESC key to close the Help window.

Get "What's This?" Help ➤ *p. 66*

1. First click the little question mark box in the upper-right corner of the window. (Note that not all windows give you this feature.) The mouse pointer will change shape.
2. Point to an object of interest and click.
3. Read the resulting text.
4. Hit the ESC key to close the Help window.

Get Help with Dialog Boxes ➤ *pp. 66-67*

Click the Help button. (Note that not all dialog boxes offer this feature.)

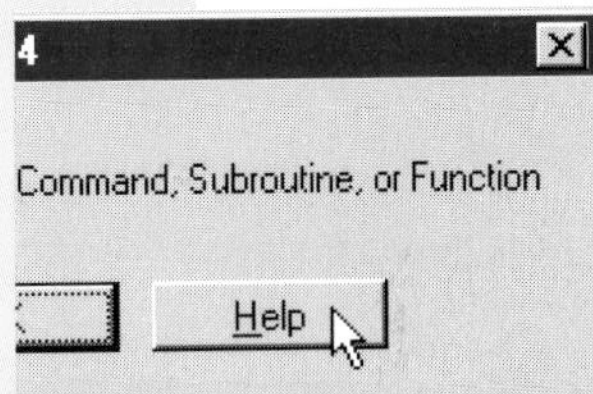

Get Help Over the Internet ➤ *pp. 69-72*

1. Connect to the Internet using your favorite service provider and browser.
2. Point your browser to **www.microsoft.com/support/**.
3. Pick **Windows 95** or any other Microsoft software topic of interest from the "Select Product" list.
4. Visit the various links offered.
5. To search for a specific topic, use the Search button near the top right of the Support windows.

Windows 95 provides very powerful online help features. For instance, you have already seen how hovering your mouse pointer over items onscreen often displays their names. In a moment you'll learn about a huge library of indexed help text and how to search it. Moreover, some Microsoft Windows applications offer program-specific online help based on observations the software makes about the way you work. Yep. You read that correctly. Some programs notice your bad habits and suggest better (or at least different) ones.

For tougher problems, Microsoft provides automated dial-up help. You can access it via telephone, fax, or data modem. Let's take a closer look at today's wide array of help options.

Where to Look for Help

Although there is much ballyhoo about users being able to focus on tasks and forget about underlying applications, we ain't there yet, campers. So the first trick is to know where to look for help.

Windows 95 has extensive online help that can show you everything from how to set your computer's clock (the topic is "12-hour clock, changing to") to the purpose of the "X" button in the upper-right corner of most Windows 95 windows (titled appropriately enuff "X button in upper-right corner of window"). But it doesn't know Shinola about printing envelopes in Microsoft Word, nor can it help you with the SUM() function in Excel or the Route command in AutoMap.

At the risk of oversimplifying, if your question is about your computer itself (the display, memory, sound, disk drives, etc.), start your journey in the Windows 95 Help system. If you have questions specific to an application (Word or Excel or whatever), try the help features provided within that program. For more obscure problems (like networking maladies, advanced font trivia, and the like), try dial-up resources like the Microsoft Network, Microsoft's WWW site, America Online, or CompuServe. These external sources of information are often more current and complete than the help files shipped with your software. And don't forget to rub elbows in the various user-to-user areas of these dial-up sites. There's nothing like learning from others' experiences.

Opening the Windows 95 Help Window

I'm guessing you want to know first about the help you can find on your very own hard disk, not some far-flung behemoth. Reach the Windows 95 Help window by pressing the F1 function key or by choosing Help from the Start menu.

EXPERT ADVICE

If you have programs running (like Word), and a window from a program is the active window, pressing F1 will usually bring up online help for the program, not Windows 95. To be sure you'll get Windows 95 Help, use the Help choice on the Start menu.

The road forks here. You can choose to see help organized in "books" (using the Contents tab), or view a list of topics arranged alphabetically (via the Index tab), or type a keyword or phrase (in the Find tab) and see what happens. Let's start with my favorite: Find.

Searching for Words and Phrases

If this is your first time using the help feature, it might display a Help Wizard asking what kind of database you'd like to set up. Click on the Next button, and then Finish, if this happens.

S'pose you want to find out about making backup copies of your hard disk files to floppies. Just follow these steps:

1. Open Windows 95 Help with the Help choice on the Start menu, or perhaps with the F1 function key.
2. Click the Find tab if necessary to bring it foremost.
3. Type the word or phrase of interest (**backup**, for example), as shown here:

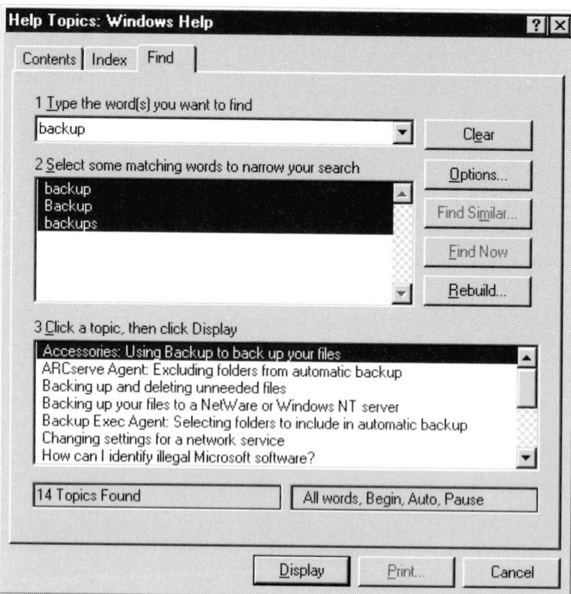

4. Either scroll through the list of topics and double-click one or type an additional word to narrow the search. Here, simply typing the beginning of the word floppy (**flo**) provides just what the doctor ordered:

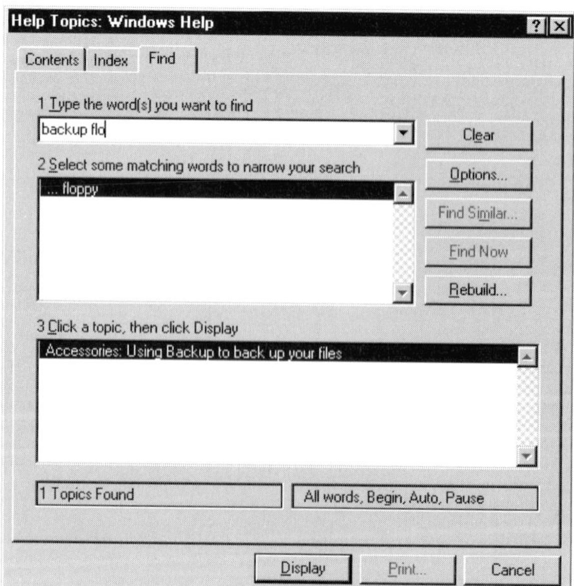

5. Double-click the topic or click once to select, then click the Display button. You'll see a screen of information about the topic you've chosen.

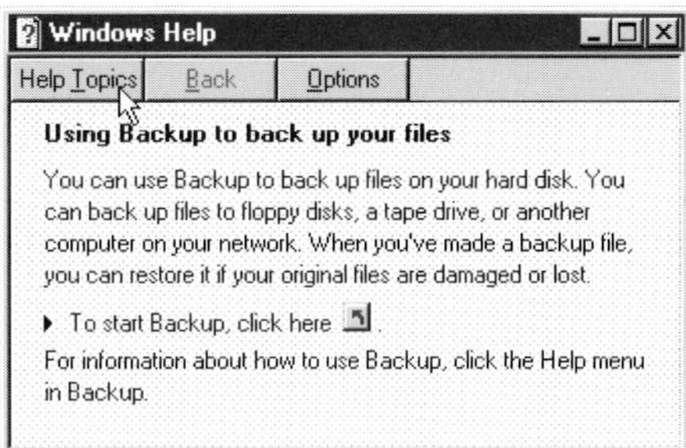

6. Use the Close box or the ESC key to quit help and get back to work. (Clicking the Help Topics button takes you back to the Find tab.)

SHORTCUT

You can often leave help topics open as you try the prescribed steps. Just drag and perhaps resize the Help window so it fits in some out-of-the-way location on your screen. This eliminates the need to memorize or (gasp!) to print.

Help Window Tricks

Windows 95 Help offers numerous, subtle features that can really assist you. This next section describes some of my favorites.

Buttons in Help Text

Many Help windows contain buttons nestled within the help text to provide additional assistance. These buttons run programs, open the control panel so that you can make adjustments, etc. For instance, in the illustration that follows, clicking the tiny button with the arrow on its face will open your display control panel.

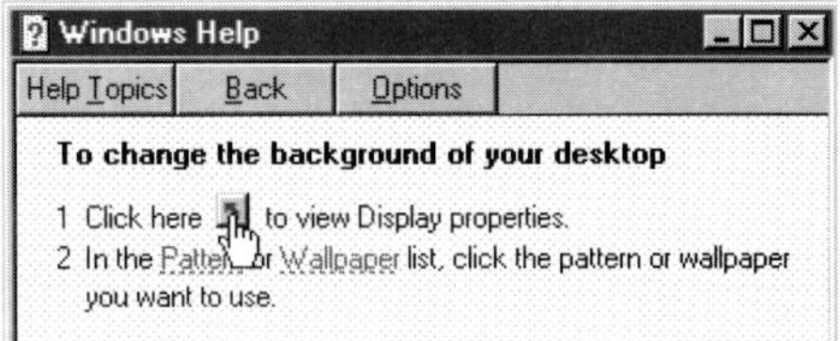

G'head. Try clicking those tiny buttons when you see them. Just remember to click Cancel in the resulting dialog boxes if things start to get out of control. (No sense needlessly formatting your hard disk just because Help makes it easy.) Read the screens and ask for additional help as you meander. And remember: You are busy, so don't get *too* distracted.

Colored Words Provide Definitions

Clicking one of the colored, underlined words in a help screen (Patterns and Wallpaper in this example) displays its definition:

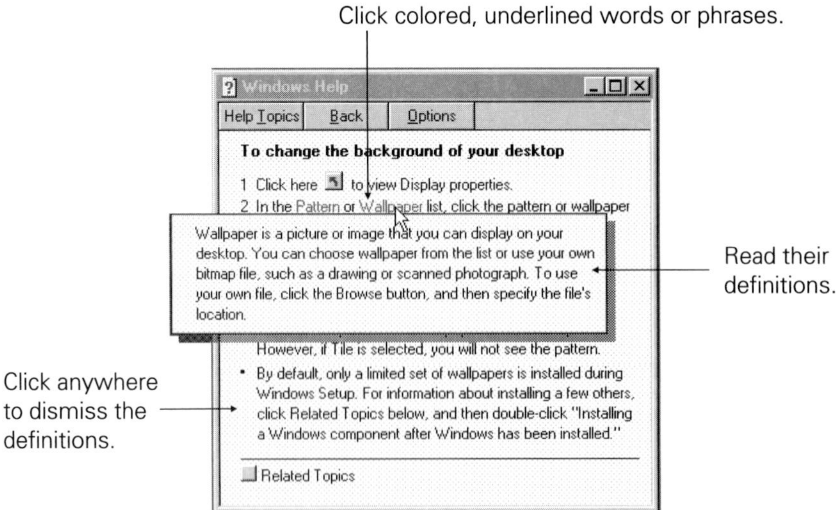

The Related Topics Button

To see related help topics, click—you guessed it—the Related Topics button. It will reveal a list of (we hope) cogent topics. Not all windows contain a

Related Topics button. But if the one you are staring at does, use it. Then double-click a topic, or select a topic, as shown here, and click Display.

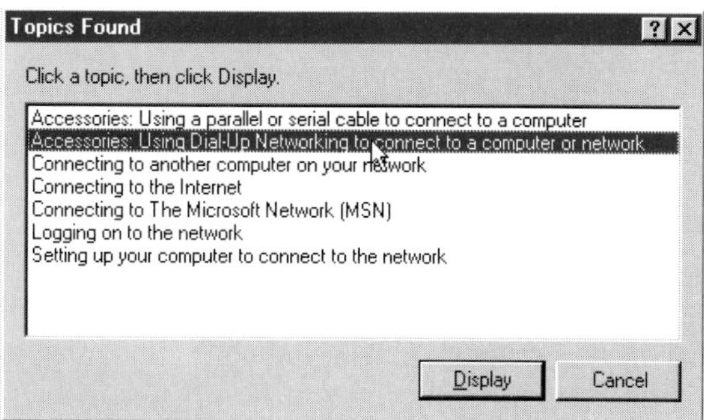

Keep Help on Top

The "Keep Help on Top" choice in most Help window Options menus lets you request that the Help window remain on top of any pile of open windows. Experiment to see if you like or dislike this feature. (It is turned off by default.)

The Index Tab

The Index tab in your Windows 95 Help window provides an alphabetical list of topics. You can scroll the list with the PAGE UP, PAGE DOWN, and other navigational keyboard keys, or with the scroll tools and your mouse, or by typing the first few characters of a topic. For instance, typing **back**, as shown in Figure 3.1, gets you in the backup neighborhood, albeit not as gracefully as with the Find tab. Once you spot your topic, you can double-click it.

Here's how to use the Index tab:

1. Choose Help from the Start menu or press the F1 function key with a Windows 95 window active. (Click the Index tab, if necessary, to bring it to the top.)
2. Type the first few letters of the word or phrase of interest.
3. Add more letters if this helps focus the search. (Backspace to delete if you've narrowed too much.)

4. Double-click on the desired topic in the list to read it. (If you get a list of topics, select from the list first.)
5. Use the Close box or the ESC key to close the Help window. (Clicking the Help Topics button will take you back to the Index tab.)

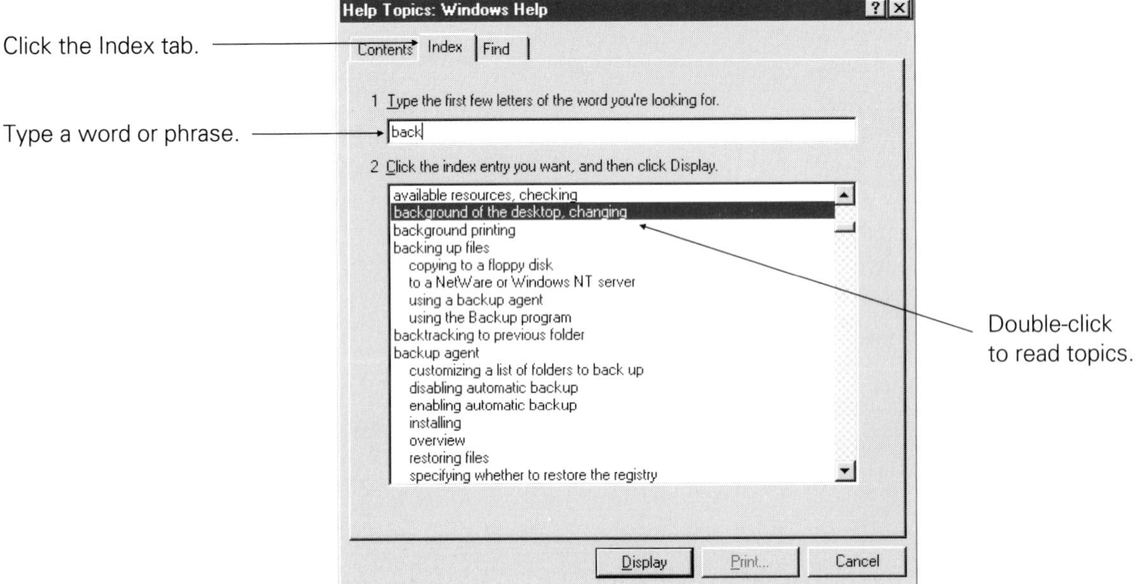

Figure 3.1 Finding help from the Index tab

The Contents Tab

The Contents tab presents you with tiny pictures of books. These books contain books within them, and the books contain little help pages upon which you click. If this is your cup of tea, here's how it works:

1. Open the Windows 95 Help window from the Start menu or with the F1 function key.
2. Click on the Contents tab, if necessary, to bring it foremost.
3. Double-click a book icon, and it will "open" to reveal a list of subtopics. Here, "How To" has been selected:

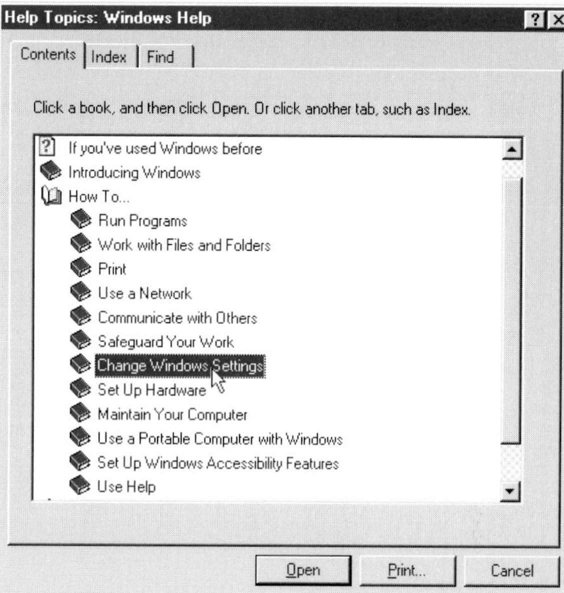

4. Double-click another book—"Change Windows Settings," for example—and you'll see even more subtopics:

5. Click a topic of interest or scroll to a different book ("Change How Windows Looks," for example), and double-click there.

6. Click on any page with a question mark to display that help topic.
7. Read (and perhaps print) the topic.
8. To learn more, click on any buttons you find in the help topic.

To change the background of your desktop

1 Click here to view Display properties.
2 In the Pattern or Wallpaper list, click the pattern or wallpaper you want to use.

9. Use the Close box or the ESC key to quit help. (Clicking the Help Topics button takes you back to the Contents tab.)

EXPERT ADVICE

I never cared for this Contents tab Zen. Too much clicking and too much guessing. For example, where does one find information about backups? In "Working with Files and Folders"? Nope. It's in "Safeguard Your Work" and "Maintain Your Computer." This frustrates me. But try it. You might like it.

Changing the Font Size Used in Help Windows

You can frequently change the size of fonts used in Help windows by following these general steps:

1. Open a help topic (search for an item of interest).
2. Click the Options button in the resulting Help topic window.
3. Pick Font from the resulting menu and a font size from the submenu.
4. Choose Small, Normal, or Large from the submenu to specify the desired font size.

Adding Your Own Notes to Help Topics

You can add your own notes to help topics and save them. For example, if you discover an envelope printing tip that works, you can add it to the Microsoft Word Envelope Printing help topic. Here are the general steps:

1. Open the help topic of interest.
2. Click the Options button in the resulting Help topic window.
3. Pick Annotate from the resulting menu.
4. Type your note in the window that appears.
5. Click Save.
6. A small paper clip will appear next to the help topic henceforth.
7. Clicking on the paper clip will display your note as shown in Figure 3.2.

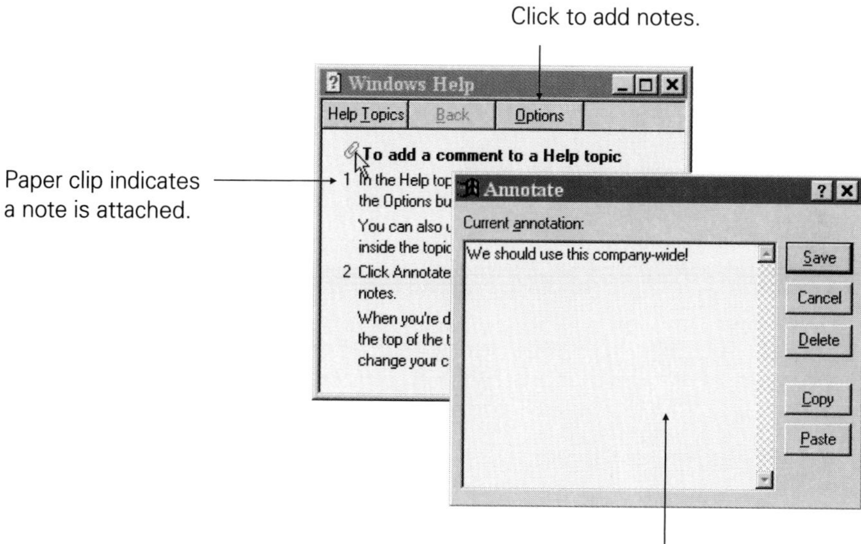

Figure 3.2 An annotated Help topic

Printing and Copying Help Topics

You can print help topics once you have them on your screen.

1. Make sure your printer is ready.
2. Click the Options button in the Help text window's button bar.
3. Choose Print Topic.
4. Make any necessary changes in the resulting Print dialog box (number of copies to print, etc.).
5. Click OK or press ENTER.

"What's This?" Help

Nothing is more frustrating than fiddling with some onscreen control when you are clueless! So, next time you see a gizmo that is not self-explanatory, look to the northeast corner of the window for a little button with a question mark like the one you see here.

When you see the question mark button, follow these steps:

1. Click it. Your mouse pointer's appearance will change. (It gets a little tag-along question mark of its own.)
2. Point to the source of your wonderment.
3. Click. You will probably get an explanation (or at least a clue).
4. Clicking a second time turns off "What's This?," so to overcome mass confusion, you'll need to repeat steps 1 through 3.

Dialog Box Help

Occasionally (some say regularly), Windows or a Windows program will ask you a bizarre question or make some disturbing proclamation.

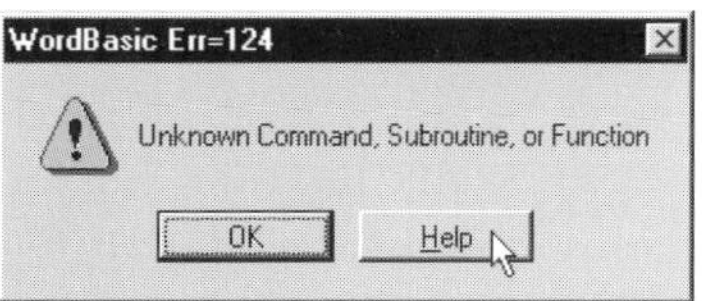

If the dialog box causing the interruption contains a Help button, give it a poke. Sometimes you'll get useful assistance. Here, look. A quick click and...

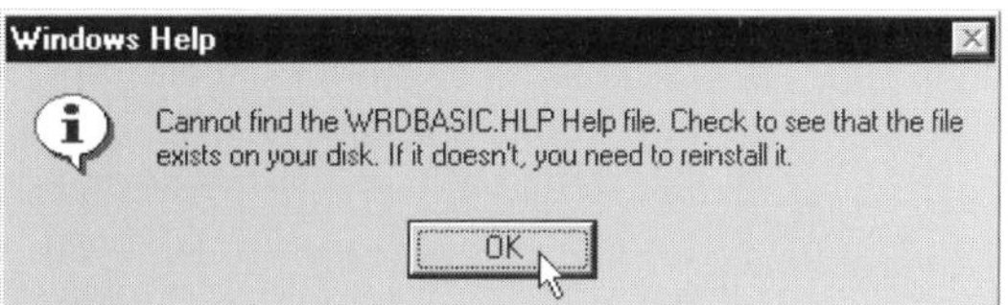

Oh. Nice. That helped a lot. Now you know why computer book authors like the words "sometimes" and "usually".

Readme Files as a Source of Help

Many disks (including your hard disk) contain text files with names like Readme.txt, or sometimes Readme.doc, or even Read.me. These information files usually contain last-minute news not found in the documentation that came with your hardware or software. It's a good idea to read these files before you install new software or hardware. They can also be a helpful source of information when you are experiencing difficulties with a product. Also, Readme files frequently contain helpful tips and suggestions.

Usually, all you need to do to peruse a Readme file is double-click its icon either in a folder window or in the Windows Explorer. (If you don't already know how to do this, Chapter 4 will give you specific steps for locating and viewing text files.)

The following table lists some help-filled Readme files that you will probably find on your hard disk. (Your disk might have different files, since one major function of Readme files is to provide "late-breaking news" between official software version changes.)

Filename	Topics
Config.txt	Modifying your Config.sys file for cranky MS-DOS programs. (This is something you should probably not need to do, thanks to Windows 95's ability to work out most of these problems itself.)
Display.txt	Potential problems with your monitor and display electronics. Read about available drivers (software) to correct display problems.
Exchange.txt	How to set up and run Microsoft Exchange, the illustrious Swiss Army knife of E-mail.
Faq.txt	Frequently asked questions about Windows 95 and the official answers.
General.txt	Potential startup problems, the programs that come with Windows 95, disk tools, disks and CDs, drivers, removable media, Microsoft Fax, and pen services. (Curiously, there's not a word about Generals.)
Hardware.txt	Known hardware problems and workarounds. (See also Printers.txt or Mouse.txt.)
Internet.txt	Connecting to the Internet. (Read this before purchasing and installing any third-party Internet software. Windows 95 might be all you'll need.) The file also provides information about where to download Microsoft's Web browser, Internet Explorer. Beware, this. It may describe obsolete procedures and versions.
Mouse.txt	Known problems and workarounds for mouse and keyboard dementia.
Msdosdrv.txt	!WONK ALERT! Syntax information for MS-DOS device drivers. (See also Config.txt.)
Msn.txt	How to connect to the Microsoft Network, Microsoft's (now defunct) dial-up competition to CompuServe, etc.
Network.txt	Read this if you plan to install and run network servers or other shared resources.
Printers.txt	Known printer problems and solutions.

Filename	Topics
Programs.txt	Known problems with selected Windows-based and DOS-based programs running under Windows 95.
Support.txt	How to get additional support for Windows 95. (Tragically, there is no 12-step support program for the Windows-addicted.)
Tips.txt	Assorted tips and tricks for using Windows 95 (most of which you will find in this book).

Using Microsoft's Fast Tips Service

Microsoft provides 24-hour, 365-day technical support via fax and prerecorded voice tips. You access these tireless droids from any touch-tone phone, fax, or modem. Since all busy people have fax machines, I've assumed you do too:

1. From any phone (it need not be your fax phone), dial (800) 936-4100 for help with desktop applications (Word, Excel, etc.), or (800) 936-4200 for Windows 95.
2. Listen to the choices (and admire the perfect diction, thank-Q).
3. Use your phone's touch-tone pad to request a "map" or catalog of available documents and recordings.
4. Enter your fax telephone number when prompted to do so. (Be sure the fax machine or modem is ready to receive.)
5. When you have been told that the document will be faxed, hang up and watch another tree fall on your behalf.
6. Call back with map in hand and request the desired information.

The Internet as a Source of Help

Microsoft and others are now providing online help for Windows 95 and other software via the Internet. Let's look first at Microsoft's offerings, then at some of the others.

Microsoft's Web Site as a Source of Help

Microsoft has a mind-boggling array of online help resources, most of them available for free to the general public. You can use your own Internet service provider and a browser like Microsoft Explorer or Netscape, or you can get to most of the information other ways via America Online, CompuServe, etc. For now, let's assume you are good boys and girls using Microsoft Explorer.

1. Connect to the Internet using your favorite service provider and browser (Microsoft Explorer in this example).
2. Type **www.microsoft.com/support/** in the Address blank in your browser and press ENTER.
3. Pick **Windows 95** or any other Microsoft software topic of interest from the "Select Product" list shown in Figure 3.3.
4. Visit the various links offered (a sampling is shown in Figure 3.4).

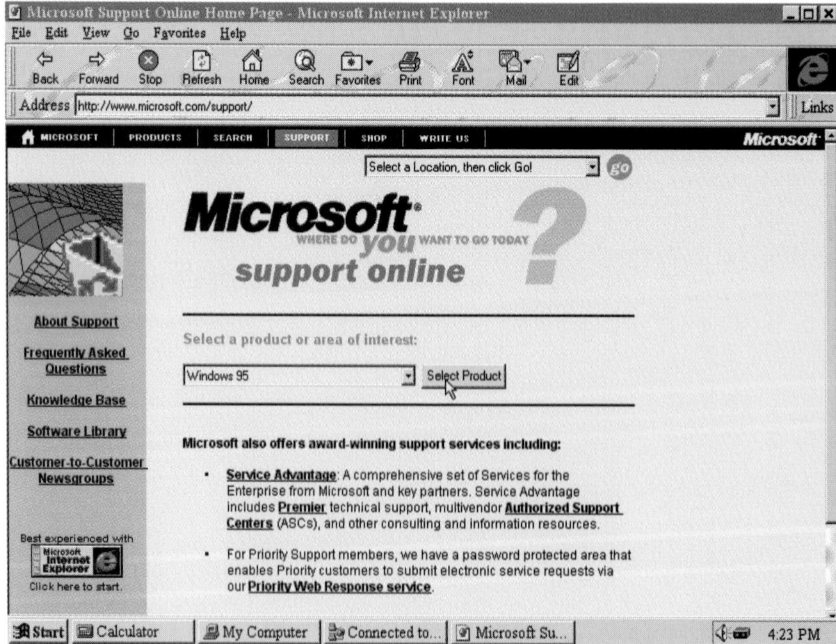

Figure 3.3 Specifying Windows 95 as the support topic of interest

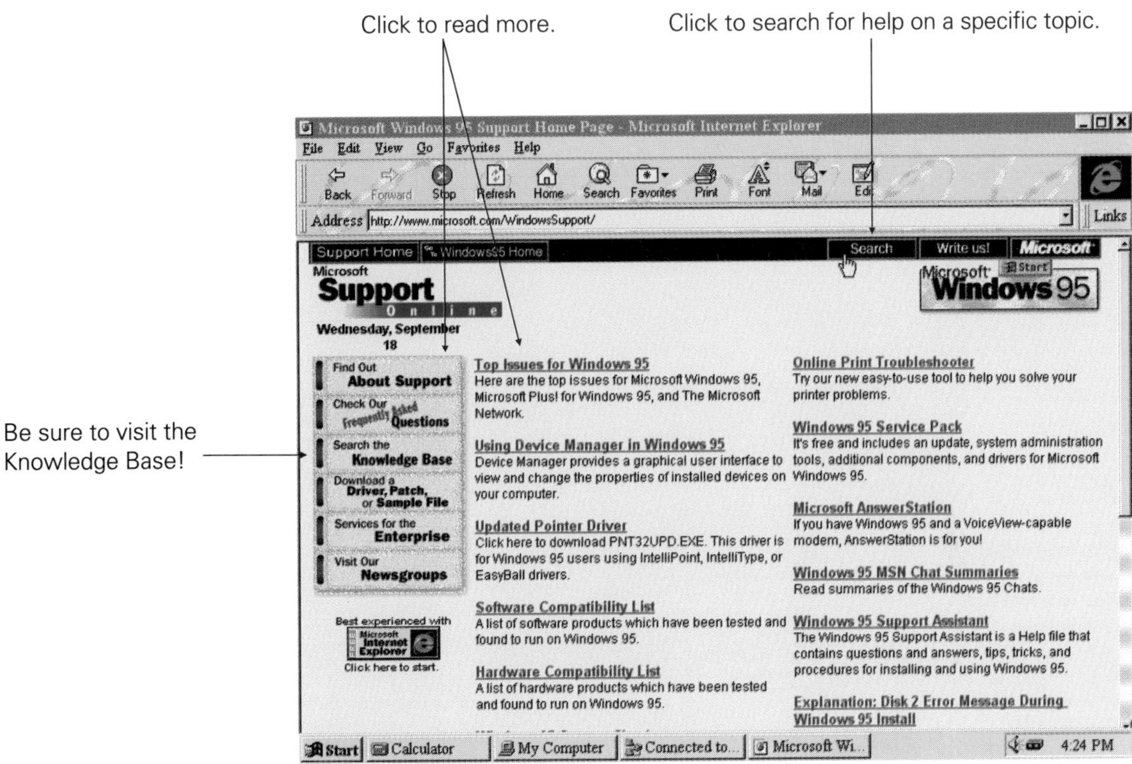

Figure 3.4 Typical support topics. Click on the links and buttons to learn more

5. To search for a specific topic, use the Search button near the top right of the Support windows. (You can see it in Figures 3.3 and 3.4.)

Other Sources of Automated Help

There are perhaps a thousand or more online sources of Windows 95 and Windows-application-related help. Many of these resources provide lists of other places to graze. For example, Figure 3.5 shows a web site that collects bugs and workarounds. The main purpose of this site is to get you interested in their newsletter aimed at tech support folks and others.

Figure 3.5 BugNet (www.bugnet.com) gives you the inside scoop on quirky software. Worth a visit!

There are thousands of folks offering Windows 95 and related software advice. Some are experts, some are clowns. Use your head! Here are a few usually helpful sites to get you started:

Resource	Reach It Via	Notes
Microsoft Knowledge Base and Software Library	America Online, CompuServe, the Microsoft Network, Microsoft's WWW site (see below), and others	An amazing collection of tips, workarounds, bug reports, files, and more.
Microsoft's World Wide Web Server	**http://www.microsoft.com/**	Where do you want to go today? Even job postings can be found here!
User Groups	The Computing sections of America Online, CompuServe, Prodigy, and others. (Many neighborhood user groups have their own BBSs too.)	Don't confuse the experts with the wannabe experts. Advice in these groups runs the gamut from genius to dangerous.

Take a few moments now to learn something new about Windows. Pick a topic—printing, perhaps, or modems. Use all of the help techniques described in this chapter to learn more about the topic. Print some of the information you find. Add your own note to one of the help topics. Explore the Microsoft web site if you are able.

When you are confident that you know where to go for answers and assistance, you're ready for one of the longest—and nitty-grittiest—chapters in this book. Chapter 4 will teach you effective disk management and help you organize your work in files and folders.

CAUTION

CHAPTER

4

Working with Disks, Folders, and Files

INCLUDES

- Types of disks
- Seeing disk contents and viewing files
- Organizing disks with folders
- Creating folders from within applications
- Filenames and types
- Moving, copying, and deleting files
- Associating file types with programs
- Formatting disks

View a Disk's Contents ➤ *pp. 84-93*

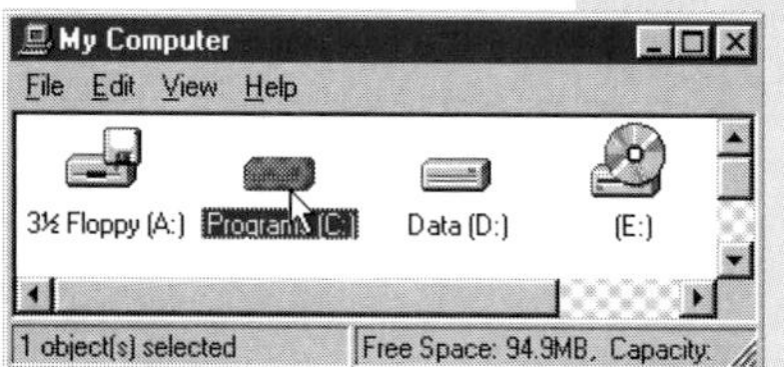

You can use any of these methods to look at the contents of a disk:

- Double-click the disk's icon in the My Computer window.
- Hold down the SHIFT key and double-click on a disk or folder icon to launch the Explorer.
- Use the Windows Explorer command found in the Programs submenu on the Start menu.

Quickly View a File's Contents ➤ *pp. 90-93*

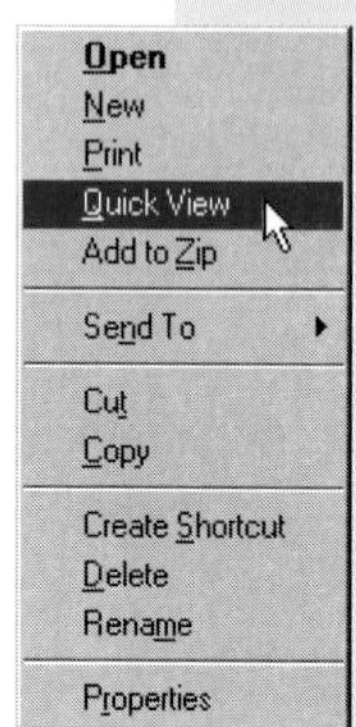

1. Be sure Quick View is installed on your computer. (Quick View won't be listed on your menu unless it is installed.)
2. Click the icon for the file you wish to examine.
3. Right-click.
4. If Windows recognizes the file type, you will see Quick View in the shortcut menu. Choose it. Otherwise, choose Open With and specify an application.

Create a Folder with Windows 95 ➤ *pp. 95-97*

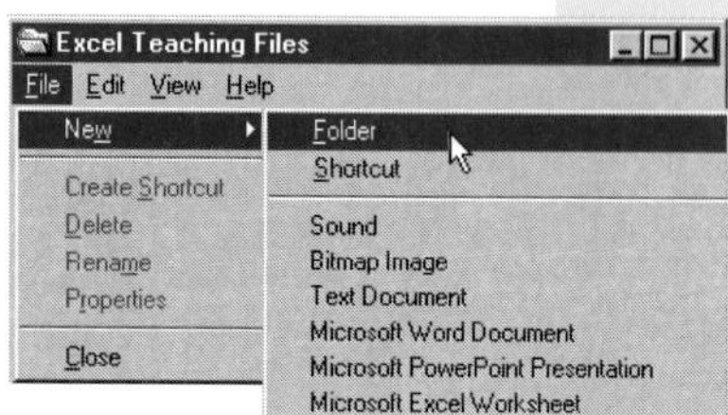

1. Open the disk or folder window where the new folder will be created.
2. Choose New from the window's File menu.
3. Choose Folder from the resulting submenu.
4. Type the name of the folder.
5. Press ENTER or click outside of the folder icon.

Create a Folder from within an Application ➤ *pp. 97-98*

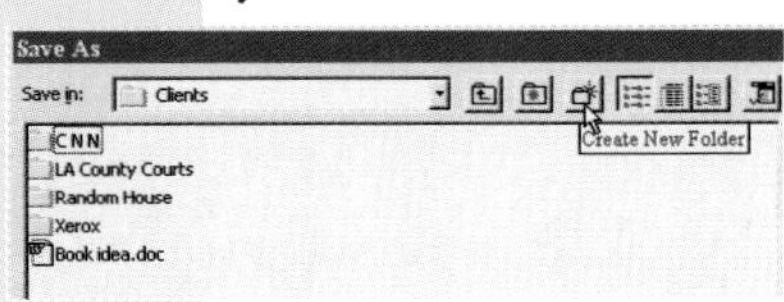

1. While in the Save As box in any Windows 95-savvy application (Microsoft Word, for example), navigate to the location where you want to place a new folder (within another folder, for example).
2. Click the Create New Folder button.
3. Type the name of the new folder.
4. Click OK. Windows will create the folder.

Name or Rename a Folder or File ➤ *pp. 97, 106-108, 112-113*

1. Click to select a file or folder icon.
2. Select the icon's name by clicking on it or pressing F2.
3. Use your mouse and keyboard to edit the name.
4. Click outside of the icon or press ENTER to save your changes.

Copy or Move Files and Folders ➤ *pp. 98-102*

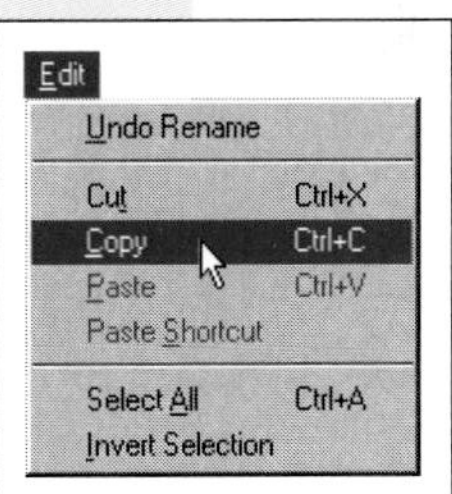

1. Select an icon.
2. From the window's Edit menu, choose Copy to copy or Cut to move an item.
3. Activate (open) a destination window or folder.
4. Choose Paste from the Edit menu.

Alternately you can:

- Drag icons elsewhere on the same disk to move them.
- SHIFT-drag icons to a different disk to move them.
- CTRL-drag icons elsewhere on the same disk to copy them.
- Drag icons to a different disk to copy them.

Delete Files and Folders ➤ *pp. 102-105*

1. Select the icon(s) for files to be deleted.
2. Press the DELETE key, or select Delete from the file menu. Hard disk-resident files are moved to the Recycle Bin (floppy and network files are simply deleted).

Recover Deleted Files and Folders ➤ *pp. 102-104*

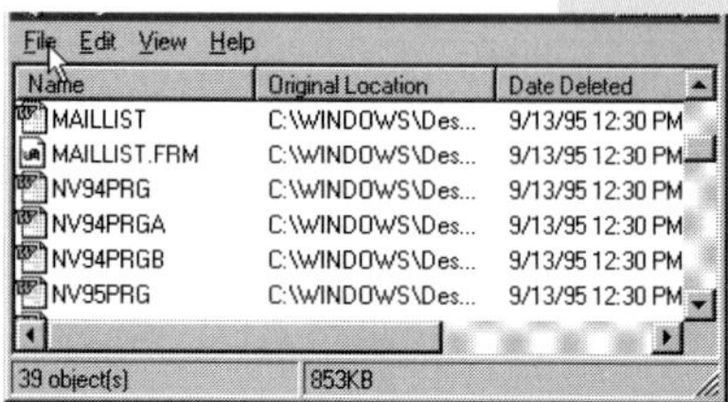

1. Open the Recycle Bin window by double-clicking the Recycle Bin icon.
2. Choose Restore from the File menu or drag the files and/or folders to the desktop or elsewhere.

Determine Available Disk Space ➤ *pp. 105-106*

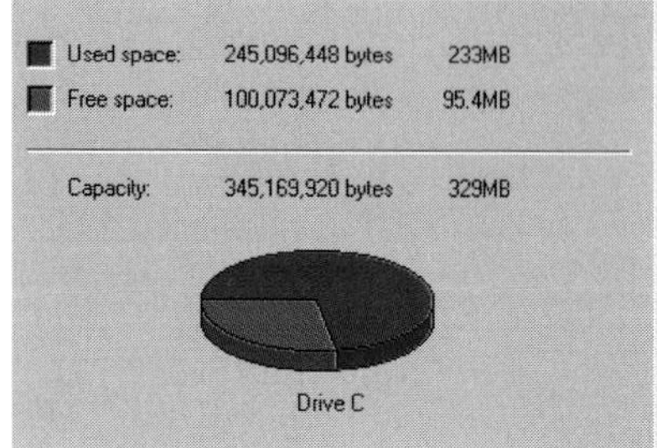

1. Right-click the disk icon to reveal the shortcut menu.
2. Choose Properties from the shortcut menu.
3. If necessary, click the General tab to bring it foremost.
4. Read the space statistics.

Associate Files with Programs ➤ *pp. 110-112*

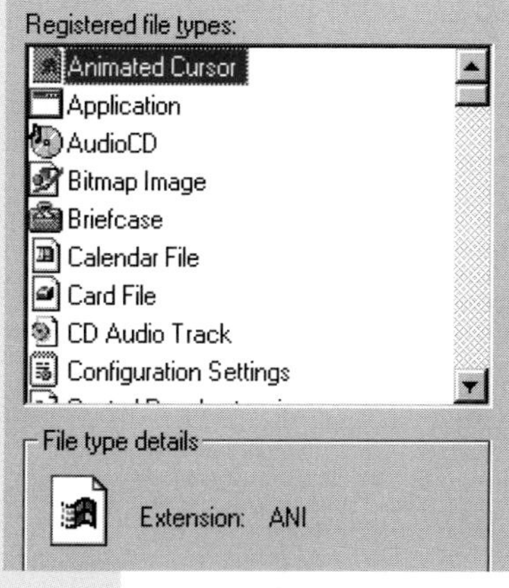

1. Open a disk or folder window.
2. Choose Options from the window's View menu
3. Click the File Types tab.
4. Choose New Type to display the Add New File Type dialog.
5. Type a description and extension (**old files** and **.old,** for example).
6. Click New to display the New Action dialog.
7. Type **Open** in the Action box.
8. Type an application name and path or browse and click on the program's icon.
9. Click OK to close the New Action dialog.
10. Click Close to close the Add New File Type dialog.
11. Double-click on a file of the type associated with the program to test it. Windows should launch the program (or bring it foremost) and use the file if all goes well.

Format and Name a Disk ➤ *pp. 113-114*

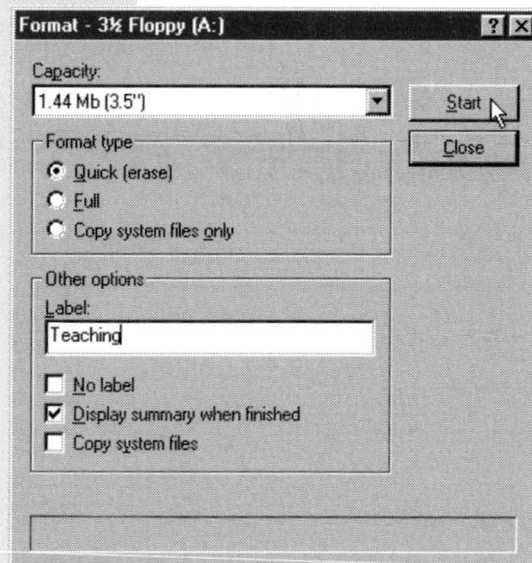

1. Insert a removable disk.
2. Click to select the disk's icon in the My Computer window.
3. Choose Format from the window's File menu.
4. Select appropriate formatting options (disk capacity, etc.).
5. Click Start.

For the last few decades, computer users have stored their important information on disks (which has made manufacturers of paper tape and punch cards very unhappy). Whether floppy or hard, removable or fixed, hidden in your computer or closeted in some huge networked server, disks all exist for one purpose: to retain quasipermanent copies of your important information and programs.

In this chapter we'll look at some ways to prepare disks and organize your library of disk-based computer files. With this knowledge under you belt you'll be prepared for Chapter 5, which will help you find lost files, and Chapter 6, which will provide some important disk housekeeping tips.

A Few Disk Terms You Should Know

A 25-cent review of disk-related jargon is in order. You store computer information on *disks* or *diskettes* (or even *discs* if you have a CD-ROM drive). *Data* is stored in *files* on the disks. *Disk drives* are the hardware devices that read and write to disk files. Disk drives have *drive letters* (A:, B:, C:, etc.), and disks themselves can be given *volume names*. Some disks are *removable* and can be swapped (like floppies and CD-ROMS, and Zip or Jaz disks); others are *nonremovable* or *fixed* disks.

DEFINITION

executable files: *Wonks often call program files "executable files" or simply "executables" (as in "Hey, bro, check out the executables on that mother!").*

Some files are called *document files* (memos, reports, spreadsheets, checkbook ledgers, etc.); other files are *programs* or *application files* (like Microsoft Word, Excel, etc.).

Your computer and Windows also create other files for their own purposes. We'll call them *system files.* These computer-managed system files keep track of settings you've specified, lists of hardware and software you've installed, and so on.

You are free to modify, move, and delete many, but not all of the files on your disks. You can read, but not change the contents of some files, for example. Many system files are out in plain view for you to see, whereas others are *hidden* (albeit not very securely). These restrictions are often referred to as parts of a file's *attributes.* It is a good idea to leave system files untouched unless you know exactly what you are doing.

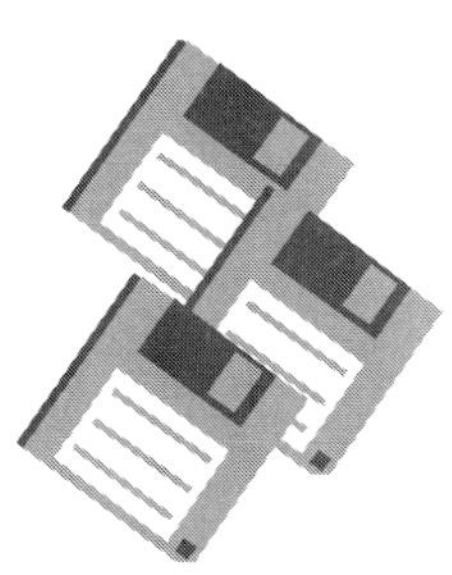

As you can see, the many files on your disks serve different purposes. Files are often created in different ways—some by you, others by Windows 95, and still others by your application software. Many file types can be identified by three letters at the end of their filenames. These three letters preceded by a decimal point are called *filename extensions.* Examples include .doc, .ini, and so on. Extensions can give you clues about the type and source of the files. You'll learn more about the various *file types* later in this chapter.

Because a hard disk can have tens of thousands of files, it is necessary to categorize and organize them even beyond adding extensions to filenames. All but the smallest disks are usually subdivided into *directories* (or in Windows 95 parlance, *folders*).

Although Windows itself and the various software setup utilities you run when installing new programs automatically create their own new folders on your behalf, you will want to create additional folders to better organize your disk(s). For example, you might create some folders where you'll store your correspondence, other folders for your budget-related files, more folders for client files, personnel records, and so on. Folders also can contain other folders. For instance, you might create a personnel folder containing additional folders for each employee, or a budget folder with separate folders for each year—each year's folder could contain 12 more folders, one for each month of the year. The trick is to devise a disk (or folder) organization strategy that is helpful without being too cumbersome.

Figure 4.1 gives you a peek at part of the disk organization of one of my computers. It has a floppy drive (A:) and two hard disks. The first hard disk (C:) is named Programs; this is where I keep my programs and Windows 95 itself. The second hard disk (D:) is where I store some of my manuscripts, client files, databases, and so on. You can't see all of my files and folders in this illustration, but you can get a sense of how the client files have been organized using folders within folders.

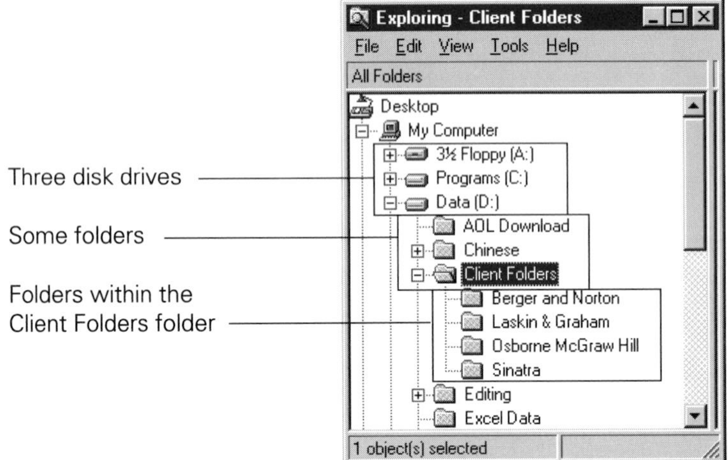

Figure 4.1 The disks on my system

upgrade note

I've used the Windows Explorer to create Figure 4.1. It's the replacement for the File Manager in earlier versions. You'll find it in the Start menu (under Programs), and it's described later in this chapter.

Disk storage capacity is an issue, particularly now that we work with huge operating systems like Windows 95; powerful, bloated suites of programs like Microsoft Office; and enormous graphic and multimedia files. Seemingly large hard disks purchased a few years ago are inadequate today. Why, when I was your age... Never mind.

When shopping for a new computer, consider doubling the salesperson's recommended hard disk size. Trust me. Salespeople are so afraid their price will be too high that they will often undersell (and users will often underbuy) this key component.

Disk storage capacity is usually measured in *kilobytes*, *megabytes*, and *gigabytes*:

- A kilobyte (K) is roughly 1,000 bytes (characters) of information.
- A megabyte (MB) is about equivalent to one million bytes.
- Gigabyte drives are all the rage now, so you should know that a *gigabyte*, or *gig* (GB) is about a thousand megabytes. (Incidentally, there is a rumor that the next inevitable increment in disk sizes—a thousand gigabytes—will be named the *Gatesabyte*.)

Today you'll probably need a *minimum* of 500+ MB to comfortably run Windows and a suite like MS Office. It can be done with smaller hard disks, but it's not a pretty sight.

Disk Types

Although a full treatment of disk standards is beyond the scope of this book (and any normal human's attention span), suffice it to say that Windows 95 supports all the important disk standards, including most floppy disk types, most hard disks, and most CD-ROM discs and drives. Windows 95 by itself can access many different networked disk drives as well. And, with the help of third-party software like Mirimar's Personal LAN Connection, Windows 95 can even read and write files created on competitive systems and networks like Apple's Macintosh AppleShare.

"The nice thing about standards," someone once wrote, "is that there are so many of them." Perhaps that engineer/philosopher worked for a disk manufacturer.

In the lion's share of cases, new Windows-ready computers are equipped with 3½-inch floppy drives capable of reading and writing around 1.44MB of data per diskette. Your computer might have one or more of the older 5¼-inch floppy drives designed to work with diskettes capable of storing between 360K and 1.2MB of information per diskette.

EXPERT ADVICE

Consider purchasing a CD-ROM drive if for no other reason than installing and upgrading software. A CD-ROM drive can completely eliminate time-consuming screen staring and floppy swapping. You can do other work while your machine tends to the drudgery. CD-ROM-based software installation strikes me as much faster and more reliable too. Treat yourself.

The trick is to know which disk standards are supported by your computer's disk drives. This way you can purchase the right kind of blank or preformatted floppies, and order the correct media (disk type) when purchasing new software. A trip to your hardware manuals should tell you the details.

Virtually all CD-ROM drives found in Windows-capable machines support today's CD-ROM standards, although there are folks busy trying to screw up (umm, I mean *advance*) this set of standards too.

Seeing What's on Your Disks

Windows 95 provides several ways to see what's on your disks. Two of my favorites include:

- Viewing the contents of a disk by double-clicking first on the My Computer icon, and then on the disk's icon.
- Using the Windows Explorer.

Icons for some drives that have removable media (like CD-ROM drives) will often tell you the name of the volume currently in the drive. Other drives (like floppy drives) don't. And to make things more confusing, sometimes Windows doesn't notice that you've swapped removable disks, and will not always display the correct volume name. Macintosh users scratch their heads when they see this.

Disk Icons and Their Windows

Someday I am going to have T-shirts printed with the phrase "When in doubt, double-click." You'll learn a lot from Windows by double-clicking. For example, to see how many drives you have, and to learn their names, double-click the My Computer icon. Try it. Here's what happens when I do that on my Pentium:

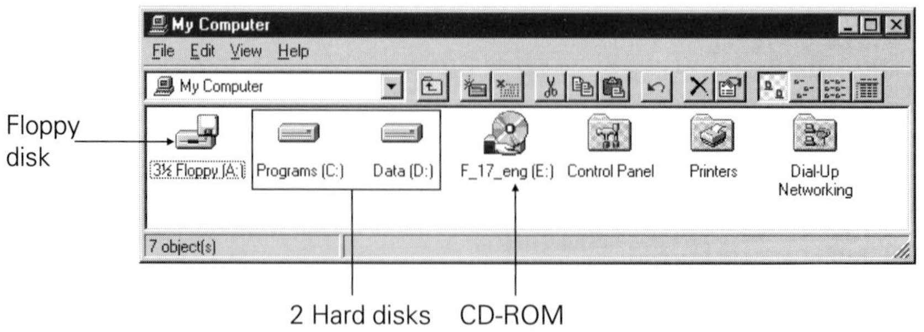

The My Computer Window

The My Computer window displays icons for each of your disk drives (and additional icons we'll ignore for the moment). For example, on my Pentium the only floppy drive is a 3½-inch unit labeled "3½ Floppy (A:)". As you can see above, there is a hard disk labeled Programs (C:) and another labeled Data (D:). The icon with the CD-ROM-looking disc (Drive E:) is, in fact, a CD-ROM drive. At the moment, it contains a CD-ROM titled "F_17_eng".

Seeing a Drive's Contents

Once you've displayed the drive icons by opening the My Computer window, you can see the "top level" of a disk's organization by double-clicking the disk's icon. Figure 4.2 shows what happens when I double-click my D: drive. There you can see icons for some of my folders. They look like little paper file folders, one containing artwork, another with examples for this book, and so on. And there are icons for some files as well. The appearance of file icons varies based on the program used to create the files.

Figure 4.2 What's on my D: drive

CAUTION

Remember that double-clicking a disk icon will not show you all of the folders and files on your disk! It shows only the "top layer" of the disk's organization. You might very well have additional folders within folders, and hopefully you'll have files in those folders. So don't panic if you double-click a disk icon and don't see your résumé file. It's probably in a folder that's not even in view yet. Read on.

To see what's in other folders, double-click them. This will reveal the next level of organization for each folder. As an example, here's what is shown when I double-click the folder called "Client Folders":

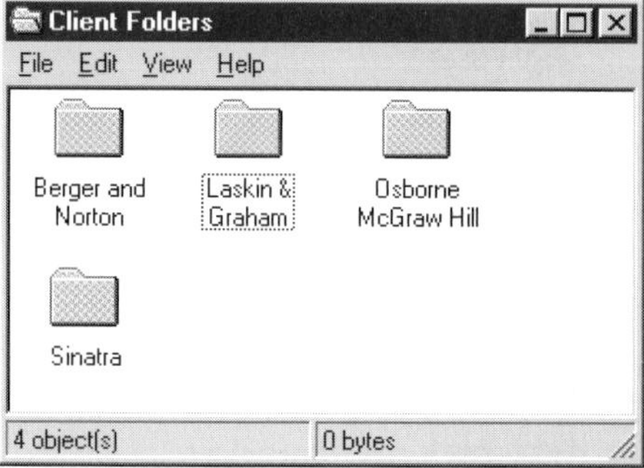

Changing the Appearance of Disk Windows

Because you may have chosen a different View option in the disk window, the *layout* and *appearance* of your disk window might be different from mine. You can change the appearance of disk windows with the View menu. It's pretty easy to figure out the effect of various View menu choices by simply experimenting.

EXPERT ADVICE

Clicking on a column heading in a disk window sorts the file list by column. For example, clicking the Modified heading sorts the list by the date last modified, so the most recently changed file or folder will appear first in the list. Repeated clicks toggle the sort order.

- The **Toolbar** choice adds or removes a series of buttons duplicating the various menu commands. (To learn about the buttons, turn on the toolbar and hover the mouse pointer over each button to read its name and function.)
- The **Status Bar** choice lets you turn off the status bar at the bottom of the window to make more room for listings.
- The **Small Icon** and **Large Icon** choices display files and folders as small or large icons.
- The **List** choice lets you view large numbers of files in less space.
- The **Details** choice lets you view file size, type, and date information. In Details view, you can sort listings by filename, file type, size, and date. You can also use the various choices on the Arrange Icons submenu and drag the edges of column names to change the widths of columns.

Name	Size	Type
AOL Download		File Folder
Artwork		File Folder
Chinese		File Folder
Client Folders		File Folder

SHORTCUT

To close a disk window, click on the Close button in the upper-right corner of the window. Holding down the SHIFT *key when you do this closes related windows as well.*

Using Refresh to See Recent Changes in Disk Content

The Explorer displays a snapshot of the disk you are exploring, based on the disk or folder's contents when you started the exploration. If that disk or folder changes while you are exploring, you might need to refresh the snapshot for the display to be accurate. For example, if you are exploring a diskette in a floppy drive, and then you remove the diskette and insert a different one, the Explorer will still show the contents of the previous (now removed) diskette. Networked drives and folders have a habit of changing behind your back as well.

To refresh the Explorer, either click on the disk or folder or choose Refresh from the Explorer's View menu, or better still, mash the F5 function key, good buddy.

The Windows Explorer

The Windows Explorer is a separate program shipped with Windows 95. Its purpose is to help you get "the big picture" of your computer's file structure. Like a plain old disk window, the Explorer can help you find lost files, move items around on your disk, and navigate your network. But perhaps its primary advantage over simply opening a disk window is that the Explorer can show you a "tree view" of your nested folders:

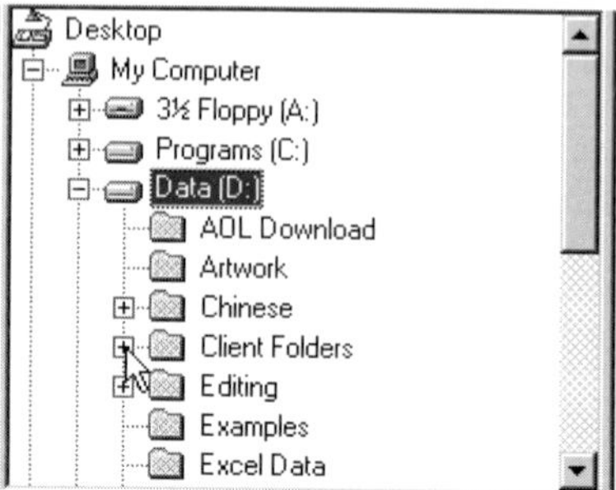

SHORTCUT

Hold down the SHIFT key and double-click a disk or folder icon to launch the Explorer.

The left pane of the Explorer window displays icons for all of the disks available to your computer (including networked drives). The top-level folders are shown for each drive, and when a folder contains additional folders (as is the case with my Clients folder), a little boxed plus mark to the left of the folder indicates that there are nested folders (or folders within folders within folders). Clicking the plus mark reveals the next level of folders.

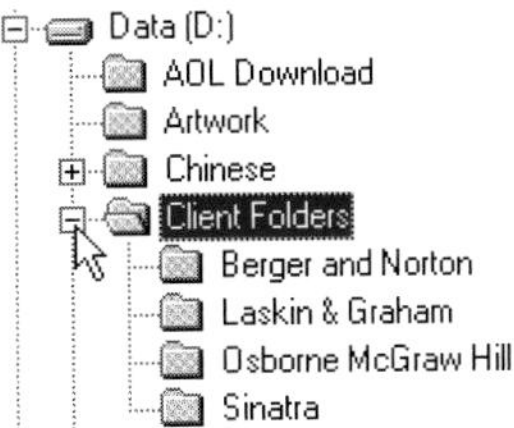

As shown in Figure 4.3, the *right* pane in an Explorer window contains a list of the contents of the folder (or drive) selected in the left pane. For example, selecting the Client Folders folder lists the various folders in my Clients folder. (Sorry, I once worked in the department of redundancy department.) Selecting one of the client folders reveals its contents—files, in this case.

Take a moment to run the Explorer and browse your disks.

1. SHIFT-click your hard disk icon (probably named C: or D: or whatever). The Explorer window will open.
2. Click a folder or two.
3. Close the Explorer window. (Use the Close box, or minimize the Explorer window if you want it to disappear but remain on the Taskbar.)

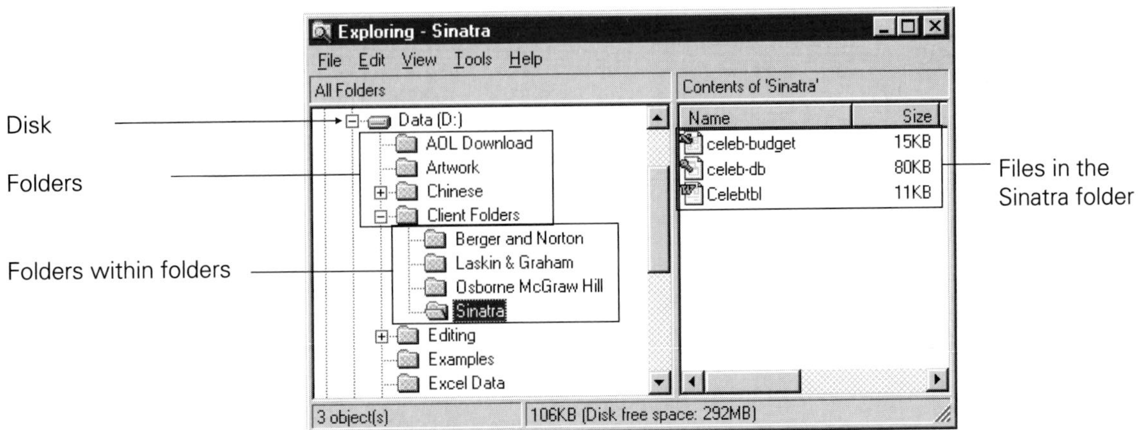

Figure 4.3 The open Sinatra folder

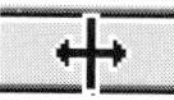

Changing the Appearance of the Explorer Window

Use the View menu to alter the appearance of file listings in the Explorer window just as you do in disk windows. Clicking list headings sorts them as you'd expect. Remember that you can drag list headings to change the widths of columns and reveal or hide long text entries. And you can change the width of the two panes by dragging the thick gray border that separates them, just as you can in a disk window.

Quick View works with text and graphics files, but not multimedia files (sounds, video clips, etc.). You can preview these by using the Play command that appears in the File and shortcut menus when you select multimedia files. See Chapter 13 for details.

Quick View: Examining a File Without Using Its Program

Quick View is a command that, if installed, lets you quickly examine the contents of files without launching the programs that created the files. The Quick View command will appear in the File menu of disk windows and the Explorer when you select a file icon that Quick View recognizes. That is to say, if Quick View doesn't know how to display a file, you won't see the Quick View choice on your menus.

Seeing Whether Quick View Is Installed

Quick View recognizes most text and graphics file formats. Unfortunately, to save hard disk space, the Windows 95 installer does not always place the Quick View program on your disk automatically. To see if Quick View is installed, simply select a known, recognizable file's icon and see if the Quick View choice appears in the disk window's File menu. For example, here's how you can check for Quick View with one of the Windows 95 graphics files:

1. Open the disk window for your C: drive by double-clicking the drive icon.
2. Double-click the Windows folder to open it.
3. Scroll if necessary to locate a graphics file labeled Argyle (or perhaps Argyle.bmp).
4. Right-click once on the Argyle icon to select it.
5. If Quick View is installed, you'll see the Quick View choice in the shortcut menu:

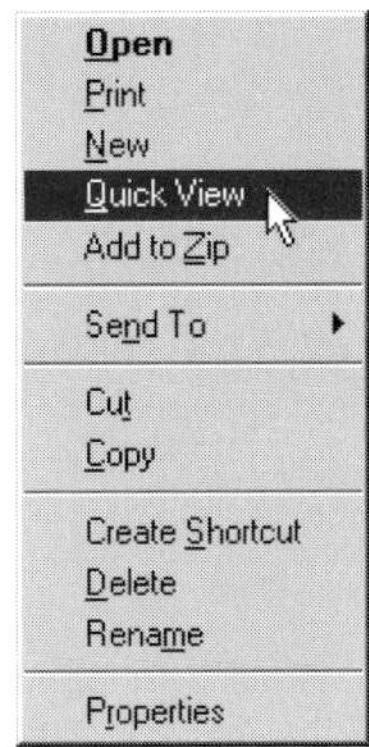

6. If you see the Quick View choice, it's already installed and ready to use. Jump to the zippy blue box over on the next page, where you'll learn to use Quick View step by step. If you don't see the Quick View choice, read the following installation instructions.

CAUTION

You often can edit items once you open them with the viewer. To do this, choose the "Open File for Editing" choice in the Quick View viewer window. But if you don't know a file's purpose, do not edit it. It is very easy to render your computer brain-dead by changing the contents of system files (.ini. files, batch files, etc.). When in doubt, don't.

Installing Quick View

If Quick View is not already installed, try this:

1. Have your Windows 95 installation CD or floppies available.
2. Choose Settings from the Start menu.
3. Pick Control Panel.
4. Double-click on Add/Remove Programs.
5. Click the Windows Setup tab if necessary to bring it foremost.
6. Double-click the Accessories choice. (You might need to scroll to see it.)

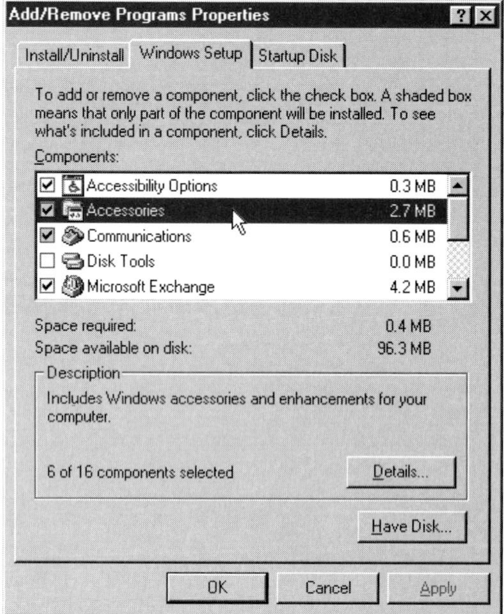

You can test to make sure you've installed Quick View successfully. Flip back a couple pages to "Seeing Whether Quick View Is Installed," and follow the instructions there.

7. Click to place a checkmark in the Quick View box. (Again, you might need to scroll to see it.)

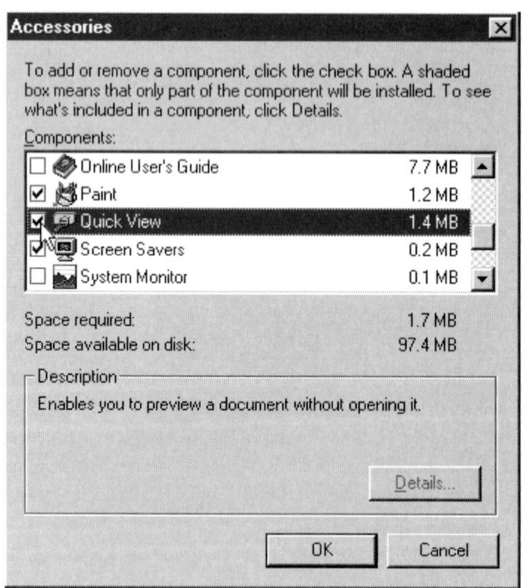

8. Make any other software addition or removal choices.
9. Click OK to close the choice's List window.
10. Click OK in the Add/Remove Program Properties window.

STEP BY STEP Using Quick View

2 Choose Quick View from the File menu, or right-click on the icon and choose Quick View from the shortcut menu. If the file is a text file, you'll see the text. (Graphics files will open in a graphics window, and so on.)

3 Click the Quick View window's Close box when you're done viewing the file.

1 Select the icon for any file you wish to view (in a disk window or the Explorer).

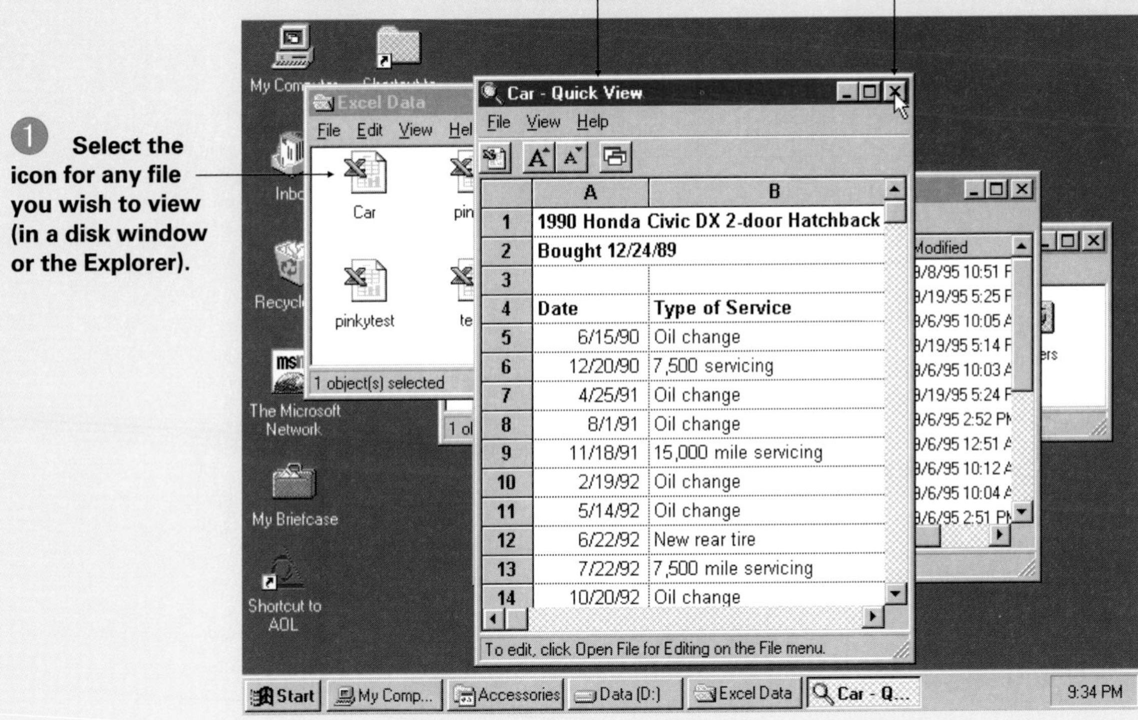

The Open With Dialog Box

Sometimes, when you double-click a file icon in a disk window or Windows Explorer window, you'll see the Open With dialog box, shown in Figure 4.4. Windows is telling you that it does not know which program to use with the file in question. This usually happens if you don't have the program used to create the file (because you got the document from someone else), or because the filename's extension is missing or has been changed. (File extensions are discussed later in this chapter.)

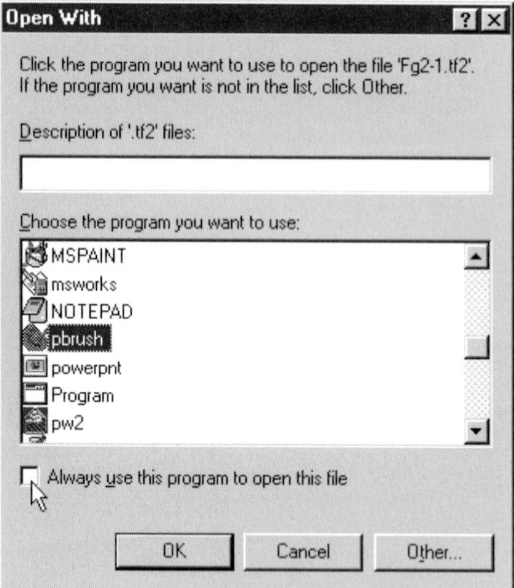

Figure 4.4 The Open With dialog box

If you see the Open With dialog box:

1. Scroll through the list of programs displayed there.
2. If you see the name of the program that you know was used to create the file, select it in the list and click OK. If you don't see the program,

click the Other button and browse your hard disk(s) looking for possible programs.

3. When (if) you see a program that you think was used to create the file (or that might be able to use files of this type), select the program, making certain that the "Always use this program to open this file" choice is unchecked.
4. Click OK. With any luck, the file will open and you will be able to use it.

Creating and Naming New Folders

To create a new folder, simply tell Windows where you want the folder to live and specify the new folder's name. Both folder names and filenames can contain up to 255 characters (but don't get that carried away). Spaces and punctuation are permitted, but do not include any of these characters:

/ \ ? ; : "<> * |

These have special meaning to Windows.

Here are the steps for creating a new folder:

1. Open a window for the disk where you want to create the new folder by double-clicking on the disk's icon.
2. If you wish to place the folder in the top level of the disk's organization, skip to step 4.
3. Double-click to open the folder in which you plan to place the new folder. For example, if you want to add a new client to your Clients folder, open the Clients folder. (Repeat this step as necessary until you reach the folder that will hold the new folder.)
4. Choose New from the File menu, and Folder from the resulting submenu.
5. A new folder will appear, selected and temporarily named New Folder.

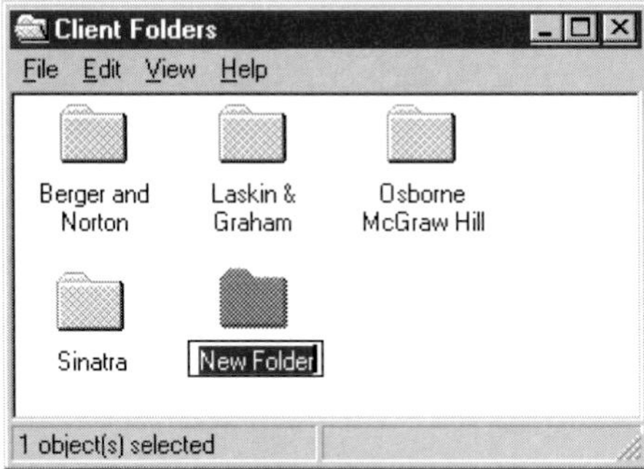

6. Type a meaningful folder name over the temporary name, which can include spaces, punctuation, etc. In this example, I've chosen the name "Disney":

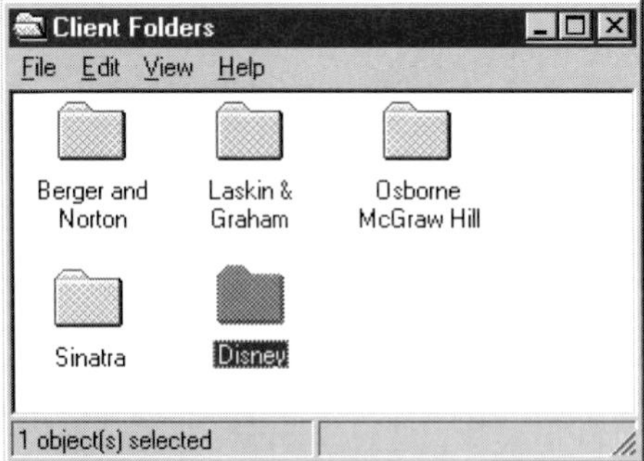

7. Click anywhere outside of the new folder to save the new folder name.

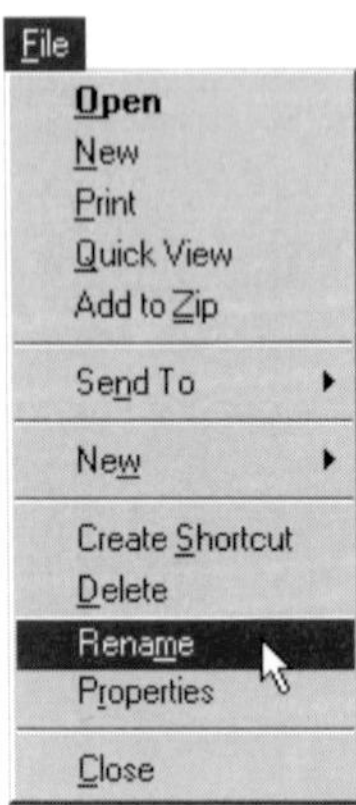

To rename a folder, follow these steps:

1. Click once to select the folder.
2. Press F2 or click on the folder's name to select the name (or choose Rename from the File menu).
3. Edit or replace the name using your keyboard and mouse.
4. Click outside of the folder or press ENTER to save the name change.

Creating New Folders from Within Applications

When using Windows 95-savvy programs, you will be able to create new folders while saving a document. For example, suppose you write a letter to a new client and when you get ready to save the letter, you wish you had a new folder specifically for that client's documents. You can create the new folder right from Word's Save As dialog box. Here are the steps (use the Save As command in any Windows 95-savvy program).

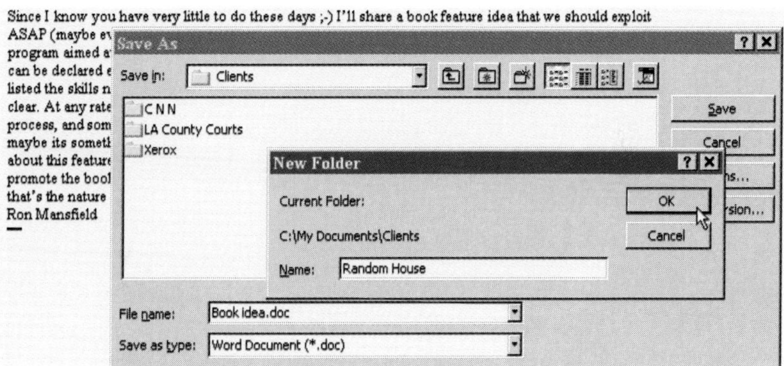

1. While in the Save As box in any Windows 95-savvy application (Microsoft Word, for example), click the Save in list or the Up One Level button as necessary to navigate to the location where you want to place a new folder (a new client folder within your Clients folder, for example).

2. Click the Create New Folder button.
3. Type the name of the new folder.
4. Click OK.
5. Windows will create the folder.

Moving and Copying Folders and Files

This is all very simple, although it may seem a little confusing. It is tempting to discuss just one method for each task, but I'll include several here instead. The different techniques and subtleties are worth learning, since they can save you time once they become second nature. Try them all. Keep the techniques you like best. Here goes.

Generally, you can move or copy folders and files by using any of these methods:

- Dragging to move them, or CTRL-dragging to copy them, to a new location on the same disk.
- Dragging to copy them, or SHIFT-dragging to move them, to a different disk.
- Selecting them and using the Copy, Cut, or Paste command.
- Selecting them and using the Send To command (to copy only).

Whether your actions result in copying or moving things often depends upon where the files or folders are when you start, and their destination. For example, when you select a folder icon and drag it to a new location on the *same* hard disk, you *move* the folder and its contents. But if you select a folder icon and drag it to a different disk (from a hard disk to a floppy, for instance), you *copy* the folder and its contents, rather than moving it. This makes sense when you think about it. Here are some specific recipes for copying and moving files and folders.

Moving Files or Folders by Dragging

To move a folder or a file to a different place on the same disk (into a different folder, for instance):

1. Click once on the icon for the file or folder to be moved. This selects it.

If you are dragging a file *icon, the file will move to the new location. If you are dragging a* folder *icon, the* folder and all of its contents *will move to the new location.*

2. Drag the icon to the new location (drag the icon over the destination folder, for example).

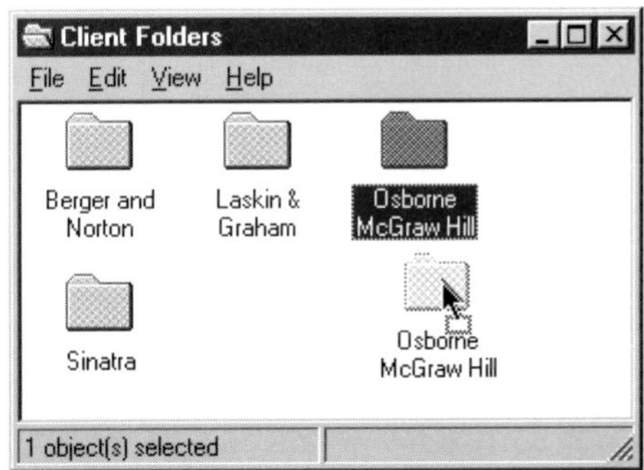

To move a folder or a file to a different disk:

1. Click once on the icon for the file or folder to be moved. This selects it.
2. Hold down the SHIFT key while you drag the icon to the new location (drag the icon over the destination disk, for example).

Copying Files and Folders by Dragging

You can copy files and folders either to different folders on the same disk, or to different disks. Since you cannot have two files with the same name in the same folder, and you cannot have two identically named folders within the same folder or at the top level of a disk, you must always copy to different folders or disks. (If you try to copy a second file or folder using a duplicate filename in one location, Windows will rename the second file or folder.)

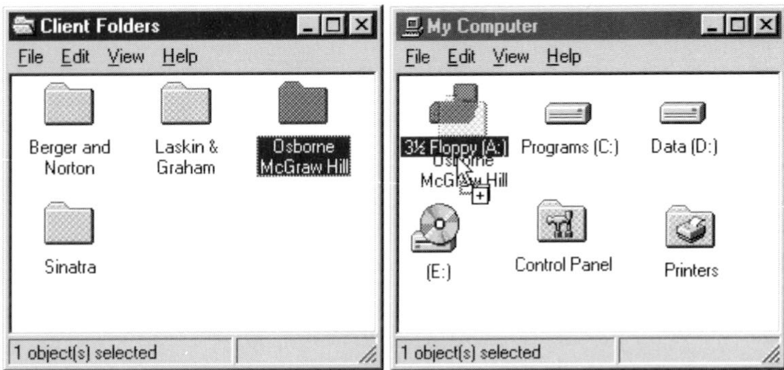

To make a copy of a file or folder and its contents while leaving the original intact:

1. Click once on the icon for the file or folder to be copied. This selects it.
2. If you're copying the item to a different disk, simply drag the item to the icon representing that disk.
3. If copying to someplace on the same disk, hold down the CTRL key while you drag the icon to the icon representing the new location. (Drag the icon over the destination folder, for example.)

If you are dragging a file icon, the file will be copied at the new location. If you are dragging a folder icon, the folder and all of its contents will be copied at the new location.

Moving or Copying Files and Folders with Copy, Cut, and Paste

You can use the Copy, Cut, and Paste commands in disk windows and the Explorer window, but I don't recommend it, particularly if you are also hard at work on some other project that might be using the Clipboard (a Word or Excel document, for example). The process of selecting and copying or cutting folder icons is quite straightforward, BUT it destroys the prior contents of your Clipboard (text or spreadsheet cells or whatever). Still, if you are feeling confident,

1. Select the file(s) or folder(s) of interest (use the CTRL key to select multiple items).
2. Choose Copy from the Edit menu or press CTRL-C if you plan to copy files or folders; choose Cut or press CTRL-X to move files or folders. This places the files and folder on the Clipboard.
3. Select the destination folder (or disk) and choose Paste from the Edit menu or use the CTRL-V keyboard shortcut.

The Send To Command: A Moving and Copying Shortcut

Here's one of those powerful features you'll love once you get the hang of it. And it becomes even more useful if you personalize it. The Send To command is found in the File menu in disk and Explorer windows, and on the shortcut menu when you right-click a disk, folder, or file icon. This command offers one or more destination choices, based on your computer's configuration and on how Windows is installed. Here, the choices are 3½ Floppy [A:], Fax Recipient, Mail Recipient, and My Briefcase.

Why is this feature called "Send To" and not "Send a Copy to?" (When I buy Microsoft some heads are gonna roll.)

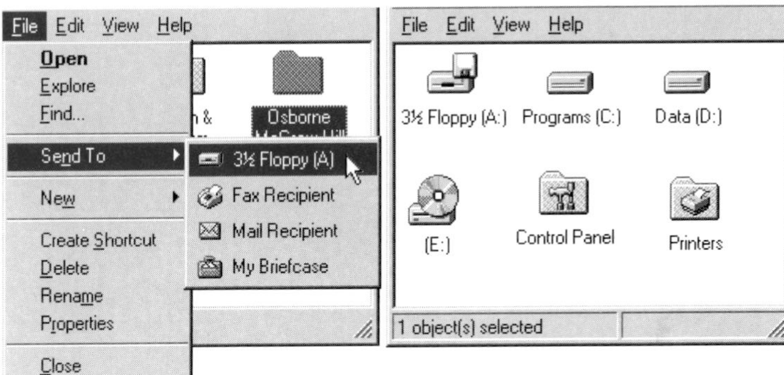

So, for example, to send copies of selected folders or files to a floppy disk, you might take this tack:

1. Select the item or items to be sent (copied).
2. Choose Send To.
3. Choose the desired destination (Floppy [A:] in this example).

Windows will send copies of the file(s) or folder(s) to the selected destination.

CAUTION

Before you send files out of the universe, consider how difficult it might be to retrieve them. It's a good idea to keep things in the Recycle Bin and make sure that you don't need them before you truly delete them. Also, be aware that when you delete files from floppies or network drives, they do not go to the Recycle Bin! They go irretrievably to Butt-Head's house, or someplace like that. Huh. Huh. Yeah.

The cool thing about Send To is that you can add your own destination choices. For example, you could create choices for shared network resources (disks, folders, etc.), or printers, or fax modems, and so on. You do this by placing shortcut icons for these destinations in a folder called Send To. It is located in your Windows folder. You'll learn more about shortcuts and shared resources later in this book.

Deleting Folders and Files

You can delete files either by selecting their icons in disk or Explorer windows and pressing the DELETE key, or dragging icons to the Recycle icon on your desktop. Or, if you like menus, the File menu in disk and Explorer windows both have Delete commands.

For example, you would follow these steps to delete a folder and all of its contents (files and other folders within the folder):

1. Click on the folder you wish to delete.
2. Press the DELETE key.
3. When asked if you want to send the folder and its contents to the Recycle Bin, click Yes, or press ENTER.
4. The folder and all of its contents will be sent to the Recycle Bin where they will remain until you empty the bin, or the bin gets too full.

To delete just a file, follow the same steps, but select a file rather than a folder. Remember, you can select multiple files and/or folders by dragging, SHIFT-clicking, or CTRL-clicking.

As you can see, files and folders are not deleted immediately. They get moved to the Recycle folder where they linger until you tell Windows to empty the Recycle Bin or until your hard disk gets so full that it empties old items by itself. The bad news is, you don't get back that extra disk space until the Recycle Bin is emptied. The good news is, if you accidentally delete something worthwhile, you *might* be able to retrieve it from the Recycle Bin. To learn how, follow these steps:

STEP BY STEP Recovering Accidentally Deleted Files

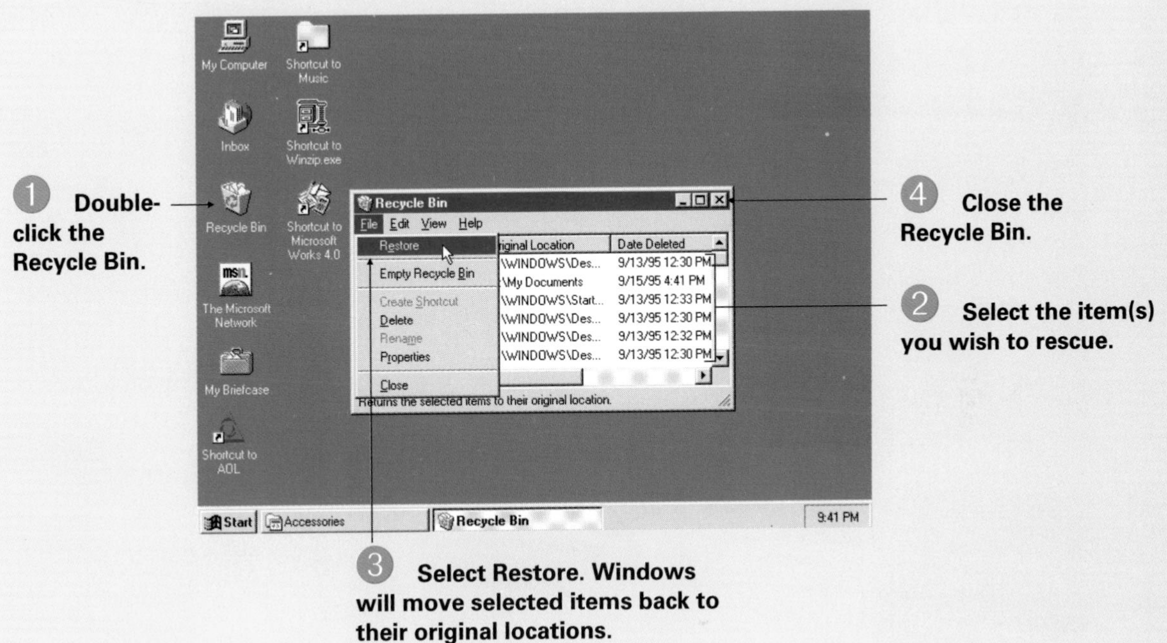

Other Emergency Recovery Methods

Even after you have emptied the Recycle Bin, there is a slim chance that you can recover deleted items if you are lucky and quick about it:

1. Stop what you are doing. Don't save new things on the disk. Don't even shut down if you can avoid it.
2. Get thee to the source of special disk utility software like Norton Utilities. (Make certain you have a version that is fully compatible with Windows 95. Even fairly recent versions of many disk recovery utilities are not Win 95 savvy, and these can do more harm than good.)

3. Read the directions carefully and follow them exactly. Try to use the emergency floppy shipped with some utilities. These make it unnecessary to install the new recovery software on your hard disk. (The less you muck with the problematic disk, the better your odds of successful recovery.)
4. Phone Microsoft's or the disk utility maker's phone support if necessary.
5. If that fails, ask yourself if you have a recent backup.

Nope? I feel for ya. Been there. Done that.

Emptying the Recycle Bin

When you are certain that the Recycle Bin contains nothing of value, you can empty it and reclaim some disk space thusly:

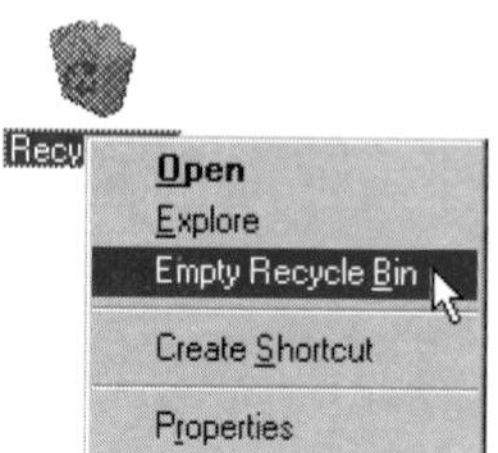

1. Click the Recycle Bin icon to select it (or double-click to open and examine it).
2. If the Recycle Bin window is not open, right-click the bin icon to bring up the shortcut menu.
3. If the Recycle Bin window is open, visit its File menu.
4. In either case, choose Empty Recycle Bin.
5. Read the warning, and confirm the deletion by clicking Yes or pressing ENTER, if that's in your best interest. Otherwise, click No to keep the items, then flip back to that last blue box and review the steps for "Recovering Accidentally Deleted Files."

EXPERT ADVICE

Always, double-click the Recycle Bin and examine its contents before emptying it. Are you sure you can live without all that stuff?

Deleting Things Without Moving Them to the Recycle Bin

Sometimes you might want to delete things without leaving them in the Recycle Bin—for example, if you were short of disk space and wanted to immediately reclaim some. Or, perhaps the things you are tossing are confidential and you don't want to leave them sitting in the bin where others can easily retrieve them. If you hold down the SHIFT key when deleting, the deleted item will not be saved in the Recycle Bin.

Or you can empty the bin immediately after deleting files by right-clicking on the Recycle Bin and choosing "Empty Recycle Bin" from the shortcut menu.

Incidentally, if you delete files from someone else's disk over a network connection, the deleted files wind up in his or her Recycle Bin, not yours. To undelete them, open the co-worker's Recycle Bin. (You can do this only if co-workers share their entire disks or their Recycle Bins.)

How Much Disk Space Is Left?

"How much disk space do I have left?" Ever said that out loud? I do nearly every day, lately. The answer can be found the same way whether you need answers about hard disks, floppies, or whatnot.

1. Right-click on the disk's icon to reveal the shortcut menu.
2. Choose Properties.
3. Click the General tab, if necessary, in the resulting Properties window. The total storage capacity of your disk, the space used, and the space available are displayed both numerically and graphically, as you can see in Figure 4.5.
4. Press ESC to dismiss the window.

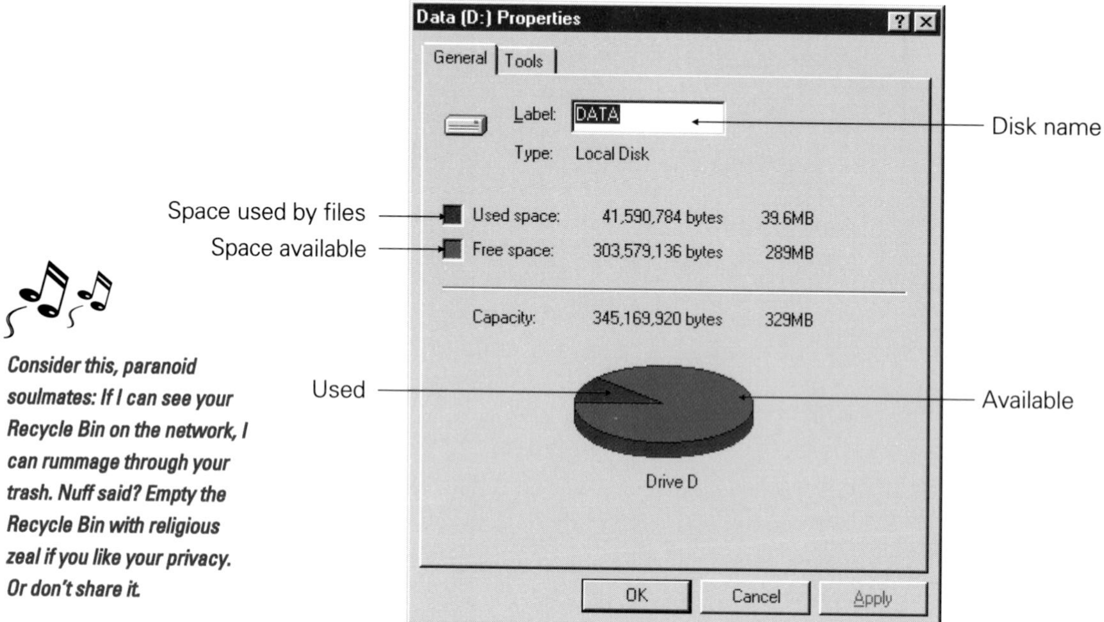

Figure 4.5 Finding out how much disk space you have

Consider this, paranoid soulmates: If I can see your Recycle Bin on the network, I can rummage through your trash. Nuff said? Empty the Recycle Bin with religious zeal if you like your privacy. Or don't share it.

Naming Files

We use filenames to identify, save, and later find our files. Windows 95 adds some new wrinkles to the name game. The good news is that Windows lets you assign longer filenames. This makes it easier to identify your work. The bad news is that older programs don't know diddly about long filenames, won't let you create them, and won't display them properly when it finds them. So, in order to maintain backward compatibility, Windows keeps two filenames for each file you create—your long one and a computer-generated short one.

If you can always use software that is compatible with long filenames, and if you never play "pass the floppy" with owners of old programs, you can always use long filenames, and your life will be blissfully simple. But you can't, and you will, you won't be able to, and it won't be. So keep reading.

New Long Filenames in Windows 95

In the old days, MS-DOS and Windows filenames could be no longer than eight characters, a decimal point and a three-character file extension. Windows 95 filenames can be up to 255 characters in length. Unlike earlier filenames, Windows 95 names can include spaces and some (but not all) punctuation marks. Do not include any of these characters in your filenames:

/ \ ? ; : "<> * |

You need to be careful how you use periods in filenames, as you will see when you read about filename extensions in a moment. And, as in earlier Windows and DOS versions, you cannot have two files with identical filenames in the same folder (directory) for obvious reasons.

CAUTION

Don't use older disk recovery and disk defragmenting programs on Windows 95. There is a good chance older disk utilities will clobber your long filenames, or worse...

Long Filenames and Older Programs

Computer-savvy cocktail party pests are always talking about things like "config-dot-sys" or "autoexec-dot-bat files." When they say "dot" they are referring to the period between the filename and its extension.

Although long filenames make things easier, there are some gotchas, particularly because virtually no programs shipped prior to the release of Windows 95 (including Word 6 for Windows and its siblings) support long filenames. To overcome this, Windows automatically assigns and saves short (eight-character) filenames each time you assign a long name. These 8+3 names are also called DOS filenames. For example, if you name a file Letter to Ron, and another Letter to David, Windows 95 will name the first one LETTERTO and the second one LETTER~1. If you then create a file called Letter to the SOB that hit my car, it will be nicknamed LETTER~2, and so on. As you can see, this might be more confusing than human-assigned short names like LTR2RON and LTR2DAVE and LTR2SOB, but then, that's what happens when you let computers do your thinking for you.

Remember, this problem only rears its ugly head when you use older programs to open files created with Win 95-savvy apps. So get out there and spend lots of money on all new software, okay?

In the interim, you can stick with short filenames if you like. Windows 95 does not force you to use long names. But it sure is nice when you get used to it.

File Types in Windows 95

Earlier I mentioned filename extensions such as .doc and .bat. Windows, DOS, and application programs all use these extensions to identify file types. Windows 95 uses them too, of course, but right out of the box, it hides many of the filename extensions from you. If you use your computer only for everyday word processing, spreadsheets, E-mail, and so on, you probably don't give a whit about filename extensions (and I envy you). Leave them turned off. Skip the next topic. But if you really want to know, here's the scoop.

By identifying files of different *types* or functions with different *filename types,* you and your computer can more easily identify the source and function of your files. In Windows 95, as in MS-DOS, many files are identified with *filename extensions,* a series of three letters at the end of filenames. All Microsoft Word document files end with the extension .doc, for example, whereas Excel spreadsheet files end in .xls. Because manufacturers have more or less agreed to use industry-standard extensions to identify specific types of files, it is often possible to associate specific file types with specific programs via their extensions.

Thus, if you or a computer program encounters a filename that ends in .doc, it is usually safe to assume that the file can be opened (used) by programs that can read and write Microsoft Word files. By the same token, files ending in .xls are normally Microsoft Excel-compatible. Other files created and used by Windows 95 end with their own proprietary filename extensions like .ini, .sys, .bat, etc. Windows expects to see these files in specific locations on your disk, and awful things can happen if you move, delete, or change the names of system files.

Usually, Windows and your programs (Word or whatever) handle assigning filename extensions. In fact, with Windows 95 you often won't even see filename extensions on your screen unless you change some of the standard Microsoft settings.

Displaying Filename Extensions

Windows 95 keeps track of information regarding the programs you use in a place (a file actually) called the *Registry.* If you've properly installed your programs, Windows 95 knows which file extensions are used by the various programs (.doc for Word, etc.). In cases where Windows recognizes a file's extension, it will display the appropriate icon for the program used to create the file. Thus Word file icons will look like little Word pages, etc. For example, the following icon, "Things I do know," is actually a Word document.

Things I do know

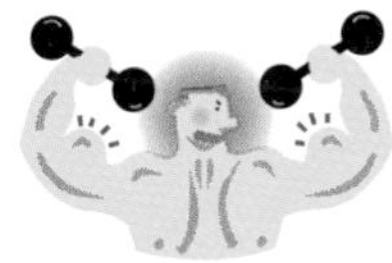

DEFINITION

Registry: *A database automatically maintained by Windows 95, containing information about your programs, setting, and more. Busy people should never mess directly with their Registries. Let Windows 95 and Setup do that. The Registry is reportedly more robust than earlier devices for collecting all of your computer's vital trivia. Time will tell.*

If Windows doesn't recognize a file extension, it displays the extension. If you want to have Windows always display file extensions:

1. Open the disk window where you want to see extensions.
2. Choose Options from the View menu.
3. Click the View tab if necessary to bring it foremost, as it is in Figure 4.6.
4. Remove the checkmark from the box next to "Hide MS-DOS file extensions for file types that are registered."
5. Click OK.

Things I do know.doc

Your filenames now will all have extensions. Notice that the filename "Things I do know" is now "Things I do know.doc."

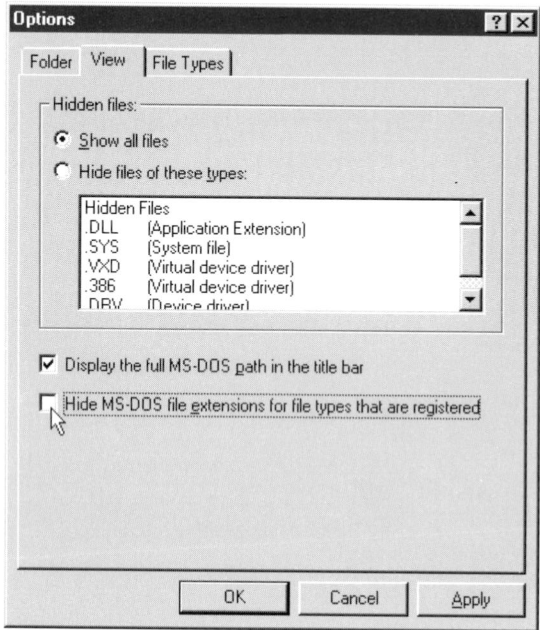

Figure 4.6 Displaying filename extensions

Associating Files with Programs

Now that you know about filenames and extensions, you will understand the process of associating file types with programs. If you double-click an icon for a file created by a program not in your Registry, Windows will pop up the Open With dialog box that says in effect "What the heck is that?"

If you know of a program that is installed on your computer that can work with the file in question, take it from here. (If you don't know of a useable program, you'll need to find one and install it before continuing.)

1. Scroll through the list of programs displayed in the Open With dialog box.
2. Click to select the program you want to use to open the file.

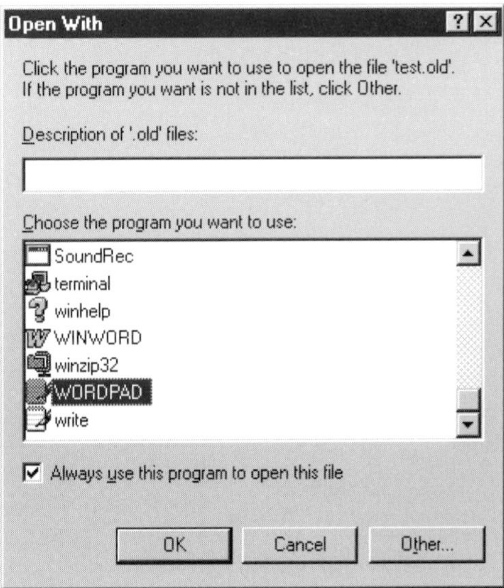

3. Unless you are 100 percent certain that you have chosen the right program, remove the checkmark from the "Always use this program with this file" option.
4. Click OK.
5. Windows and the chosen application will attempt to open the file.
6. If all goes well, you'll be able to see and use the file.

Once you know that files of a certain type can be opened by a particular program, you can leave the box checked in step 3.

Changing Associations Between Programs and File Types

There are a number of reasons to change the association of a file type with a program. You might get a better program that you want to use (a better graphics program, perhaps). Or maybe you associated the wrong program with a file type and hate the way Windows nags about this each time it fails to open. Follow these steps to change associations:

1. Choose the View menu and then Options in either the Explorer or a disk window.

2. Click the File Types tab.
3. Choose the type of file you want to change from the scrolling list and read the current settings.
4. Click the Edit button to display the Edit File Type dialog box.
5. In the Actions box, click "open."

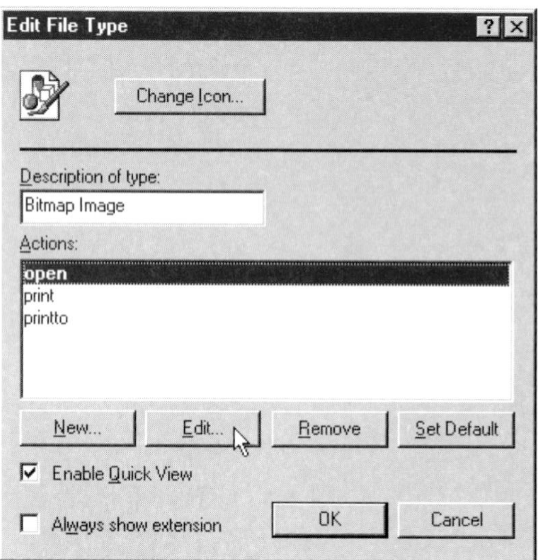

6. Click the Edit button.
7. Specify the program you want to open files with this extension. (Use the Browse button if necessary to find the program.)
8. Click OK.

Renaming Files

If you know how to rename folders, you know how to rename files. Here's the recipe anyway, just in case. To rename a file, do this:

1. Open a disk window or use the Explorer to locate the file you wish to rename.
2. Click once to select the file's icon.
3. Either press the F2 function key, or click on the file's icon name to select the name (or choose Rename from the File menu).

4. Edit or replace the name using your keyboard and mouse.
5. Click outside of the file's icon or press ENTER to save the name change.

Formatting Disks

Generally, you will need to format your hard disk only if you purchase a new one that has not been formatted, or if you have had some major calamity. When in doubt, consult the documentation provided with the drive, and perhaps get some technical assistance.

Some floppy disks come from the factory without being fully prepared to accept data. The process of preparing disks to store data is called *formatting*. Where floppies are concerned, the busy person is best served by purchasing preformatted disks. They cost only pennies more than unformatted disks. Besides saving time, buying preformatted floppies frees up your computer and saves some wear and tear on the disk drives. If you do need to format floppies, here's how:

1. Place the unformatted disk in a compatible floppy drive.
2. Double-click the My Computer icon if necessary to display the icons for your disk drives.
3. Right-click to bring up the shortcut menu and choose Format (or click Format from the File menu). You will see the Format dialog box.

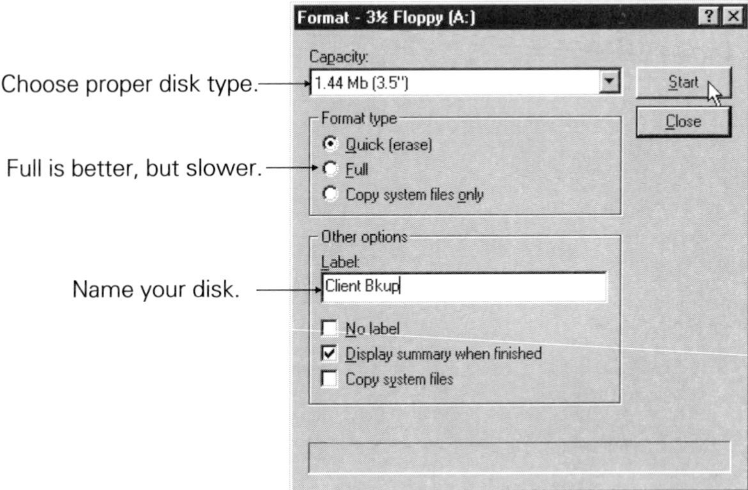

4. Choose the correct capacity given the type of diskette you are using (1.44, 720, etc.).
5. Choose "Quick (erase)" if you are in a hurry and plan to store relatively unimportant things on the disk.
6. Choose Full if you want Windows to inspect the entire disk for flaws while it formats.
7. Type a disk label (name) if you wish. (Disk labels can contain up to 11 characters including spaces.)

Naming and Renaming Disks

To rename a disk, follow these steps:

1. Right-click the icon for the disk you wish to rename.
2. Choose Properties from the resulting shortcut menu.
3. Click on the General tab if necessary to bring the tab topside.
4. In the Label box, edit or replace the name of the disk using your keyboard and mouse.

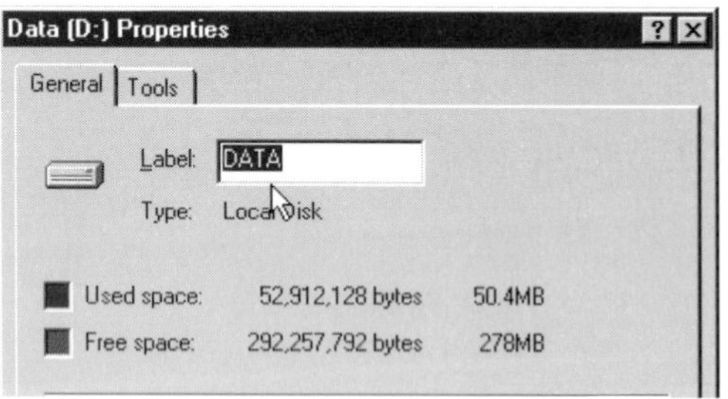

5. Click OK.

This chapter contains some very, very important skills! Take some time now to practice what you've learned. Before moving on, be certain that, at a minimum, you can:

- Format floppies
- Copy files from a hard disk to a floppy
- Create a new folder
- Move files from one folder to another
- Delete files
- Recover files from the Recycle Bin
- Associate file types with programs

If you've made it to the end of this chapter, busy reader, and you can accomplish at least the tasks listed above, then you are well on your way to becoming a disk management whiz. And it's a good thing, too, because our next topic, lost files(!), is enough to bring both unsuspecting newbies and pros to their knees.

MEMO:
RUSH!

CHAPTER

5

Finding "Lost" Files

INCLUDES

- Looking in the Recycle Bin
- Using the Find command
- Narrowing your searches

Check the Recycle Bin ➤ pp. 120-121

1. Double-click on the Recycle Bin icon.
2. Click column headings if desired to display by date, name, etc.
3. Choose Restore when you find your files, or drag them to an appropriate location.

Use the Find Command ➤ pp. 121-122

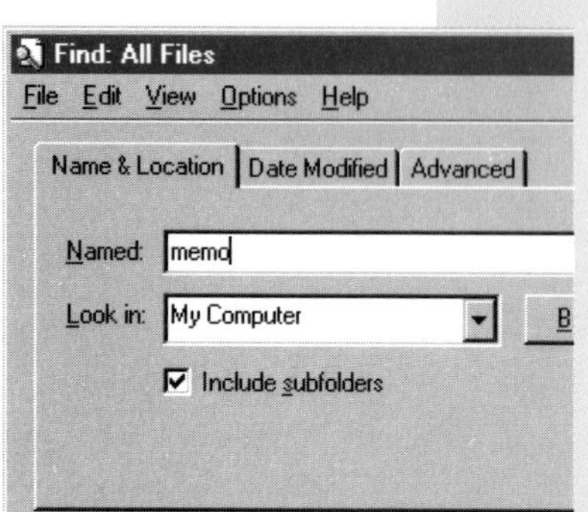

1. Choose Find from the Start menu.
2. Pick Files or Folders.
3. Specify a partial filename in the Named text box.
4. Specify where to look by selecting a location from the Look In drop-down list (a particular disk, My (entire) Computer, a particular folder, etc.).
5. Add date, file type, and other modifiers only if you know they won't obstruct the search.
6. Click Find Now.
7. Make the Find dialog box wide enough to show file details.
8. Click column names to sort if that will help.

Narrow Your Search ➤ pp. 124-126

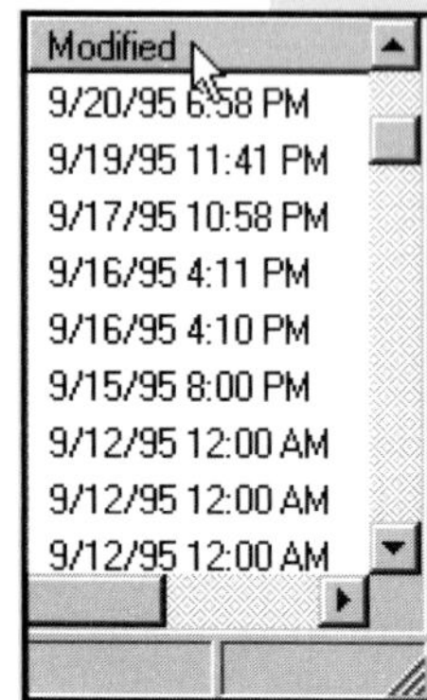

- Use the Date Modified tab in the Find dialog box to specify a date or date range for the file(s).
- Use the Of Type list on the Advanced tab to specify a type of file to search for.
- Modify your search string with wildcard characters.
- If you simply don't know the filename, search for a text string within the file.

Ever said anything like this? "This (bleeping) computer lost my file! It's gone. Lost. I'm roadkill on the information superhighway!" Well, chances are very good that you have felt this way at one time or another. And chances are equally good that you, not the computer, misplaced the file. On the brighter side, odds are that you can find it. And really, if you've read and understood Chapters 1 through 4 of this book, you already know everything necessary to find lost files.

But misplacing an important file is so traumatic that I figured it deserved its own, easy-to-find chapter. So take a deep breath, relax, and let's see if we can find that missing file or folder.

Where Files End Up When They Go Astray

It's not wanderlust that leads them afield, honest. Files usually end up wherever we tell our computers to put them. And if we aren't specific, our computers often put things right where we put the last things we saved. So if you've been working with a specific folder on your hard disk, that's a great place to start looking for a lost file. If you've been working with things on a networked drive, your missing file might be in Tonawanda, New York, instead of on your hard disk in Maui. A bummer, granted, but usually easy to fix. Another good place to look is the Recycle Bin. This is particularly true if you've been housekeeping.

Some programs have default places where they put things, so if you don't intervene, saved files go there. For example, CompuServe's CIS (dial-up) program puts things you download into a folder called Download in the CompuServe folder unless you protest. Become familiar with your various programs' habits in this regard. Many programs let you specify default save locations. This is often worth exploiting.

Some Questions to Ask Yourself

When I'm not talking to my computer, I sometimes talk to myself (quietly if others are around). Here are some of the things I say when looking for a file:

- Where was I last working (which folder, disk, network device, etc.)?
- Was I using my desktop machine or my portable? (Honest, I've done that one, busy person.)
- Might I have misspelled the name of the file when saving it?
- Could I have dragged the file or folder into some other folder erroneously?
- Could someone else have renamed or moved it?
- Did I save the file with a long filename, and am I now using a machine or program that's only capable of displaying short filenames? (This is gonna be the big problem of the decade!)
- Did I accidentally select an icon's filename and replace it with some garbage characters? (Yep, I've done that too.)
- Did I mess with the filename's extension?
- Is the Open dialog box in my program (Word or whatever) set to display the correct file type?
- Why am I talking to myself like this?

Check the Recycle Bin

When you're running low on disk space and in a cranky mood, it's easy to get carried away with file trashing. Did you accidentally delete an important file? Visit the Recycle Bin and see if you can find it there.

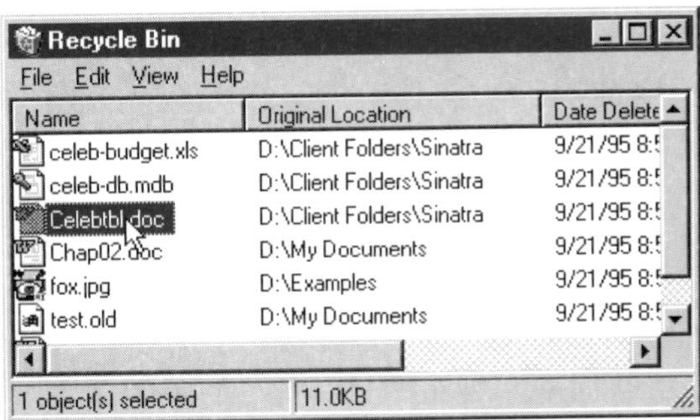

If you know you deleted that sucker and then emptied the bin, either go for your backup file, or stop everything and try a disk recovery utility like Peter Norton's.

CAUTION

Remember that old disk recovery utilities can wreak havoc with Windows 95 disks. Make certain any utility you employ specifically states that it is Windows 95 compatible!

Using the Start Menu's Find Command

You can also open the Find command from the Explorer's Tool menu. Find works the same way there as when you open it from the Start menu.

After manually looking in the more or less obvious places, it's time to bring out the big guns. I like to start with the Start menu's Find command. For your searches to be effective, you'll need to specify at least part of the filename (or a text string contained within the file), and tell Find where to look:

1. Choose Find from the Start menu.
2. Pick Files or Folders from the submenu. You'll see the Find dialog box shown in Figure 5.1.

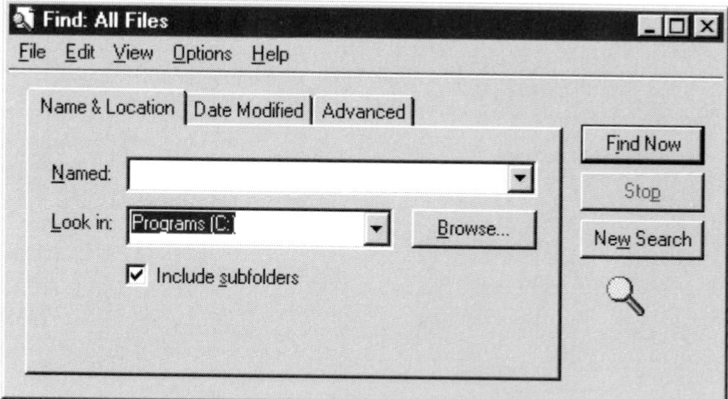

Figure 5.1 The Find dialog box

Specifying the Filename

Ideally, you'll always be able to enter the exact filename and extension. (Yeah, right!) In the real world, however, the Find command will help you find files even if you don't know their exact names. The trade-off is, you'll probably see a long list of files that are not what you want. To find a program called "setver", you can type **set** in the Named portion of the dialog box and then click Find Now. Find will list the program Setver.exe, but as you can see in Figure 5.2, it will also show Setuplog.txt, Setuplog.old, ~mssetup.t, and any other files with names containing "set". If there are duplicate "setver" files, they will all appear in the list as well.

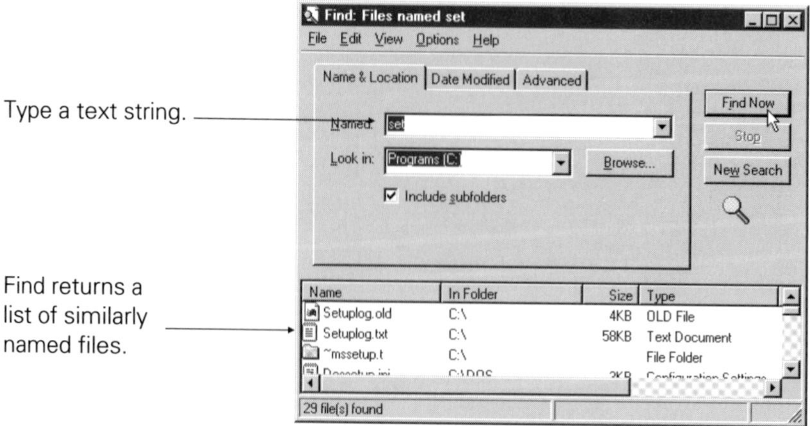

Figure 5.2 If you specify only part of your file's name, Find will likely return a list of similar files

DEFINITION

hit list: *A list of all the items that match your search criteria. Also a to-do list for very bad guys. See also* Pulp Fiction.

In Figure 5.2, the hit list is manageable. Notice that Find has listed every filename containing the character string set, regardless of where that string occurred in the name (beginning, middle, or end). At times this can be very handy; at other times the false hits can be overwhelming.

Specifying Where to Look

Where you look is as important as what you are looking for. You can ask Find to inspect just one disk, or every volume on your computer. If you are networked, you can search every accessible machine in your organization or, if you work for NASA, probably darn near every disk in the solar system. The wider your search, the longer it will take, and the more false hits you will see listed. So start small, but not too small. Ask yourself those questions listed earlier, then begin by specifying the My Computer choice, perhaps, in the Look In box. It will inspect all of the disks on your computer.

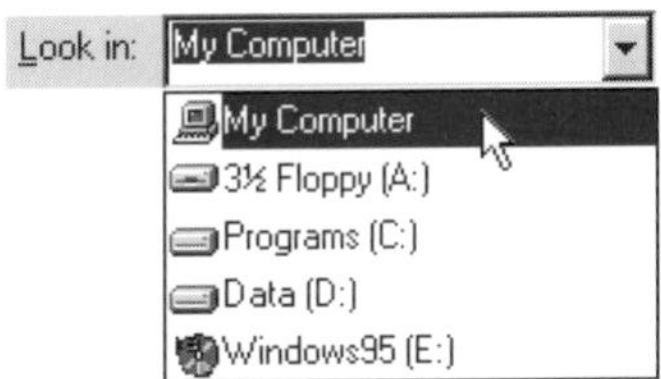

CAUTION

If your computer has a CD-ROM drive but you know the file is not on a CD-ROM, then make sure the drive is empty before you use the My Computer option. Otherwise you'll waste a lot of time.

Once you've specified what and where to search, you can actually start searching. Use the following steps:

STEP BY STEP Running and Viewing the Search

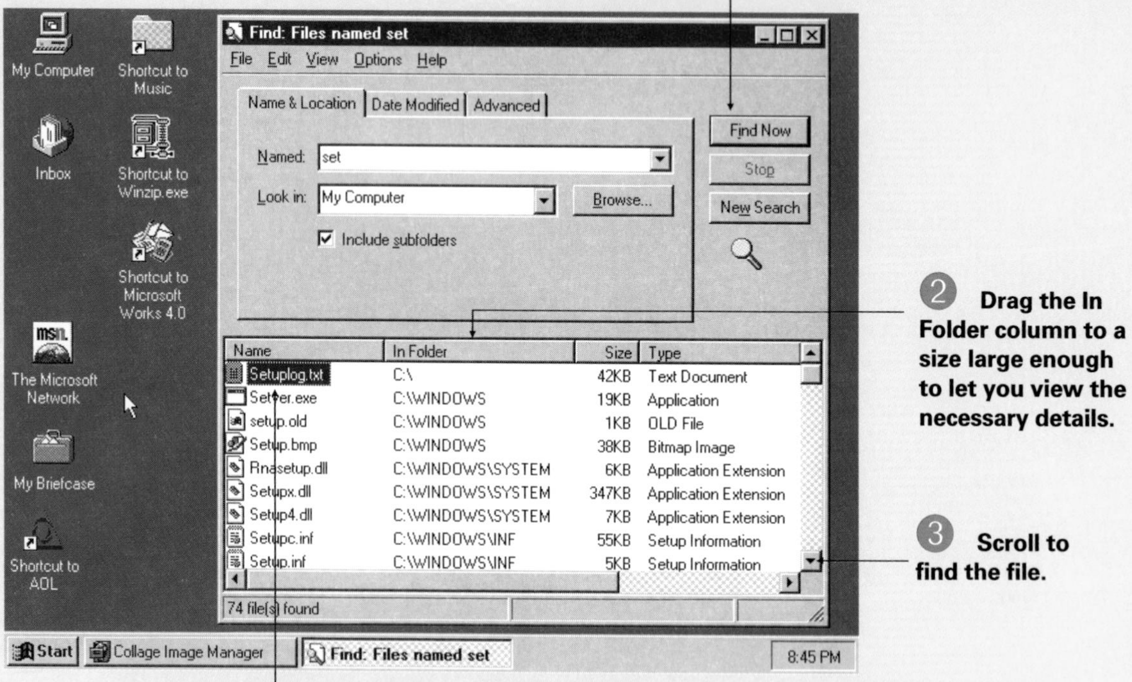

Using Dates and Other Filters to Narrow Searches

When a hit list gets too long, you can use dates to narrow the search. If you know with certainty the date when the file was last modified (remember, it might have been modified by someone else), you can use the Date Modified tab in the Find dialog box to specify a date or date range, and then rerun the search, as shown here:

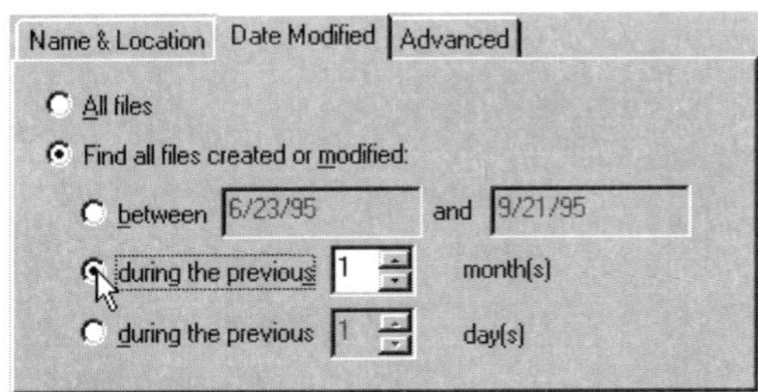

Or you can simply sort the long list by date with a click of the mouse on the Modified column (remember: clicking again toggles the order):

EXPERT ADVICE

If your search is for a particular kind of file (a graphics file or an Excel file or whatever), choose the file type from the Of Type list to narrow your search. The Of Type list is on the Advanced tab of the Find dialog box.

See how these few skills get used over and over once you learn them?

Searching with Wildcards

You can narrow your searches by using the wildcard characters * and ?. For example, searching for ***th*** will find the string "th" anywhere in a filename or extension. **?th** will find "th" in a name or extension IF the name does not begin with "th".

Finding Files When Filenames Are a Mystery

Things get a little trickier if you haven't a clue about a file's name. One way around this problem is to have Find look for text strings within the files themselves. Here's how you do it:

1. Display the Name & Location tab in the Find dialog box (see Figure 5.1).
2. Specify the place to look (My Computer, for example).
3. Make sure the Named field is empty (because you want Find to check all files).
4. Switch to the Advanced tab.
5. Make sure All Files and Folders appears in the Of Type box.
6. Enter the text string for which you want to search. Here I'm trying to find out where I put Mia Farrow's phone number.

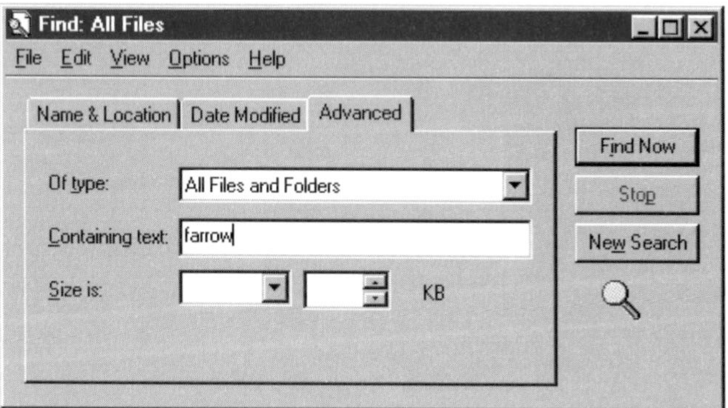

7. Click Find Now and be patient. This will take a while.

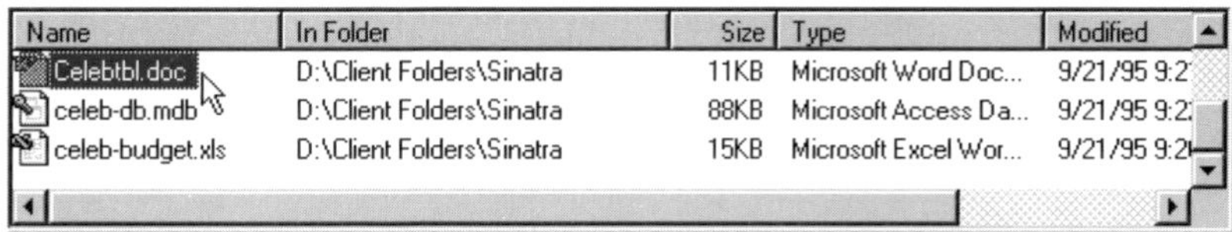

Name
In Folder
Size
Type
Modified
Celebtbl.doc
D:\Client Folders\Sinatra
11KB
Microsoft Word Doc...
9/21/95 9:2
celeb-db.mdb
D:\Client Folders\Sinatra
88KB
Microsoft Access Da...
9/21/95 9:2
celeb-budget.xls
D:\Client Folders\Sinatra
15KB
Microsoft Excel Wor...
9/21/95 9:2

Oh yeah. I put her phone number in two word documents and a FileMaker database. These searches take a very long time, so if you can restrict them to a disk or two, do it.

Specifying Case Sensitivity

This feature can be a little confusing since it only works in the "Containing text" box (located in the Advanced tab of the Find dialog box). The Find feature always ignores capitalization when searching filenames, regardless of the setting you specify in the Case Sensitive option (located on the Options menu). If, however, you know exactly how the text you are looking for is capitalized within a document, you can choose the Case Sensitive option in the Options menu and Find will only list files containing text exactly matching your specification. With this feature enabled, a search for "Ron" will not find "ron" or "RON" within files, but will still show you filenames containing "Ron", "ron", "RON", and even "rOn".

Take a moment now to try some searches. For example, look for files on your hard disk ending with the extension .txt. Sort them by date modified. View one or two. Now search for files containing your name within them. If you've had your computer for any length of time, you'll be amazed at how many document files (and even programs) have your name, buried as text, within.

Once you've found all those important files, you'll want to take good care of them. In Chapter 6, you'll learn how to back up important files with Windows 95. You'll also find out how to keep your disks functioning soundly so you'll have safe, reliable space for storing and working with your data.

DO NOT
RUSH!

CHAPTER

6 Caring for Your Files and Disks

INCLUDES

- Backing up important files
- Disk integrity checks
- Defragmenting disks
- Protection from viruses
- Disk compression

Start the Backup Program ➤ pp. 133-134

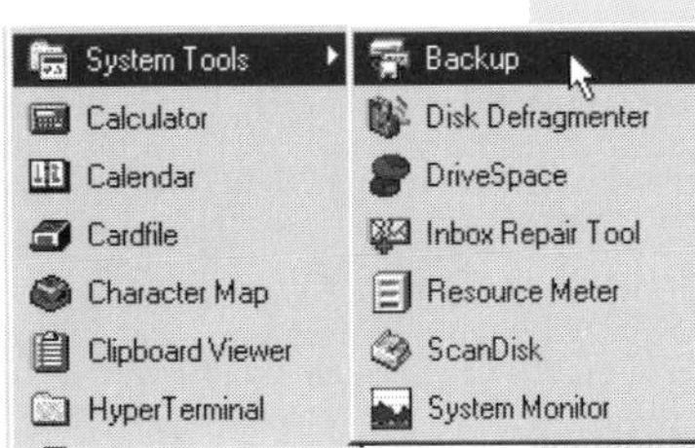

You can access the Backup program quickly by first adding it to your Start menu (see Chapter 10). If you haven't done this, follow these steps to start Backup:

1. Choose Programs from the Start menu.
2. Choose the Accessories option.
3. Choose System Tools.
4. Select the Backup program from the System Tools menu.

Back Up Your Files ➤ pp. 135-136

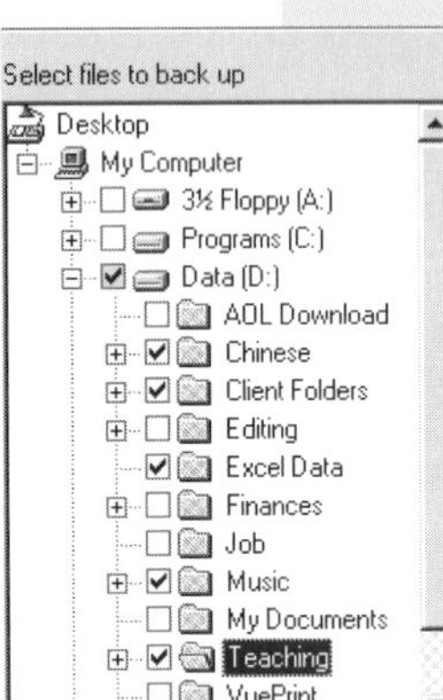

1. Start the Backup program.
2. In the Microsoft Backup dialog box, select the files and folders you wish to back up.
3. Click the Next Step button.
4. Select a location (floppies, tape, etc.) for the backup copies.
5. Click Start Backup.
6. Assign a name to your set of backup files.
7. If you are backing up to floppy disks, insert blank disks when prompted as the backup progresses.

Restore Backed-Up Files ➤ pp. 136-138

1. Start the Backup program.
2. Click the Restore tab in the Microsoft Backup dialog box.
3. Click the icon for the device (tape drive, floppy disk drive, etc.) that contains the storage set.
4. Double-click the icon for the storage set.
5. Select a folder.
6. In the folder's file list, put checkmarks next to the items you wish to restore.
7. Repeat steps 5 and 6 as necessary.
8. Click Start Restore.

Check for Disk Errors ➤ *pp. 138-139*

1. Start the ScanDisk program, which you'll find in the System Tools menu.
2. Select the disk or disks to be scanned.
3. Select the type of test you want to run, and change the testing options as necessary.
4. Click Start.
5. If ScanDisk offers to fix any disk errors that it finds, either click OK or seek further advice from a technician or other knowledgeable source.

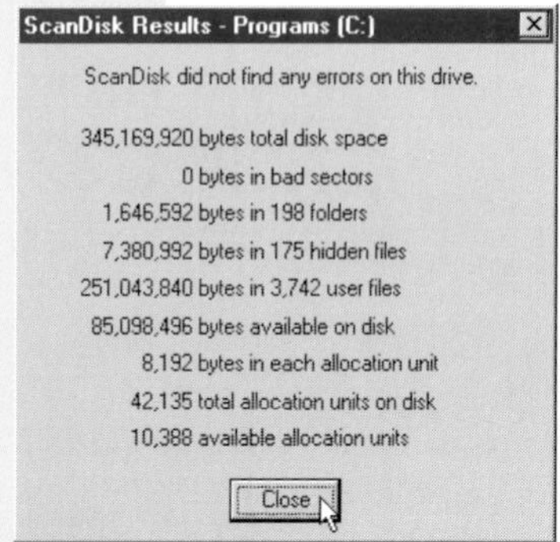

Defragment a Disk ➤ *pp. 140-142*

1. Make sure you've exited any disk utilities and backed up all your critical files.
2. Start the Disk Defragmenter program, available from the System Tools menu.
3. Select the disk to be analyzed and click OK. Eventually, the Defragmenter will display a report showing its recommendations for your disk.
4. If you wish to defragment your disk, click Start.

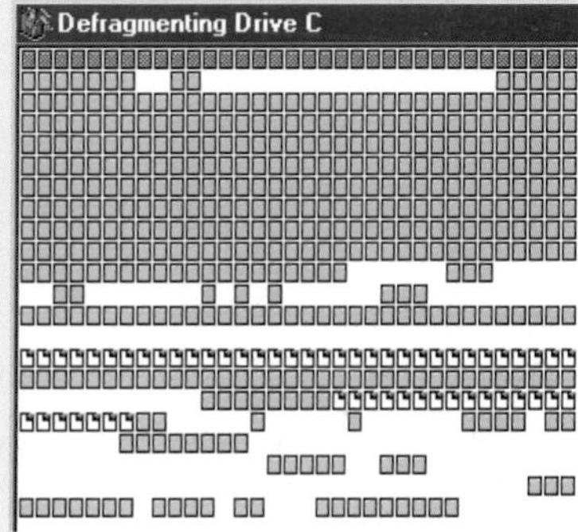

Prevent Virus Infection ➤ *pp. 142-144*

- Know the sources of your programs and documents (Word, Excel, and other documents containing macros can be infected).
- Check new programs and documents with virus detection software prior to opening or running them.

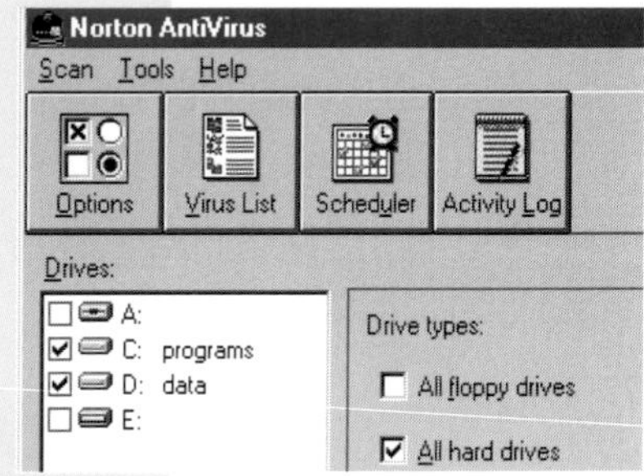

Disasters happen. I've personally lived through floods, wildfires, power outages, disk failures, a burglary, several earthquakes, and a screening of the film Ishtar. Except for Ishtar, all of these events threatened my computer files. Once a broken water pipe did trash some data. Another time my hard disk simply ground to a halt. Trust me ... if your data has not been at risk, it soon will be.

The best protection is to regularly make copies of important files and store them in another ZIP code. It also helps to keep your hard disks error- and virus-free. Let's have a look at some options.

Backup Plans: An Overview

In a very small office your backup plan can be pretty simple. You might drag copies of your few mission-critical documents to floppies on some kind of a schedule, and take them someplace else. *Someplace else* means a reasonable distance away from the computer. A different neighborhood is good. Bank safe deposit boxes work for some folks. When I worked at home I had a little fireproof safe with a handle on it. The backups went in there (at the far end of the house), and the safe evacuated with us whenever the flames licked the hills or the ground shook. Not perfect, but good enough. (Usually my publishers and clients have additional copies of my important files.) Now that I have an office in town, I take my *office* backup disks and tapes *home*, and the *home* computer backups to the *office.*

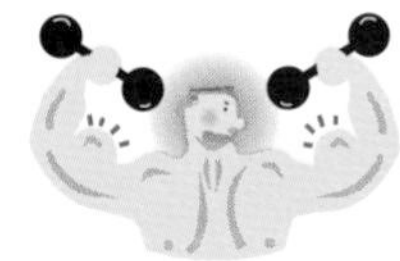

DEFINITION

back up: *To copy important files to disks, tapes, or other media for safekeeping and retrieval in the event that original files are damaged or lost.*

How often you back up and what medium you use are also important. Start by asking yourself how many days worth of work you can afford to lose in a worst-case scenario. In most medium-sized organizations, even losing a day's work is too much. That's why smart users back up daily. And they rotate the backup media (tapes, disks, etc.) so that the risks of worn-out backup tapes or disks are minimized.

If you work in a large organization, you probably have policies and procedures governing what you must back up, how, and how often. Please find out about these rules and comply. Nothing you read here should dissuade you from doing things the way your organization wants them done. And if there is no plan, make your own, and then stick with it!

The Windows 95 Backup Program

Windows 95 ships with a backup program called Backup. It might not have been installed on your computer though. To see if it has, follow these steps:

1. Choose Programs from the Start menu.
2. Pick Accessories from the Programs submenu.
3. Pick System Tools from the Accessories submenu. If you see Backup in the System Tools submenu, as you do here, you are in luck.

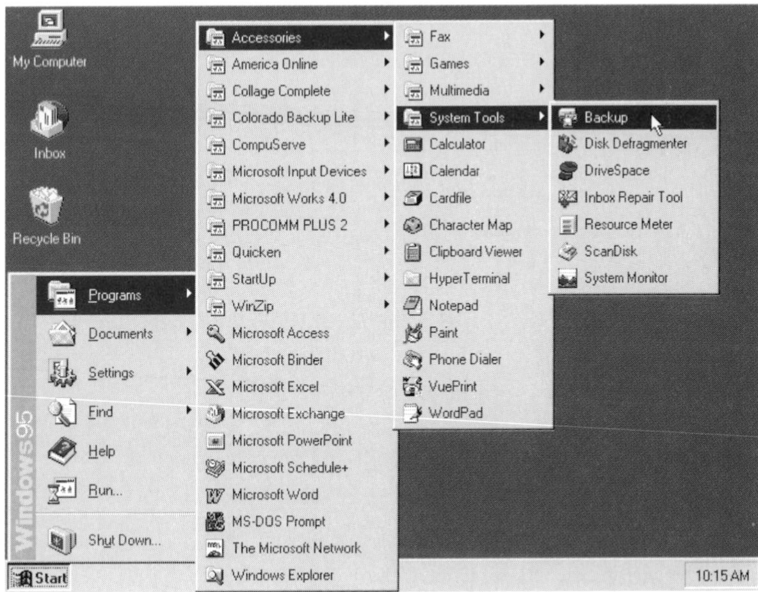

Phew! Now, *there's* a program that needs to be on the top level of your Start menu. (And Chapter 10 will show you how to put it there.)

If you don't see Backup in the System Tools submenu, keep chugging ahead:

1. Use the Start menu's Settings selection to access the control panel.
2. Double-click the Add/Remove Programs icon. Be sure you have your Windows 95 CD-ROM or floppies handy.
3. Click the Windows Setup tab.
4. Double-click Disk Tools.
5. Click to place a checkmark in the Backup box.
6. Click OK.
7. Click OK again and follow the directions.

Once Backup is installed, run it from the Start menu. The exact litany you see will vary based on your system and choices you or the installer might have made earlier. In any case, read the dialog boxes carefully.

EXPERT ADVICE

It makes very little sense to back up programs that you have on CD-ROMs or floppies, or stuff that you should have deleted years ago, or (in my opinion) Windows 95 itself. These things are almost always more reliably reinstalled from scratch. But again, if you work someplace with a different set of guidelines, decide what to back up based on those.

I personally don't use the full System Backup, and you probably shouldn't either without professional help. So if the Microsoft Backup dialog box appears with a message that says "To back up your entire hard drive..." ignore it for now. In fact, a click in the "Don't show this again" box is really in order here.

SHORTCUT

Normally, you'll want to back up only important documents, spreadsheets, databases, checkbook ledgers, custom artwork, difficult-to-obtain multimedia files, etc.

Backing Up Your Files

Follow these steps to back up your work:

1. In the Microsoft Backup dialog box, select the files and folders you wish to back up. Place checkmarks next to their names by clicking in the appropriate boxes, as shown here:

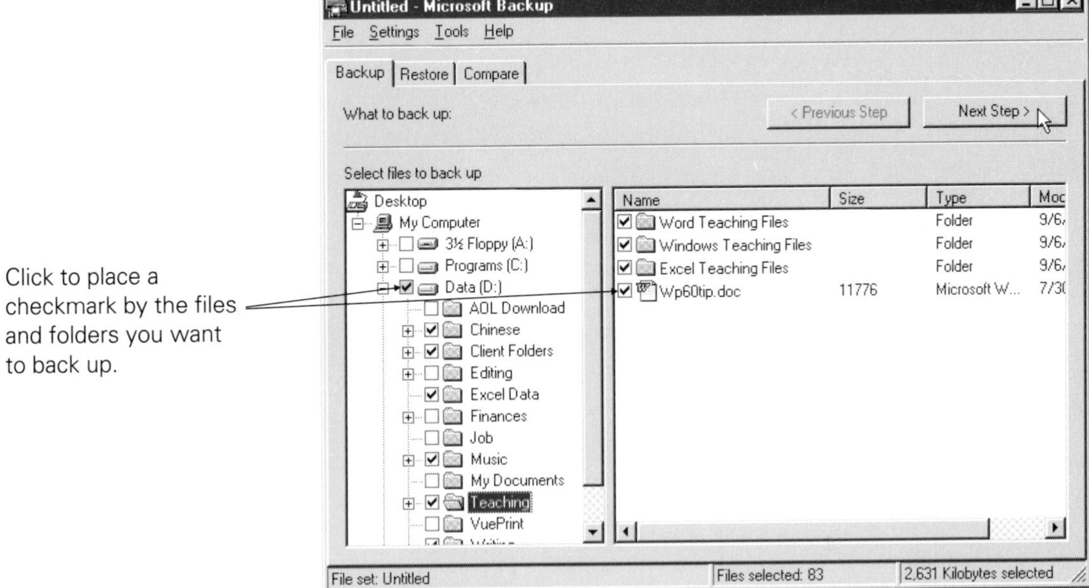

2. When you've selected everything of importance, click the Next Step button. The program will ask you where to put the backup copies. You might use floppies (slower than other backup media, but cheap and ubiquitous), tape, removable hard disks, writable CD-ROMs, a remote network server—whatever you have available. Again, based on your choice you might need to take other actions (formatting backup tapes, for instance).
3. When you are ready to go, click the Start Backup button.
4. The backup file set you are creating must be named. Choose a name that's meaningful to you and in keeping with your backup strategy.

Here I'm using days of the week:

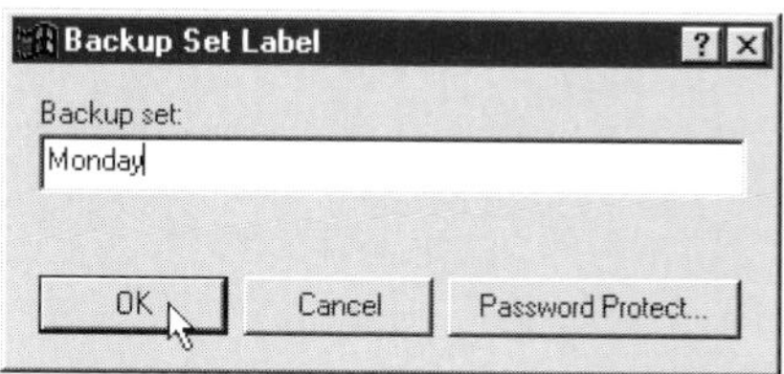

5. Click OK. As the backup progresses you get to watch a little animation and some statistics. Unfortunately, you don't see a list of filenames, so you won't be able to tell if the wrong things are getting backed up (or worse still, if the *right* things are *not* getting backed up).
6. If you are using disks for your backup, you'll be prompted now and then when it is time to feed the Drive Gods...

Once you've run a backup (particularly the first few times), it can't hurt to check your work. To do this, use the Restore feature to view the names of the files you've stored and confirm that the backup was successful. You can then exit the program without actually restoring any files.

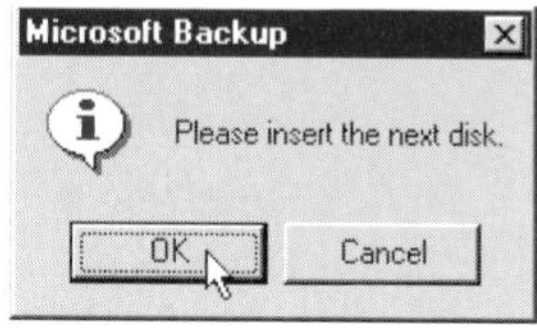

...but eventually, the process will be done.

Restoring Backed-up Files

Of course the real beauty of the backup feature is that it lets you restore your backed-up files when you need them. In times of crisis, the Restore feature can draw tears of joyous relief from some busy people. Here's how to use it:

1. Start the Backup program (if it is not running already).
2. In the Microsoft Backup dialog box, click the Restore tab:

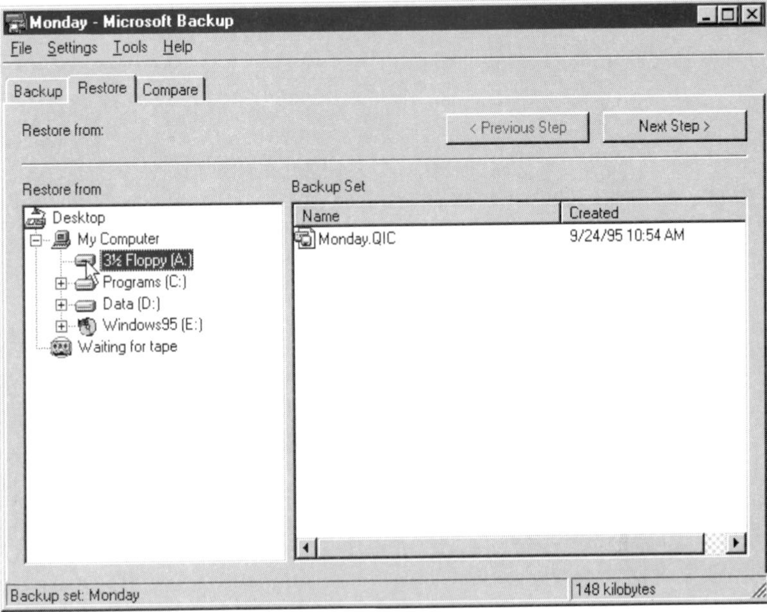

3. Click the icon for the device (tape drive, floppy disk drive, etc.) containing the backup.
4. Double-click the icon for the storage set.
5. Double-click a folder icon of interest. You will see a file list something like this one:

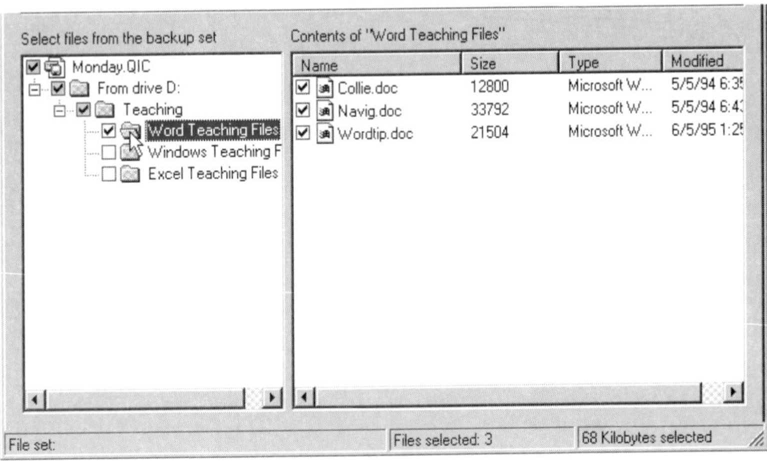

6. Put checkmarks next to the items you wish to restore.
7. Repeat steps 5 and 6 until you've checked every item you want back.
8. Click the Start Restore button, and the files and folders you've selected will be restored to their original locations.

Checking for Disk Errors

With anything as complex as a computer, errors are bound to creep in. Disk files are particularly susceptible. And although some errors are trivial, others can be major, or foreshadow big hardware problems. For all of these reasons, it is important to run a Windows 95 utility called ScanDisk from time to time. I do it about once a week.

EXPERT ADVICE

You can start ScanDisk the hard way by clicking the Start button, choosing Accessories, choosing System Tools, and finally choosing ScanDisk, or you can create and use a Start menu shortcut. (See Chapter 10.)

To run ScanDisk, follow these steps:

1. Choose ScanDisk.
2. Choose the disk or disks to be scanned (CTRL-click all of your hard disks, at a minimum).
3. Make a selection in the Type Of Test list (Thorough is a good idea).
4. Change options if you know what you are doing—otherwise, leave them as is.
5. Click the Start button and wait. You should hear your disk drive a-hummin'.

You might get an error message something like this one:

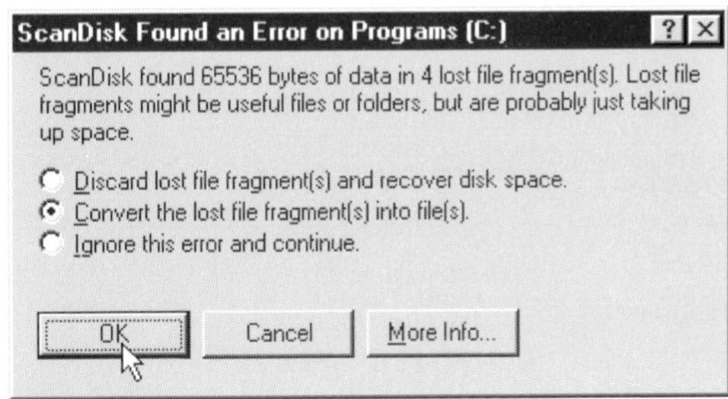

6. ScanDisk might offer to fix the problem. If this sounds reasonable, click OK. If you have doubts, seek technical advice or write down what you see and cancel out of ScanDisk until you can get advice.

Eventually, if you continue, you'll get a report like this one:

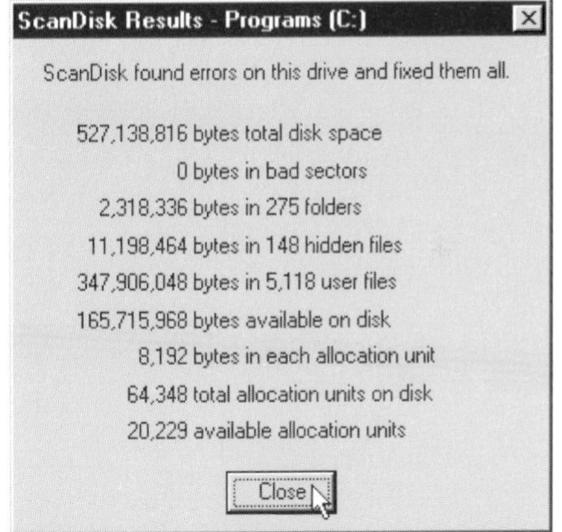

SHORTCUT

If you purchase and install the optional Microsoft Plus! software, you can use it to automate ScanDisk sessions on a schedule you define.

Defragmenting a Disk

Again, if this disk utility was not installed, use the Add/Remove Programs control panel icon and your original Windows 95 disks or CD-ROM.

Files don't get stored contiguously. Windows 95 makes the best use of available space by putting parts of files here and there on your hard disk. Eventually, this slows down your computer as the drive goes hither and yon looking for parts of your files. A defragmenting utility shipped with Windows 95 can tidy up—and speed up—your disk.

Running the Defragmenter

Before you actually run the Defragmenter, make sure you've exited any other disk utilities (like ScanDisk). Also, you should strongly consider backing up all of your critical files, just in case. Once you can proceed safely, follow these steps:

1. Choose Programs from the Start menu, make your way to the System Tools choice, and choose Disk Defragmenter.
2. Select the disk to be analyzed and possibly defragmented and click OK. The Defragmenter will tell you what it thinks:

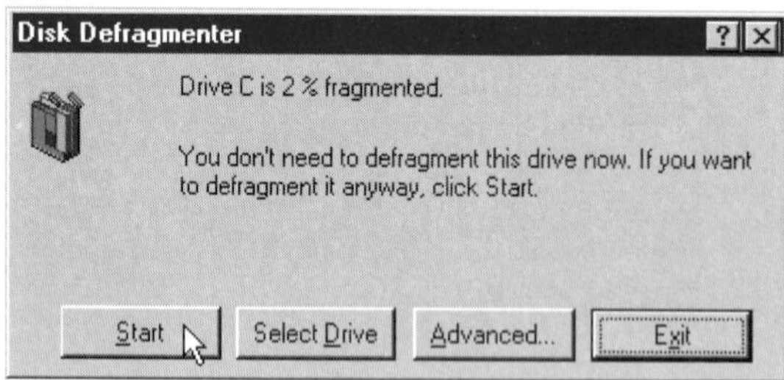

3. Now it's time to make a decision, based on the Defragmenter's report:
   - If your disk is in pretty good shape, busy person, you may just want to click Exit.
   - If you'd like to select another disk for analysis, click Select Drive.
   - If you'd like to defragment your disk, click the Start button. You'll see a progress report. Be patient! This might take some time.

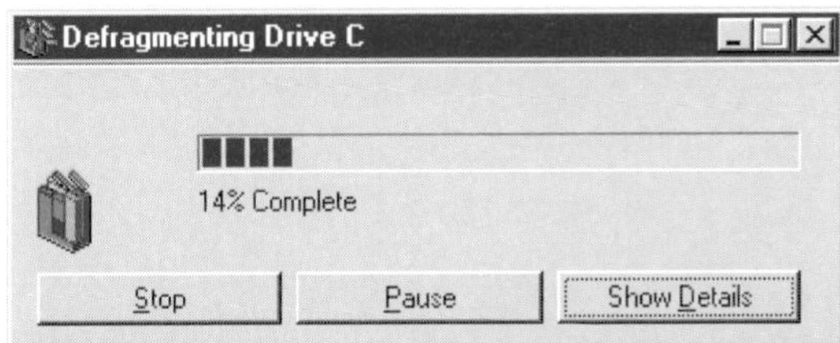

EXPERT ADVICE

Before clicking Start to begin the defragmentation process, you may want to click the Advanced button to check out the options for customizing the procedure.

4. To view the Defragmenter's progress, choose Show Details. You'll see a graphic illustration of your disk, showing fragmented file data, unused space, and eventually a growing section of defragmented disk space, each indicated by different-looking boxes:

If you get dizzy watching all these tiny boxes zip around your screen, you can always click Hide Details—or better yet, get away from your computer screen for awhile and open your mail, straighten your desk, or take a stress-reducing walk outside!

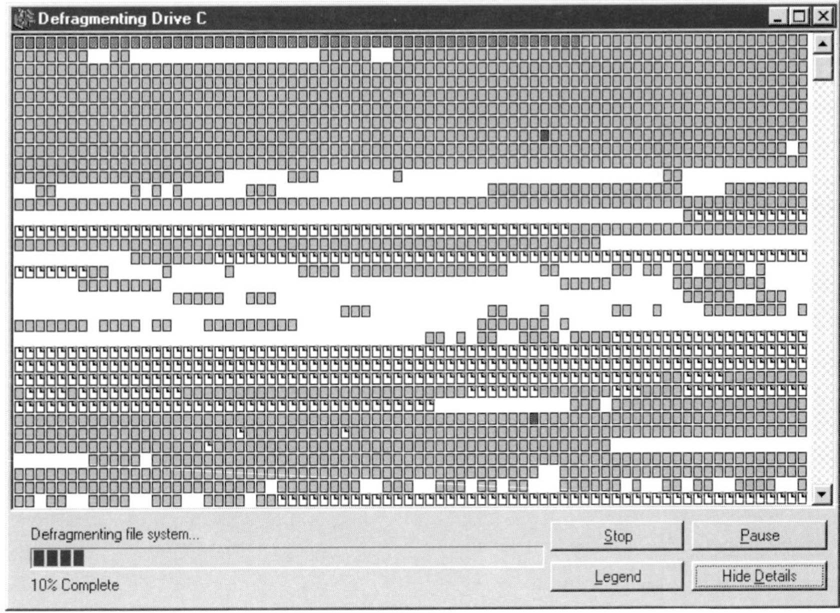

You can click Stop or Pause from the detailed graphic display if, for any reason, you change your mind or need to interrupt the process. Your safest bet, though, is to just let the Defragmenter run its course.

Virus Protection

There are twisted programmers who get their kicks from writing and passing around programs (and now, Word, Excel, and other documents containing destructive macros) that vandalize your disks. These annoyances are generally referred to as viruses, although there are subtle variations (Trojan Horses and such). The technical distinctions are not worth exploring here. What you do need to know is how they can spread—and how to protect your computer.

CAUTION

Until recently, you could only get a virus by loading a copy of an infected program onto your hard disk and running it. Now, you can get infected by simply opening Word documents, Excel spreadsheets, and, in very rare cases, E-mail.

Virtually all infections come to you disguised as free programs or, nowadays, documents passed via floppy or over America Online, CompuServe, the Internet, your in-house network, etc. Schoolchildren bring them home. Churchgoers give them to their priests. Girl Scouts give them to Boy Scouts. Even one of the world's largest software manufacturers... umm... residing in the Pacific Northwest has inadvertently distributed them on CD-ROMS!

The only sure way to avoid a virus is to never load any programs or documents on your computer. (As Johnny Carson used to say "You'll be safe from earthquakes if you always stand in a doorway, but your life will be p-r-e-t-t-y boring.") The next best thing is to restructure your entire life around the following principles:

- Know your software and document sources (don't take floppies from strangers).
- Never steal copies of commercial software.
- Purchase and religiously use an up-to-date virus scanner to scan new programs before running them, and scan your disk(s) on a schedule.
- If you use programs that support macros (like Microsoft Word, Excel, Word Perfect, etc.), be sure that the virus detection software you purchase can protect you against infections spread via macros.
- Make regular backups of your disks just in case.

CAUTION

Old virus protection software created prior to Windows 95 will not *work, and may even damage your files. Purchase new, Windows 95-savvy utilities.*

Sources of Virus Protection Software

There is free shareware available for virus protection, but I think your best bet is to purchase a good virus checking program from a known commercial vendor. Examples include *Norton's AntiVirus* offered by Symantec or the *Anti-Virus Toolkit* from Dr. Solomon. You can purchase these things locally, or via mail order from places like PC Connection. Because I know you are busy, and only to save you some time, I'll give you PC Connection's phone number here. (800-800-1111). I own no stock in the company, and have used plenty of other fine vendors.

Sources of Viruses Information and Updates

Since virus hunting is a constantly changing art, once you receive and install your anti-virus software, you must keep it up-to-date by regularly downloading "patches" or new virus hunting definitions. You will also want to keep abreast of changes in threats. It was only recently, for example, that macro infections became a significant problem. Here are several sources of virus information:

Dr. Solomon's Virus Central	**http://www.drsolomon.com/vircen/**	**Great source of info and updates for Dr. Solomon's virus detection software.**
Computer Virus Help Desk	**http://iw1.indyweb.net/~cvhd/**	Another good forum. Way more than you've ever wanted to know. (Sadly, this is a good thing.) You'll even see what NASA has to say about their virus problems.
Symantec's AntiVirus Research Center	**http://www.symantec.com/avcenter/index.html**	Source of hot topics and updates for Norton's AntiVirus software.
Microsoft Knowledge Base	**http://www.microsoft.com**	Search the Knowledge Base for the term **Virus**. This site is a little disappointing and (at least at the time this was written) somewhat outdated.

upgrade note

Unlike Windows 3.1, Windows 95 does not come with a virus detection program. You'll need to buy a separate package from Norton or from somebody else.

Disk Compression: Ten Pounds in a Five-Pound Sack?

This will be short and sweet. Windows 95 comes with a utility that compresses your files so that they take up less space on your disk. However, I have never met a compression program that I liked. Disk drives are too cheap, life is too short, and the risks are just too great when you compress stuff. If you want to learn about disk compression schemes, check your Windows manual and online help.

If you haven't already done so, take a minute now to purchase and install commercial virus protection software. Make a backup plan and write it down. If you are a supervisor or have coworkers, work with these folks to establish plans for the entire organization. Make a backup of your important files. Check to see if your disk(s) need(s) defragmenting.

Next, in Chapter 7, you'll learn some timesaving tips and techniques that can add hours to your free time. Just take a look.

FIRST CLASS
OVERNIGHT
MEMO
RUSH!

CHAPTER

7 Important Techniques and Timesavers

INCLUDES

- Using the second mouse button
- Swapping mouse buttons
- Keyboard shortcuts
- Dragging and dropping
- Scraps
- Shortcut icons
- Properties
- OLE and ActiveX

FAST FORWARD

Use the Second Mouse Button ➤ pp. 151-153

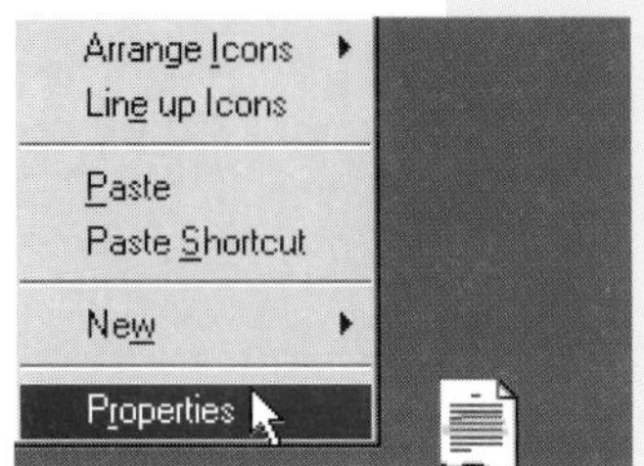

1. Click with the second (normally, the right) mouse button to select things like folder icons, file icons, the Start menu, etc. You will see a shortcut menu listing possible actions.
2. Use the menu as you'd expect.

Swap the Functions of the Right and Left Mouse Buttons ➤ p. 153

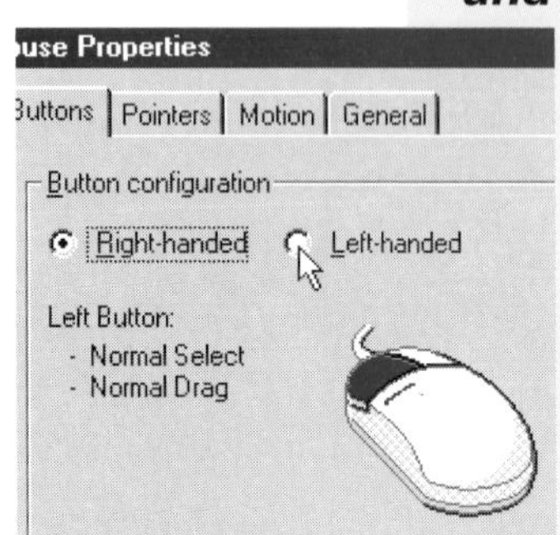

1. Choose Settings from the Start menu.
2. Choose the Control Panel option.
3. Double-click the Mouse icon.
4. Click Left-handed or Right-handed.
5. Click OK.

Use Keyboard Shortcuts ➤ pp. 154-157

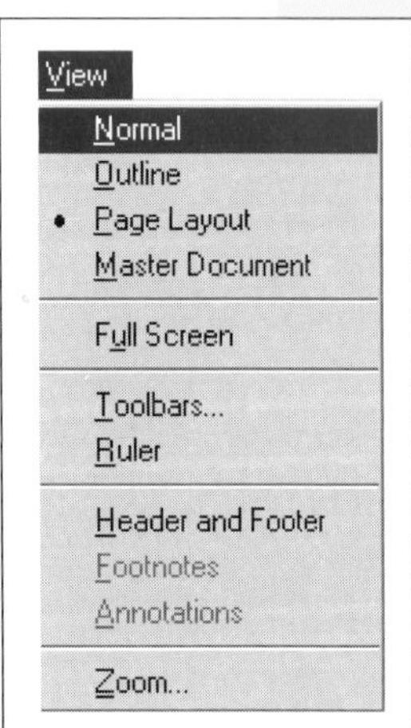

1. Press and release the ALT key.
2. Press the underlined letter of the desired menu title (the V in View, for example).
3. Press the first underlined letter of the desired menu choice (such as the N in Normal or the U in Full Screen).

Many programs also assign special keyboard shortcuts for frequently used features (like CTRL-C to copy). These shortcuts are usually listed on the program's menus.

Drag and Drop to Copy or Move Information ➤ *pp. 157-159*

1. Make sure the program you are using supports drag-and-drop.
2. Select the information to be moved or copied.
3. Point to the selected information and hold down the mouse button.
4. The mouse pointer will change shape.
5. Drag to the desired insertion point.
6. Release the mouse button.

The information should move. (If you hold down the CTRL key while dragging, the information gets copied, not moved.)

Use Scraps to Copy and Reuse Items ➤ *pp. 160-161*

- Select information and drag it to the desktop or into a folder.
- To reuse scraps, drag them into documents.
- To view the contents of scraps, double-click.

Examine Properties to See and Change Settings ➤ *pp. 163-165*

1. Click to select the object of interest (file icon, folder, etc.).
2. Right-click to produce a shortcut menu.
3. Choose Properties from the shortcut menu.
4. Click the appropriate tab if necessary to view the property of interest.

Change Properties ➤ *pp. 165-166*

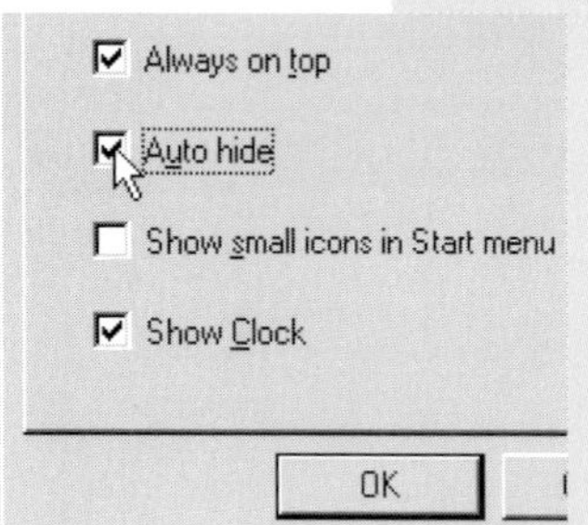

1. Open the desired dialog box.
2. Click buttons, slide sliders, and/or type changes.
3. Click OK.

(Remember: Not all properties can be changed by mere mortals.)

Link Objects to Automate Updating ➤ *pp. 166-167*

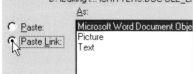

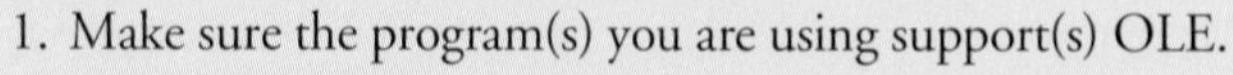

1. Make sure the program(s) you are using support(s) OLE.
2. Select the information you wish to link.
3. Copy (use CTRL-C).
4. Switch to the destination window.
5. Choose Paste Special from the File menu.
6. Specify the desired paste option.
7. Reformat the linked object if necessary.

Embed Objects ➤ *pp. 167-169*

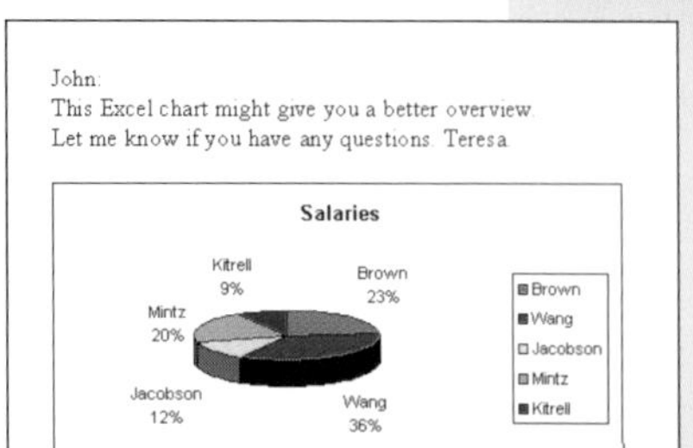

1. Make sure the program(s) you are using support(s) embedding.
2. Select the information you wish to embed.
3. Copy (use CTRL-C).
4. Switch to the destination window.
5. Choose Paste Special from the Edit menu.
6. Specify the desired paste option.
7. Reformat the embedded object if necessary.

As the old saying goes, "Having lost sight of our objectives, we redoubled our efforts." If you are like me, you are usually so busy that you fail to learn new tricks that could make you a more efficient computer user. We form bad habits and live with them, knowing full well that there must be a better way. This chapter has some tricks and techniques worth adopting.

If you don't have time for this whole chapter now, bite off a topic today, put a Post-it™ note where you stop, and come back tomorrow.

The Second (Non-Primary) Mouse Button

For years that second (a.k.a. *non-primary* or *secondary* or worse, still, *Button 2*) mouse button lingered forlornly, longing for useful and predictable work. Well, it's official. The extra clicker on your mouse, or trackball, or laptop palmrest, or whatever (usually the right button) now brings up little "context" menus in Windows 95 and well-behaved programs. It is also used for "special dragging" (whatever that is).

Even Microsoft isn't in complete agreement about the name of context menus. You'll often see them described as "shortcut" menus. I prefer that term, myself.

Using the Second Button

If you know how to use the primary mouse button, you know how to use the other one (granted, you'll probably need to employ a different finger). The trick is to use the second button with any screen element that responds to right-clicking. Not all objects react to pokes of the second button, but many do. For example, slide the mouse pointer over any visible portion of your Windows 95 desktop and press the secondary button.

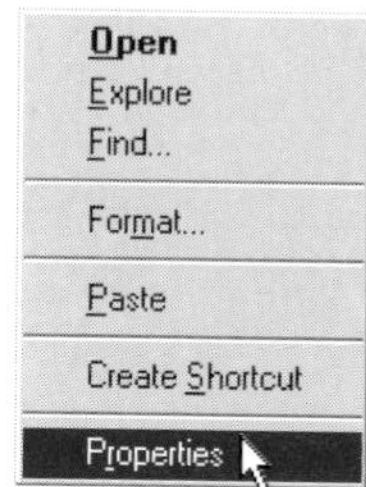

Quicker than you can say "Bill's a billionaire," you'll see a small context, or shortcut menu. Use the mouse to select a menu item (let's try Properties, for example).

And here's where it gets weird. Clicking with either the right or left button will execute the menu choice. In this example, I click Properties on the shortcut menu. The result: I got the Display Properties window.

Don't panic. We'll visit the wonderful world of properties to learn more about them very soon.

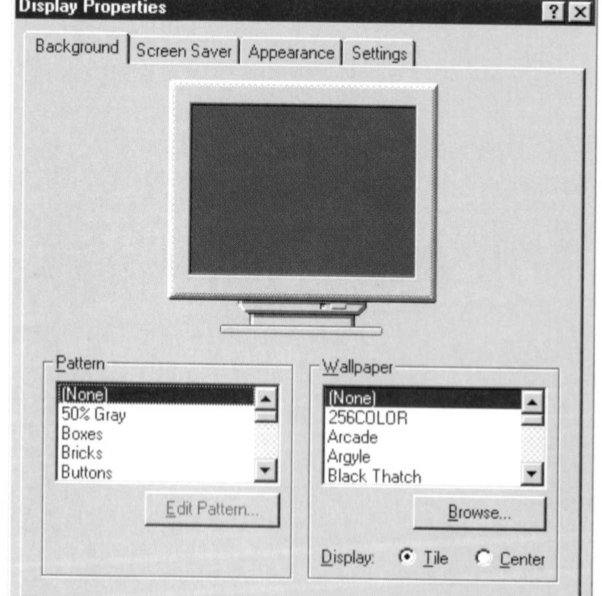

That rules, huh? The right mouse button just saved me a trip to the Start menu and then a submenu and then a double-click. There are a zillion places to visit with the second mouse button. Someday, someone will give a prize to the person who's come up with the longest list of things to do with the second button, so prepare for this. Experiment. At a minimum you'll find enough new spots to one-up the competition at the coffee machine.

Swapping Functions of the Primary and Secondary Button

Some of my best friends are left-handed. Even my dog tends... well, never mind. To swap button functions, follow this recipe. (You'll learn more about personalizing Windows 95 in Chapter 10.)

1. Choose Settings from the Start menu.
2. Pick Control Panel from the resulting submenu.
3. Double-click the Mouse icon.
4. Click the Buttons tab if necessary to bring it topside.
5. Click to select either Right-handed or Left-handed. (Right-handed is the standard Microsoft setting.)

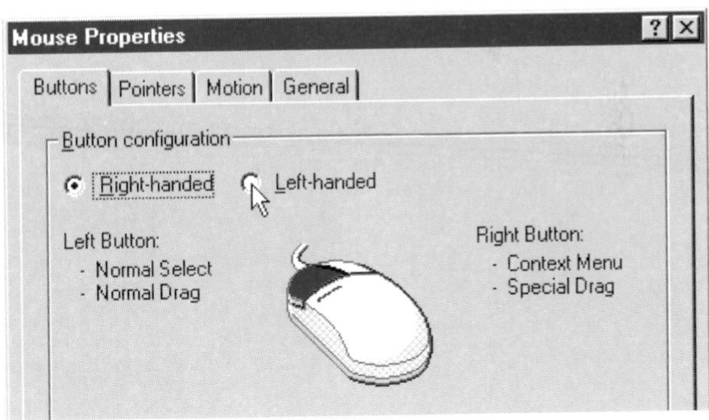

You needn't be a lefty to benefit from swapping mouse button functions. Try it. See what you think. (Or use this information to drive an unsuspecting co-worker crazy...)

6. Click OK.
7. Try it. If you hate the results, repeat steps 1 through 6.

Keyboard Shortcuts for Menu Choices

You know this, so I'll just remind you in passing. There are two brands of keyboard shortcuts—one set for virtually all menu items (ALT followed by the underlined letter in the name of a menu item), and another, more efficient way to execute just those special few commands Microsoft thinks we use all the time. Keyboard shortcuts save you (the informed, busy user) a trip to the menu bar. Remember these?

Popular Keyboard Shortcuts

Many of the things you do regularly can be accomplished with key combinations and/or function keys. Table 7.1 lists some of my favorites.

Programmers often list helpful keyboard shortcut key combinations next to their corresponding commands in menus, so check menus and make your own cheat sheets whenever you buy a new program.

The ALT Key and Underlined Menu Letters

You can reach virtually any menu choice and activate it sans mouse. This is particularly good to know if your little rodent dies at 35,000 feet, and you want to watch the in-flight movie. Here's what to do:

1. Press ALT. Sometimes, but not always, the first menu name in the active window gets highlighted (Edit in the case of this calculator example):

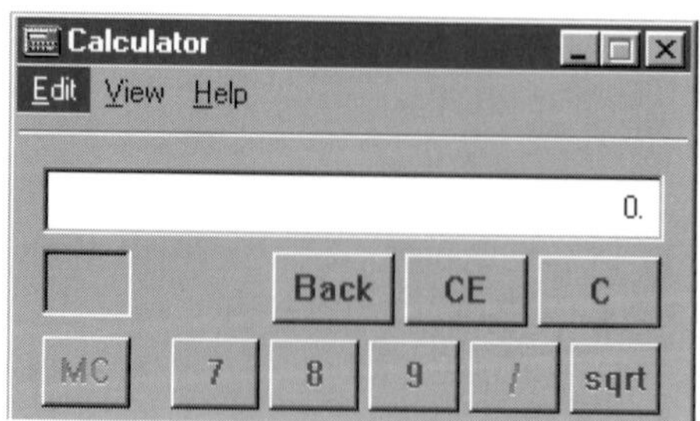

Action	Shortcut
Copy	Use CTRL-C to duplicate things you've selected. This leaves selected item(s) intact, and places a copy on the Clipboard (destroying the Clipboard's prior contents).
Cut	Use CTRL-X to move selected item(s) to the Clipboard (destroying the Clipboard's prior contents).
Paste	Use CTRL-V to paste contents of the Clipboard at the insertion point.
Help	Use F1, but first make sure the program of interest or a child window of that program is active.
New	Use CTRL-N to open a new document.
Open	Use CRTL-O to display the Open dialog box so you can choose from existing files.
Print	Use CTRL-P to start the printing process.
Quit	Use either ALT-F4 or CTRL-W. (Have you saved your work?)
Close document window	Use CTRL-F4. (Have you saved your work?)
Save	Use CTRL-S to save your work to disk.
Undo	Try CTRL-Z, but note that not all programs undo.
Switch between document windows	CTRL-F6 works in most programs.
Display the Start menu	Use CTRL-ESC, and then arrow keys and ENTER to highlight and execute Start menu choices.
Navigate and issue commands	Use tab keys to move around in most dialog boxes and ENTER to make choices.
Close dialog box	Press ESC.
Move from application to application	Press ALT-TAB and release the keys when the onscreen box surrounds the icon for the desired program.

Table 7.1 Useful Keyboard Shortcuts

2. Press the letter key of the underlined letter for the desired menu. For example, to get to the Help menu in the Calculator, press H.

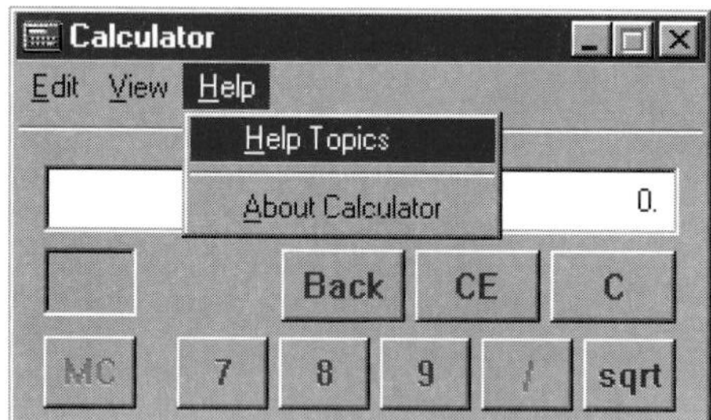

3. Press the underlined letter of the desired menu item (A for About, as an example).
4. To close informational windows, try pressing ESC.
5. To quit programs that don't have an Exit choice on their File menus, try ALT-F4.

If, after pressing ALT, you don't see the first menu drop, type the underlined letter of the desired menu.

upgrade note

Microsoft is changing the way shortcut menus work. This will take some getting used to. Watch the screen as you work because merely pressing ALT will no longer highlight a menu name in newer programs.

Using the Keyboard to Activate the Start Menu

To use the Start menu from your keyboard, follow these steps:

1. Press CTRL-ESC.
2. When the Start menu appears, press the first letter of the desired menu choice (or if there is an underlined letter, press it). In cases where there are two Start menu choices beginning with the same letter, press the letter key repeatedly to highlight the desired choice.

3. When you've highlighted the desired choice, press ENTER. If the choice is executable, the program will run, the document will open, the network connection will be made, and all will be right with the world. If the choice leads to a submenu, you'll see the next menu level.

You also can use the up arrow, down arrow, left arrow, and right arrow keys to navigate once you display the Start menu with CTRL-ESC.

EXPERT ADVICE

Precede your favorite Start menu item with numbers (1. CompuServe, 2. America Online, etc.). This makes it easy to launch programs from the keyboard. For example, CTRL-ESC, 1 would run 1. CompuServe, CTRL-ESC, 2 would run 2. America Online, etc. See Chapter 10 for instructions on renaming Start menu items.

Moving or Copying by Dragging and Dropping

Recent versions of Windows-approved programs (like Word 6 and up or Excel 6 and newer) support drag-and-drop copying and moving. You can drag and drop within one program, or you can drag stuff from one program to another.

Dragging and Dropping in the Same Window

In general, to *move* information you just take these steps:

1. Select information to be moved.
2. Point to the selected information, and then hold down the mouse button and watch the mouse pointer change shape.

3. Drag to the desired location.
4. Release the mouse button. The selected stuff moves.
5. Choose Undo or press CTRL-Z if you don't like the results.

To copy rather than move, hold down the CTRL key while dragging. Usually, the icon will have a plus sign (+) added to it if you will be copying rather than moving. Isn't that something?

Dragging and Dropping Between Windows

Dragging and dropping often works between windows even if they are not children of the same parents. Again, both programs need to support the new drag-and-drop feature. Let's call the window containing the information you want to move or copy the *source* window and the window receiving the information the *destination* window. Here are the general steps:

1. Display the two windows you plan to use. Figure 7.1 shows a Word document in one window and an Excel worksheet in the other.
2. If necessary, switch to the destination document and prepare the area where you want the information to be dropped (add a blank line to make room, or whatever).
3. Switch to the source document and highlight the information to be copied or moved.
4. Hold down the primary mouse button and drag the selection from the source window to the destination window. (If you want to copy

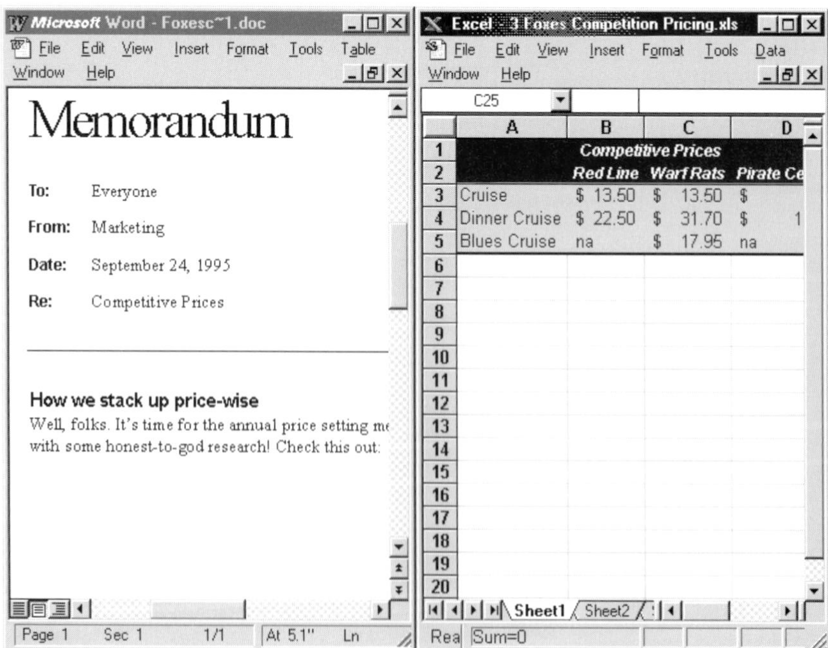

Figure 7.1 Getting ready to copy data between windows

the information, instead of moving it, hold down the CTRL key while dragging.)

5. Release the mouse button and see what happens. In Figure 7.2, the Excel table has been copied into the Word memorandum.

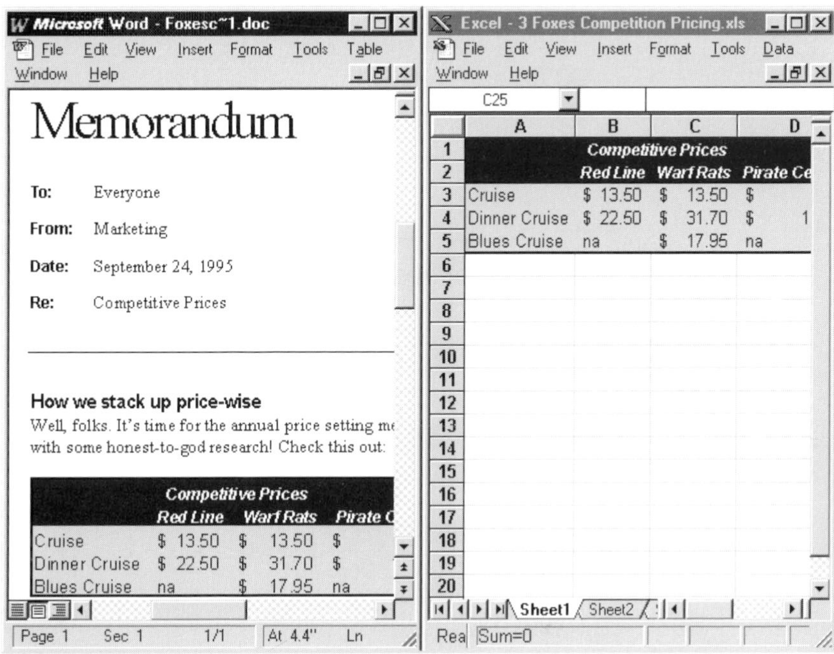

Figure 7.2 Data copied successfully!

Again, the end results depend upon a host of factors, including the type of source and destination programs used, the settings and formatting options in the source and destination windows, decisions made three years ago by a Microsoft programmer who now can't remember what was decided, and on and on.

CAUTION

While copying, cutting, dragging, and dropping can be fun, they can really alter your documents. Before experimenting, take a moment to save both the source and destination documents, then don't save them again until you are sure that all is well.

Moving or Copying by Creating Scraps

If an application supports Object Linking and Embedding (described later in this chapter), you can use this feature to collect scraps of information that you can temporarily store on your desktop or place in a folder for future reference and reuse. Once you've created scraps, you can insert them into documents more or less as you please.

A scrap might consist of a word or a few text paragraphs, some spreadsheet cells, a graphic, or combinations of just about anything you can see in an OLE-savvy window. For example, you could have a scrap containing your mailing address or an entire signature block for letters (complete with "Very truly yours" and your scanned signature).

STEP BY STEP Creating a Scrap

1 While in a program that supports this feature (like Word or Excel), select an item to be copied.

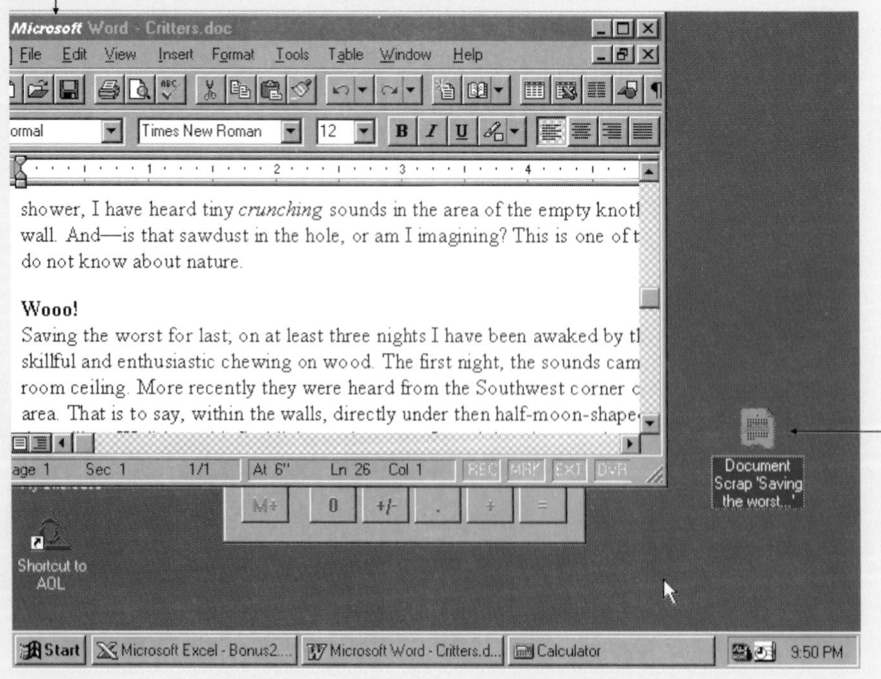

2 Drag the selection either out to the desktop or into a folder of your choosing. An icon will appear with the word *Scrap* in its title. If the scrap contains text, you'll see the first few characters or words. Spreadsheet scraps will show text from the first field or two. Graphics and other scraps might just have the word *Scrap*, and perhaps a sequential number.

To see the contents of a scrap file, double-click it. This will launch the program associated with the scrap and display it. (If Windows 95 doesn't know which program it should use to open the scrap, it will ask you for help.)

To use the contents of a scrap in a document, drag the scrap to any open window. If the window can accept the insertion of your scrap, the mouse pointer will contain a little gray insertion point that tells you where the scrap will be inserted. Usually a copy is inserted, and the original scrap remains intact and in its original position. Alas, not all programs behave the same way when you drag scraps in and out of them. Experiment. It's a brave new world.

EXPERT ADVICE

Use the Clipboard when you just want to keep things around for a few minutes. Use scraps when working with things you'll use over and over again (logos, art, boilerplate text, etc.).

Shortcut Icons: Powerful Timesavers

You need to free your mind to deal with this topic. It's a tad esoteric, but worth the effort. Here goes.

In a graphical environment like Windows 95 it can be a pain to burrow through a bunch of windows and folders to find things you use a lot. This is particularly true if the object of your desire is on some far-flung networked server. And when I say "thing" I don't just mean some file you edit regularly. I mean just about anything that can be represented with an onscreen icon—printers, folders, control panel icons, you name it. Let's look at a few examples.

Folder, Disk, and Network Shortcut Icons

Suppose you have a folder where you keep all of your correspondence. Suppose further that you like to visit that folder regularly, where you double-click on files of interest, perhaps to reuse or update them. (True, you *might* find the file you need on the Start menu's Documents list, but then again you might not.) Without a shortcut to that Correspondence folder you'll need to slog through a bunch of windows or use the Explorer or some other roundabout technique to reach the file you need.

Instead, you can put a little picture of your correspondence folder (a shortcut to it) on your desktop. Clicking the little shortcut picture of your Correspondence folder will cause Windows 95 to go get the folder and open its window for you. Even if you are in Hawaii and your Correspondence folder is on some networked server in Buffalo, clicking the shortcut will work. (In theory, anyway.) Here's how to create a folder shortcut:

1. Find the folder of interest using the Explorer or other techniques discussed in Chapters 4 and 5.
2. Select the folder (click once to highlight).
3. Press the second (usually the right) mouse button.
4. Pick Create Shortcut from the resulting menu.
5. When the shortcut icon appears in the active window, drag it to the desired location (the desktop, perhaps). To test your new shortcut, keep going.
6. Close the window(s) you opened while finding the actual folder.
7. Double-click the shortcut icon to see what happens.
8. You should see the window containing your real folder. Very Mac-like, huh?

EXPERT ADVICE

You can drag shortcuts to the Start menu if you like. Simply drag them over the Start button. Too easy.

Other Ideas for Shortcut Icons

You needn't limit yourself to creating folder shortcuts. You can use the same basic trick to create shortcuts to a specific file in a folder, or a shortcut to a computer on your network, or to various printers, or whatever.

And get this! Suppose you have a favorite haunt on the Microsoft Network. You can visit the forum or file area or whatever, create a shortcut for that place on your desktop, then just double-click the next time you want to get back there. If you are not connected to the Microsoft Network when you click the shortcut, Windows will run the necessary communications software and dial in for you, then navigate the rat's nest of choices automatically.

This is a rare but not unheard of technique. It requires that the application software support shortcutting. Expect other programs to support these tricks as time goes on. If you click on a graphical element on your screen with the second mouse button and you then see the Create a Shortcut choice, give it a try.

CAUTION

Nothing as cool as shortcuts can work flawlessly. If you make shortcuts for networked resources, and then if those resources become unavailable (because you unhook your laptop from the network, for instance), the shortcuts will not work. Sometimes changing folders or filenames or access privileges can complicate things too.

Deleting Shortcuts

You delete shortcuts as you would any other item of disdain. Click to select the shortcut and press DEL. This moves the shortcut to the Recycle Bin, but does *not* affect the item to which the shortcut points.

Properties: An Important Windows Catchall

Sometimes Microsoft falls in love with a word. Such is the case with *properties.* The term is used many different ways at Camp Bill. Unfortunately, we need to understand the divergent concepts to which the term is applied. Perhaps some examples will help.

What Are Properties?

Just about everything in and on your computer has properties. Starting simply, each file on every one of your disks has properties unique to itself. A file's properties include the file's name, its size, its type (Word, Excel, etc.), rules about sharing, and so forth.

Moving on up, folders also have properties, which, in most cases, are similar to a file's properties (name, size, sharing rules, etc.).

Here's where it starts to get confusing. Each of your disks has properties too, including its name; the amount of available and already used storage space; its type (local, networked, floppy, etc.); engineering trivia about how information gets laid down on the spinning magnetic platters; and so on. All these things are elements of your disk's (and/or disk *drive's*) properties.

And, different hardware devices obviously have different properties. Your monitor's properties include things like the number of dots it can display, and the speed at which it can refresh the screen's image. Different devices, different lists of properties. Not so bad, huh?

But wait. It gets worse. Sometimes when hardware and software work together to produce desired results, you specify things called properties to define your expectations. For example, when you wish to change the pattern on your Windows 95 desktop from, say, Microsoft logos to bricks, you change the display's *Background* properties. There's that word again. Or, when you tell Windows your local telephone area code so that it can help with modem dialing, you fiddle with modem settings called—you got it—*Dialing Properties.* In these cases, you are telling software your desires and they are being stored as properties. Even shortcut icons have interesting properties worth exploring. A shortcut's properties tell you the location (the path and filename) of the item the shortcut is pointing to.

Seeing and Changing Property Settings

To see a file or a folder's properties, try this:

1. Right-click a folder or file to display the shortcut menu.

2. Choose Properties.
3. Read the folder or file's properties (and click the resulting tabs to see more).

As you can see, some properties are under your direct control, whereas others are not. You can change a file's properties (from read/write to read-only in this example), but you can't change its size by just typing some new number. Different objects will offer different properties, some of which you can change, and some you cannot.

EXPERT ADVICE

Windows lets you read about (and sometimes change) an item's properties in a slew of dialog boxes and windows—via the Properties choice in shortcut menus, with Properties buttons in dialog boxes, and whenever Windows or an application program asks you for a properties setting.

Seeing and Changing Display Properties

Let's use the Display Properties window to illustrate a couple of concepts. You can reach Display Properties quickly by right-clicking anywhere on the Windows desktop and picking Properties from the shortcut menu. Alternatively, here is a more regimented approach:

1. Choose Settings from the Start menu.
2. Pick Control Panel next (slide to highlight, then click).
3. Double-click Display.
4. Choose the property tab of interest—the Screen Saver tab of the Display Properties dialog box is shown here:

5. View and possibly change a variety of properties.
6. Close the dialog box with the OK or Cancel button.

Whoa! You can see and change a lot in the Display Properties box, huh?

CAUTION

If you were born to experiment, you'll probably love the Display Properties dialog box. You can really screw things up here. Remember that the Cancel button can often get you out of trouble.

Object Linking and Embedding

Object Linking and Embedding (OLE) is a collection of standards and tools designed to let you automate the sharing of information between files. This can be particularly useful when your data is frequently updated and used in a variety of documents.

"Examples, please," I hear you groan.

Okay. Suppose you have a master company phone list that you maintain as a Microsoft Word document. People's names and their extensions are always changing. You have other Word documents that include lists of employee names and phone numbers. OLE can let you keep all of those documents up to date whenever you update the master phone list. (Well, maybe it can.)

Another example? You keep a sales budget spreadsheet in Excel, and use PowerPoint to make slides for monthly staff meetings. Wouldn't it be nice to have the slide show automatically updated each month? OLE can do that (perhaps).

As you can probably tell, I have a love/hate relationship with Object Linking and Embedding. It reminds me of my old Triumph TR7. Hell of a car when it would start. Nearly killed me.

The Risks and Rewards of OLE

If you are disciplined and in control of your life, and if you have a pretty fast computer, AND if you are a careful proofreader, OLE is a thing of beauty. Otherwise it's a beast.

If you move or rename files, you can cause problems. If you are not careful about telling Windows when to update links, things might not get updated when they should—or they might get changed when they shouldn't. There are formatting issues, and security issues, and...! Whole books have been written about this fledgling technology. For now, here's the TV guide version, best read at arm's length.

The Basics of Linking

First, you need one or more OLE2-savvy programs, like Word 95, Excel, Access, or PowerPoint. You can link info within the same document or between two documents from the same program (like two Word documents), or if you really like life on the edge, link stuff from one program to another. Here...I'll show you. The instructions provided in the "Linking Information Between Two Programs" Step by Step will link information between an Excel spreadsheet and a PowerPoint slide.

The Basics of Embedding

Embedding works a lot like linking, except that instead of just pointing to parts of other documents, you insert copies of the documents and lots of other stuff in the destination document. Embedded files are often very big—an important consideration if you plan to play pass-the-floppy with embedded documents.

STEP BY STEP Linking Information Between Two Programs

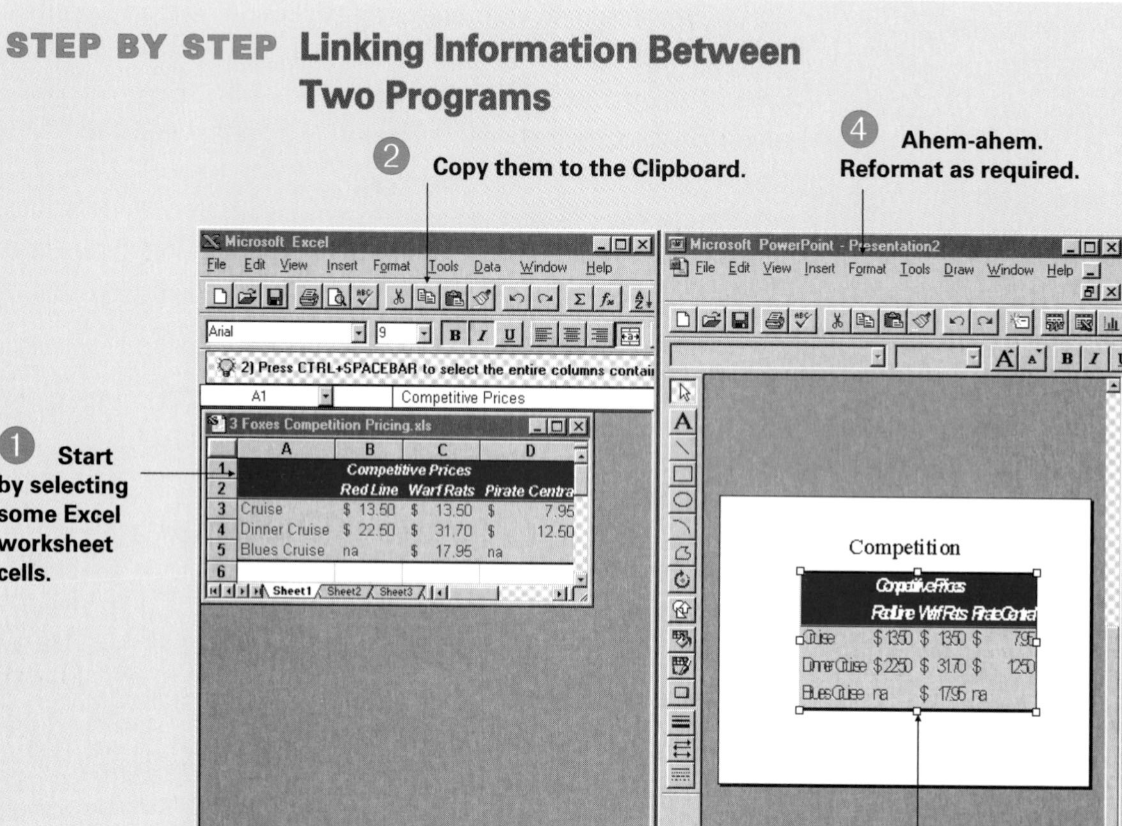

1 **Start by selecting some Excel worksheet cells.**

2 **Copy them to the Clipboard.**

3 **Use the Paste Special or Insert command to link the selected cells in the PowerPoint slide.**

(Looks like hell, huh? You can improve things by adjusting the size and shape of the PowerPoint insertion, or changing fonts, but Geez! As you can see, the creators of this new technology still have work to do.)

4 **Ahem-ahem. Reformat as required.**

On the other hand, recipients of documents with embedded information need not possess the actual applications that were used to create the embedded elements. That is to say, you needn't have Excel installed on a machine to see a PowerPoint slide with an embedded chunk of Excel spreadsheet cells. (You will need PowerPoint, however.)

What's ActiveX and Should You Care?

You may have recently heard or read about a new Microsoft-developed technology called *ActiveX.* I mention it here because it's an outgrowth of Object Linking and Embedding. Primarily used for web page development, ActiveX lets programmers create things called *controls.* Microsoft calls ActiveX the "glue" that enables programmers to add multimedia and interactive elements to web pages. Unless you are a programmer, or intend to become one, all you really need to know for now is that in order to take advantage of ActiveX enhancements, you will need to use recent versions of ActiveX-compatible software like the latest versions of Microsoft's Explorer web browser.

Reality Check and Where to Learn More

OLE and ActiveX are headed in the right direction, but I dunno. Personally, I'm too busy to make OLE work reliably and quickly enough for my needs. Decide for yourself. If OLE holds a lot of potential interest for you, check out *Making Microsoft Office Work*, by Ralph Soucie.

ActiveX advantages will come your way without any extra work on your part, but only if you use an ActiveX-savvy web browser, and only when you visit web sites where programmers use ActiveX technology. To learn more about ActiveX, and to see it in action, visit Microsoft's web site (**www.microsoft.com**).

We've covered a lot of diverse ground in this chapter. It would be a good idea to actually try putting all this stuff to use before you move on. Here are some suggestions:

1. Experiment with the second mouse button. Right-click on the desktop. Right-click on some file and other icons. Open a program that supports right-clicking (like Microsoft Word) and experiment there too.
2. Try some keyboard shortcuts both in Windows 95 and in the programs you use most. Write down five of your favorites on a Post-it™ note and keep the cheat sheet next to your computer until they become second nature. Then pick five more to learn, and so on.
3. Practice dragging and dropping. Run Microsoft Word or another drag-and-drop-savvy program or two. Select some text or worksheet cells or graphics and try dragging the selected items within a document, and then from one document to another.
4. Create some scraps and then reuse them. For example, open Microsoft Word and type your name, mailing address, phone number, fax number, and E-mail address. Create a scrap of this text and put it on your desktop. This can save you a lot of retyping in the future.
5. Take a moment to explore the properties of various objects found around your computer. (Remember how? Right-click and choose Properties from the shortcut menu.)
6. If linking and embedding technology intrigues you, open a program or two and experiment. Word and Excel are great places to start.
7. Finally, if you are a web nut and have Microsoft's Internet Explorer version 3.0 or later, visit the Microsoft web site (**www.microsoft.com**), where you can learn more about ActiveX.

You're now well on your way to being a Windows 95 power user. Chapter 8 will take you a step further. There you'll learn how to install (and remove!) Windows utilities as well as the application programs of your choice.

CHAPTER

8

Installing and Removing Programs and Hardware

INCLUDES

- Adding and removing Windows 95 utility accessories
- Installing application programs
- Upgrading software
- Removing unwanted programs
- Tips to ponder before using programs found online and in the public domain
- Adding new hardware

FAST FORWARD

Install Windows Utilities ➤ pp. 155-157

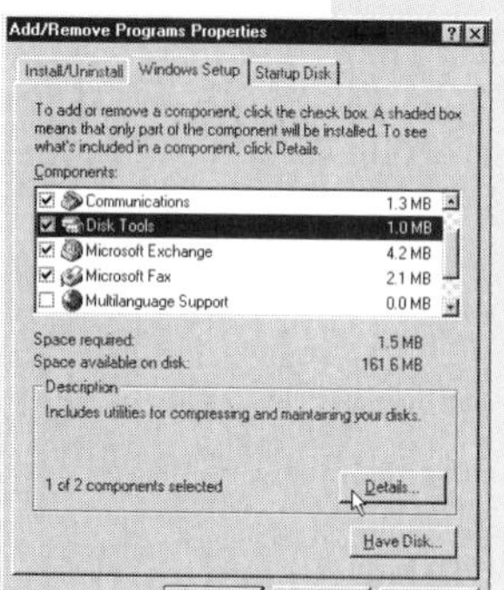

1. Choose Settings on the Start menu.
2. Choose the Control Panel option.
3. Double-click the Add/Remove Programs icon.
4. Click the Windows Setup tab.
5. Scroll then click to choose a category.
6. Click the Details button.
7. Add or remove checkmarks to add or remove programs.
8. Click OK.
9. Insert disks or CDs when prompted.

Install New Applications ➤ pp. 158-159

1. Read installation instructions.
2. Check for and review Readme files.
3. Either choose Run from the Start menu and type the appropriate command, or double-click the icon for the disk or CD containing the installer program and double-click the disk's or CD's Setup or Install icon.

Upgrade Software ➤ p. 159

A version of 3D Home Architect already exists in the destination directory on your computer. Do you want to be prompted before each file is overwritten? (If you wish to cancel the installation, press the Esc key).

1. Explore potential compatibility issues.
2. Back up important data files.
3. Run the new software's installation program.
4. Choose Upgrade or an equivalent option.

Remove Unwanted Programs ➤ *pp. 159-160*

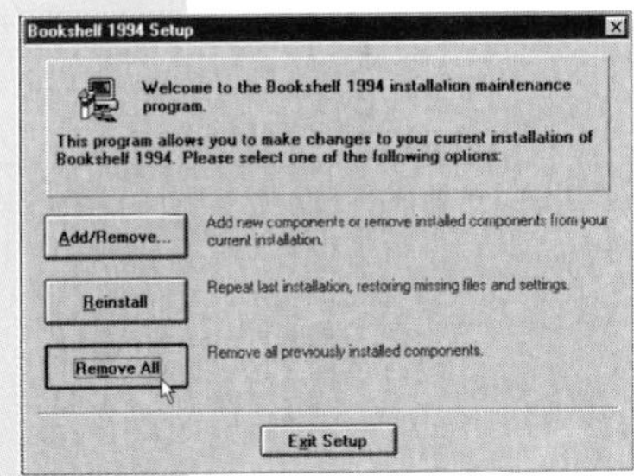

- Check the program's documentation.
- Use the Windows 95 Uninstall feature if it is compatible with the software being removed. (Use the Install/Uninstall tab of the Add/Remove Programs Properties window.)
- Avoid using third-party "uninstallers" unless they are certified Windows 95-compatible.

Add New Hardware ➤ *pp. 163-166*

- Check the hardware documentation. Follow Windows 95 procedures if they are provided.
- You might not need the software provided with the hardware if Windows 95 recognizes the hardware.
- Use the Windows 95 Add New Hardware feature in the Windows 95 Control Panel whenever possible.
- Read the onscreen directions carefully and follow them exactly.
- Check the hardware maker's tech support sites to see if new drivers are offered.

The process of installing and removing programs and hardware affects your computer in a number of ways. Some installations and removals will be straightforward, ten-minute affairs. Others can be very involved, and downright frustrating. There are some questions you should ask yourself before you begin. Let's take a look at the risks, rewards, and Zen of installing and removing software and hardware.

CAUTION

Sometimes just sticking a new disk in your machine and clicking the program's icon runs an installer without your consent. Free and low-cost multimedia "disc magazines" often do this. Read the documentation that comes with the discs before turning over control of your computer to some marketing genius.

Do You Really Need to Install Something New?

There are risks involved in adding new software or hardware to your computer, especially if you are busy. As you'll see in a moment, even a simple installation creates new folders, modifies system files, and uses valuable disk space. Sometimes an installation can temporarily put your computer out of commission, or at least distract you from your real work for days. So, before I install something new, or remove some old, trusted program or hardware device, I ask myself the following questions:

- Will this new product make me more productive or provide worthwhile entertainment?
- Do I have the time *right now* to troubleshoot for hours if things go terribly wrong?
- Do I have time in the next few days to learn how to use the new product?
- Will the new hardware and software work with my old files, and is this an important consideration?
- Will it change the way I collaborate with others, and can I still exchange files with co-workers after the installation or removal?
- Will changes interfere with the functioning of my other hardware or software?
- What's the buzz on the street? Is the product I am about to install reliable?
- Is this the most recent *reliable* version of the software?
- Is this the complete package or some watered-down trial version? (I hate demos.)
- Will what I am about to add work with my computer hardware configuration and Windows 95?
- How much disk space is required, and do I want to devote that much to this product?
- What time is it at the manufacturer's tech support center, and are they available now?
- When was the last time I backed up my important stuff?
- Am I alert, sober, and willing to be patient?
- Do I really want to sit at my computer any longer today?

As you've probably guessed from this list, I don't install new hardware or software very often.

What Happens When You Install a New Program?

Let's put off the subject of adding hardware until later in the chapter, and concentrate on software for a moment. Since many hardware upgrades necessitate software upgrades as well, this is a logical progression. Virtually all commercial software packages (and many created by amateurs) come with installer programs that should do most or all of the following:

- Check your computer for potential compatibility problems.
- Check for sufficient available disk space.
- Create necessary folders (directories) needed by the software.
- Prompt you to load and unload your disk drives.
- Decompress compressed files.
- Make necessary changes to your (numerous) system files.
- Add new fonts and drivers needed by the program.
- Advise you of the success or failure of the installation attempt.

Some fancy programs lead you through other steps such as automated product registration, personalizing software settings, guided tours, and so on.

What Happens When You Remove an Old Program?

In a perfect world, the process of removing software would undo every action listed in the preceding section. Yeah, right. And people would come to a complete stop at stop signs.

Not very many software packages even provide "uninstall" commands. As a result, users often just delete the folders that are obviously associated with unwanted programs and hope for the best. Sometimes this works out fine. Other times, you get back most of your disk space, but your overall system performance suffers due to unnecessary, inaccurate, inefficient, and even conflicting system settings left behind by the unwanted programs. In certain instances, after removing old software, you'll see recurring warnings and error messages as your computer goes looking for files and folders that are no longer available. Once in a while your computer may simply turn to the electronic equivalent of stone—usually because you've deleted or changed some critical file, folder, or setting.

CAUTION

Because installing and removing programs affects so many aspects of your computer, read all of the documentation and any Readme files provided on the disks before you run the installer. And, when installing, contrary to my advice elsewhere in this book, if in doubt, don't double-click.

Readme or Weep

The printed manuals and installation sheets that come with new programs are sometimes pretty old. That's why many installation disks have last-minute text files containing cautions, tips, compatibility news, and more. It is very important that you get in the habit of reading these Readme files before you attempt any new installation. Here are the general steps:

1. Insert the first new installation disk in the appropriate drive (floppy, CD-ROM, etc.).
2. Double-click the My Computer icon if necessary to open the My Computer window.
3. Double-click the disk containing the installer software.
4. Look for icons entitled Readme (or perhaps Read_me, or Read Me First, or Readme.txt, etc.).

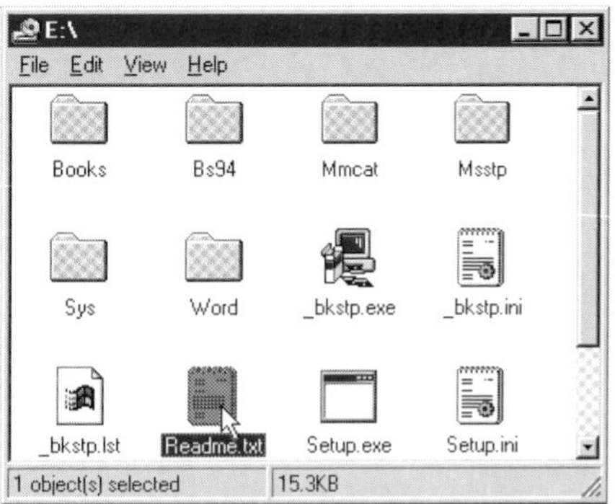

5. Double-clicking the Readme icon should launch the Windows Notepad or WordPad and display text. Read, heed, and consider printing the news. In this case, it is a warning about potential multimedia problems:

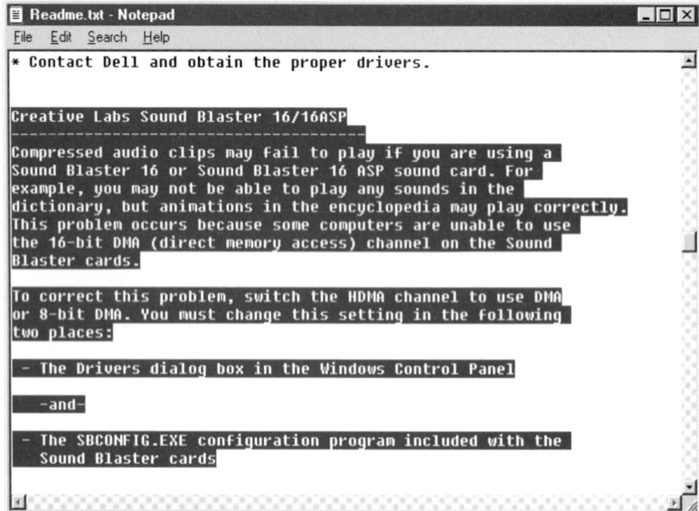

Readme.txt - Notepad
File Edit Search Help
* Contact Dell and obtain the proper drivers.
Creative Labs Sound Blaster 16/16ASP
Compressed audio clips may fail to play if you are using a
Sound Blaster 16 or Sound Blaster 16 ASP sound card. For
example, you may not be able to play any sounds in the
dictionary, but animations in the encyclopedia may play correctly.
This problem occurs because some computers are unable to use
the 16-bit DMA (direct memory access) channel on the Sound
Blaster cards.
To correct this problem, switch the HDMA channel to use DMA
or 8-bit DMA. You must change this setting in the following
two places:
- The Drivers dialog box in the Windows Control Panel
-and-
- The SBCONFIG.EXE configuration program included with the
Sound Blaster cards

6. Make sure there aren't any other Readme files.
7. Quit the Notepad or WordPad.
8. Begin the installation *only* if that seems prudent after steps 1 through 6.

EXPERT ADVICE

Unfortunately, some vendors ship their Readme.txt in compressed files. You'll probably need to wait until after installation to read them. Get in the habit of looking for Readmes a second time, after you've installed the software.

Installing and Removing Windows 95 Accessories

In order to save you some disk space, the Windows 95 installer leaves out some accessories when it initially sets up your system. For instance, the Quick View program described in Chapter 4 takes 1.5MB of disk space, and is not automatically installed. Other accessories such as the Clipboard viewer are on your installer disks, but probably not on your hard disk unless you or someone else has put them there. Windows 95 also comes with extra sounds, screen savers, and other toys that you might want to install if you have the disk space and love distractions.

Conversely, you may find that some Windows 95 utilities languish unused, just hogging disk space. The control panel's Add/Remove Programs icon holds the answer to these two different dilemmas.

Seeing and Changing What's Installed

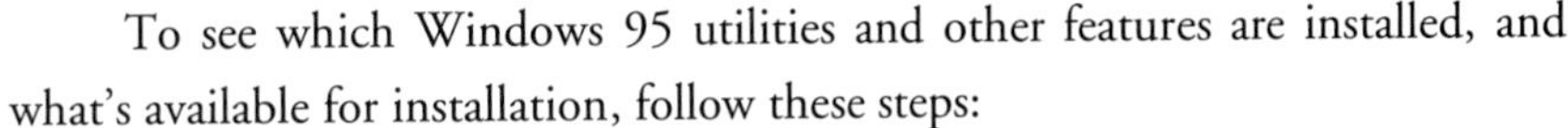

To see which Windows 95 utilities and other features are installed, and what's available for installation, follow these steps:

1. Have your Windows 95 installation CD or disks ready if you plan to add any accessories, sounds, screen savers, etc.
2. Choose the Control Panel option from the Settings submenu on the Start menu.
3. Double-click Add/Remove Programs.
4. Click the Windows Setup tab shown in Figure 8.1.
5. Scrolling through the list shows categories of accessories (Accessibility Options, Accessories, Communications software, etc.).
6. Scroll, if necessary, and select the category of interest.
7. Read the Description section of the dialog box to see what the category does and how many of its items are installed. For example, in

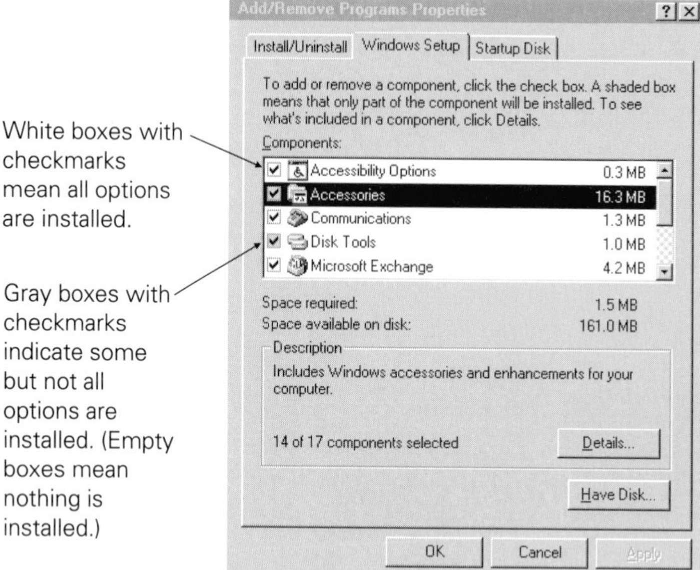

Figure 8.1 Checking out what's been installed

Figure 8.1 the Accessories category is selected, and 14 of the 17 available accessories have been selected (installed).

8. Click the Details button for a list of the available and installed accessories. Items with checkmarks next to them are installed. Items without checkmarks can be installed on your hard disk, but currently are not.

9. To add an item, click to place a checkmark in its box. To remove an item, click to remove the checkmark.
10. Click OK to close the category's dialog box.
11. Pick other categories that you want to inspect and possibly change.
12. When finished, click OK in the Windows Setup tab.
13. You will be prompted to insert a diskette or CD-ROM. Do so, and click OK. (If using a CD-ROM, you might need to give the drive a chance to spin up.)
14. Click OK.

The software should be properly installed and/or removed.

CD-ROM Add/Remove Icons

Some new CD-ROMs (including Windows 95 installation discs) have an Add/Remove Software icon in the lower-right corner of their initial screens. Clicking it is often a shortcut to the appropriate installer.

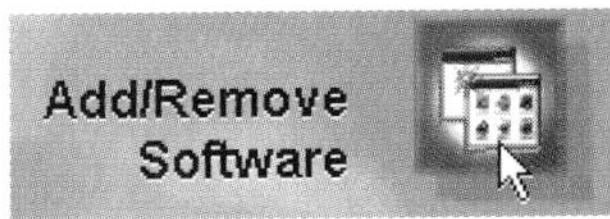

You also can run the Setup Wizard by visiting the Add/Remove Programs icon in the control panel. Click on the Install button in the Install/Uninstall tab to get the Wizard started. Optionally, you can follow the manual steps outlined next.

EXPERT ADVICE

If you are connected to a network, your network administrator might want you to install your new software via the network rather than with floppies or CD-ROMs. Be sure to ask, and then carefully follow any directions you receive.

Installing New Programs from Floppies and CD-ROMs

You install most contemporary programs (such as Word, Excel, or whatever) using similar techniques. The software is shipped on either floppies or CD-ROMs. Somewhere on the first floppy or on the CD-ROM is a program called either *Setup* or *Install.* Running this installation program starts the process.

To install a new program, use these handy steps:

1. Make backups of important files.
2. Read any installation instructions shipped with the software, including any Readme files.
3. Either choose Run from the Start menu and type the appropriate command (**a:\install**, **d:\setup**, or whatever), or double-click the icon for the disk containing the installation program, then double-click the Install (or Setup) icon.

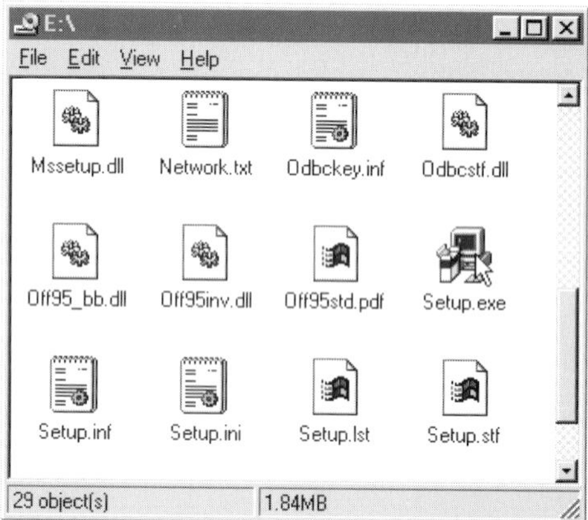

4. Follow the onscreen directions. Once installation is done, you may be instructed to reboot.

When installing from floppies, I like to check first to see that I have all the necessary disks, and I place them in order (1, 2, 3, etc.) before starting the installation. Given a choice, I always install from CD-ROMs. CD-ROM installations are faster and seem generally more reliable than floppy installs.

Upgrading to New Versions of Programs

Begin by doing the research suggested in my list of questions at the beginning of this chapter. Will the new software be compatible with your old files? Will you still be able to share files with your co-workers? If you suspect that there might be compatibility problems, check the new program's documentation to see if it is practical (or even possible) to keep the old and new versions of the application installed on the same computer simultaneously.

CAUTION

A new version of your favorite program might modify your old files in such a way that older versions of the program won't ever be able to read them again! Always back up your files before using them with new software releases.

Removing Unwanted Programs

As is the case with any form of surgery, the trick is to remove the unwanted while keeping the patient alive and robust. Some new programs, such as the latest version of Microsoft Office, have uninstaller commands. Sometimes there are "uninstall instructions" in your user manuals. Quite often, however, you are on your own.

To see if the programs you want to remove can be uninstalled by Windows 95, visit the Install/Uninstall tab of the Add/Remove Programs Properties window and see if the program is listed there. If the program you wish to remove is listed, click to select the name in the list, and then click the Add/Remove button. Follow the onscreen prompts, which might ask you for the original disks.

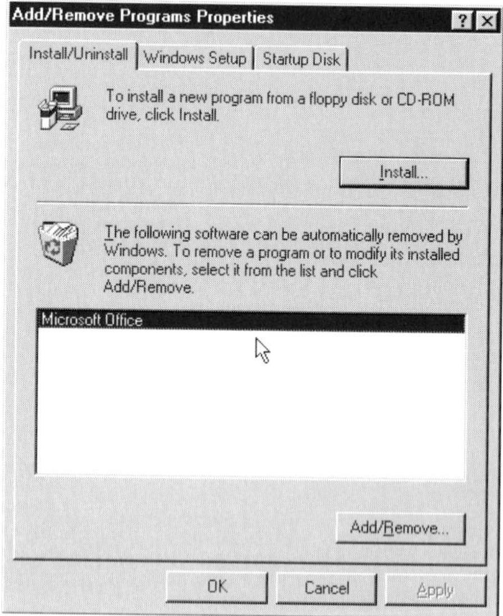

By the way, some badly behaved programs don't remove the names of old versions when you install new versions over them. Then when you try to remove what you think is the old version, you remove the new one. Cute, huh?

CAUTION

There are some "universal uninstaller" programs on the market that claim to handle the details of removing old software, changing back your system files, etc. If you purchase one of these, be certain that the one you choose was designed to work with Windows 95. Older uninstallers could make your life a soap opera!

Considering Online and Public Domain Programs

We've all been tempted to download free or low-cost programs from America Online, CompuServe, the local user group BBS, etc. And, heck, there's some great software out there. But you will also find some real disasters waiting to happen. And you might need additional software to "unpack" the program prior to installing it. Although it's impossible to cover all the scenarios, here are some hard-learned tips:

- Find out if the software is Windows 95-savvy before you run it. Most programs, but not all, are compatible with Windows 95.
- Know your source. You sleep with dogs, you're gonna wake up with fleas. The chances of getting a virus are very good at a computer swap meet, and slim (but not nil) at places like the big online libraries. Commercial sites such as America Online and CompuServe are somewhat more reliably policed. And Lord knows what you'll find on the Internet. So, next time you find something cool-sounding at http:\\pirates.against.corporate.america.alt, don't walk away—run!
- Use a virus checker regularly if you obtain programs online or from acquaintances.
- Ask around. Who do you know who is using the software successfully? Are they running Windows 95?
- Find out what else you need to install the software. Many programs are "compressed" to save disk space and speed electronic transmission. These need to be expanded before they can be used. You might need additional utilities (like WinZip) to do the expanding. These can almost always be downloaded at little or no cost. If you have questions, leave an E-mail message for the library's moderator before you obtain the program.
- Pay registration fees for programs that you use. It keeps people interested in creating more useful stuff.

CAUTION

The steps in this section can ruin your life if you don't know what you are doing. Get professional assistance if you have any doubts about completely trashing your hard disk and starting over.

The Scorched-Earth Reinstallation Approach

If you are forced to continually install, and uninstall, and upgrade software (as I am in my profession), eventually your system files will get so messed up that your computer will run like my '67 Pontiac Tempest (in other words, not at all).

The best solution in cases like this is often to scrap everything and start from the beginning. You will probably want to have some professional help before undertaking this task:

1. Be sure you have a boot floppy if you are going to install Windows from DOS. If you'll be installing from a CD-ROM, then your boot floppy should have CD_ROM driver software. (See your computer manual.)
2. Make sure you still have all of your program disks (for Word, Excel, etc.).
3. Make sure you have the latest Windows 95 disks or disc and any upgrade releases. If you plan to install from DOS, make sure you have a "full" Windows 95 package, not one designed only to upgrade from prior Windows versions.
4. Back up just your document files (not the old Windows and program files).
5. Make sure the backup worked.
6. Insert a boot floppy.
7. Format your hard disk.
8. Reinstall Windows 95.
9. Reinstall your applications.
10. Restore your document files.

EXPERT ADVICE

I have one hard disk for Windows 95 and my programs, and a second disk for all of my document files. This makes it quicker to reinstall Windows and my other programs, and I avoid the painful and risky business of purging and reinstalling document files.

Installing New Hardware

Installing new hardware can be as simple as slipping a credit card-sized modem into your laptop's PCMCIA slot, or it can involve removing screws, sheet metal, and brackets while spending a good deal of time on your hands and knees. While I try sincerely to avoid wasting time and money on new hardware, irresistible new toys seem to appear here daily—video cameras that let us see people over the Internet, hard drives with removable cartridges capable of storing gigabits of information, CD-ROM recorders that let us make our own audio and data CD-ROMs, and on, and on.

The first step should always be to make certain that you purchase the proper hardware given your situation. If the device will be used externally (a printer, for example), have you ordered the correct cable(s) given your setup? There are several kinds of serial and parallel port connector options, for instance. Which kind do you have, and can you get the correct cable or at least an adapter? If the device requires an extra serial port, do you have one? If the device requires the use of an extra expansion slot within your computer, is there an empty socket of the correct type? You get the idea. Think ahead. Research the hardware requirements, and know the specifications of your system. If you do not like to tinker, consider taking your computer to someone who installs hardware for a living.

EXPERT ADVICE

It is almost always worth paying a little extra to shop at a place offering a money-back guarantee and real live technical support. Flea markets are great places to buy vintage clothes, but you'd better know what you are doing if you purchase hardware from any vendor located next to a Vegematic booth!

Plug and Play

Windows 95 ushered in the *plug-and-play* era (cynics have dubbed this "plug and *pray*"). With reasonable success (given that making hardware and software work together at all is like herding cats), Windows 95 notices if you've installed new hardware and tries to make it work. You stand a much better chance of achieving your goal if both your computer and any new toys you buy all claim to be plug-and-play-compatible. The second-best approach is to look for new hardware that boasts "Windows 95 compatibility" without mentioning plug-and-play. As a last resort, older hardware with boxes and documentation silent on the subjects of Win 95 and plug-and-play will often work anyway, albeit sometimes only after a little coercion.

CAUTION

Before you add new hardware, read the instructions! Search for and read "README.TXT" and other text files. It's very easy to screw up if you purchase hardware originally designed to work with Windows 3.x and fail to follow (the often well hidden) alternate installation procedures required under Windows 95!

The Add New Hardware Wizard

Unless the instructions that come with your hardware tell you otherwise, begin by turning off the computer and other accessories before installing any new hardware. Then turn all of your hardware back on—so, if you have external disk drives, modems, video cameras, and the like, turn them *all* on, along with the new device.

Sometimes Windows 95 will automatically recognize the new hardware, and ask if you want to complete the necessary installation steps. If that doesn't happen, and if the new hardware does not automatically work as you'd expected it would, and unless the hardware instructions say otherwise, visit the Windows 95 Control Panel and double-click the Add New Hardware icon. Follow the onscreen instructions, and agree to the choices the Wizard proposes.

Computer Hangs After Installing New Hardware

In some cases, adding new hardware will cause your computer to hang. This is most often due to "resource conflicts" that occur when the new hardware and the old hardware both try to use the same wiring, or memory or other computer assets. If this happens, turn off the computer and skip ahead to the Hardware Troubleshooting section of this chapter.

Device Drivers: Software for Your Hardware

Device drivers (or simply *drivers*) are programs that run pretty much unobserved. Their function is to make your computer, its accessories, and perhaps your applications software (Microsoft Word or whatever) all get along. Windows 95 comes with a huge library of drivers. That partially explains all those floppy disks, or the need for a Windows 95 CD-ROM. Usually the Add New Hardware Wizard, mentioned earlier, will locate and install the appropriate drivers automatically. But you should be prepared to feed the appropriate Windows 95 floppy (or, if you purchased Windows 95 on a CD-ROM, the CD-ROM).

In some cases, your new hardware will come with a floppy disk or two containing driver software. Don't assume that because the hardware came with a disk you need to use it! For example, if you install a network card, Windows 95 might prefer to use its own network drivers rather than those provided by the network adapter vendor. Read the documentation carefully. When in doubt, contact a technician.

In rare instances, you might need to download new driver software either from Microsoft's web site (visit their Windows Driver Library, also known as WDL), or from the hardware maker's web site or BBS. Get help if you need to take these extra steps.

Hardware Troubleshooting

Whole books have been written on the Zen of hardware troubleshooting; and while I could spend a chapter or two here telling you how to get a System Resource Report, and interpret the findings, and change the resource settings, it would be too much and too little information at the same time. Here are some general tips. If the following steps fail, you should get help immediately, preferably from the place you bought the new gear; or failing that, from the hardware manufacturer.

- Check the installation itself. Are the cables in properly? Did you follow the instructions *exactly*?
- If it's an external device (a printer or scanner or whatever), is it plugged in and powered up? Are the ready lights lit?
- Restart the computer and rerun the Add New Hardware Wizard. Sometimes it takes two or even three tries. Dunno why, but it does.
- Write down the contents of any error messages you see on your screen. They might look like Greek to you, but a technician will often be able to quickly interpret them and solve your problem.
- When all else fails, try the Hardware Conflict Troubleshooter as described next.

The Hardware Conflict Troubleshooter

Windows 95 comes with a Wizard designed to detect and correct many common hardware installation problems. Here's how to use it, assuming your computer starts and Windows 95 runs after you add the new hardware, of course:

1. Visit Windows 95's online help.
2. Type **hardware trouble** in the Find tab.
3. Double-click Troubleshooting hardware conflicts in the topic list.
4. Read the resulting help screens, use the buttons they provide, and perhaps take notes as you work.

Well. Here we are at the end of another chapter. Before moving on, try installing a new Windows 95 program or two, like some games, then remove them. If you've been putting off a software upgrade, and if you have the new software handy, and the necessary time and patience, give it a try.

Printing is the next stop. In Chapter 9 we'll turn our attention to printers, fonts, and other related issues.

CAFÉ
KING
CAUTION

CHAPTER

9

Printing and Fonts

INCLUDES

- Installing printers
- Printing to fax modems and files
- Changing printer settings
- Using the print queue
- Solving printing problems
- Font facts and techniques
- Using special characters and symbols
- Printing from DOS programs

Install a Printer ➤ pp. 197-202

1. Choose Settings from the Start menu.
2. Choose Printers.
3. Double-click the Add Printer icon in the Printers window, and click Next.
4. Choose Local or Network.
5. Select your printer's manufacturer and model, and click Next.
6. Specify the port (LPT1, COM1, etc.) where your printer is connected, and click Next.
7. If you are installing a default Windows printer, click Yes.
8. Click Next, and then click Finish.
9. Insert your installation disks (or CD) according to the onscreen directions.
10. When the procedure is finished, click OK.

Print a Document ➤ pp. 202-203

- Use the Print command from within your application.
- Click the Print button in your application's toolbar.
- Select the icons of the documents you want to print, and simply drag them over a printer's icon (or its shortcut icon).

Switch Between Multiple Printers ➤ pp. 203-204

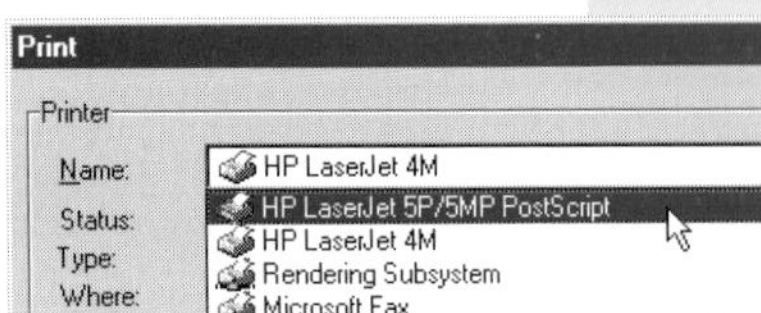

1. From within your application choose Print (or press CTRL-P).
2. Select the printer from the Name box in the Printer section of the dialog box.
3. Click OK.
4. Pick Page Setup from the File menu and check the settings.

Print to a Fax Modem ➤ p. 204

If your fax modem software permits it, or if you want to use the Microsoft Fax service, choose the Fax modem option in any Print dialog box. (You'll need to have Microsoft Exchange installed.)

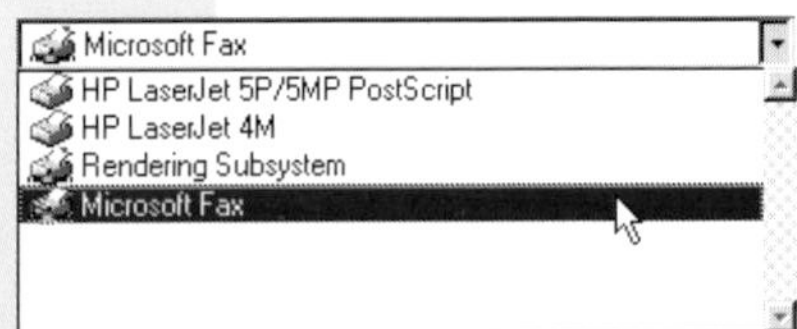

Change Your Printer's Settings ➤ pp. 205-208

1. Choose Settings.
2. Select Printers.
3. Right-click a printer icon.
4. Choose Properties.
5. Pick a tab, and change its settings as necessary.
6. Click OK.
7. Repeat steps 5 and 6 until the printer is configured according to your needs.

Monitor Printing Progress ➤ pp. 208-210

1. Choose Settings.
2. Select the Printers option.
3. Double-click the desired printer icon to see the print queue.

Share Your Networked Printer ➤ p. 211

1. Right-click the printer's icon (NOT its shortcut icon).
2. Choose Sharing from the Shortcut menu.
3. Click Shared As, name the printer, and choose other options as needed.

View and Print Font Samples ➤ pp. 214-215

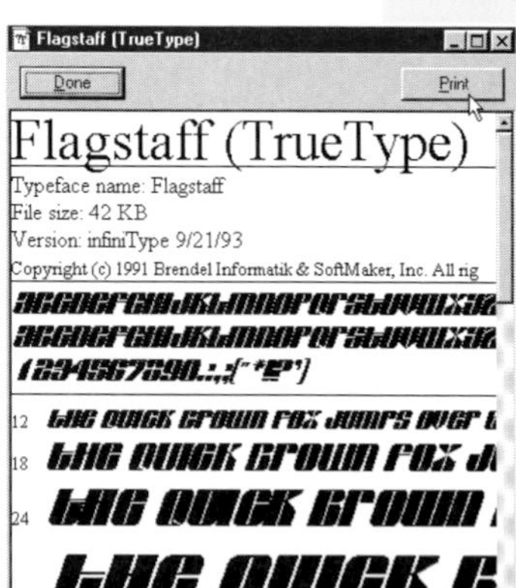

1. Choose Settings, and then pick the Control Panel option.
2. Double-click the Fonts folder.
3. Select a font or CTRL-click to select multiple fonts.
4. Right-click to reveal the Shortcut menu.
5. Choose Open.
6. Scroll to view the sample.
7. Click Print.

Add and Remove Fonts ➤ pp. 215-216

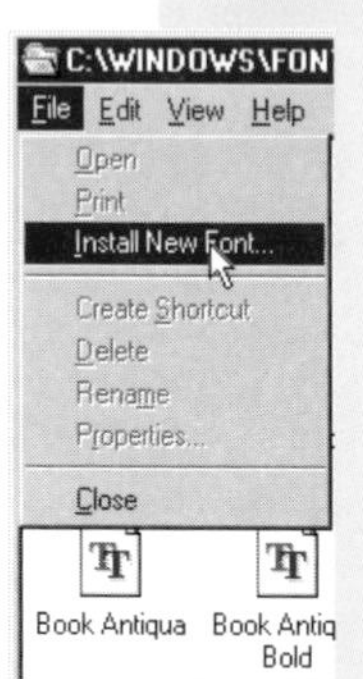

Follow the directions that came with the fonts, or follow these steps:

1. Choose Settings, and then select the Control Panel option.
2. Double-click the Fonts folder.
3. If you're deleting fonts, select the ones you want to delete.
4. Select Install New Font from the Font folder window's File menu if you're installing fonts, or choose Delete if you're removing fonts.

Insert Special Characters into Your Document ➤ pp. 217-218

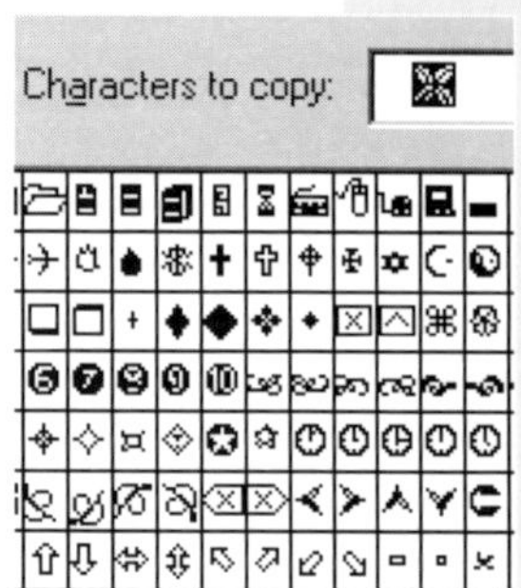

1. Choose Accessories from the Programs level of the Start menu.
2. Pick Character Map.
3. Make sure the correct typestyle is selected.
4. Click to magnify characters or double-click to add them to the list of characters to be placed on the Clipboard.
5. Click Copy to replace the current Clipboard contents with the special character(s).
6. Click Close.
7. Paste the character(s) into your document.

If your printer is already installed and working, and if you have only one printer, skip ahead to "The Importance of Page Setup." The rest of us are going to learn how to install and use our printers.

Twenty years ago, paper company executives were wringing their hands over the coming of the paperless office, which was to be spurred on by personal computing. Well, I wish I'd purchased some stock in paper companies back then...and I'm glad I'm not a tree. This chapter discusses ways to get the most out of your printers, forests, and fonts. We'll even explore "printing" to a fax modem.

Today's seemingly endless variety of printers serve many different tastes and budgets—from lowly dot-matrix line printers to color laser tree killers and typesetting service behemoths that can cost ten times as much as the computers that drive them. Remarkably, Windows 95 knows what to do with most of these devices.

Installing with the Add New Printer Wizard

Some printers are shipped with installation disks containing drivers and other necessary or at least helpful software. Read the documentation that came with your printer and pay particular attention to any Windows 95 information.

Every type of printer has unique communications requirements—so before Windows and your programs can print, the software needs to know which printer model or models you have. Microsoft copes with this by providing *printer drivers*—software created for hundreds (or perhaps thousands) of different printer types. Because many printers have a variety of options (envelope feeders, quality settings, etc.), each driver displays slightly different options in the various printing dialog boxes you see.

To save hard disk space, Windows 95 only installs drivers for the printers you specify. If you want to add a new printer to your stable, you use something called the Printer Wizard, with these steps:

1. Have your Windows 95 installation disc or disks handy. Take a deep breath.

2. Make sure your printer is connected to the desired port (computer connector) and that it is powered up, and not paper- or toner-challenged in any way.
3. Choose Settings from the Start menu.
4. Choose Printers from the resulting submenu.

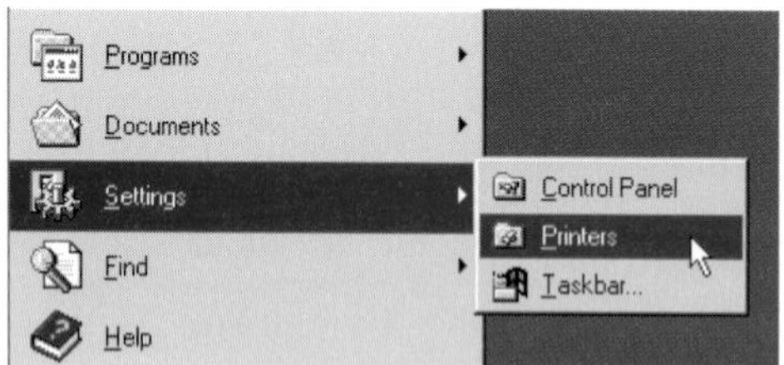

5. Double-click the Add Printer icon in the Printers window.

6. You'll see the first page of the Add Printer Wizard, which basically tells you what the Printer Wizard does. Click Next.
7. If you are given a choice, choose Local or Network depending upon how your printer is attached to your computer. (See Chapter 11, and check with your network administrator for help with networked printers.)
8. Scroll through the list of printer manufacturers in the left list. Choose the correct company.

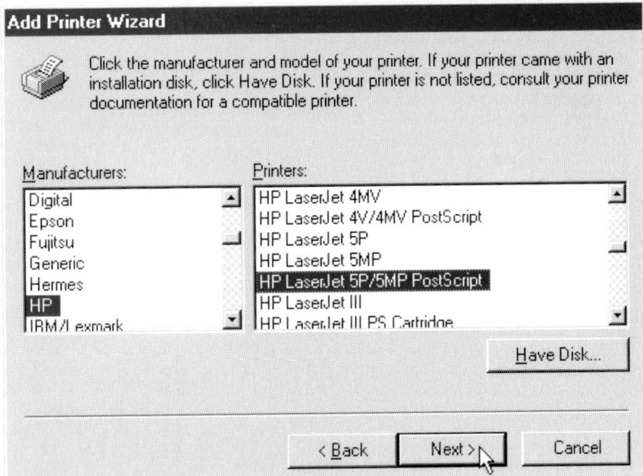

If your printer supports PostScript printing, and if you are offered a PostScript choice, use it. You often will be rewarded with faster, or at least better looking, output.

9. Scroll through the resulting, company-specific list of models on the right. Pick the correct model. (If you don't see your printer listed, flip to the topic "If Your Printer Is Not Known to the Wizard," then return here.)
10. After you have specified the correct printer make and model, click Next.
11. Choose the port (LPT1, COM1, etc.) corresponding to the computer connector where your printer is attached.

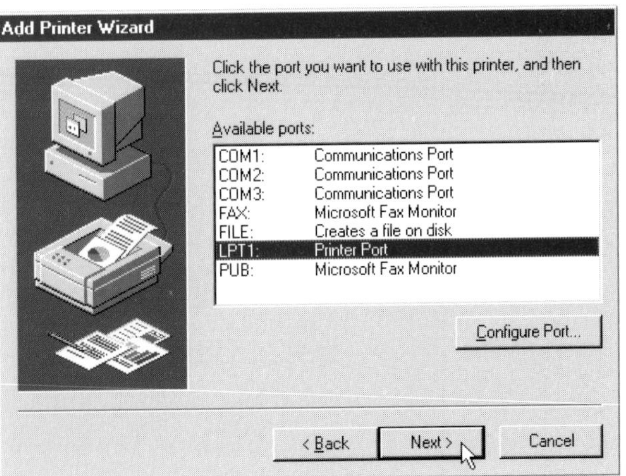

12. After you've specified a port, and perhaps reconfigured it, click the Next button.
13. You can type a new name for the printer icon associated with this printer, or keep the descriptive (but boring) Wizard-provided name. As much as I love to name printers Sleepy, or Grumpy, or Thelma, or Louise, it's really best to keep the default names, at least for a while.

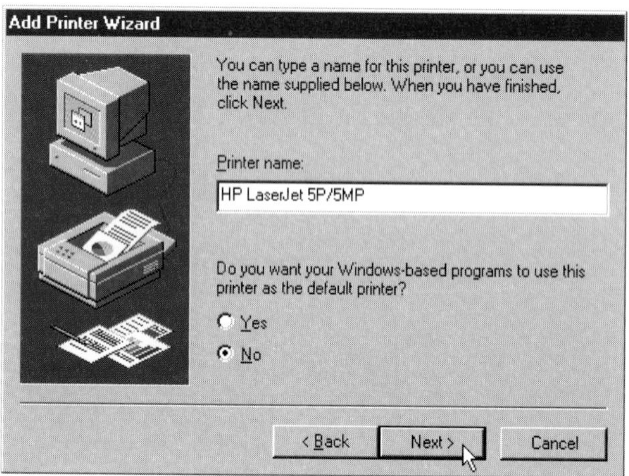

In rare cases, you might need to "configure" the port where your printer is attached, thereby telling Windows about your printer's communications requirements. The Configure Port button takes you down that path. See your printer and computer manuals if this is confusing. (First, of course, try leaving the configuration as is.)

14. If this is to be your everyday printer, click the Yes button to make it the default Windows printer. (Don't worry, you can always change your mind about this later.)
15. Click Next. You'll be asked if you want to print a test page.
16. Click your heels three times, leave the Yes button selected, and click Finish—or Swedish, perhaps, if you live in another country. (A little international humor there.)
17. You will be asked to insert a disk(s) or disc and click OK. Follow the onscreen directions. Files will move from the installer disk(s) or disc to your hard disk. Electrons will flow.
18. If you've elected to print a test page, with luck, technology will prevail and you'll see printed paper emerge after several moments of blinking lights and whirring hardware. If you are seeing red instead, jump ahead to the section "Troubleshooting Common Problems."

19. If the test page prints successfully, admire your work, then jump either to "Quick and Easy Printing" or "Choosing from Among Multiple Printers."

If Your Printer Is Not Known to the Wizard

Sometimes the Wizard won't list your printer. This is either because the printer is so brand-new that its drivers were just a gleam in someone's eye when your version of Windows 95 shipped or because your printer is so darn old that only Western Union and the Navy still use it.

- If you have an installation disk that came with your printer, read its accompanying documentation and follow the instructions therein. Frequently, all that's required is to insert the disk and click the Have Disk button in step 9.
- Sometimes, Microsoft electronically distributes new and improved printer drivers for free (see Chapter 3), or not so free with interim Windows 95 releases.
- Many printer manufacturers maintain forums and libraries at CompuServe, America Online, the Microsoft Network, etc. Some manufacturers have their own bulletin boards and Internet sites. These are all potential sources of wisdom and Windows 95 printer drivers.
- Another alternative is to read your printer documentation to determine which printer type(s) it can *emulate.* That is to say, some printers can be made to behave like HP LaserJets or Apple LaserWriters or whatever. If this is the case, and if you can figure out how to make your printer take on one of the personalities known to the Windows 95 Add Printer Wizard, go for it. Set the printer to emulate, then lie to the Wizard. You can't hurt anything, and it might work.
- Failing that, try selecting Generic from the Manufacturer section of the Add Printer Wizard dialog box.

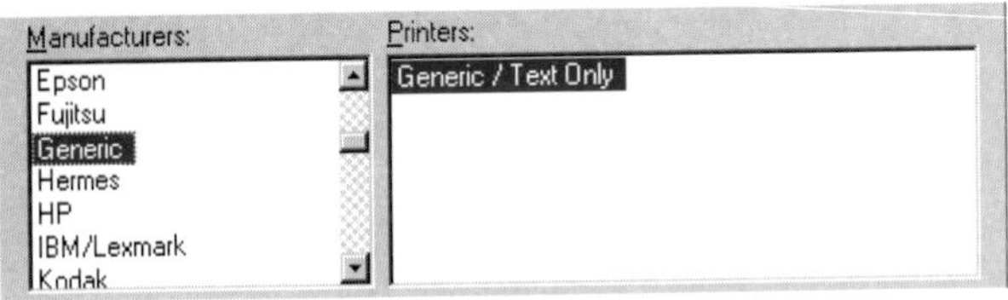

- Call the printer manufacturer's tech support line and listen to "It's a Small World" while you wait your turn on hold. Microsoft's support line is another option, particularly if you like that northwestern grunge music and perky disk jockeys (or is that *disc* jockeys?)

Quick and Easy Printing

If you've led a good life, and if the printer gods smile upon you, once you've installed a printer or two, all you need to do is choose the Print command found in virtually every Windows-savvy program, answer a few questions like the ones in the Print dialog box shown in Figure 9.1, or settle for the default settings, and finally click Print or press ENTER.

If you have any trouble printing (page-orientation problems, text ending in midsentence, etc.), try visiting the Printer Properties dialog box, and/or your program's Page Setup dialog box, as described later in this chapter.

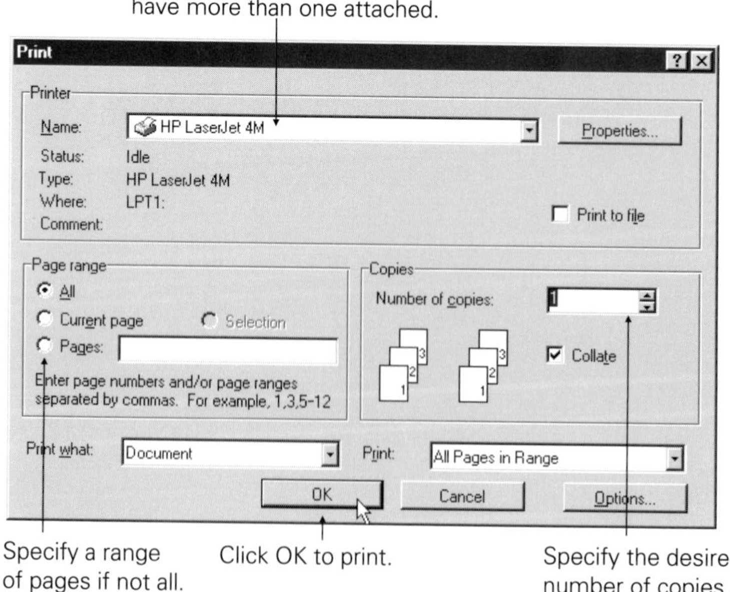

Figure 9.1 A Print dialog box for a Hewlett-Packard printer

Dragging to Print

If your software supports drag-and-drop (as current versions of most Microsoft products do), you can simply select icons of documents you want to print and drag them over a printer's icon (or its shortcut icon). This will start the application, if it's not already running, and print one copy of each document in its entirety.

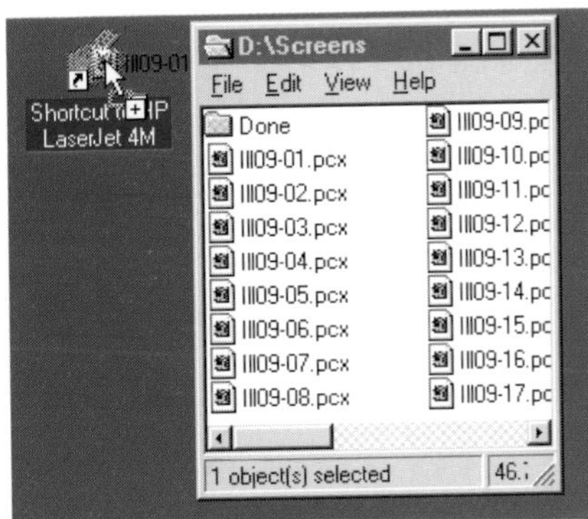

SHORTCUT

Many programs have Print buttons in their toolbars. These buttons are often the quickest way to print. Some programs automatically print a single copy when you click the Print button; others bring up the Print dialog box.

Choosing from Among Multiple Printers

Multiple printers are handy. You can use one just for printing envelopes, set another for oversized paper, and so on. Or maybe you have a slow, costly color printer and a high-speed draft printer. Windows lets you connect an almost endless collection of printers and choose different ones for different tasks.

1. From within your application, choose Print, either via the File menu or with the CTRL-P shortcut.
2. Select the desired printer from the list in the Print dialog box.

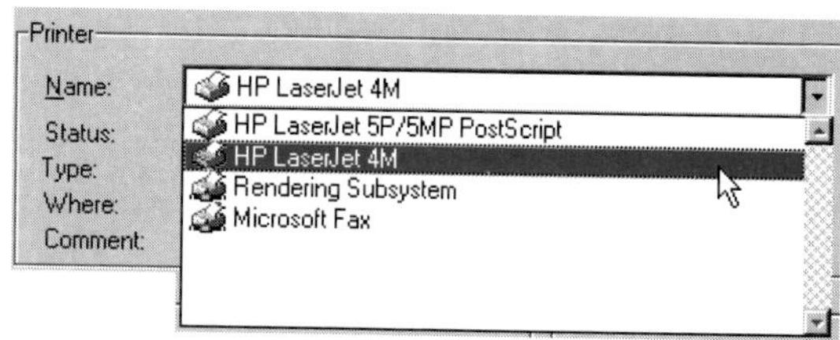

3. Click OK to start printing.

See Chapter 12 for the skinny on modems and on Microsoft Exchange, a necessary ingredient if you plan to use Windows 95's fax printing facility (as opposed to the one that came with your modem).

Printing to Fax Modems

Although the subject of fax modems is covered later in the book, it is worth mentioning that you can set some fax modem drivers to behave like printers so that you can send print jobs to the modem. The modem then dials the specified fax number(s) and printing happens at the other end o' the line. If you've ever arrived at a hotel with your laptop sans printer, this can be a lifesaver. Fax yourself a document to the front desk.

Printing to Files

When working on complex documents that you hope to print on specialty printers (like the typesetters at service bureaus), you can have Windows 95 direct your print jobs to disk. You then deliver these special files to the service provider, either on disk or over a modem, and if all goes well, you get back your phototype, or brochure, or whatever.

The problem is the hundreds of little details. Like how big are the files, and what kind of disk do you put them on? What fonts will be used and does the service bureau have the same ones you've used? So, here are a few tips:

- If you are going to work on an important job (an annual report or a sales presentation, for example), test the whole process of printing to files and then outputting to film (or whatever). Do this very *early* in the process.
- Use samples that closely approximate the final documents. There are potentially thousands of complications.
- Try a few different shops if you have that luxury.

- Find someone at each service bureau who is both knowledgeable and patient.
- Write down those phone extensions when you meet Mr. or Ms. Right.

Printer Settings

First, a rant. Five years ago, we all complained about the lack of printer flexibility and limited choices for settings. Now, there are *too many* options, and too many ways to *make* those choices. Sometimes, you need to check in to multiple dialog boxes to get things to work. Other times, if you change options in too many dialog boxes, things won't work as you'd expect, because settings can overrule or fight each other.

Take the simple act of telling your computer that you want to print in landscape or portrait mode—that is to say, use the paper wide and short or tall and narrow. You can select portrait or landscape mode from the Printer Properties dialog box, or from within your application, or even from the buttons on the outside of many printers.

Envelope feeding is another one of those enigmas. Your printer, and the application, and oft-times Windows all need to know how you plan to jam the blank envelope into the printer. Will you place it sideways down the middle? In the main tray, or the upper tray? To the right? cattywhompus?* Or what?

Here's the deal. You will need to experiment. And, you'll need to write down your findings, much as you did in fifth-grade science class. What follows are some general tips and suggestions to get you started. Then we will look at how to reach the various dialog boxes and how you use them.

The main printer settings for any Windows 95 printer can be reached by visiting the printer's Properties dialog box, as described in the following steps:

1. Choose Settings from the Start menu.
2. Pick Printers.
3. Click once to select the icon for the printer of interest.
4. Right-click to view the Shortcut menu.
5. Choose Properties.
6. Visit the tab(s) of interest and make changes.
7. Click OK.

**A technical term beyond the scope of this book.*

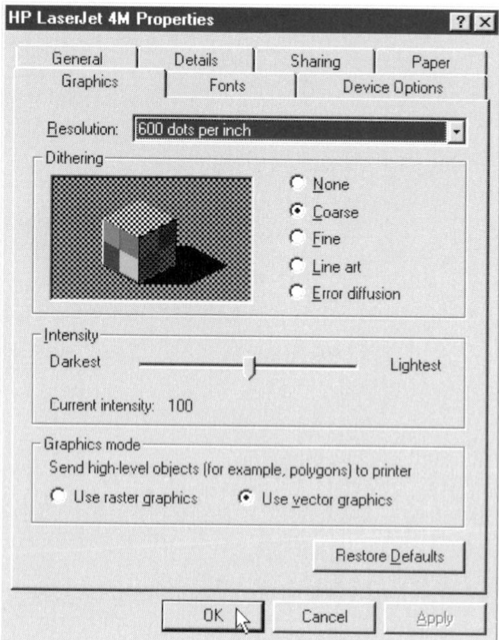

Available choices will vary from model to model. Sometimes using the What's This button can also be helpful. (See Chapter 3.)

Useful Printer Setup Tips

These are just a few tips to help in setting up your printer:

- If possible, don't mess with the printer's menu buttons (the plastic ones on the printer itself). Leave the printer set the way it came from the factory. (True, your software will change the printer's settings anyway, but if you leave them alone you always can do a printer reset and be back where you started.)
- Try to leave the settings in the various tabs of the Windows 95 Printer Properties dialog box at their factory defaults, or at least to settings you want to use all of the time.
- Make most of your printer setting changes from within the program *and the document* you are planning to print. In other words, if you are setting the printer to print an envelope created with Microsoft Word,

try to make the printer setting changes with the envelope window open in Word and foremost on your screen. (Make the envelope the active window.)

- Write down recipes that work when you discover them, and keep these notes someplace handy.
- Put little stickers on your printer with arrows and diagrams showing how to orient envelopes, odd-sized DayRunner organizer pages, and other curiosities.
- If you share printers or templates with co-workers, try to reach an agreement about how to set up printers and documents. Write down the end result to minimize confusion and training time.

The Importance of Page Setup

Most popular Windows 95-compatible programs (like Word and Excel) let you preview printed pages on your display prior to printing. This saves time, money, and trees. However, in order for the screen previews to be accurate, Windows and your programs must know which printer you will be using, the paper size you'll be printing to, and much more. This information is used to compute things like line endings, page breaks, etc. So, whenever you start a new project (particularly if you have multiple printers or frequently diddle with printer settings), visit your program's Page Setup command or its equivalent. It's usually located on the program's File menu. Make sure to select the options you plan to use when actually printing the job.

Changing an Application's Page Settings

Different programs (Word and Excel, for example) have different printing options. Many of these options can be found in the Page Setup dialog box. Other times, buttons in the Page Setup dialog box will take you to additional options.

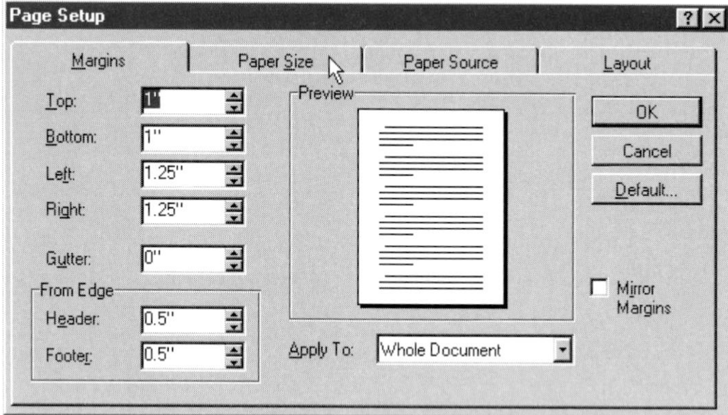

1. From within the application, choose Page Setup from the File menu.
2. Pick the tab of interest.
3. Make the desired changes. (If the dialog box has a preview feature, watch it as you work.)
4. Click OK.
5. Use Print Preview, if available on the application's File menu, to see the results of your proposed changes.

Printer Hardware Settings

Although many printers let you change their default settings, doing so can cause confusion upstream. Many software drivers expect the printers to behave a certain way. Try to avoid changing hardware settings.

Using Print Queues and Checking Progress

Because printing long, complex documents can take time, Windows 95 *spools* them to your hard disk so that you can work on other things while you're waiting. Your computer then "steals" some processing time and prints "in the background." Think of it as the computer equivalent of chewing gum and walking at the same time. If the chosen printer is already busy printing something else (or out of paper, or constipated, or whatever), new printing jobs get stored on the hard disk in *queues* where they wait their turn. Each printer has her own queue.

DEFINITION

***spooling:** Sending print jobs to disk first and then from the disk to your printer. Although this makes you wait longer for your pages to come out, it lets you do other work while you are waiting. (See also* bureaucracies.*)*

Usually, all this spooling and printing takes place without your attention. But you might want to intervene—to check the status of a job or change its priority, for example. Here's how you do it:

1. Select Settings from the Start menu.
2. Choose Printers from the submenu.
3. Double-click the icon of the desired printer to see and alter the queue.

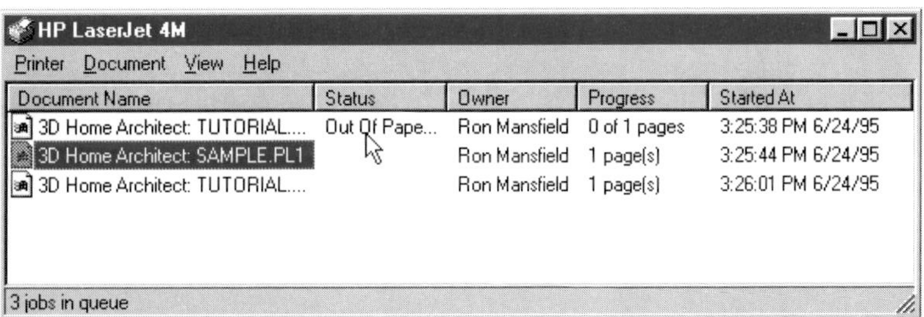

4. To cancel or pause a job, select it and choose Cancel Printing or Pause Printing from the Document menu. (On networked printers you can only control your own jobs.)
5. To cancel or pause all jobs, choose Purge Print Jobs or Pause Printing from the queue's Printer menu. (Again, on networked printers you can only control your jobs.)

6. To change a job's position in the queue, select, then drag it.

SHORTCUT

If you are printing, double-click the Printer icon at the right end of your Taskbar to reveal the Printer dialog box.

As I mentioned earlier, if your programs support drag-and-drop, you can drag document icons from disk folders or the Explorer onto the printer icon for printing. To create a printer icon, follow these steps:

STEP BY STEP Creating a Printer Shortcut Icon

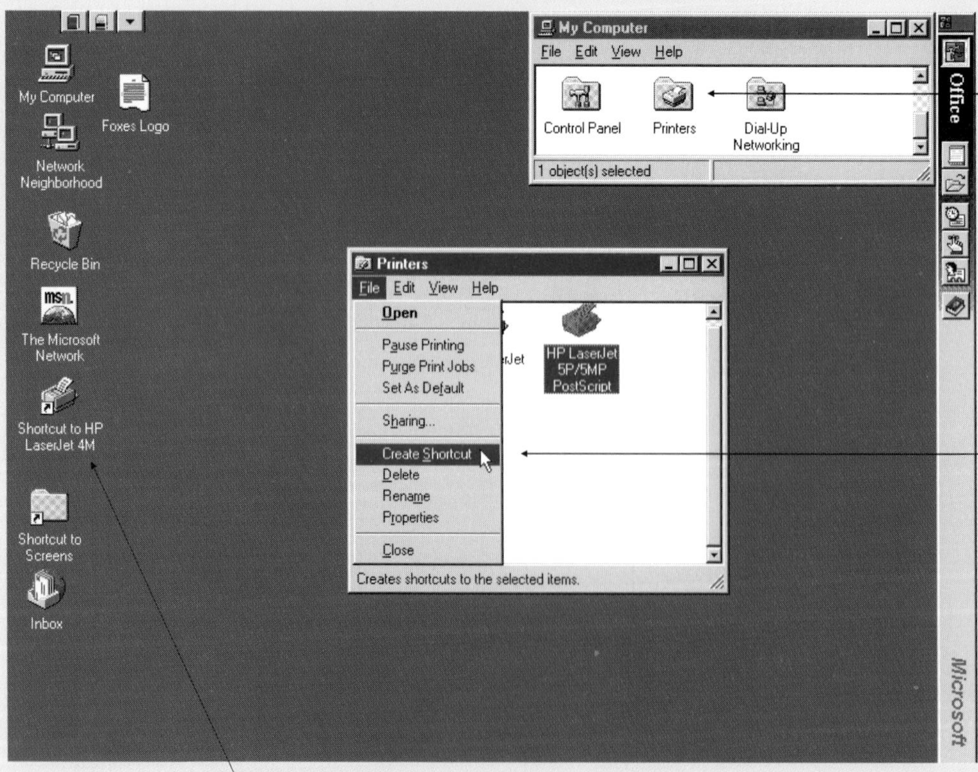

1 **Select the printer icon (either via the Start menu or by opening the Printers folder in the My Computer window) and right-click.**

2 **Choose Create Shortcut from the Open menu. You will get yelled at by Windows for following my instructions, but click Yes, unabashed. You are doing the right thing here.**

3 **The shortcut icon will appear on your desktop. Drag it to a cozy spot.**

Sharing Printers

If your computer is on a network, and if you are a very nice person, and if you have competent, considerate co-workers, you can let them send their print jobs over the network to your printer. Sounds great, huh? The phone rings. "Hey, Ron. Can you toss an envelope in the upper tray?"

Two minutes later, a visitor. "How does that headline look? Is it too big?"

The phone rings again. "I need to do some two-sided printing. Would you mind flipping each page quickly when it comes out?"

Your response? "Right. And I'll lend you my car, so you can go to lunch while I'm flipping your pages. I'm *busy*, can't you see? Get a budget."

Fortunately, there are some gotchas that might preclude shared printing altogether, so you might want to get your network person involved from the start if you plan to share printers. For example, not all network configurations gracefully support printer sharing. You or your co-workers might need to make some fancy settings choices to "capture" the printing port. The leeches—that is, *folks* who want to share your printer—won't be able to print if your computer is shut off, or if you've moved it to, let's say, your tray table at 30,000 feet.

At any rate, printer sharing can be done, but maybe not by busy people. See Chapter 11 and online help if you want to give it a try.

Capturing Printer Ports

Many DOS programs expect to see, and must be able to use, a specific *printer port*—typically LPT1, LPT2, LPT3, COM1, COM2, or COM3. These port names (LPT1 and so on) normally refer to the various parallel and serial connectors on the back of your computer. You can "trick" programs into thinking they are sending printing jobs directly to those connectors on the back of your computer and even route the printing to *networked* printers located elsewhere. The process is called *capturing a printer port.*

Once you've set up your system, Windows 95-savvy programs let you select printers without worrying about port designations, but many DOS programs (even when you run them under Windows 95) want you to tell them the name of the port (LPT1 or whatever) where the desired printer is connected.

If you didn't tell Windows 95 that you wanted to print from DOS programs when you installed your printer(s), you weren't asked to capture ports, and you might have trouble printing from DOS programs if you can only print to a networked printer. In this case you will probably need to "capture" a printer port.

Here are the basic steps:

If you are unfamiliar with shared networked printers, you might want to check Chapter 11 as well. Since capturing a printer port can be a little confusing, and is only relevant if you share printers on a network, you might want to enlist the aid of your network manager or help desk before proceeding.

1. Visit the Control Panel and double-click the Printers icon.
2. Right-click on the icon for the printer you intend to use.
3. Choose Properties from the resulting shortcut menu to see the printer's properties.
4. Click the Details tab.
5. Click the Capture Printer Port button.
6. From the Device list, select the port you want (LPT1 through 9, for example).
7. From the Path List, choose the desired shared printer.
8. If you always want to capture the shared printer at startup, make sure there is a checkmark in the Reconnect at logon box.

Troubleshooting Common Problems

As printers become more versatile, problems become more plentiful. Some are pretty easy to solve. Table 9.1 lists some tips.

Working with Fonts

Fonts are collections of stylized characters (letters, numbers, symbols, and punctuation marks) displayed and printed by your computer. They change the appearance of your work, both onscreen and in print.

Although not 100 percent traditionally accurate, the following definitions are close enough to the truth for a busy person. (Unless, of course you are a busy typographer.) Font *names* (Times New Roman, Playbill, etc.) are used to differentiate different *type styles*, or *designs*. There are quite a number of font technologies available to Windows 95 users; however, the majority of your work will probably

Problem	Try This
Nothing Prints.	Check the printer power and paper tray. Is the online light (or the ready light, or whatever) lit? Why not? Is someone else printing? If this is a network printer, is the network functional? The printer's not jammed, is it? If this is a new installation, or if you've just reconnected your printer, double-check basics (such as cables being firmly connected and electrical cords all plugged in). Try restarting both the printer and the computer. (Shut down Windows, then physically switch off both your computer and printer. Don't use "soft" Restart and Reset commands.)
Everything prints sideways, or parts of the image are cut off.	Check the printer setting against the application's Page Setup settings. Paper size, orientation, and margin settings should agree.
Printed fonts don't match the screen.	Use TrueType fonts or fonts that match those contained in your printer (or print cartridge) whenever possible. Sometimes just printing a second time will fix mysterious problems.
You get "Out of Printer Memory" warnings.	Some older programs do this unnecessarily. Before you buy more printer memory, consult with the software maker about things like Page Protection options.
Instead of my document I get page after page of gibberish.	Your computer is trying to send PostScript commands and your printer doesn't know it, or can't print PostScript. Be sure you've chosen the correct printer driver, and that your printer is set to print PostScript. Some older printers need PostScript cartridges. Does yours? Is it properly installed?

Table 9.1 Solutions to Some Common Printing Problems

be done with *TrueType* fonts. Fonts are usually stored in a Fonts folder on your hard disk, although it is possible to use fonts stored on a network, or in a printer, or even fonts shipped along with a document, under certain circumstances.

DEFINITION

TrueType fonts: *Fonts that use the same technology to display text on the screen and to print it (the screen fonts provide a very close approximation of printed characters). TrueType font names are preceded by two Ts in many font lists and dialog boxes, making them easy to spot. They are automatically installed when you set up Windows.*

Viewing and Printing Font Samples

1. Choose Settings from the Start menu.
2. Select the Control Panel option.
3. Double-click the Fonts folder.
4. Double-click the font of interest, or hold down the CTRL key while you click once on all but the last font you wish to examine, then double-click *it.*

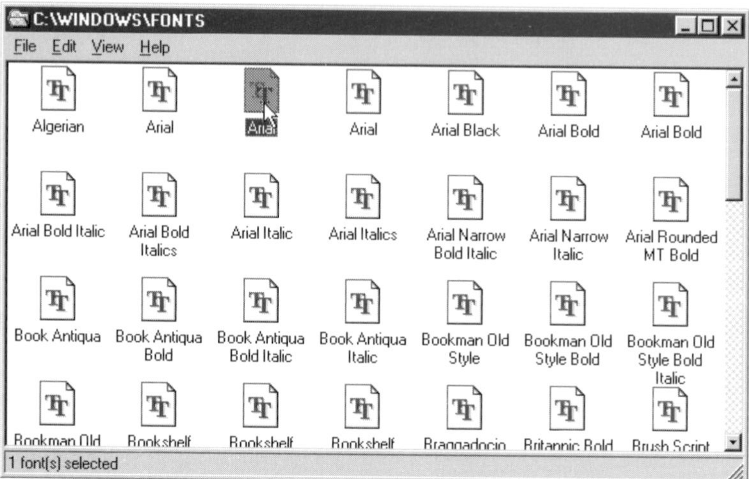

5. A window or windows will open displaying the selected font(s). Resize the windows if you like, or scroll to see everything.
6. To print a sample, click the Print button. (If you have multiple printers, select the printer of interest first, since it can have an effect on the outcome.)

Installing Fonts

Sometimes software and printer installation programs install new fonts automatically. Other times you will be asked if that's okay. You also can purchase fonts from software stores, download them via modem, and play pass-the-floppy with friends (assuming, of course, that the fonts are shareware).

If the fonts you purchase come with installation instructions for Windows 95, follow them. Otherwise, use this general procedure to install a new font:

1. Place the font disk in a drive (or, if the fonts are already on your hard disk, but are not yet installed, find out where they are hidden—in CompuServe's Download folder might be a possibility, for example).
2. From the Control panel, open the Font folder by double-clicking its icon.
3. Choose Install New Font from the File menu.
4. In the Add Fonts dialog box, show Windows the way to the new fonts by clicking the appropriate choices in the drive, and possibly the folder lists. (Be patient while Windows builds the list of font names.)
5. Double-click a single font name to install it or CTRL-click to choose multiple fonts; or click, then SHIFT-click, to choose a continuous range of fonts.
6. With the font(s) selected, click OK to complete the installation.

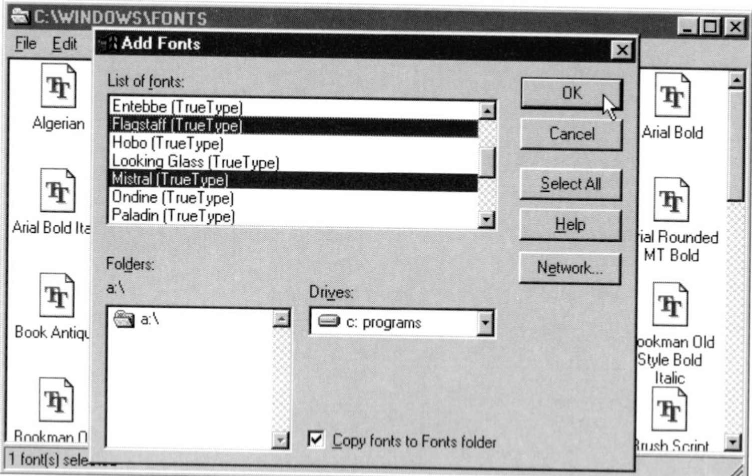

Removing Fonts

To remove fonts, follow these steps:

1. Open the Font window (double-click the Fonts folder in the control panel).
2. Select the font(s) to be deleted by clicking or CTRL-clicking.
3. Choose Delete from the File menu.

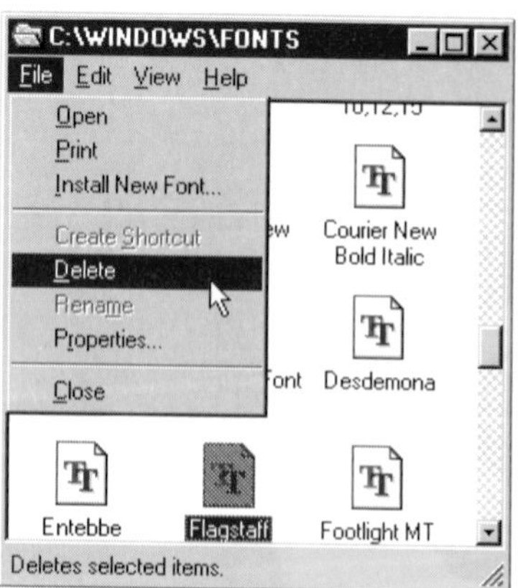

Using Special Characters and Symbols

To see and perhaps insert special characters (international accents, trademark symbols and the like), try this:

1. Choose Programs from the Start menu.
2. Pick Accessories, and then Character Map.
3. Make sure the font listed in the Font box matches the font you are using in your document (change it if necessary).
4. Click once on a character to magnify it, or twice to add it to the Characters to Copy box.
5. Click Copy, then Close.

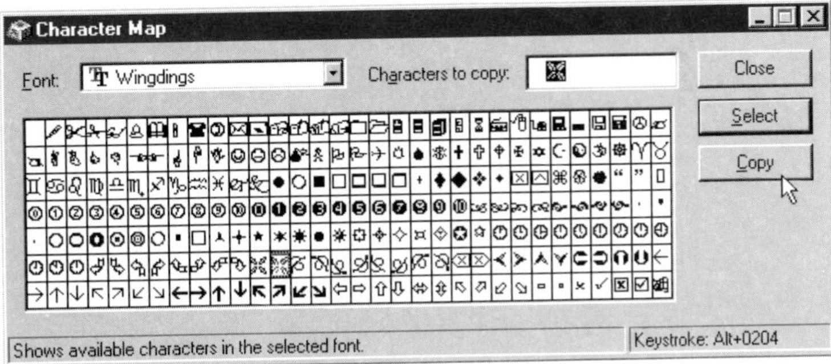

CAUTION

Using the Character Map steps described here replaces the contents of your Clipboard with the selected special characters.

See the Keystroke message in the lower-right corner of the Character Map window? Pressing that key combination will insert the currently selected character. Hold down the ALT key while you use the numeric pad to enter the code.

Back in the document, make sure your insertion point is positioned where you want the special characters to appear, and then paste (use CTRL-V).

EXPERT ADVICE

Some programs (like Microsoft Word, but curiously not Excel or PowerPoint) have a Symbol choice on their Insert menus. This is often a quicker way to insert special characters.

We've covered a fair amount of ground here. Fortunately, if your computer was properly set up for you, most of the hard work is done. If you need to add a new printer, this would be a good time to give it a try. Or, you could experiment with the print queue. Turn off your printer and try to print several documents from Word or some other Windows 95-savvy program. Visit the print queue and rearrange the order of the jobs waiting in the queue (because the printer is turned off). You get to kick off your shoes in the next chapter. We'll look at ways to personalize the look and feel of your computer. You will get a chance to set up a few things just once to make your computing easier or at least more enjoyable. It'll be fun! Keep reading.

CHAPTER

10 Stuff to Do Once to Make Your Life Easier

INCLUDES

- The Welcome screens and tips
- Changing items on the Start menu
- Regional settings and number formatting
- Mouse personalities and keyboard behavior
- Customizing sounds and screen appearance
- Dialing preferences
- Accessibility options for physically challenged users

FAST FORWARD

Disable the Welcome Screens and Tips ➤ pp. 224-225

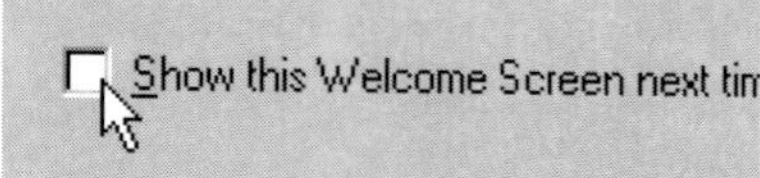

Remove the checkmark from the Welcome screen by clicking on the checkmark. (Clicking in the box when there is no checkmark places one there.)

Add Items to the Start Menu ➤ pp. 226-229

Drag icons to the Start button, or:

1. Right-click the Taskbar.
2. Choose Properties.
3. Click the Start Menu Programs tab.
4. Click the Add button.
5. Type the path to the desired filename, or click Browse to locate the desired file and click to select it.
6. When the Create Shortcut Wizard appears with the desired file listed, click Next.
7. Click the folder where you want the Shortcut (menu item) to appear and click Next.
8. Type the desired name for the Start Menu item (the name you wish to see in the Start Menu).
9. Click Finish.

Repeat steps 5-10, then click OK when finished.

Remove Items from the Start Menu ➤ pp. 231-232

1. Open the Start Button Properties dialog box by right-clicking on the Taskbar.
2. Choose Properties.
3. Click the Start Menu Programs tab.
4. Click the Remove button.
5. Scroll to see the item you wish to remove.
6. Click to select it.
7. Click the Remove button.
8. Repeat steps 5-7, then click Close when finished.
9. Click OK in the Taskbar Properties dialog box to close it.

Set Your Computer's Date and Time ➤ *pp. 233-236*

1. Double-click the Time in your Taskbar.
2. You'll soon see the Date/Time Properties dialog box.
3. Change settings by clicking and typing.
4. Click OK.

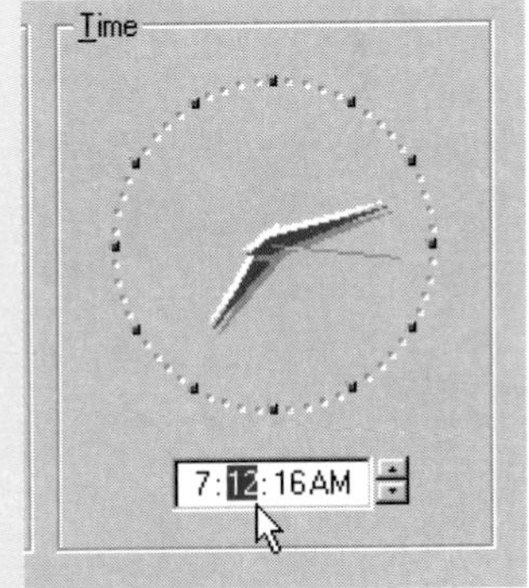

Select Number and Currency Formatting ➤ *pp. 236-237*

1. Choose Settings from the Start menu.
2. Choose Control Panel.
3. Double-click the Regional Settings icon.
4. Click the desired tab (Currency, Date, etc.).
5. Change settings by clicking and typing.

Change Mouse Settings ➤ *pp. 237-242*

1. Choose Settings from the Start menu.
2. Choose Control Panel.
3. Double-click the Mouse icon.
4. Pick the desired tab.
5. Change settings by clicking and typing or dragging.
6. Preview settings in the test areas.
7. Click Apply to test changes.
8. Click OK to save changes.

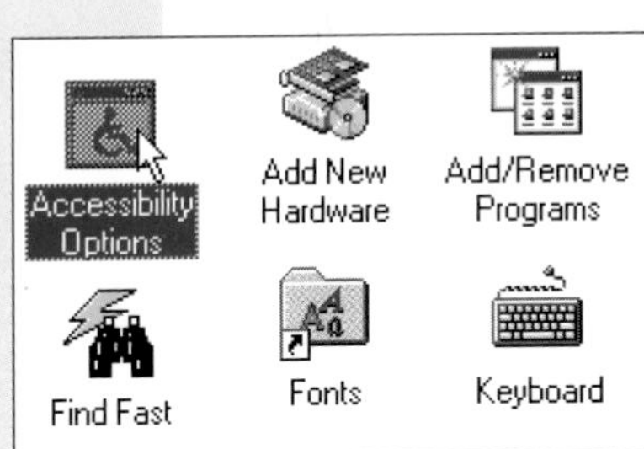

Change Keyboard Settings ➤ *pp. 242-244*

1. Choose Settings from the Start menu.
2. Choose Control Panel.
3. Double-click the Keyboard icon.
4. Pick the desired tab.
5. Change settings by clicking and typing or dragging.
6. Preview settings in the test areas.
7. Click Apply to test changes.
8. Click OK to save changes.

Change Screen Properties ➤ *pp. 244-252*

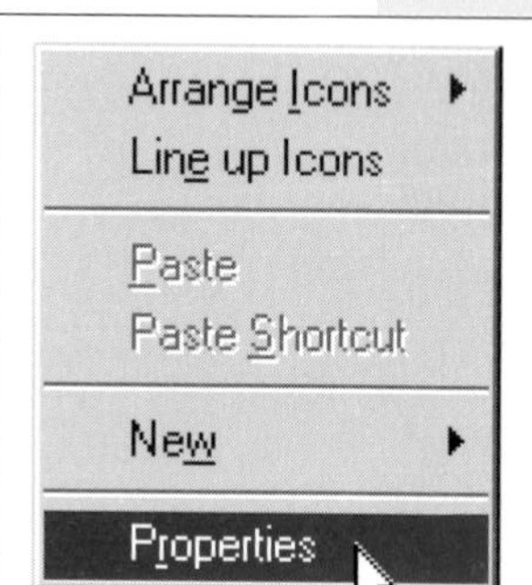

1. Right-click on the desktop.
2. Choose Properties from the Shortcut menu.
3. Pick the desired tab.
4. Change settings by clicking and typing or dragging.
5. Preview settings in the test areas.
6. Click Apply to preview changes on the whole screen.
7. Click OK to save changes.

Choose Sounds for Events ➤ *pp. 252-256*

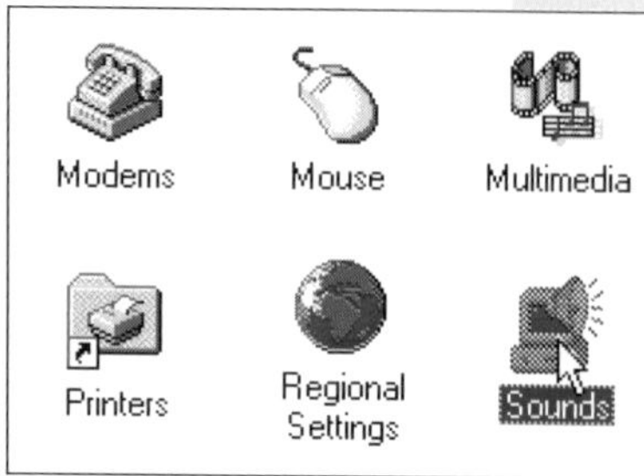

1. Be sure your computer is sound-equipped and properly functioning (speakers cabled, powered up, etc.).
2. Choose Settings from the Start menu.
3. Choose Control Panel.
4. Double-click the Sounds icon.
5. Scroll to see events that can initiate sounds (opening Windows, etc.).
6. Scroll to see lists of available sounds, or browse your hard disk for files ending with the extension .wav.
7. Preview settings by selecting them and pressing the Preview button (a triangle).
8. Click Apply to test changes.
9. Click OK to save them.

Preview Sound Files ➤ *p. 254*

Double-click sound files ending with the extension .wav. (Use the Find command to search for *.wav to find all the sound files.)

Define Modem Dialing Preferences ➤ *pp. 256-258*

1. Choose Settings from the Start menu.
2. Choose Control Panel.
3. Double-click the Modems icon.
4. Pick the General tab.
5. Click the Dialing Properties button.
6. Change settings by clicking and typing or dragging.
7. Optionally save these settings under a different name (On the road, Cellular, etc.).
8. Click OK to save changes.

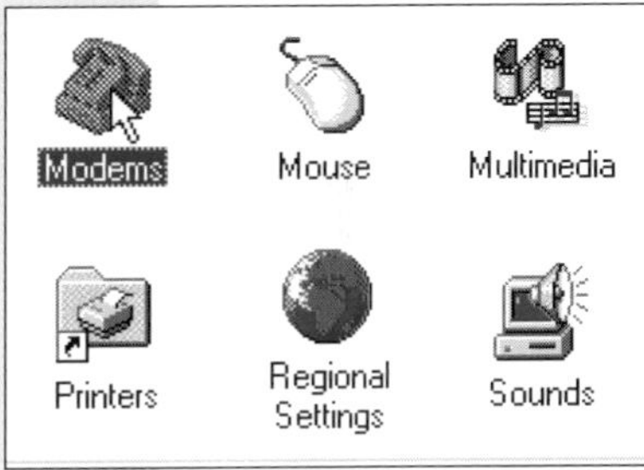

Enable Accessibility Options for Physically Challenged Users ➤ *pp. 258-259*

- Search for the topic Accessibility in online help.
- Double-click the Accessibility Options icon in the control panel to customize the system according to the user's needs and preferences..

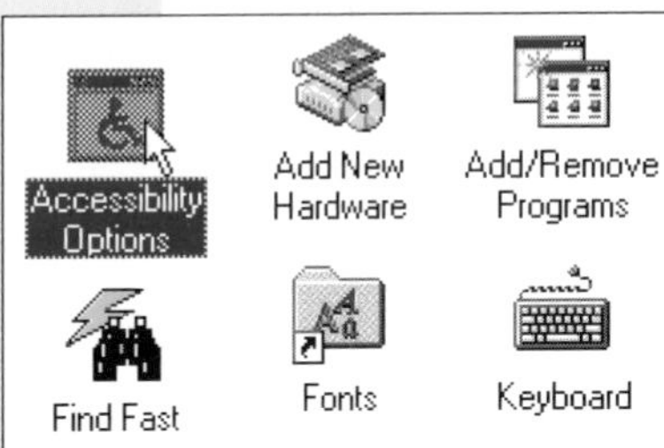

There are some things that you can do once (or perhaps once in a while) that can make using your computer easier and more enjoyable. Many of these things fall into the category of personalizing Windows 95. Since *personal* is the first word in the term "personal computers," it seems fitting that we can personalize the appearance and behavior of our silicon servants.

Windows 95 offers even more flexibility than its predecessors. You can change the way your computer looks and sounds, how it dials the phone, and so much more. Alas, there might be rules where you work about personalizing the "company's machines," and it is even possible for the computer police to shut off many of the features you'll read about here. Sometimes that's a good thing, because it makes mission-critical software work better. Other times it's just the old power game. So, if you can't personalize the company machine, get your own machine—or better yet, get your own company. For now, let's play.

DEFINITION

computer police: *Bright, earnest, helpful, underpaid office employees hired to enforce policies, keep things running, help you when your computer crashes, and take all of the fun out of personal computing.*

The Welcome Screen and Tips

If you get sick of those initially helpful tips of the day and the attendant Welcome Screen after seeing them 20 times, do this. Click to remove the checkmark from the "Show this Welcome Screen next time you start Windows" box:

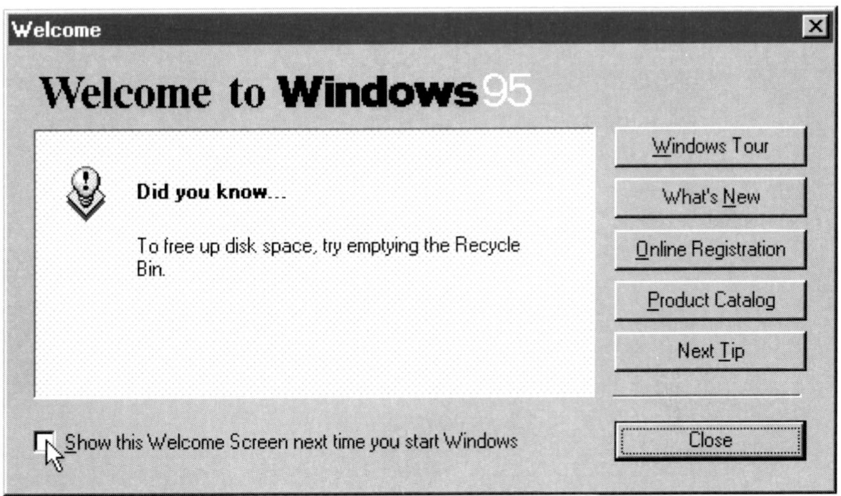

Reactivating the Welcome Screen

To turn the Welcome Screen back on (for someone else, perhaps?), try this:

1. Choose Help from the Start menu.
2. Pick the Index tab.
3. Type **welcome.**
4. Double-click "Welcome screen, viewing".
5. When the Welcome help window opens, click the little in-text button, shown here:

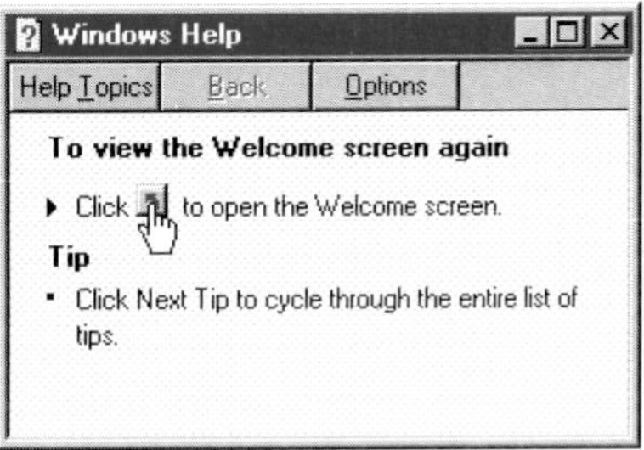

6. When you see the Welcome screen, click to place a checkmark in the "Show this Welcome Screen next time you start Windows" box.
7. Click the Close button.

The next time Windows starts, you should see the Welcome screen and tips.

Changing the Start Menu

The Start menu is a handy place to personalize your system. By making a few simple changes, you can make your Start menu your own. Here are some examples of things you might want to do to the Start menu:

- Add programs and other items
- Rename Start menu items
- Remove programs and other items
- Move items
- Clear the Documents menu

Let's take 'em one at a time. In order, even!

Adding Items to the Top of the Start Menu

The quickest way to add an item to the "top level" of the Start menu is to drag the item's icon over the Start Menu button. This is a very powerful tip, and you needn't limit it to program icons. You can drag document icons (like an icon for your favorite Word template or Excel spreadsheet), or folder icons, or even Windows 95 shortcut icons for shared resources. And, you can drag from just about anywhere—like the Explorer, or disk windows, or your desktop.

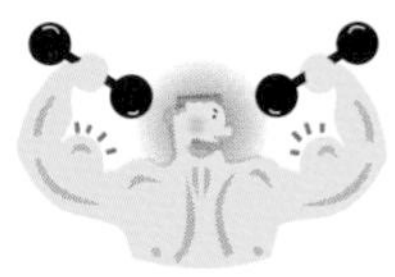

DEFINITION

Windows 95 shortcut icon: *Little picture of a folder, printer, computer, or other resource. With any luck, these rascals remember the original item's location. Double-clicking or otherwise selecting a shortcut icon takes you to the actual item without a lot of rummaging. (Too bad these don't work on wooden desktops too...)*

For example, let's add the Calculator icon to the "top level" of your Start menu (this will save you a trip to the Programs submenu each time you need the calculator):

1. Choose Find and then choose Files and Folders from the Start menu.
2. Type **calc.exe** in the Named box.

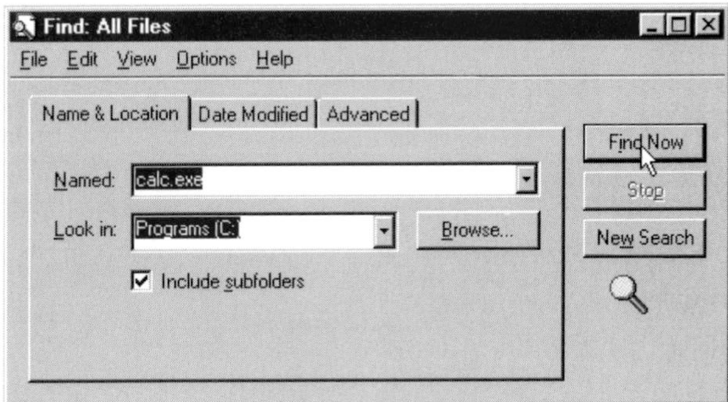

3. Make sure the drive containing your Windows folder is listed in the Look In box (if you are not sure, choose My Computer for this box instead).
4. Make sure the "Include subfolders" box has a checkmark.
5. Click the Find Now button.
6. You should see an icon for the file Calc.exe (It might just say "Calc"). Click on it and drag it to your Start Menu button. (If you can't see the Start Menu button, drag to the lower-left corner of the screen and the button will appear.)
7. Watch the pointer's shape change as you drag, particularly when you get to the Start button's position. (It's telling you where you can and cannot drop things you drag.)
8. Release the mouse pointer when you reach the Start button. Windows will create a shortcut icon for the Calculator program (Calc.exe) and place it on your Start menu (near the top of the list).
9. Check out the new icon:

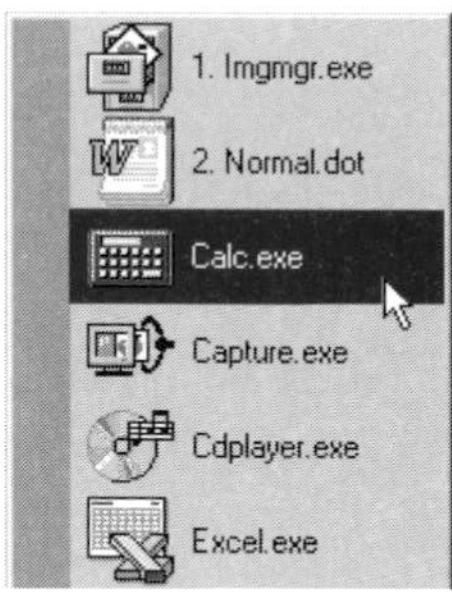

Later in this chapter, you'll see how to change the name of any Start menu items to something less wonkish.

Adding Items to Specific Spots in the Start Menu

There's another, more tedious way to add items to the Start menu that's helpful if you want to place things in a particular location. Suppose, for example, that you wanted the Calculator shortcut to appear in your Programs menu instead of at the top level of the Start menu. Here's one way to do that:

1. Find the Calc.exe program using steps 1 through 6 in the preceding exercise.
2. Right-click on a portion of the Taskbar that does not contain a button (the high ground between buttons, for instance).
3. When you see the Shortcut menu, choose Properties. (This takes you to the Taskbar's properties.)

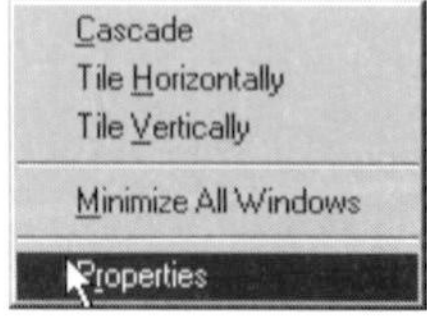

4. Click the Start Menu Programs tab, if necessary to bring it forward. At this point you could click Add and type the path to the program (**c:\windows\calc.exe**), but I prefer the trick in the steps that follow.

5. Click the Advanced button on the Start Menu Programs tab. You'll see a window containing icons for items on the Start menu.

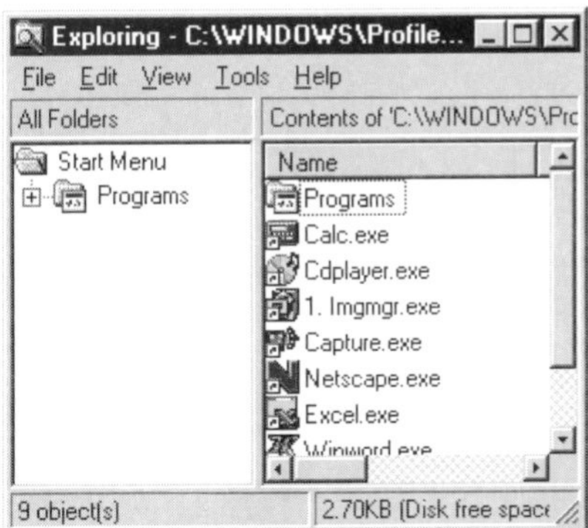

6. Click the Calc.exe icon in the Find window and drag it, as shown in Figure 10.1, over the Programs folder in the Exploring window.
7. A new Calc.exe shortcut will be created in the Programs folder. Check the Start Menu Programs submenu, and you should see the shortcut (named "Shortcut to Calc.exe").

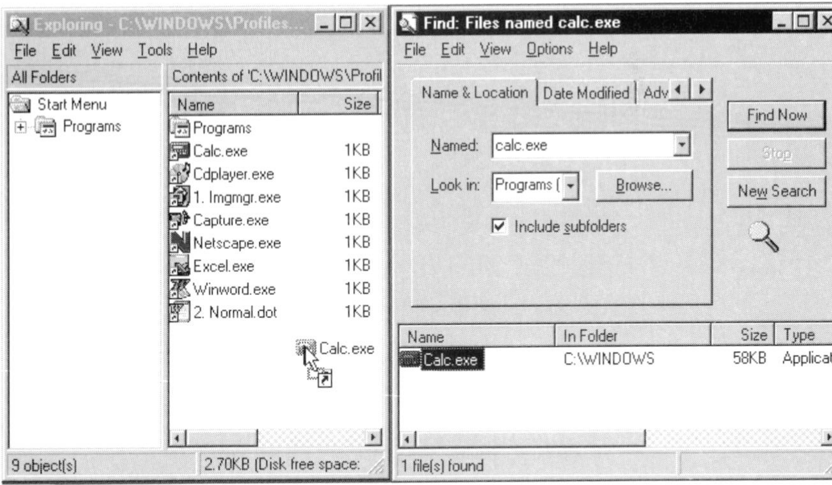

Figure 10.1 The Find feature's Advanced option lets you drag and drop a filename to a new menu

Renaming Start Menu Items

You start the renaming process by opening the same Exploring window used in the previous exercise. If yours is still open, skip steps 1 through 3 here.

Obviously, Start menu choices like "Shortcut to Calc.exe" are pretty obnoxious (unless you think that showing off like this gets you somewhere with the people looking over your shoulder).

1. Open the Taskbar's Properties window by right-clicking on a non-button portion of the bar and picking Properties from the Shortcut menu.
2. In the Taskbar Properties window, click the Start Menu Programs tab if necessary to bring it forward.
3. Click the Advanced button.
4. Select the icon you wish to rename (double-click on one or more folders if necessary to reveal the icon of choice).

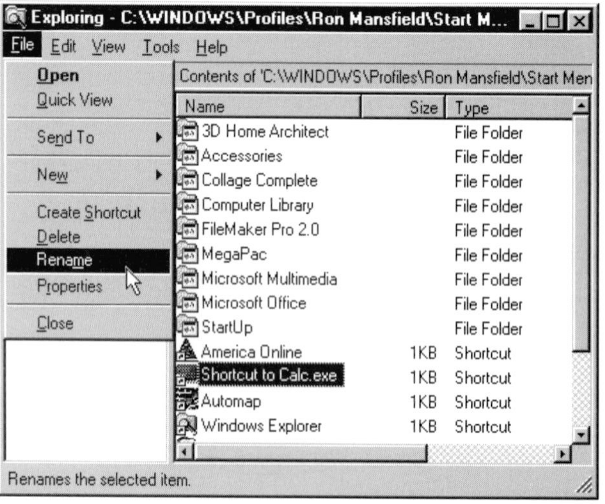

5. Either choose Rename from the File menu, or click on the icon to select the name.
6. Edit the name.
7. Rename other icons if you want, then close the Explorer window.
8. Check the names in the Start menu. They should be properly modified.

Removing Items from the Start Menu

You remove items from the Start menu by following the same steps to get to the Start Menu Programs tab in the Taskbar Properties window. Then you use the Remove button, mouse, and DELETE key. The following steps will tell you how:

1. Open the Taskbar's Properties window by right-clicking on a non-button portion of the bar and picking Properties from the Shortcut menu.
2. In the Taskbar Properties window, click the Start Menu Programs tab if necessary to bring it forward.
3. Click the Remove button. The Remove Shortcuts/Folders window appears.

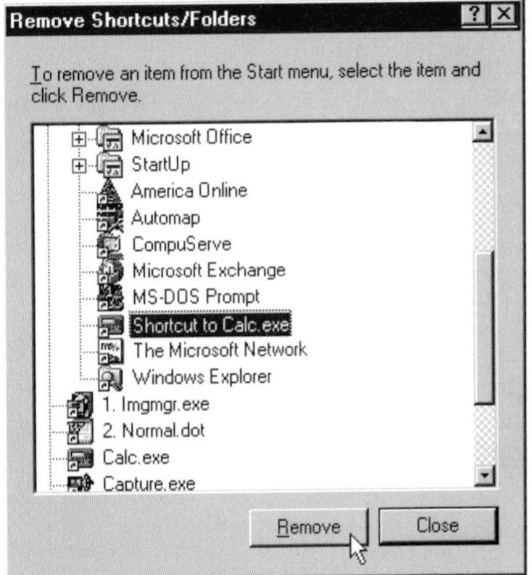

4. Select the icon you wish to remove (click on the + signs next to folders if necessary to reveal the icon of choice).
5. Click Remove. The item will be squirted like a watermelon seed out of the Universe (and there is no Undo here, Captain).
6. Remove other icons if you want, then close the Remove Shortcuts/Folders window.

Now...remember earlier when we talked about the hazards of leaving the names of confidential files in your Documents submenu? If you work with files that others shouldn't see, get in the habit of clearing the Documents submenu.

STEP BY STEP Clearing the Documents Submenu

1 Right-click on a non-button portion of the Taskbar and pick Properties from the shortcut submenu to bring up the Taskbar Properties dialog box.

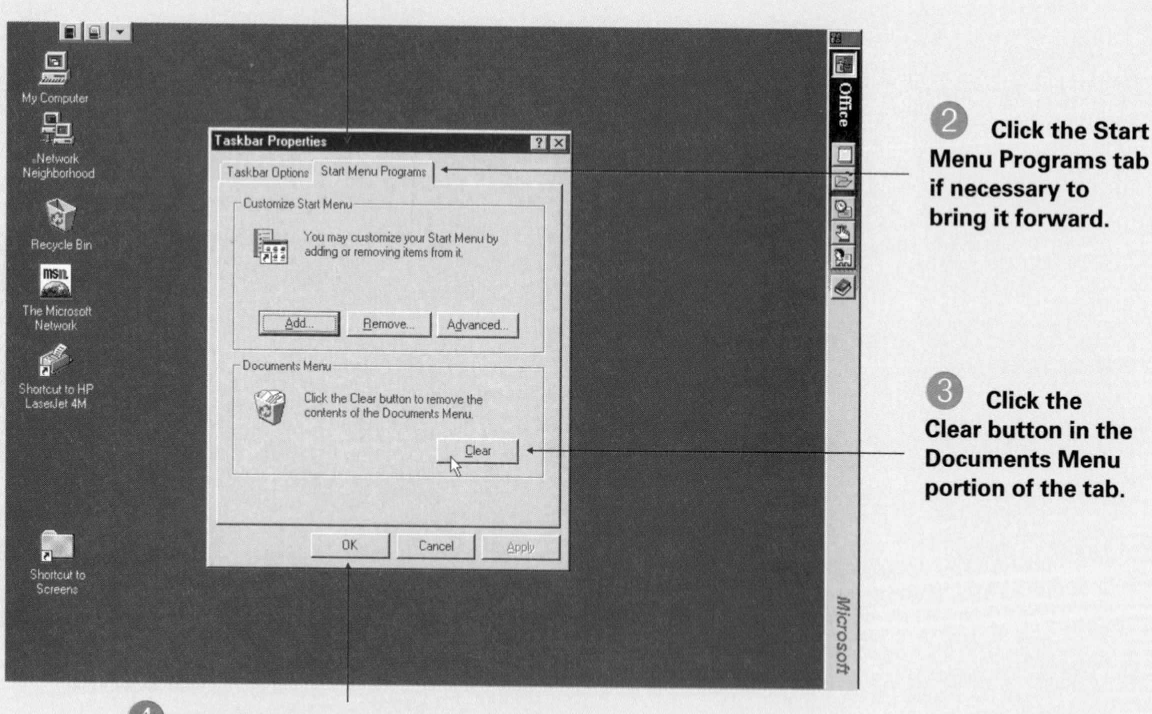

2 Click the Start Menu Programs tab if necessary to bring it forward.

3 Click the Clear button in the Documents Menu portion of the tab.

4 Click OK. Check the Documents choice on the Start menu. It should say "(Empty)."

Moving Things Around on the Start Menu

Well, this isn't as much fun as it could be. Start menu items always want to display themselves alphabetically. After I purchase Microsoft, you'll be able to drag things around in the Explorer window and organize the Start menu any way you like. But until then, here are some tricks you can try.

Number your icon names in the Explorer. For example, if you want the calculator on top followed by a phone dialer, you might name the calculator icon "1. Calculator" and the dialer "2. Phone Dialer," and so on. This is a pain when you want to insert something new, but, hey.

Or, you can use prefix words or letters to group related icons together. For example, to group all your flying software, templates, and so on, you could start each icon name with "Fly," then create shortcuts to a database file called Fly Logbook, another to a spreadsheet called Fly Budget, a shortcut to a folder with Word documents labeled Fly Stories, and so on.

SHORTCUT

Remember that you can create folder shortcuts and have them appear in your Start menus. So if you organize your disk carefully, you can get to just the right spot by picking a folder icon from the Start menu.

Clock, Calendar, Regional Settings, and More

Your computer has a built-in clock/calendar chip complete with battery backup. Windows uses the information from this gizmo to date-stamp files, to run scheduled activities (like backups), to show the time and date in your Taskbar, and much more. PC clocks vary in accuracy from awesome to comical. And, although you probably won't die from an inaccurate computer clock (unless you use it to navigate), it's a good idea to keep your clock at least in the neighborhood of the correct time.

CAUTION

Some software, including backup programs, group collaboration software, etc., gets really confused when you stamp things with the wrong date or time, particularly if you're connected to a far-flung network.

STEP BY STEP Setting the Date and Time

1. Double-click on the Time icon in your Taskbar (or choose Settings from the Start menu, click Control Panel, and double-click the Date/Time icon) to bring up the Date/Time Properties dialog box.

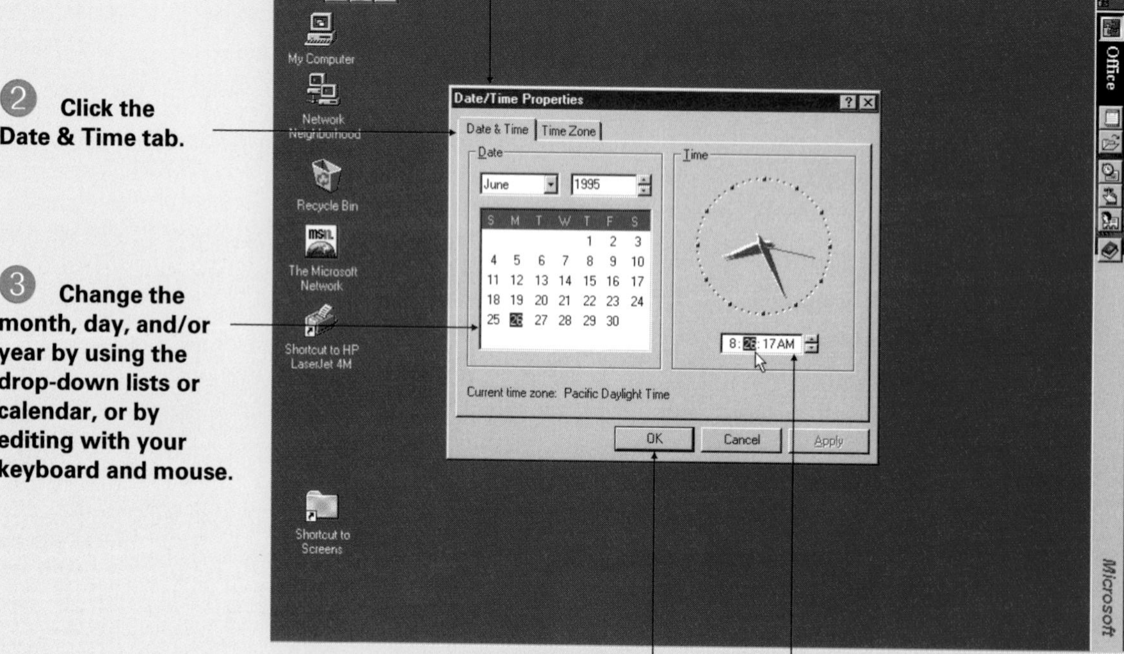

2. Click the Date & Time tab.

3. Change the month, day, and/or year by using the drop-down lists or calendar, or by editing with your keyboard and mouse.

4. To set the time, select the numbers you wish to change and edit with your keyboard and mouse.

5. Click OK or move to the Time Zone tab to work there.

Time Zones

You may never have to deal with time zone settings at all—or they might be a real mind-bender that you have to attend to on a daily basis. If you take your laptop on the road (and your frequent flyer miles are up there), then the Time Zone tab of the Date/Time Properties window can be a lifesaver when it's time to change your computer's clock and calendar. It can also tell you what time it is in other time zones.

To see and possibly change your time zone setting, follow these steps:

1. Double-click the Time icon in your Taskbar. (If the time is not displayed on your Taskbar, choose Settings from the Start menu, click Control Panel, and double-click the Date/Time icon.)
2. Click the Time Zone tab if necessary to bring it forward.

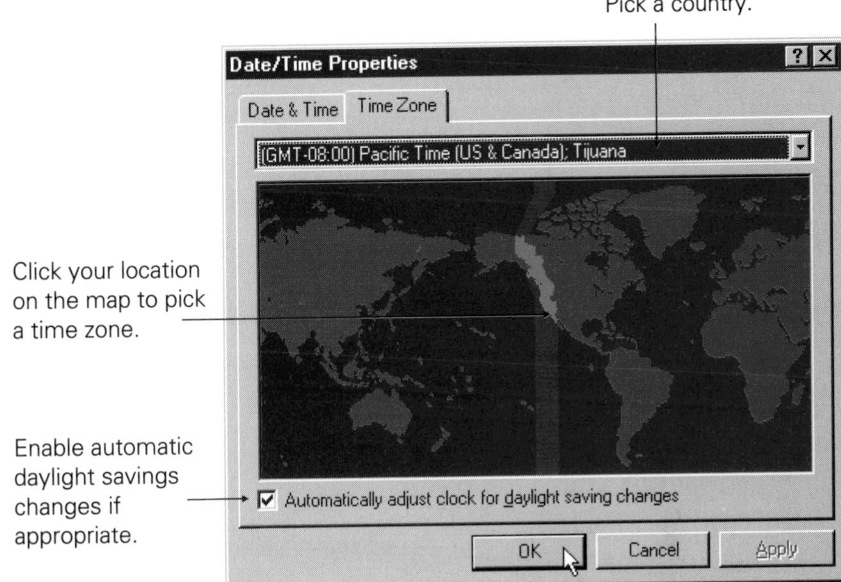

3. The current zone setting is highlighted (usually in green on color displays), and the name of the current zone is displayed above the map. If the correct zone is not selected, change it using any of these techniques:
   - Pick a new time zone from the drop-down lists.
   - Move the highlight with your right and left arrow keys (or just grab the green bar and drag with your mouse).
   - Click on the zone's location in the map.
4. Click OK or move to the Date & Time tab to work there.

CAUTION

When the year changes from 1999 to 2000, bad things will happen to good people. Many (many, many) programs will not know what to do when the Times Square ball drops. Ask programmers of your mission-critical software if they've tested it with this in mind.

Daylight Savings Time

If you must deal with daylight savings time, Windows 95 can automatically set the clock forward and back at the appropriate instant. When you select a time zone that honors daylight savings time, you'll be able to add or remove the checkmark controlling automatic daylight savings adjustments. It's located in the Time Zone tab of the Date/Time Properties window:

Normally you'll want to keep a checkmark in this box unless you live in one of those enlightened midwestern American towns (or most of the rest of the world) where people think that DST is hogwash.

Regional Settings

Being worldly folk, programmers at Microsoft have built in the ability for Windows 95 and regionally savvy programs to display and use international variations of numbering, date, currency, and calendaring schemes. You can specify and customize these settings in the Regional Settings Properties window, shown in Figure 10.2.

The key phrase here is *regionallysavvyprograms.* In order for the settings in the Regional Settings Properties window to matter, your software must know what

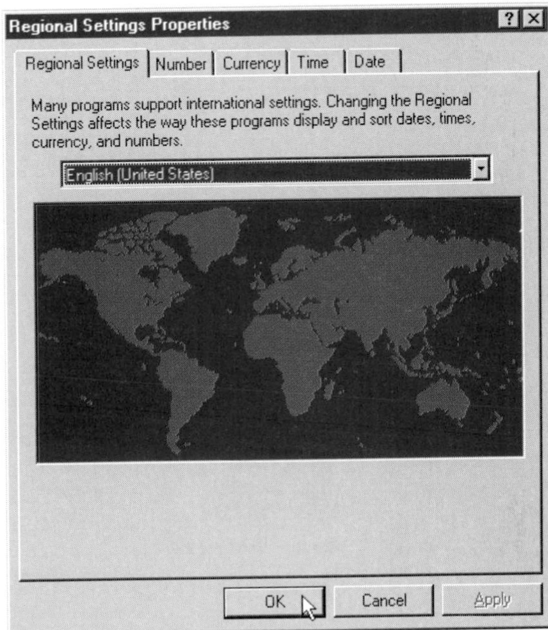

Figure 10.2 Use the Regional Settings Properties window to specify region-specific number, currency, and calendar settings for your programs

to do about them. To reach, and possibly experiment with regional settings, follow these steps:

1. Choose Settings from the Start menu.
2. Click on Control Panel.
3. Double-click the Regional Settings icon.
4. Click a tab to bring it forward.

Mouse Behavior

As you might recall, it's possible to swap the function of your mouse buttons. Even though the feature was designed primarily to make clicking easier for left-handed people, some of my right-handed friends prefer to swap buttons too.

What you might not know is that you can also control the double-click speed, and modify other point and click parameters. To avoid repeating myself, let's open the Mouse Properties window once, and then just deal with each of the four tabs.

Opening the Mouse Properties Window

Although I refer to mice in this section, you can just as easily make similar adjustments to the performance of trackballs, touchpads, and those little thingies found in the middle of keyboards on some notebook computers. Unless there is a specific Control Panel icon for your pointing device, use the Mouse icon.

Follow these steps to open the Mouse Properties window:

1. Choose Settings from the Start menu.
2. Click on Control Panel.
3. Double-click on the Mouse icon.

The Mouse Properties window shown in Figure 10.3 will open, and you'll see four tabs that you can click on to initiate changes to your mouse's functions:

- The *Buttons* tab lets you change button functions and click-speed sensitivity.
- The *Pointers* tab lets you change the appearance of onscreen mouse pointers (not recommended).

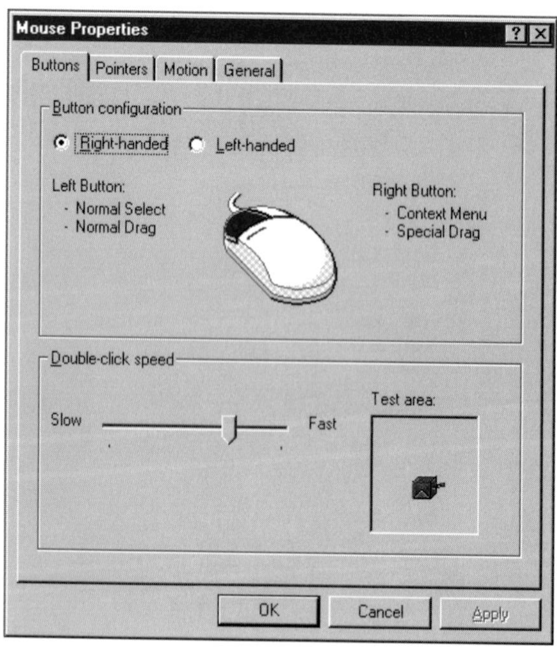

Figure 10.3 The Mouse Properties window

- The *Motion* tab lets you adjust pointer speed and add pointer "trails" for portable computers.
- The *General* tab lets you pick from a variety of mouse drivers.

Swapping Mouse Buttons

Normally, the left mouse button (sometimes the top button on laptops) is used for everyday pointing and clicking, while the right (or bottom) button is used for special tasks like revealing shortcut menus. To reverse the buttons, follow these steps:

1. Open the Mouse Properties window.
2. Click the Buttons tab if it is not already in the foreground.
3. Choose Left-handed to reverse the normal button functions.
4. Click Apply.
5. Click OK.

If you accidentally swap buttons (or intentionally swap them and then realize that you hate it), you will need to tell your brain to use the "wrong" button long enough to get back to the Mouse Properties Buttons tab. Button swapping is a mean trick to play on someone. Just don't say you learned it here.

Setting Double-Click Speed

By measuring the time lapse between your two clicks, Windows decides if you've truly double-clicked, or just clicked twice. Beginners sometimes fail to double-click because they don't click twice quickly enough. Impatient people like to be able to double-click really quickly and then click twice rapidly without *that* act being construed as double-clicking. There's a setting in the Buttons tab of the Mouse Properties window that tells Windows which type of clicker you are. Unfortunately, it is not labeled Beginner and Impatient but Slow and Fast:

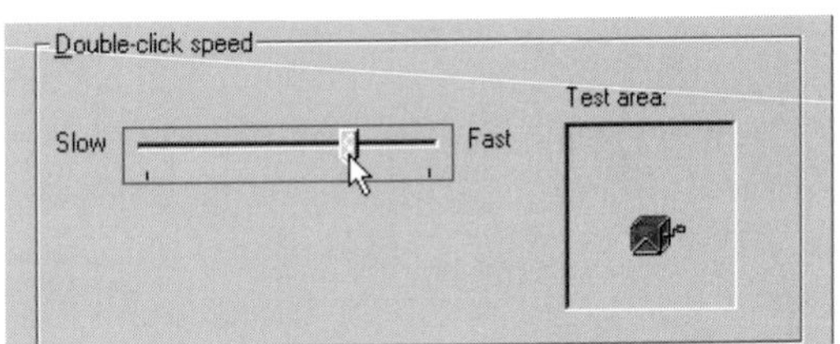

Move the slider toward Slow if you are a beginner, or toward Fast if you are a hotshot. Be forewarned that the extreme right setting is so fast that you might need to change your medication to accomplish a successful double-click. Fortunately, there is an amusing way to test various click settings. Read on.

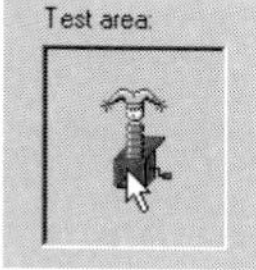

The Clicking Speed Test Area

The little jack-in-the-box icon contains—you're ahead of me, huh?—a boy named Jack. When you double-click properly on Jack's box (given the current speed settings), Jack appears. Click properly again and that boy's outta here. If you click too slowly, you get Jack ——. Well, you know. Jack does not behave. Try various double-click speed settings while seeing if you can get Jack to come out and play. Set the slider for the fastest (right-most) setting that you're comfortable with. Click OK to save the setting and close the dialog box.

Pointer Schemes

You can change the appearance of pointers both in Windows and in your applications by adding or changing pointer schemes. Why, I do not know. Life is already so confusing that the last thing *I* need is pointers that look different from those in all my manuals. Skip the Pointer scheme and go out for a walk or a beer or something. Geez.

Pointer Speed

Now here's a setting tab I really appreciate! The Motion tab lets you adjust the corresponding motions of your mouse and the onscreen pointer:

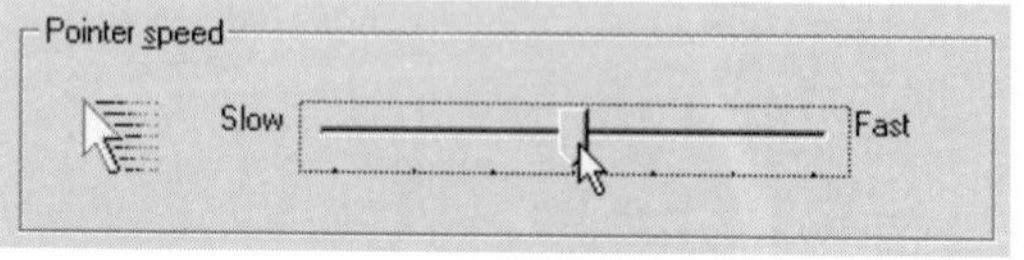

That is to say, with the slider set to the left end of the scale, you've gotta move your mouse a fair distance to get the onscreen pointer to move perceptibly. This is great for beginners, or for close work, or for shaky hands. Moving the speed adjuster to the *right* makes the old mouse pointer fly. This is great if you have a big screen and a diamond cutter's hand-eye coordination. To experiment with different settings, try this:

1. Click the Motion tab if necessary to bring it forward.
2. Remember where the Pointer speed gizmo is currently set.
3. Drag it right (Fast) or left (Slow).
4. Click the Apply button to preview the change in speed.
5. Test by moving the mouse pointer around on the screen. Point first to the top and then to the bottom of your screen. Now point to something tiny.
6. Play for a while. Give your eyes and hand a chance to get calibrated. What do you think? If you hate the change, return to the original setting and click Apply again.

CAUTION

If you purchase a new trackball or other pointing device and install the software that comes with it, the pointer settings might be controlled by that software. Be sure to check the manual.

Some brats refer to pointer trails as "mouse droppings." Ehew!

Pointer Trails

Some laptops have displays that can't keep up with rapid motion—like the movement of the mouse pointer. Sometimes the pointer seems to disappear on these machines. It's crazy-making. If you turn on mouse trails, you'll see multiple mouse pointer images giving you some indication of where the pointer has been, and perhaps even a clue as to where it is going:

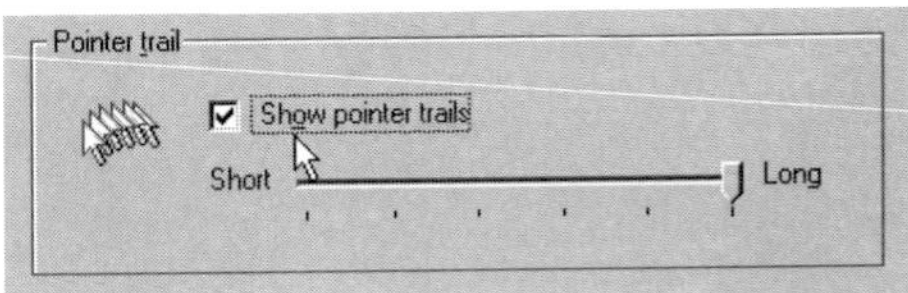

The General Tab in the Mouse Properties Window

You use the General tab to change the mouse driver software used with Windows 95.

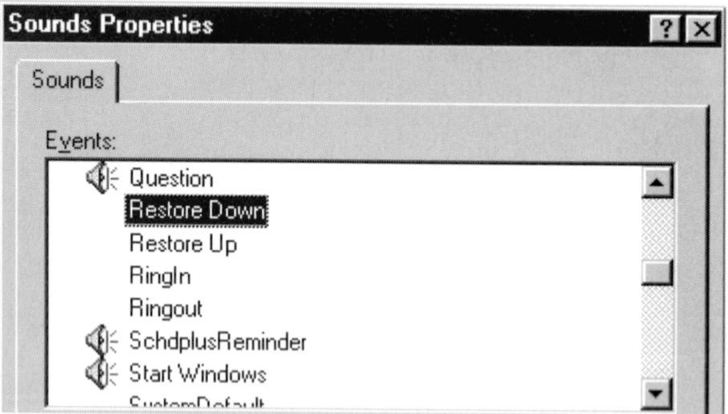

Chances are you can live a long and happy life without ever visiting this tab. But 'cha never know. When installing a new pointing device, check its documentation to see if you must make any changes herein.

Keyboard Behavior

The Keyboard Properties window lets you change repeat-key rates, keyboard layouts for different keyboards, language settings for international keyboards, and get this—the blink rate of your insertion point. (No, I don't know why, so please don't ask.)

Opening the Keyboard Properties Window

Here are the four simple steps you use to open the Keyboard Properties window shown in Figure 10.4:

1. Choose Settings from the Start menu.
2. Click Control Panel.
3. Double-click the Keyboard icon.

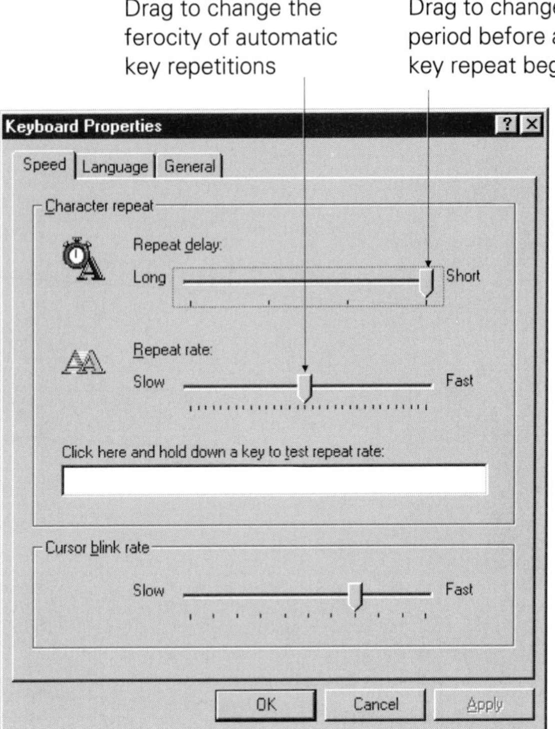

Figure 10.4 The Keyboard Properties dialog box

Key Repeat Delay

In most programs, if you hold down a key long enough, the key will start generating its corresponding character over and over until you let up on the key. For example, in a Word document if I type "Oh, baby" that's what I get. But if I want to imitate Barry White, I could hold down the H key for a while and get "Ohhhhhhhhhh, baby." The length of time I need to hold down the key before the groanin' begins is the *repeat delay* time. The speed with which those breathy h's appear on the screen once they get started is the *repeat rate.* I like the default settings just fine, but if you're in a mood for change, you can follow these steps:

1. Visit the Keyboard Properties window.
2. Choose the Speed tab.
3. Move the Repeat delay slider left to increase the time before the machine gun action starts, or right to start the repeating sooner. (Again, left for beginners, right for the impatient.)

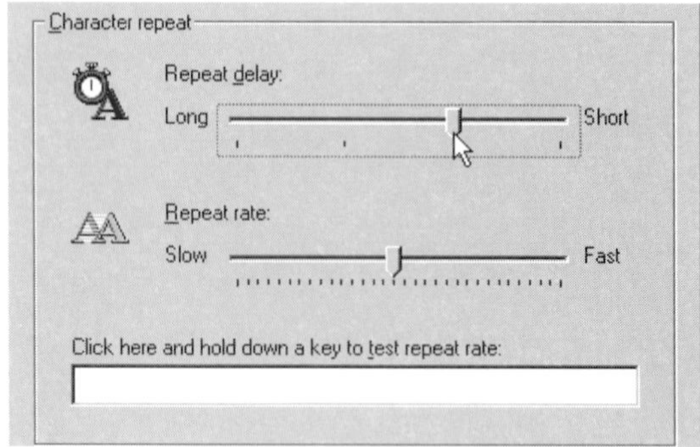

4. Click in the "Click here and hold down a key" box to test the delay time.
5. Change the repeat rate too, if you like. You can test this effect also.
6. Ohhhhhhh, baby, baby.

Screen Appearance

"Cool screen. How'd you do that?" Have you ever suffered from screen envy? The ultimate computer facelift is to change the background, screen saver, and the colors of various onscreen elements.

Changing your screen's appearance can also burn up a lot of precious time. Why, some government employees I know spend all day playing with this stuff. (Which might be a good thing for our country, come to think of it.)

So, busy person, are you gonna skip this section and get back to learning productive stuff? I didn't think so. I'll keep it brief.

You make the changes in the Display Properties window, which is easily reached with the right mouse button. Follow these steps:

1. Right-click anywhere on the desktop.
2. Choose Properties in the resulting shortcut menu. The Display Properties window appears.
3. Click various tabs to explore the possibilities (described next).

Desktop Patterns and Wallpaper

You redesign your desktop's appearance either by picking patterns and colors or by choosing graphic files containing pictures of the wife and kids, or your favorite firefighter, or your boat, or whatever. You can also combine these effects so that, for instance, you can superimpose a photo on a patterned desktop.

DEFINITION

***graphic files**: Files containing images. Frequently made up of dots and with a filename ending with the extension .bmp. Created with paint or drawing programs, or imported with a scanner or other image-capturing device.*

Using Desktop Patterns

Windows comes with a selection of desktop patterns. Choose one from the Pattern list in the Background tab of the Display Properties window. (Phew!) Some of the possibilities, like the one in Figure 10.5, make me dizzy.

Here's how to select a desktop pattern:

1. Scroll and click to pick a pattern in the Pattern list.
2. Your selection appears in the sample monitor.
3. If you like it, click Apply.

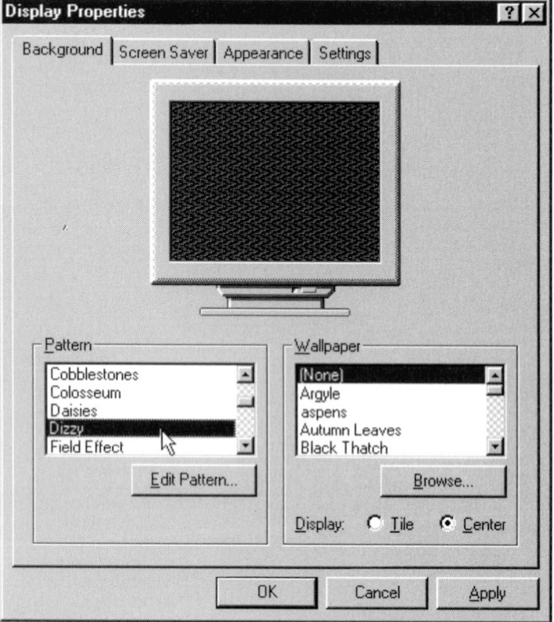

Figure 10.5 Windows 95 offers a truly dizzying variety of desktop patterns

CAUTION

The background settings should not be so distracting that you can't see your icons and read their names. Restraint is often a good thing.

Using Wallpaper

You specify wallpaper by picking a graphic file, then choosing to either center the graphic or repeat it over and over and over until it fills the screen:

1. From the Background tab of the Display Properties window, select a wallpaper style from the Wallpaper list.
2. Click on Tile to repeat the pattern all over your desktop.

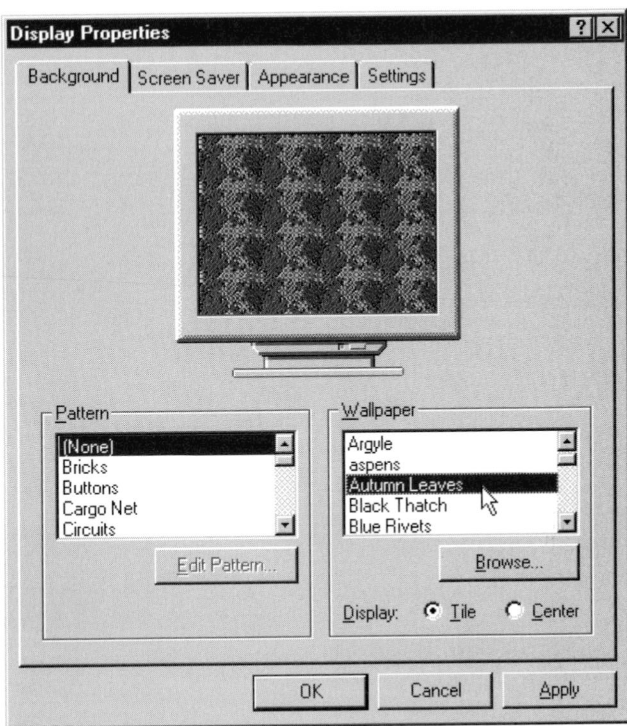

As you will soon see, you can also change the color of patterns and wallpaper and such. (See the upcoming section "Windows Color Schemes.")

3. Watch the sample, but realize that the big desktop will look quite different.
4. Click Apply to see the wallpaper on your desktop.
5. Choose another wallpaper style, or click OK if you are happy.

If the wallpaper you've chosen doesn't cover the whole desktop, you will see a border defined by the Patterns setting described earlier. Oh yes, color settings come into play, too.

Editing Screen Patterns

Here's a great time waster. You can edit patterns by following these steps:

1. Select a pattern in the Pattern list.
2. Click Edit Pattern. The Pattern Editor window appears.

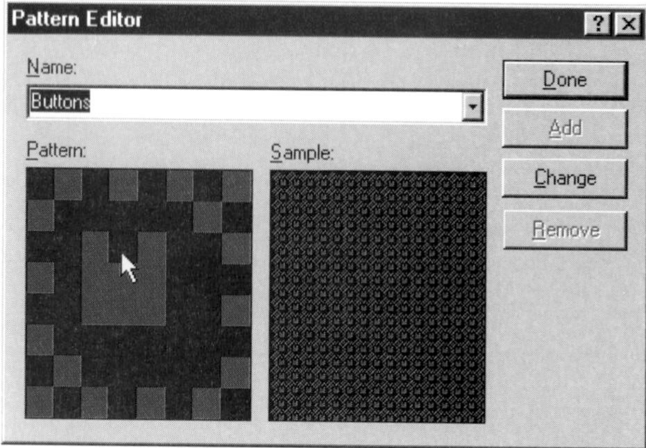

3. Click in the Pattern window to toggle off/on the little squares corresponding to each pixel in the pattern. Keep one eye on the Sample window to see how your edits affect the look of the pattern.
4. Click Change, and then click Done to close the Pattern Editor window.
5. Click Apply to apply the edited pattern to your desktop.

EXPERT ADVICE

Of course, your screen doesn't have to have a desktop or a wallpaper pattern! For truly busy people who don't have time to fiddle with such things, or who don't want to use system memory displaying ornamental graphics, each of these lists contains a (None) option.

Using Graphic Files as Desktop Images

If you would like to display a graphic (a photo or whatever) on your screen as part of your desktop decoration, follow these general steps:

1. Make sure the graphic file is a bitmap file with the file extension .bmp.
2. It's nice, but not necessary to have this file (or a copy of it) in your Windows folder.

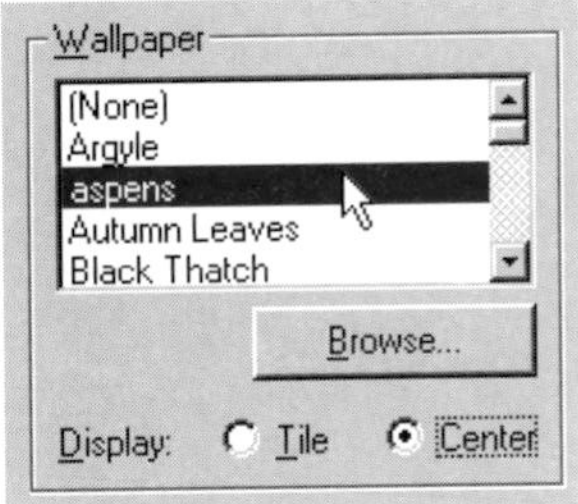

3. Scroll the Wallpaper list. If the file is in your Windows directory and is properly named, you'll see it listed. (If you don't see its name, use the Browse button to locate the file.)
4. Once you've located the file, double-click its name. You will see the file in the miniature window.
5. Experiment with the Tile and Center options. Pick one.
6. Click Apply if you wish to see the file on your full-sized desktop.
7. Click OK. Your desktop should be decorated. For example, here's a bitmap photo surrounded by a pattern:

You might want to change the Pattern setting or color scheme. If so, keep reading; we're going to show you how.

upgrade note

Windows 95 lets you change the colors of fewer screen elements than did prior Windows versions, so your options have been limited. On the other hand, the process is less confusing now.

As the easily distracted among you have probably figured out, you can change the color of individual elements of the Windows interface, and even name your own schemes. Cool, huh? Now GET BACK TO WORK!

Windows Color Schemes

Windows lets you change many of the colors used for things like title bars, onscreen text, etc. The boys and girls in Redmond have even created and named some predefined color schemes for you. See what happens if you follow these steps:

1. Open the Display Properties window by right-clicking your desktop and picking Properties from the Shortcut menu.
2. Choose the Appearance tab.
3. Click in the Scheme box to reveal its drop-down list.

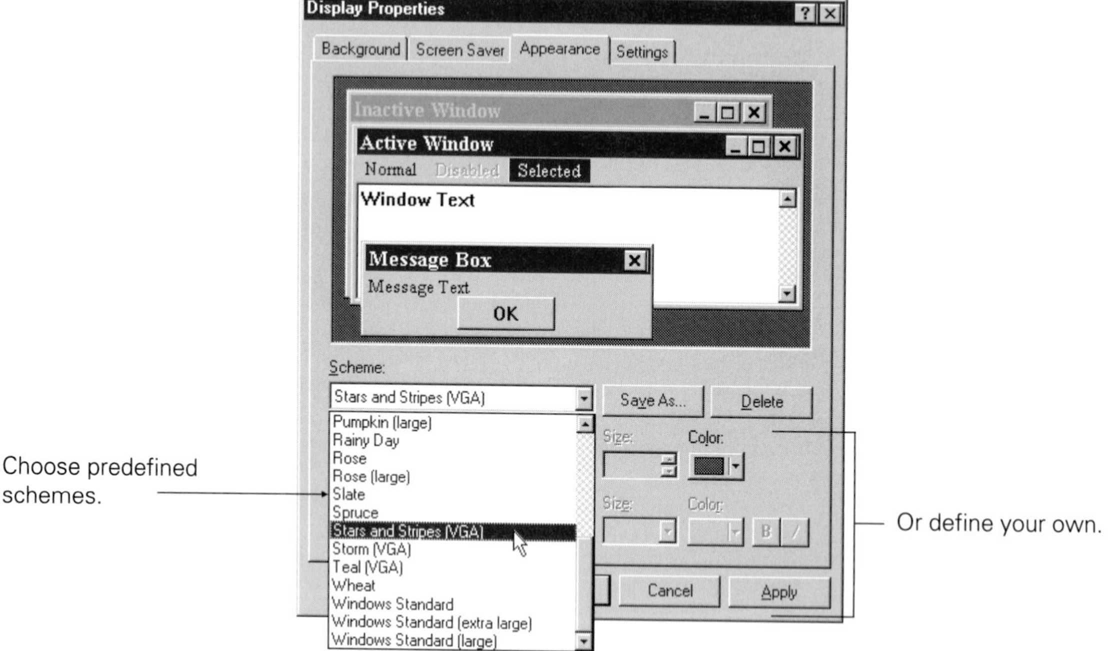

4. Scroll up and down the list to preview the various predefined schemes.
5. Press ENTER when you find one you like.
6. Click Apply.
7. Run your favorite programs and see what you think.

You can always revert back to the Windows Standard scheme if you wish by choosing Windows Standard from the Scheme list.

Screen Savers

First, let's admit this fallacy: Screen savers probably don't save screens. Mostly they entertain, and perhaps they hide your work from prying eyes when you step away from your desk. That said, here's how to pick and enable them.

1. Open the Display Properties window by right-clicking your desktop and picking Properties from the Shortcut menu.
2. Choose the Screen Saver tab.
3. Click in the Screen Saver list to reveal a drop-down list.

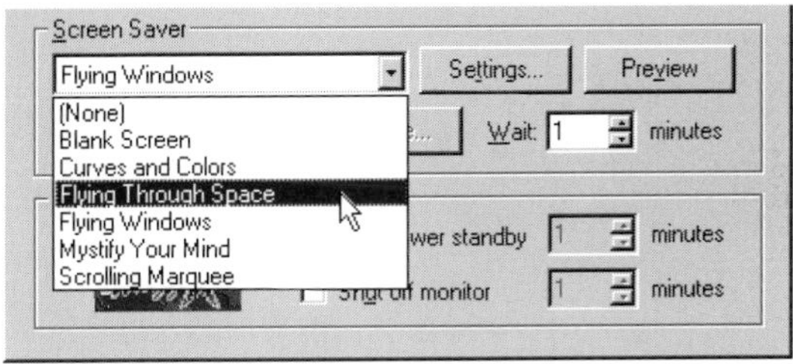

4. Use the UP ARROW and DOWN ARROW to preview the various screen savers.
5. Press ENTER when you find one you like.
6. Visit the various settings for the chosen saver by clicking the Settings button and making some choices (how many flying logos, how fast, etc.).
7. The Preview button will fill your screen with your latest plaything. Moving the mouse will bring you back to the Display Properties dialog box.
8. If your monitor supports energy-saving technology, you might want to enable it.

Shutting Off Screen Savers

To shut off screen savers, follow these steps:

1. Open the Display Properties window by right-clicking your desktop and picking Properties from the Shortcut menu.

2. Choose the Screen Saver tab.
3. Click in the Screen Saver list to reveal the drop-down list.
4. Choose (None) from the list.

Screen Resolution

Screen resolution increases or decreases the effective workspace on your desktop by either shrinking or enlarging the size of everything on your screen. The higher the resolution, the more stuff you can arrange on your desk, but the smaller it will all be.

The "standard" Windows screen resolution is 64 × 480 dots, or *pixels*. Some screen and display electronics combinations only support 640 × 480. This is the case with many of the built-in displays on laptops.

Other display configurations can support 800 × 600 or more pixels. Whether you can see anything useful at these higher settings depends upon your hardware and eyesight, and what you plan to do. I am a fan of 800 × 600 pixels on a 17-inch display.

If you constantly wish you had more landscape on which to pile windows, folders, and shortcut icons, and if your computer supports it, try increasing your screen resolution.

Assigning Sounds to Computer Events

The installer puts only a few of the many Microsoft-provided sound schemes on your hard disk. Use the Install/Remove software techniques described in Chapter 8 to add the rest if you have the inclination, time, and disk space. Microsoft Plus! offers additional sound files worth exploring.

If your computer has contemporary sound features (Microsoft-compatible, SoundBlaster-compatible, or similar audio capabilities), you can replace the boring beeps and grunts associated with various Windows events. What could be more amusing than hearing Pee Wee Herman say "I meant to do that" each time your computer crashes? Or how about a clap of thunder whenever you start Windows? Well, you can purchase files containing sound bytes like these, or use the ones Microsoft provides. You can also record your own (see Chapter 13)—but not till you get some real work done. Follow these steps to get started with existing sound files, busy person:

1. Choose Settings from the Start menu.
2. Select Control Panel.

STEP BY STEP Increasing Screen Resolution

1 **Right-click your desktop and pick Properties from the shortcut menu to bring up the Display Properties dialog box.**

2 **Choose the Settings tab.**

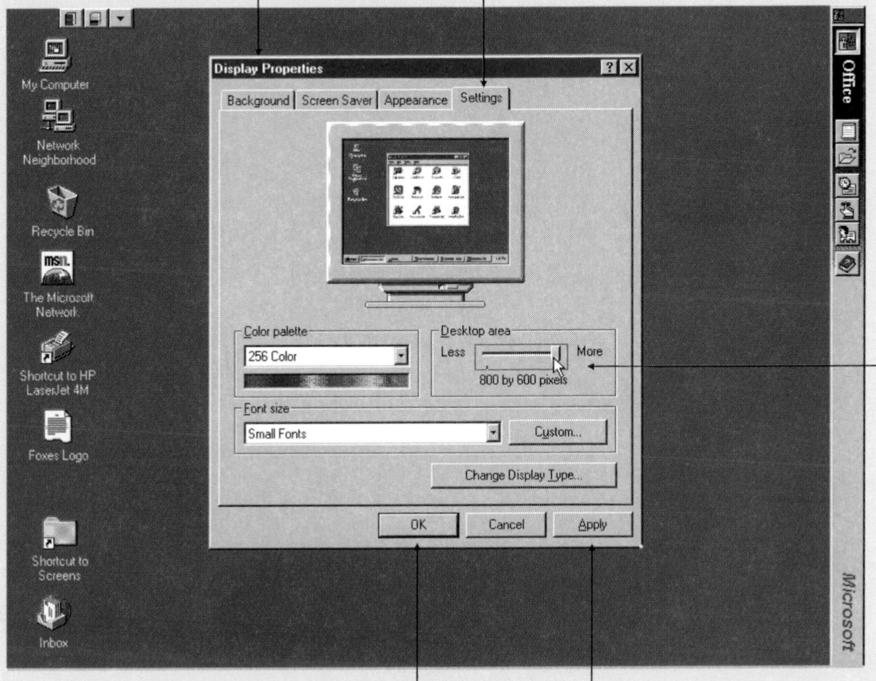

3 **Drag the "Desktop area" slider to a larger number. (Larger numbers let you display smaller pictures of more stuff, while smaller numbers enlarge what's on your screen but leave you with less room overall.)**

4 **Click Apply to see what you think. Follow the onscreen prompts while you and Windows figure out if this trick will work with your hardware.**

5 **Click OK when you've finished.**

3. Double-click Sounds.
4. If you see a list of events, and if you have useful sound hardware, some of the events will have little speakers next to them. This probably means your sound hardware is at least potentially functional.

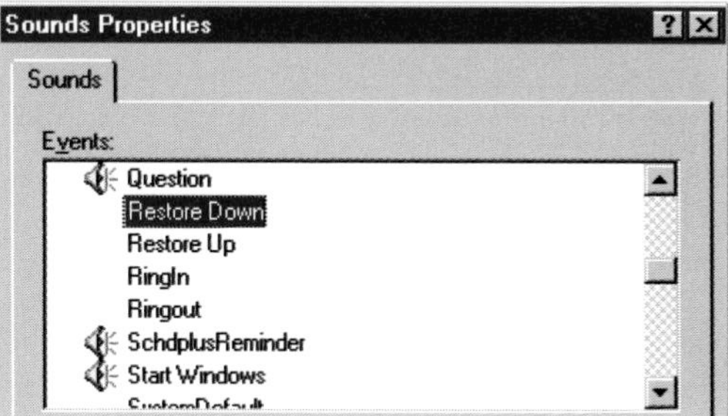

5. Scroll through the list and click an event with a speaker next to it. (If you have programs like AOL's and CompuServe's that produce sounds, their event sounds will be listed here along with Windows 95's sounds.)

Previewing Sounds

There are several easy ways to hear sounds before assigning them to events. Here's my favorite:

1. When you see a sound event with a speaker next to it, click to select it.
2. Click the Preview button.
3. You should hear the sound play through your speakers.
4. If this works, use the drop-down name list to choose other sounds, clicking Preview to hear them.
5. If you don't hear anything, make sure your volume control(s) is turned up, and if you have external speakers, check that they are properly cabled and powered.

SHORTCUT

A quick way to preview your sounds is to open your Windows folder, then open the Media folder and double-click sound icons that interest you.

Choosing Sounds for Events

If you'd like to hear a particular sound play whenever an event occurs (whenever you start or quit Windows 95, for example), here's how to set it up:

1. Open the Sound Properties window by double-clicking the Sounds icon in the Control Panel.
2. Scroll to select an event (Exit Windows, for example).
3. Scroll in the name list to pick a sound, or click Browse to locate sounds not stored in the Windows\Media folder.
4. Click to select the sound, as shown in Figure 10.6.
5. Click the Preview button to hear the sound.
6. Choose different sounds of additional events, and replace some sounds with others, if you like.
7. Click OK when done and test the sounds.

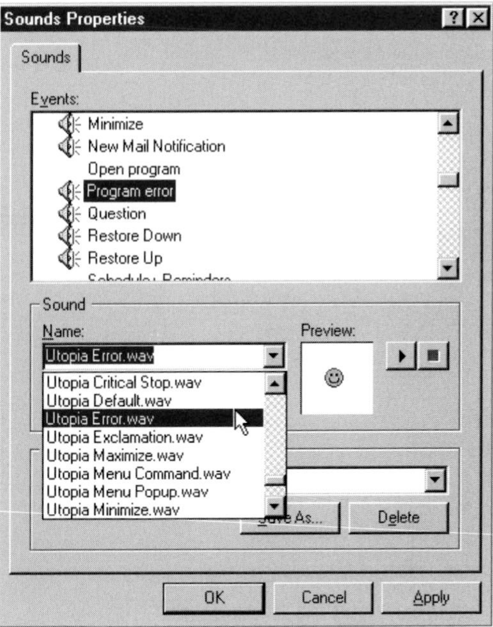

Figure 10.6 It's easy to assign different sounds to various computer events

SHORTCUT

After you've changed sound settings, you can create sound schemes by clicking Save As in the Sound Properties dialog box, and then naming the collection of sounds as a scheme. The scheme name then appears in the Schemes list, so you can easily recall the settings at any time.

Sound Schemes

You can create and save multiple sound schemes for your computer, then select them from the Sound Properties dialog box when you need them. You could have quiet, unobtrusive sounds for meetings, perhaps, and rude sounds for parties. Microsoft has provided some sound schemes for you. You'll read about these next.

Sources of Sounds

Don't miss the sound schemes provided with Windows 95. They are provided on your installation disks, but not automatically installed. These include the schemes Jungle, Musica, Robotz, and Utopia. If you've purchased Microsoft Plus!, you'll find fascinating sounds scattered everywhere on the disc. Use the Find command and search for *.wav to locate them. Double-click icons in the Find list to preview them.

The Internet, AOL, CompuServe, and most electronic flea markets are all abuzz with sound files that you can download. What you need are files with the extension .wav. Because sound files are often very large, it is common for dial-up services to distribute them as compressed files. So, you might need a utility like WinZip to expand them after downloading. Have fun!

Customizing Your Modem's Dialing Settings

You can have one or more modems connected to your computer. Windows 95's plug-and-play feature usually does a fine job of detecting modems and installing the necessary drivers and system settings.

If you've just installed a new modem and you can't get it to work, begin by reading any Readme files that came with the hardware. Then try calling tech support.

However, you *will* want to tell Windows something about your dialing preferences, particularly if you use programs that make use of this handy capability.

Locations, Area Codes, Outside Lines, and More

The Dialing Properties box lets you set up dialing instructions for various locations. These settings tell Windows what to do about getting an outside line (dial 9?, 8?).

EXPERT ADVICE

If you use a calling card to make long-distance calls, you can teach Windows the particulars of that process to save yourself the bother of reentering your account code and PIN each time you make a long-distance call.

If you have a desktop machine that never moves, you'll probably set up only one location. But if you are a road warrior, your laptop might have many location settings—one for the office; one for the pay phone in that Boulder, Colorado, jazz bar; another for your cell phone connections; and so on. When you move your computer to a new location, you'll need to visit the Dialing Properties dialog box and set up dialing instructions for that location. To learn how to do this, just follow these steps:

1. Choose Settings from the Start menu.
2. Click Control Panel.
3. Double-click Modems.
4. Click the General tab to bring it to the front if necessary.
5. Click Dialing Properties.
6. In the Dialing Properties window, either make changes to the default location, or click New to define a new location (Home, Office, etc.).
7. Click OK to save the changes.

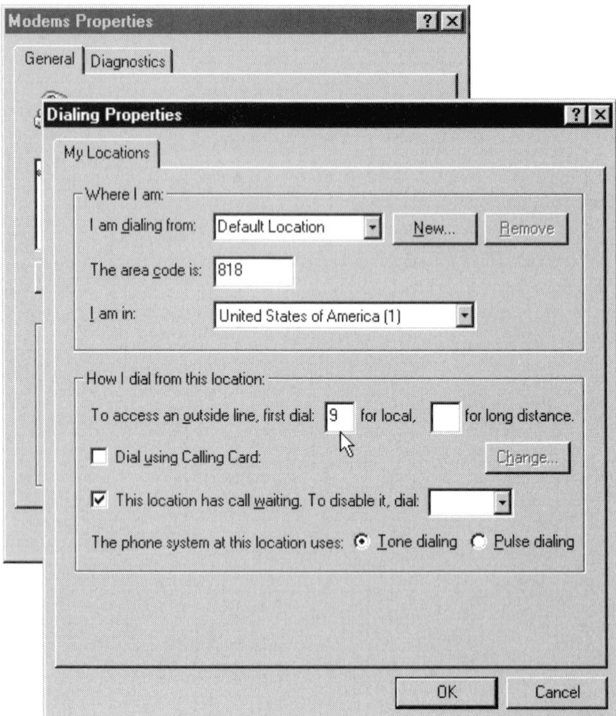

Options for Physically Challenged Users

Microsoft's Dialer accessory uses these settings too. Read about it, and more about modems, in Chapter 12.

Windows 95 can be used by people with a wide variety of physical challenges. Here are examples of the built-in assistance that Microsoft provides:

- Support for alternative input devices
- Audible signals for keystrokes
- Flashing screen elements in place of sounds
- Keyboard replacements for mouse actions (including clicking and dragging)
- Large and colorful fonts for the visually challenged
- Ways to let Windows know to ignore brief, unintentional keystrokes

To learn more about Windows 95 accessibility options, check the online help topic *accessibility*. You can also double-click the Accessibility Options icon in the control panel to display the Accessibility Properties window shown in Figure 10.7, where you'll find additional information.

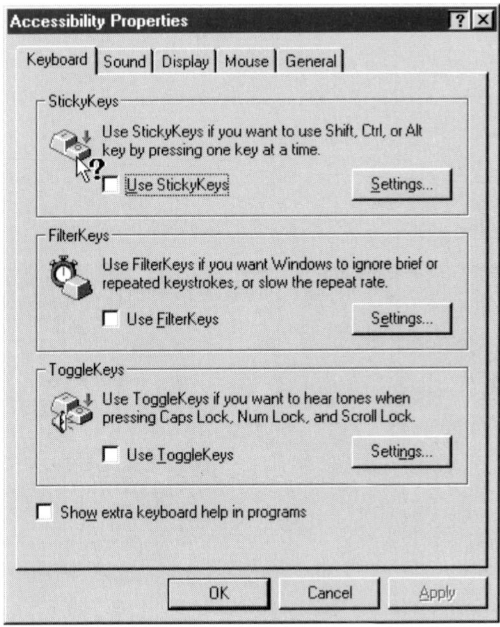

Figure 10.7 Physically challenged users can customize Windows to better meet their needs and preferences

You can find more information about Windows 95 accessibility options on a variety of Internet and other well-known resources.

Adding Items to Your Send To Menu

Fresh out of the box, your Send To menu does not offer many choices. You can quickly send things to a floppy drive, and perhaps your Briefcase (if that feature's installed), and maybe to the fax modem. But it is possible to add other choices to your Send To menu. For example, if there is a folder you use all the time (like the My Documents folder), be it on your hard disk or clear across the network, you can add that folder's name to the Send To menu. Thereafter, to copy things to the desired folder, simply select them and pick the appropriate Send To choice. Here is the general procedure:

1. Create a shortcut for the item you wish to add to the Send To menu (a frequently used folder, or some shared resource, for example).
2. Open the Windows folder by double-clicking.
3. Drag the shortcut you've created in step 1 into the Send To folder.

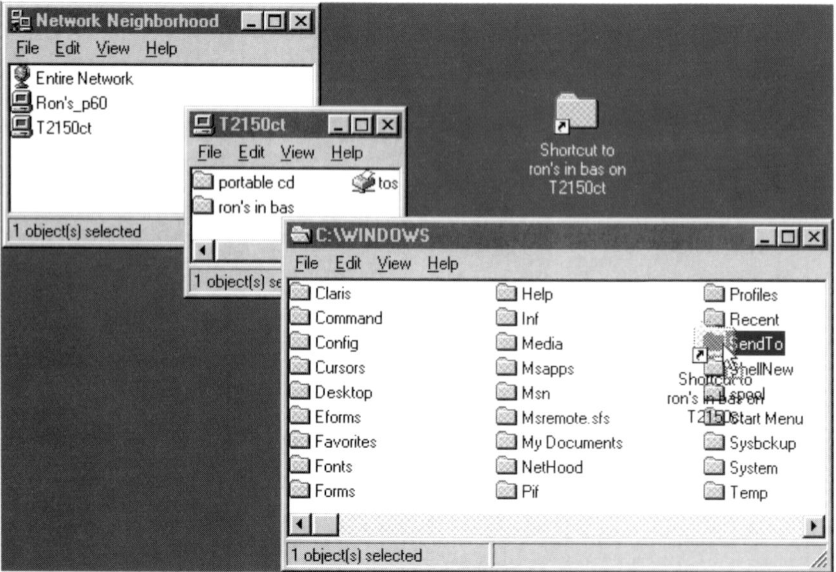

4. Rename the shortcut so that it reads the way you want it to in the submenu (perhaps remove the words "Shortcut to").

EXPERT ADVICE

It's often handy to add your own destinations to the Send To menu. For example, you can add networked disks, or a frequently used folder.

Other Ways to Improve Your Computing Experience

Here are some other things you can do to help better organize and personalize your computer:

- Develop a disk organization (folder) strategy for filing your documents. For example, create separate folders for your personal and business correspondence, and others for your home and business spreadsheets. Or, if you have many customers or clients, create folders and perhaps subfolders for each. (See Chapter 4 to learn more about organizing your disks.)
- Create a backup plan, format *and label* the necessary disks and tapes, then write down the procedures to make it easier to follow them until they become second nature. (See Chapter 6 for more information.)
- Remove unwanted programs and unnecessary files to save yourself some disk space. (Chapter 8 has the details.)
- Install all the fonts you think you might need, and remove the ones you'll never use. (See Chapter 9 for more information.)
- Create an anti-virus strategy. Purchase the necessary software and mark your calendar to remind yourself to obtain monthly (or weekly) updates that will keep your virus checker able to spot the latest threats. (Chapter 6 talks about virus prevention.)

At this point, you know most of the basics. Take some time now to personalize your computer, and set up your disks properly. Next stop—networks, where you will learn how to collaborate with your partners in crime.

CHAPTER

11

Networks

INCLUDES

- What you'll need for networking
- Terms you should know
- Sharing files
- Sharing printers
- Shutting down your networked computer
- Troubleshooting your network

Enable Peer-to-Peer Networking ➤ *pp. 268-274*

1. Install the necessary hardware and Microsoft file-sharing software.
2. Double-click the Network icon in the control panel.
3. Click the Access Control tab.
4. Pick Share-level or User-level and assign passwords or create a list of authorized users.
5. Click the Identification tab and identify your computer.
6. Click the Configuration tab and enable sharing.
7. Restart when prompted to do so.
8. Right-click the icon for the resource to be shared (hard disk, CD-ROM drive, folder, printer, etc.).
9. Choose Sharing.
10. Click the Sharing tab and enable sharing.
11. Specify sharing options and passwords.
12. Click Apply, and then OK.

Share Your Hard Disks ➤ *pp. 273-274*

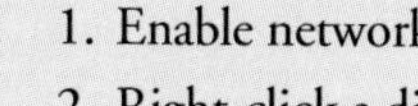

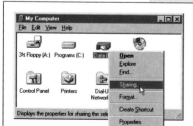

1. Enable networking.
2. Right-click a disk or folder icon.
3. Choose Sharing.
4. Click the Sharing tab in the resulting Properties dialog box to bring it to the top if necessary.
5. Choose Shared As.
6. Enter a share name, optional comments, and password(s).
7. Specify full, read-only, or password-dependent access.
8. Click Apply, and then OK. The icon for the shared item will have a hand and sleeve at its bottom.

Access Other People's Hard Disks ➤ *pp. 275-277*

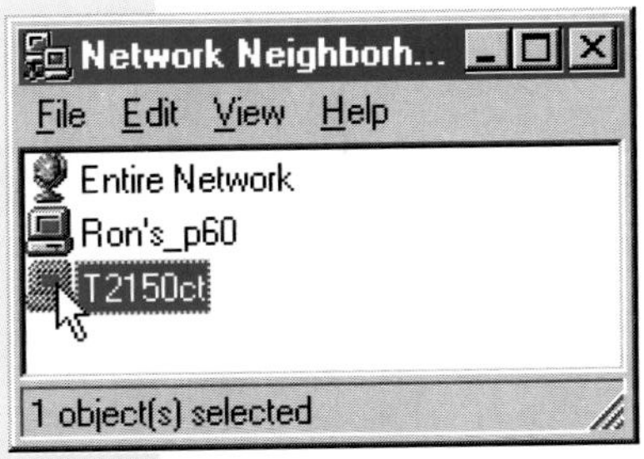

1. Double-click the Network Neighborhood icon.
2. Double-click icons for available disks and folders, opening windows as necessary.
3. Double-click files to launch applications or otherwise treat file icons as if they were your own, taking into consideration any access restrictions imposed by the owner.

Use Other People's Printers ➤ *pp. 278-279*

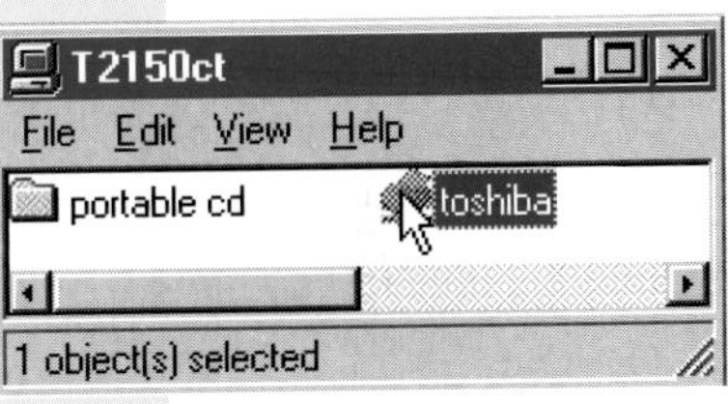

1. Make certain both computers are powered up and running Windows 95. Printer sharing must be enabled. Be sure the printer is ready.
2. Double-click the Network Neighborhood icon.
3. Double-click the icon for the computer whose printer you wish to share.
4. Windows will offer to install drivers if they are not already on your hard disk. (Have your Windows disks or CD handy.)
5. Print the optional test page when asked to do so.

Share Your Printer ➤ *pp. 279-280*

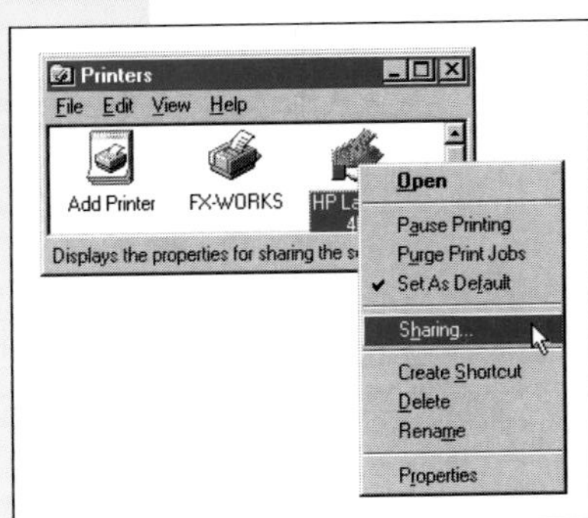

1. Right-click the icon for the printer you wish to share.
2. Choose Sharing from the shortcut menu.
3. In the printer's Properties dialog box's Sharing tab, click Shared As.
4. Name the printer something meaningful.
5. Password-protect it if you want to restrict access.
6. Click Apply, and then OK.
7. Tell authorized users the password.
8. Leave your computer and printer on during the hours when others will need to print.

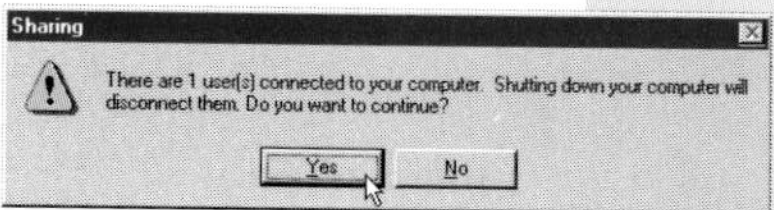

Shut Down Networked Computers ➤ pp. 281-282

- Warn other users who might be using your resources before you shut down.
- Remember that shutting down a computer while users have your files open can damage your files.

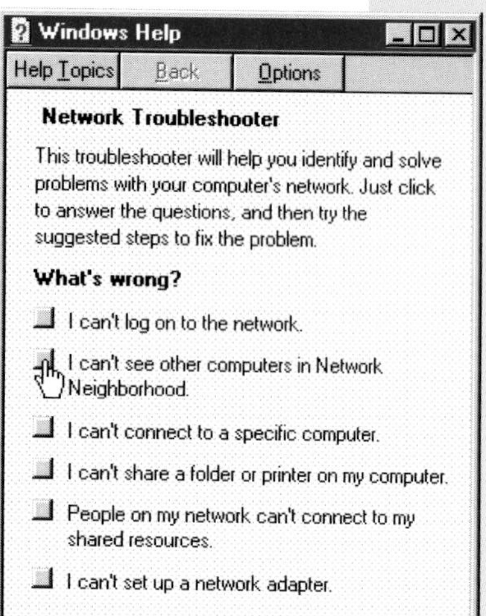

Troubleshoot Network Problems ➤ p. 284

1. Ask yourself "what's changed?"
2. Check all network cabling.
3. Check the computers of those with whom you cannot network.
4. In the Find tab of Windows online help, type **network trouble** and double-click Troubleshooting Network Problems.
5. Click the buttons that correspond to your situation, and follow the directions that appear.

Today, many large networks are a combination of multiple smaller Local Area Networks and dial-in users. These communities of often far-flung networked users are called Wide Area Networks, *or* WANs.

Network is one of those words that computerists use as both a noun and a verb. People also refer to networks as Local Area Networks, or LANs. A network refers to a collection of specially equipped computers and the wiring and software used to interconnect them. The resulting rat's nest of wires and circuits lets us share the contents of our disks with coworkers; maintain a centralized library of up-to-date forms, databases, and documents for use by everyone; share other resources (like printers, CD-ROM drives, etc.); back up files from many local hard disks to a single, centralized disk or tape; and exchange electronic mail.

This process of sharing data and equipment is often called *networking.* A network can consist of just two computers on the same desk, or a vast, global collection like those used for airline reservations systems.

EXPERT ADVICE

When ordering a new computer, purchase a preinstalled network adapter. Then it will be ready to network when you are.

What You'll Need for Peer-to-Peer Networking

To use the Windows 95 peer-to-peer networking features, you need two or more computers, and perhaps a printer; a network adapter for each computer; wiring to interconnect the network adapters; Windows 95; a sense of humor; and a little patience.

Be sure your network adapters are Windows 95 compatible, will work with your computers, and will support the wiring scheme you've chosen. Spend a few extra dollars for name-brand network adapters (3Com, IBM, etc.). If the adapter is advertised as Microsoft Plug-and-Play approved, so much the better.

A Warning About Network Card Software

One problem with network adapter cards is that many (especially those you find at swap meets) are designed to work with older systems like Microsoft Windows for Workgroups. The instructions that come with the hardware might assume that you are running Windows for Workgroups, or NetWare, or whatever, rather than Windows 95. If there is no specific section in the hardware documentation pertaining to Windows 95 installation, *disregard* the software installation instructions that come with network cards. (Leave those floppies alone, busy person!) Instead, just plug in the hardware, and restart your computer. Windows 95's plug-and-play feature will probably notice the new network card and, with luck, will recognize it and take care of the piddly details for you.

Using Modem, Serial, or Parallel Connections for Networking

If you'd like to know more about direct connections and modems, see Chapter 12; you also can search online help for the topics Direct Cable Connection and Dial-Up Networking.

In place of network adapter cards and cables, it is possible to use the serial or parallel ports on your computer for *direct* network connections. You also can access shared computers via modem. Because most folks already have their serial and parallel ports working on other things, and because modem connections, although very helpful on the road, can be slow and disruptive when used in the office, I recommend spending a few bucks on Ethernet network adapters.

Setting Up a Simple Peer-to-Peer Network

Once you have the network cards installed, and the wiring is properly connected, you are ready to enable and test Windows 95 peer-to-peer networking. At least one of the machines on your network needs to be set to share its resources (disks, printers, CD-ROM drives, etc.). Other computers on the network need to be defined as *clients* in order to use shared resources.

Each of your Windows 95 computers can share all or some of its resources. And each of your computers can act as a client with other computers on the network. Computers can both share and *be* clients simultaneously. You can specify nearly endless sharing options to suit your needs, using techniques described in this chapter. But for starters, let's get two computers working together.

CAUTION

For the following exercise, pick a computer that does not contain confidential information on its disk(s), since we are going to set up full and easy access to an entire disk for starters.

Prepare to Share

With at least two computers properly wired to each other, visit the one containing files and other resources you wish to share.

1. Save your work and quit any other applications you are running. (You will need to restart your computer at the end of this exercise.)
2. Choose Settings from the Start menu.
3. Pick the Control Panel option.
4. Double-click the Network icon.
5. Scroll through the network components list. If you see an item called "File and Printer Sharing for Microsoft Networks," you don't need to follow any more steps.

6. If you don't see "File and Printer Sharing for Microsoft Networks" (have your Windows installation disks or disc ready in case they are needed), then click the Add button.
7. Double-click the Service icon.
8. You'll see more choices in the Select Network Service dialog box, shown in Figure 11.1.
9. Click Microsoft.
10. Double-click "File and Printer Sharing for Microsoft Networks".
11. When the Select Network Service dialog box disappears, click OK in the Network dialog box.
12. Click Yes or press ENTER to restart.

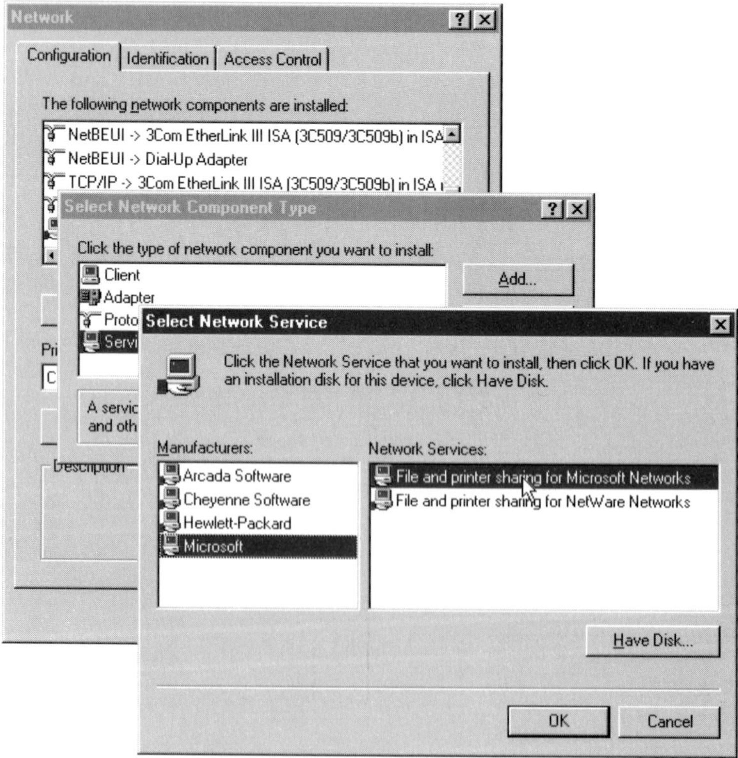

Figure 11.1 Installing a network

Specifying the Type of Sharing and Computer Identification

After you've installed the network software and restarted your machine, you must tell Windows if you want to provide share-level access or user-level access. As you probably remember, share-level lets you specify which *resources* to share, whereas user-level lets you create a list of authorized *people*. In order to enable user-level sharing, at least one of the computers on your network must be a Windows NT or NetWare server.

DEFINITION

server: *A computer dedicated to storing files and sharing common resources.*

Let's choose share-level for now, since it is simple and quick, and requires only two Windows 95 machines.

1. Choose Settings from the Start menu.
2. Pick the Control Panel option.
3. Double-click the Network icon.

SHORTCUT

To quickly open the Network dialog box, right-click the Network Neighborhood dialog box and choose Properties.

4. When the Network dialog box appears, click the Access Control tab.
5. Pick "Share-level access control" by clicking its button.
6. Click the Identification tab.

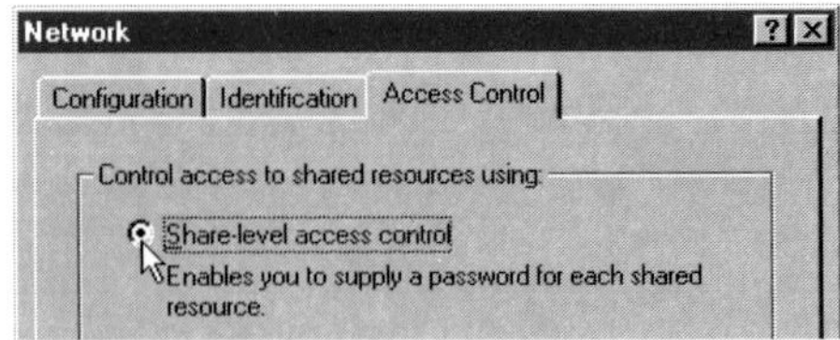

7. Enter a unique computer name that others on the network will recognize. (Once you've chosen a name, nobody else on the network can use the same name for their computer.) The name can be up to 15 characters in length, with no spaces. (If you type spaces, Windows will remove them.) You can use the following nonalphanumeric characters: ! @ # $ % ^ () _ - " { } . and ~.
8. Enter a name in the Workgroup field. (Even a network of only two computers needs a workgroup name, the primary purpose of which is to segregate large networks into more manageable subgroups of related workers.) Again, the workgroup name should be 15 characters, no spaces. In some networks an administrator might have chosen a setting that will automatically assign you to a workgroup.
9. Finally, enter an optional description to help network users determine the purpose or contents of this shared computer. Longer text and spaces are permitted here.

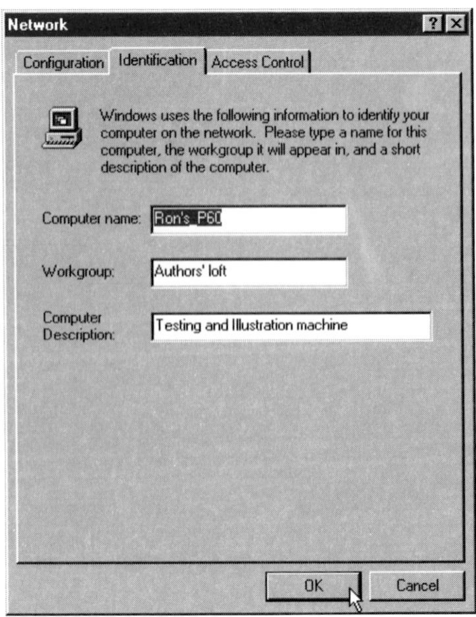

10. Click the Configuration tab.
11. Click the File and Print Sharing button.
12. When the File and Print Sharing dialog box appears, click to place checkmarks in both boxes if you wish to share both files and printers.
13. Click OK to dismiss the File and Print Sharing dialog box.
14. Click OK in the Network dialog box.
15. You probably will be prompted to restart your computer. Click Yes and wait for the restart.

CAUTION

If you share your resources, try not to change the name of your computer or the names of shared disks, folders, or printers. This can drive peers crazy as they try to find your resources on the network.

Specifying Which Resources to Share

With the network hardware, wiring, and networking software installed, you'll still need to specify which resources (disks, printers, etc.) you plan to share. For example, if you want to share your entire hard disk, follow these steps:

1. Right-click the icon for the drive that you want to share.
2. Pick Sharing from the shortcut menu. (If there is no Sharing choice, see the "Troubleshooting Network Problems" section at the end of this chapter.)
3. Click the Sharing tab, shown in Figure 11.2.
4. Choose Shared As.
5. Type a recognizable share name in the Share Name field.
6. Pick the desired access type (Read-Only, Full, or Depends on Password).
7. Enter a password or passwords and write them down.
8. Click Apply.
9. Click OK. The icon for the drive should have a little hand and a sleeve at its bottom, indicating that the drive is shared.

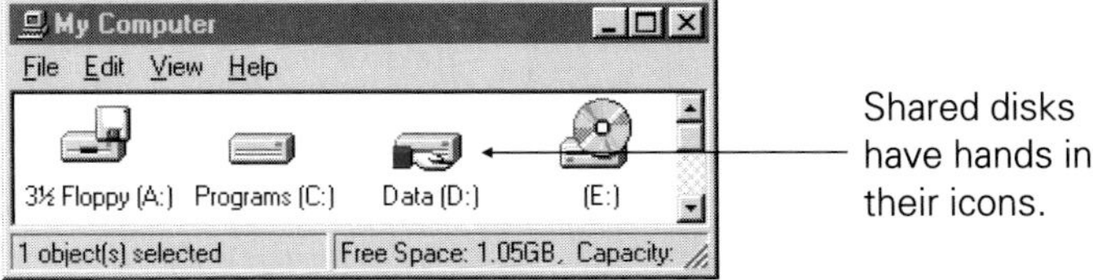

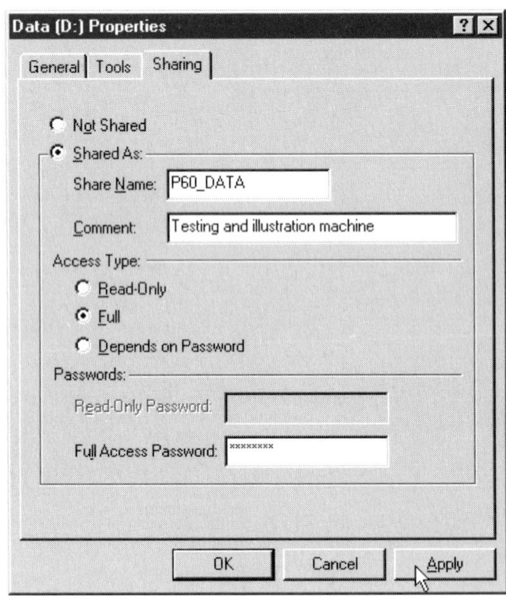

Figure 11.2 Setting up a hard drive for sharing

At this point, in order to actually test sharing, you'll need to go to a computer on the network that is already set up as a client, or set one up as described next.

Setting Up Client Machines

Before you can access other people's resources, your computer must be set up as a client. Here are the general steps:

1. Save your work and quit any other applications you are running, because you will need to restart your computer when you complete these steps.

2. Choose Settings from the Start menu.
3. Pick the Control Panel option.
4. Double-click the Network icon.
5. Click the Add button.
6. Double-click the Client icon.
7. Double-click the Microsoft icon in the Select Network Client dialog box.

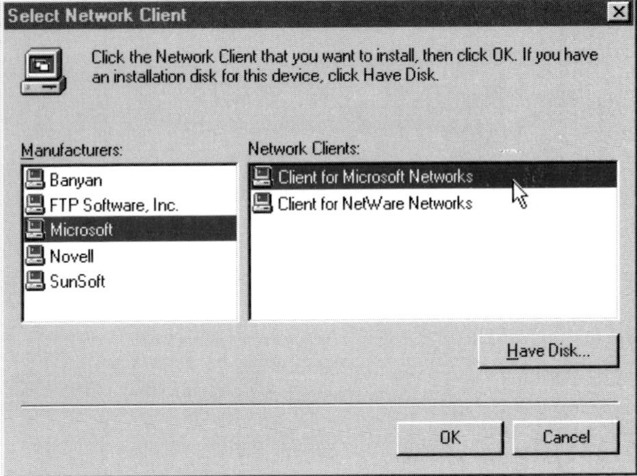

8. Double-click Client for Microsoft Networks.
9. If asked for a Windows installation disk or disc, provide it.
10. Click OK in the Network dialog box.
11. Click Yes (or press ENTER) when asked if you want to restart your computer.

The next section tells you how to access the computer that you set up to share.

Accessing a Peer's Files

With at least one powered-up machine on the network set to share, and using a second machine set up to be a client for the correct type of sharing (Microsoft's peer-to-peer networking in our example), follow these general steps.

Double-click the Network Neighborhood icon. You will see a list of shared resources (disks, folders, and the like) available to you. Double-clicking a disk icon should reveal a disk window, double-clicking a folder icon should reveal a folder window, etc. At this point, you should be able to use shared disks and folders as if they were your own, with a few exceptions (explained in the next section).

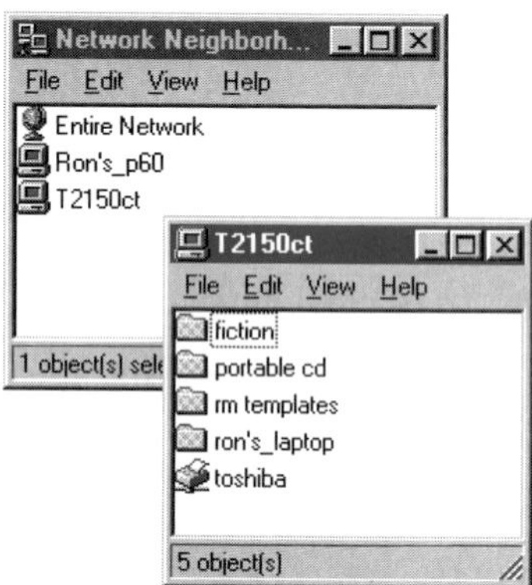

Things to Consider When Using Other People's Resources

Obviously, you'll want to treat other people's files with respect, particularly if you've been granted full read/write access. Don't change, copy, distribute, move, rename, or delete files without permission. Also keep these tips in mind when using someone else's files:

- Except when certain programs (such as databases) permit it, you will be denied access to a file if someone else is using it. This prevents two people from making changes to a file at the same time.
- You might need to know passwords to access files, folders, disks, or printers.
- Your computer might need a properly installed copy of the program that created a file (or one that can use the file).
- When naming files in a networked environment, remember that some users might have problems with long filenames.

- If you wish to see shared resources (such as networked disk drives) listed in the Open and Save dialog boxes of pre-Windows 95 versions of programs like Word and Excel, you will need to map the resources. (Newer, Windows 95-savvy versions of applications won't require mapping.) See the online help topic Mapping Networked Resources for details.

Once you have established network communications, you can use shared files from within Windows 95-savvy programs like the latest releases of Microsoft Word, Excel, etc. For example, to open a document located on a peer's machine using Word, you'd follow the steps outlined in the next blue box. Remember that you might not have full access to shared resources. For example, you might be able to open a file but not save changes you make to the file. You can, however, use the Save As command to save your own changed version of documents, even if they are read-only.

STEP BY STEP Using Shared Files from Within Applications

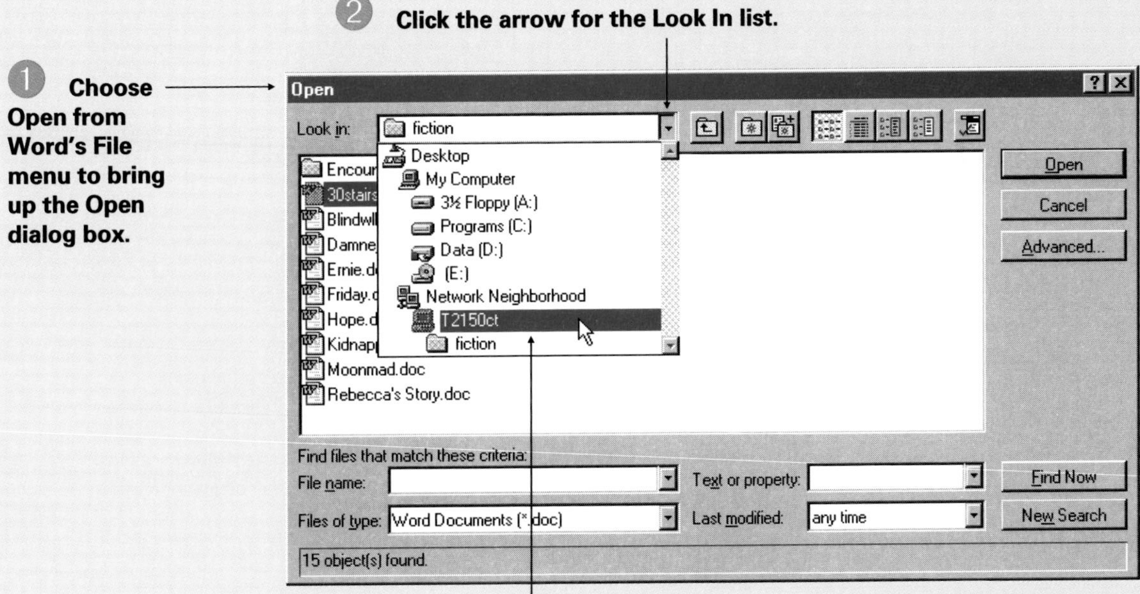

3 Choose the shared resource of interest (a networked hard drive or folder or whatever).

Using a Peer's Printer

If you need to use someone's printer other than your own, and if that person is a Windows 95 user willing to share printers, you can follow these steps:

1. Make certain the computer connected to the printer you plan to share is powered up and running Windows 95.
2. Make sure that Printer sharing is enabled on that computer.
3. Make sure the printer is ready, and that the user is willing to share it at this time.
4. Double-click the Network Neighborhood icon on your computer's desktop.

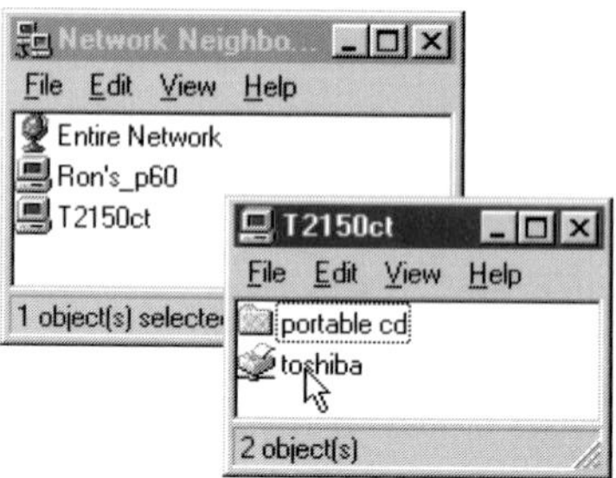

5. Double-click the icon for the computer whose printer you wish to share.
6. Have your Windows disks or CD handy. If the appropriate drivers for the chosen printer are not installed on your computer, Windows will offer to install them.

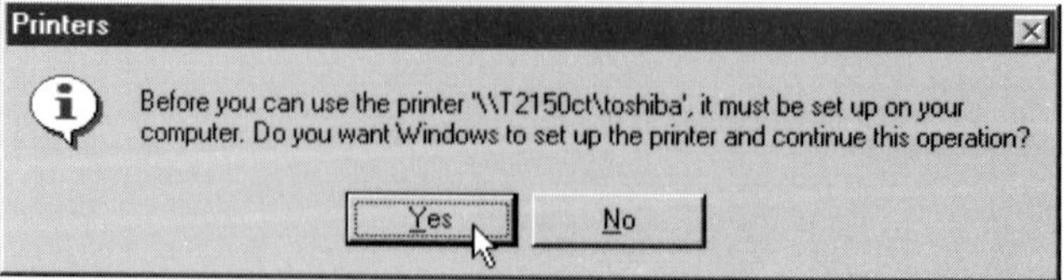

7. Print the test page when asked to do so.
8. When you wish to use this printer for a future print job, just choose the remote printer using the Printer drop-down list in the Print dialog box. (Remember that the owner's computer and printer must be on and ready when you're set to print.)

Sharing Your Printer

To share your printer, follow these steps:

1. Pick Settings from the Start menu, then Printers.
2. Right-click the icon for the printer you wish to share.
3. Choose Sharing from the shortcut menu. (If this choice is unavailable, see "Troubleshooting Network Problems" at the end of this chapter.)
4. In the printer's Properties dialog box, click the Sharing tab if necessary to bring it to the top, as shown in Figure 11.3.

Users with NetWare and Windows NT servers on their networks can share printers connected to these servers. Contact your network manager or support staff for assistance.

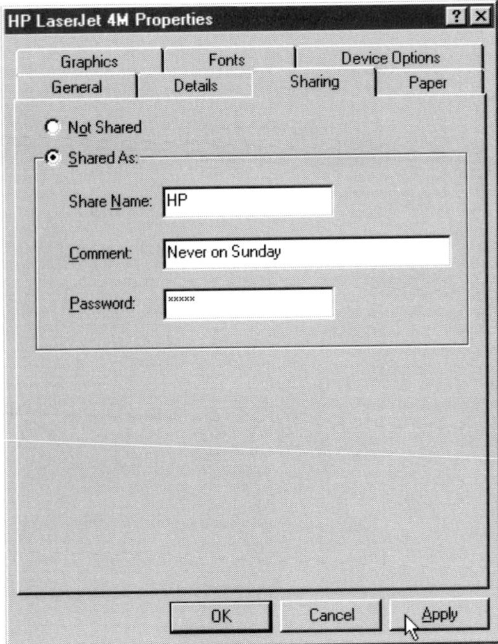

Figure 11.3 Setting up a printer for sharing

5. Click Shared As.
6. Name the printer something meaningful.
7. Add a comment if you want to tell users something about the printer. (This printer can't be used on Sunday. This printer eats more fingertips than wolverines. Whatever.)
8. Password-protect the printer if you want to restrict access to a chosen few.
9. Click Apply, then click OK.

Your printer icon in the Printers window will have a hand and sleeve at the bottom when sharing is enabled:

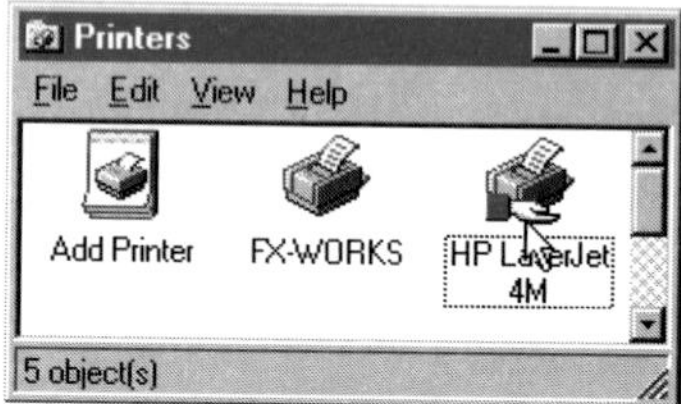

To Stop Sharing Your Printer

To stop sharing your printer, follow these steps:

1. Pick Settings from the Start menu, then select Printers.
2. Right-click the icon for the printer you wish to stop sharing.
3. Choose Sharing from the shortcut menu.
4. In the printer's Properties dialog box's Sharing tab, click Not Shared.
5. Click Apply, then click OK. Your printer icon in the Printers window will no longer have a hand and sleeve at its bottom when sharing is disabled.

EXPERT ADVICE

You can share other things besides files and printers, including CD-ROM drives. Experiment!

Setting Up User-Level Sharing

In order to enable user-level sharing, you'll need to be on a network with a NetWare or Windows NT server, containing a list of authorized users. Contact your network administrator for assistance.

Finding Computers on Your Network

It is often useful to know who, if anyone, is using your shared resources. Windows 95 comes with an accessory called Net Watcher. It is not automatically installed, so you'll need to use the Add/Remove Programs icon in the control panel to install it.

To locate networked computers, either open the Network Neighborhood window by double-clicking its icon and clicking the Entire Network Icon, or right-click the Network Neighborhood icon and enter the name of a shared computer or part of that computer's name. Another useful technique is to right-click the Network Neighborhood icon and choose Explore. You'll see a list of shared resources in the Explorer window:

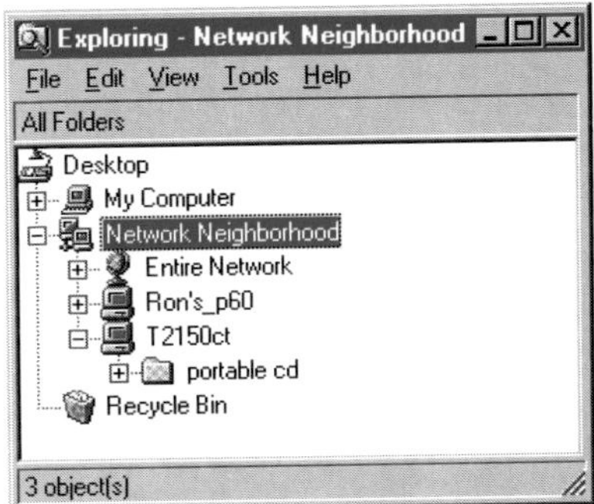

Before You Disable Sharing

Remember that if other people are using your shared resources and you shut down your computer, you disconnect them from your resources. This can be a minor annoyance (like the disruption of a print job) or a real disaster, in the case of a file that gets damaged or destroyed because it was improperly closed. And remember, the damaged and destroyed files we are talking about here are on *your* hard disk.

If you try to shut down your computer, or disable sharing while someone is sharing it, Windows will warn you. Talk to the other user(s). Use the Net Watcher if necessary to see who needs to be contacted.

CAUTION

If you disconnect a peer (or if a peer disconnects you), Windows will not tell the person using the shared resources that he or she has been disconnected from those resources. It's good manners to warn other users before you disconnect them or shut down your system. Otherwise, they'll find out the hard way when shared printers don't print, etc.

Disconnecting Others

To disconnect other networked users without shutting down your computer, open the Net Watcher accessory. Select a user from the Net Watcher list. Click the Disconnect User button in the toolbar, or use the corresponding menu choice on the Administer menu. Remember: Disconnecting users when they have your files open can damage your files!

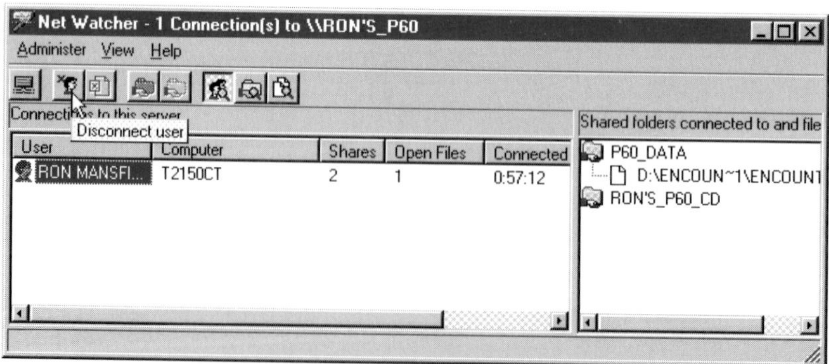

Starting Your Computer Without Logging On

To start your computer without running network services, click the Cancel button when presented with the Network login screen. You'll need to restart your computer to enable networking.

Novell and Other Non-Microsoft Networks

Windows 95 comes with client software for a number of non-Microsoft networks including Artisof® LANtastic® versions 5.0 and up, Banyan© VINES versions 5.2 and up, DEC™ PATHWORKS™, Novell® NetWare versions 3.11 and up, and SunSoft™ PC-NFS® versions 5.0 and up.

There are also built-in components for various "transports" and "protocols" including TCP/IP and IXP/SPX, RCP, NetBIOS, and more. No doubt, third-party software vendors will add more capabilities to this list. Windows 95 was designed to be easily configured for a multitude of network options.

CAUTION

Many non-Microsoft networks don't support long filenames (or long folder names, for that matter). Keep this in mind when naming files and folders (subdirectories) if you work on such a network. Windows and the network software will rename your files to make them fit, but you might not like the results. Try to use meaningful, "legal" filenames whenever possible.

Improving Network Security

In December of 1995 Microsoft started shipping an update to their network password security scheme designed to make password hacking significantly more difficult. Check with your network administrator to see if this upgrade is necessary or advisable on your computer. One place to find more information (and the necessary files for the update) is **www.microsoft.com/windows/software/servpak1/sphome.htm**.

Troubleshooting Network Problems

The built-in troubleshooter in Windows Help can help you solve many common network problems, but before you run it, run your brain for a moment and see if you can solve the problem yourself. If your computer has been running fine on the network and then suddenly quits, ask yourself these questions:

- What's changed? Have I been fiddling with the control panel or passwords or sharing settings?
- Have I unplugged a network connection intentionally or accidentally?
- Is the computer I am trying to network with operating properly?
- Has anything changed at that end?
- Does restarting my computer (and possibly the other) fix the problem?

If answering these questions doesn't solve the problem, try the Network Troubleshooting feature built into online help. Begin by choosing Help from the Start menu. Flip to the Find tab and type **network trouble**. Double-click Troubleshooting Network Problems. Read the unfolding saga, clicking the buttons that correspond to your situation. With any luck you'll be back in business shortly.

If you have the necessary hardware, this might be a good time to try setting up a small peer-to-peer network of your own. Experiment with printer sharing. Create and organize some folders on your server if you have one.

In Chapter 12 you'll visit the wonderful world of the Internet, modems, and the arts of faxing and E-mail.

CAUTION

CHAPTER

12

The Internet, Modems, Phones, Faxing, and Direct Connections

INCLUDES

- Windows communication support
- Using modems to exchange data
- An overview of the Internet and other online services
- Setting up dial-up (PPP) Internet services
- HyperTerminal
- Remote network access
- Direct computer connections sans modems
- Faxing
- Troubleshooting your connections

FAST FORWARD

Install a Modem ➤ pp. 295-298

- Turn on your modem before running the Windows 95 setup program and Windows 95 will detect it and automatically set up the modem for you.
- To install or change modems after Windows 95 has been installed, use the Add New Hardware Wizard reached via the control panel.

View and Change Modem Settings ➤ pp. 298-301

1. Choose Settings from the Start menu.
2. Choose the Control Panel option.
3. Double-click Modems.
4. Pick the modem of interest if you have more than one.
5. Visit the General, My Locations, and possibly, Diagnostics property tabs.

Access the Internet ➤ pp. 301-303

- If you work in a large or high-tech organization, ask if there is direct Internet access via your LAN.
- For dial-up Internet access, either contact an Internet access provider (ISP), or use CompuServe, America Online, etc.
- Check the Windows 95 online help.

Set Up Dial-Up (ISP) Internet Service ➤ *pp. 304-306*

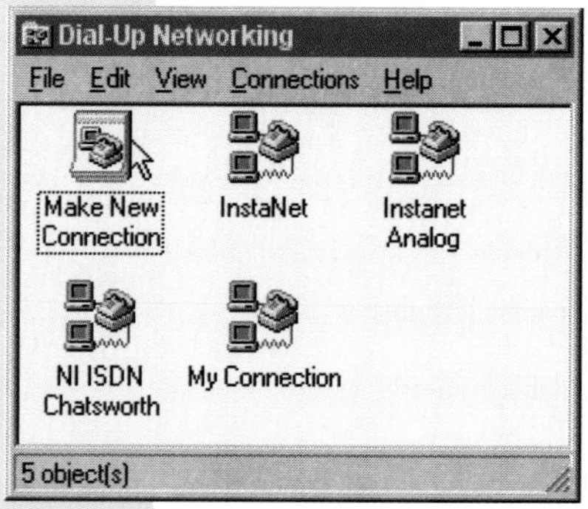

1. Obtain a Point-to-Point protocol (PPP) Internet account from a reliable Internet Service Provider (ISP).
2. Make sure you have a properly installed and functioning modem (14.4 or faster is my recommendation).
3. After the PPP account is activated (not just ordered, actually turned on and ready for you!) and you have the account paperwork at hand, begin the installation. (It is best to start the installation during hours when your ISP provides human telephone technical support.)
4. If the ISP provides an installation disk that you are certain is 100% compatible with Windows 95 and your modem or ISDN device, use it, following any instructions carefully.
5. If you don't get a Windows 95-specific installation disk from your ISP, open Windows Help and click on the Find tab.
6. Type **internet account** and double-click the resulting "Connecting to the Internet using Dial-up Networking" topic.
7. You will be presented with a series of help topics, many of them containing buttons leading you to other steps and possibly Wizards based on your situation.
8. Read each screen very carefully. Follow the steps exactly. If you have questions while installing, call your Internet Service Provider's help line.
9. If you haven't already done so, install a network browser like the Microsoft Internet Explorer or Netscape. Using the information provided by your ISP, set up your mail, news, and other features as necessary.
10. Let the games begin!

Access Commercial Services ➤ pp. 306-309

- Use the Windows 95 version(s) communications software provided by the bigger services (CompuServe, America Online, etc.), or use HyperTerminal if no specific software is provided.
- Start with free hours, then be sure you understand billing options and monitor your usage and billing carefully.
- Locate and use local access phone numbers to avoid costly toll calls. In large towns some "local" access numbers in the same area code will cost you more than others due to "unit" charges. Contact your phone company for details.
- Some services like AOL offer "800" numbers. There is an extra cost for these numbers, but it can often be less than hotel long distance or even credit card calls.

Access Other PCs and Free Services ➤ pp. 309-312

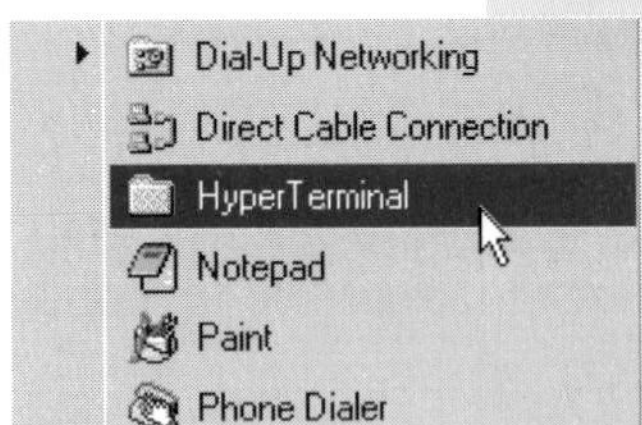

- Use the Windows HyperTerminal program or the general-purpose software that came with your modem to dial smaller and noncommercial BBS sites.
- Create HyperTerminal settings files for sites you plan to visit regularly.
- Check publications like *Computer Shopper* for listings of sites, phone numbers, and their specialties.

Dial Into Your Network ➤ p. 313

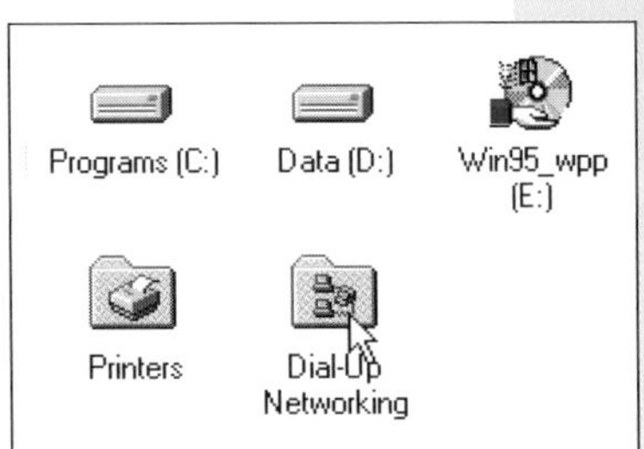

- Contact your network administrator to see if dial-in services are offered.
- To set up your own dial-in access point, use the server software add-in provided in Microsoft's Microsoft Plus! accessory pack.
- Once connected to the network remotely, use shared resources normally (E-mail, share files, etc.).
- Expect things to happen more slowly over a modem connection than when connected via Ethernet.

Connect Two Computers Directly ➤ *pp. 313-316*

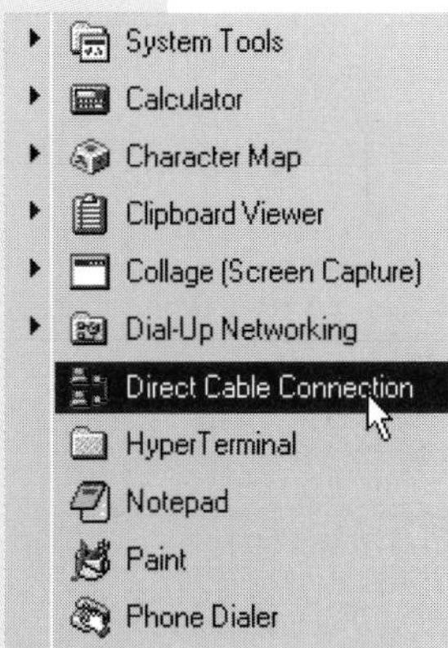

1. Both computers must have network software installed, access privileges established, etc.
2. Purchase a serial or parallel cable designed for direct computer-to-computer connection.
3. Run the Direct Cable Connection accessory (found in the Accessories submenu of the Programs menu).
4. Follow the Wizard's instructions, establishing one computer as a host and the other as a guest.
5. When connected, share resources as usual (exchange E-mail, swap files, and so on).

Send and Receive Fax Documents ➤ *pp. 316-326*

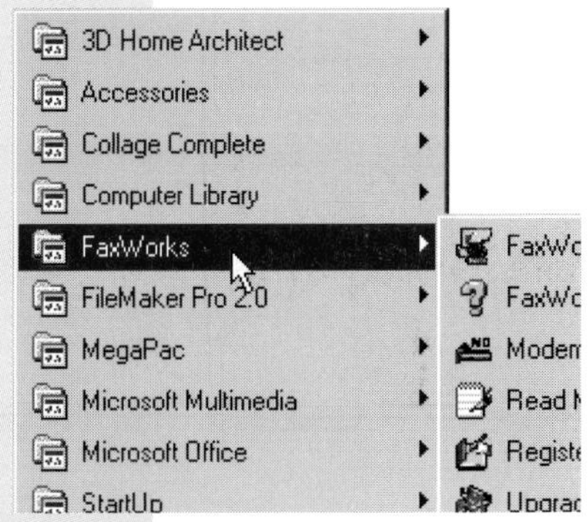

- Use the fax software that came with your modem, or use fax services available via Sprint, MCI, the Microsoft Network, and elsewhere.
- Use the fax facilities built into Microsoft Exchange or other communications packages.

Speed-Dial Your Telephone ➤ *pp. 326-327*

1. Connect your phone and modem to the same line.
2. Open the Phone Dialer accessory (in the Accessories submenu).
3. Enter commonly dialed phone numbers.
4. Click the button for the number you wish to dial.

Windows 95 puts modem installation, setup, and use within the reach of regular human beings. A bewildering array of technobabble can be virtually ignored if you use contemporary modems and communications software with Windows 95.

Modems: The Short Course

You can use modems for a variety of tasks including exchanging files with other computers, accessing commercial services like CompuServe and the Microsoft Network, prowling the Internet, sending and receiving faxes, logging onto your office network from on the road, and speed-dialing your telephone.

Modems come in all shapes and sizes. Some are built-ins, others plug into expansion slots on your desktop machines, and others are external boxes. Windows 95 will work with most contemporary modems. You can even have multiple modems installed on your computer and choose which one to use for a particular task. In some circumstances, you can send and receive over multiple modems on the same machine simultaneously. Moreover, plug-and-play can automatically recognize and configure all but the most finicky and obscure devices.

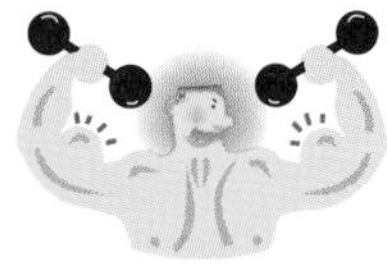

DEFINITION

modem: *(Contraction for Modulator/Demodulator) Hardware designed to convert your computer's zeros and ones into sounds, which, when sent over phone lines to other modems, are sometimes (but not always) converted back into useful computer data.*

Modem Compatibility Issues

There are a begillion modem standards and specifications in use today. They specify everything from the speed at which data flows, to the number of bits (zeros and ones) used to represent characters, to the data compression methods used, to the error correction schemes employed (or not employed). You are too busy to learn this stuff. Take comfort in knowing that virtually all *contemporary* modems are able to find some common ground in this jungle. And, with the help of Windows 95, the computers, modems, and software automatically manage most of this minutia on their own. So, again, busy person, drop a Ben Franklin or two on a nice *new* modem. Upgrade to Windows 95-ready communication software.

ISDN: Fast or Half-Fast?

Many online service providers and phone company now support high-speed ISDN connections that can move information at 10 or 20 times the speed of modems. ISDN connections can be blazing fast, and it's easy to get spoiled. Screens that take minutes to display with a 14.4 modem can sometimes fill in a few seconds with ISDN. File uploads and downloads are usually much quicker. It is even possible to make fast connections with AOL, CompuServe, and others via an ISDN line and an ISP. On the other hand, there is often the "hurry up and wait" problem associated with the Internet's growing sluggishness. You will receive little noticeable speed improvement if the Net is very busy or if the sites you visit are slow or bogged down. Try to get an ISDN demonstration from your ISP using sites you might visit during times of day you might visit them. Do a comparison, if possible.

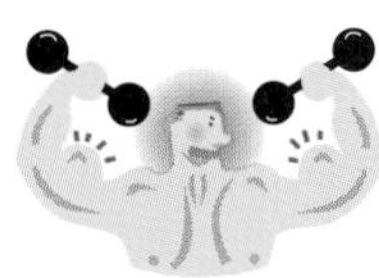

DEFINITION

ISDN (Integrated Services Digital Network): *The perfect busy person's helper, ISDN offers fully digital phone connections that promise speeds 5 to 10 times greater than modem connections for online services. ISDN service requires special phone connections and a modem-like device called an ISDN card, or an ISDN Terminal Adapter (TA).*

You will need to purchase an ISDN device (a plug-in card, or an external Terminal Adapter, also called a "TA"), and you will need to order a special line from your phone company. Sometimes your phone company can use your existing wiring, and you can make voice calls over your ISDN line, if you have the proper hardware, but be sure you maintain at least one regular old (analog) phone line for your everyday voice calls! ISDN adapters require electricity. If you don't have a regular old phone line and your power goes out, your ISDN line won't work, and you won't have a voice phone.

The ISDN device and your computer(s) will need to be configured for your ISDN phone line. ISDN can be affordable and relatively easy to install, or prohibitively expensive and a nightmare to get running. You should also realize that most ISDN devices do not have any fax capabilities. So, if you hope to use your computer to send and receive fax messages, you will almost certainly need both a traditional modem and an ISDN device. There are some cabling, COM port, and other issues you'll need to consider, so you might want some knowledgeable person's advice before you drop a bundle on an ISDN adapter and fax-capable modem.

If you are technically challenged, or in a big hurry, consider purchasing a "turnkey" installation from your phone company or ISP where someone comes out to your location and sets *everything* up for you. Be sure you know what's included and what's not. It's no good to have a working line and an ISDN device that your computer knows nothing about. A good turnkey deal should (at a minimum) include a demo of your browser connected to the Net via your ISDN line.

For more information about ISDN, visit Dan Kegel's excellent page at **http://mirror.cs.miami.edu/isdn/**. Dan is even pretty good natured about answering questions from beginners via E-mail. Just don't wear out your welcome.

The Promise of TAPI

Not to be confused with some island in the South Pacific, TAPI stands for Telephony Application Programming Interface. It's a Windows 95 feature that promises to further reduce the confusion and frustration of computing via modem. It enables Windows 95-savvy programs to control and coordinate modem use. With TAPI in the loop, you could, for example, be running fax software that is waiting to receive a fax, and decide to log onto America Online without needing to shut down the fax software. Even though both the fax and AOL software want the modem, TAPI will mediate and let the AOL software have the modem, giving it back to the fax software when you log off of AOL. So instead of seeing error messages about the modem already being in use, or unavailable, you'll get connected and do your thing. Or at least that is how it is supposed to work.

You see, all of your communications packages need to be TAPI-aware for this to work seamlessly. Most pre-Windows 95 programs don't know TAPI from Shinola. Again, get thee to a software store and say "I want my TAPI-savvy software" if this feature intrigues you.

EXPERT ADVICE

If you plan to dial up other computers, or send and receive fax documents, and if your modem is more than a few years old, consider spending the under $200 it will cost to get yourself a sexy new 28.8 or faster screamer, then update your communications software to make it Win 95-savvy also.

Installing a Modem

If, when you first install Windows 95, you have a modem connected to your computer (and if it is powered up), the setup program will detect the modem, and probably make most of the necessary settings for you.

If you later add a modem (or turn yours on after the installation), you will probably need to visit the Add New Hardware Wizard (reached through the control panel). Otherwise, the first time you try to run a communications program, Windows will take you to the Add New Hardware Wizard. In any case, the Wizard will ask you for some dialing trivia that Win 95-savvy programs will use to make your life much easier. This process is called *defining your location.*

Defining Your Location

When you first install a modem, or any time you move your modem-equipped computer to a new location, it is a good idea to tell Windows 95 the country and area code where you are located, as well as whether you need to dial a number like 8 or 9 to reach an outside line, and so on. Windows remembers these details and uses them to simplify your communications tasks.

You enter this location information either with the help of the Installation Wizard or via the Modem Properties dialog box. If the Installation Wizard asks you for location information, you'll see one set of question and answer screens; if you use the Modem Properties to define location settings, you'll see virtually the same questions as the Wizard asks, only in a slightly different presentation.

You can set up and save information for multiple locations. The place you spend the most time with your computer (your home or the office, for instance) should be your *default* location. If you never move your computer, you'll only need to enter default settings. If you travel, or take a laptop to a variety of locations with different dialing needs, you can have dozens or even hundreds of location settings.

You create and modify location settings in the Dialing Properties window, which you access through the Modems Properties window.

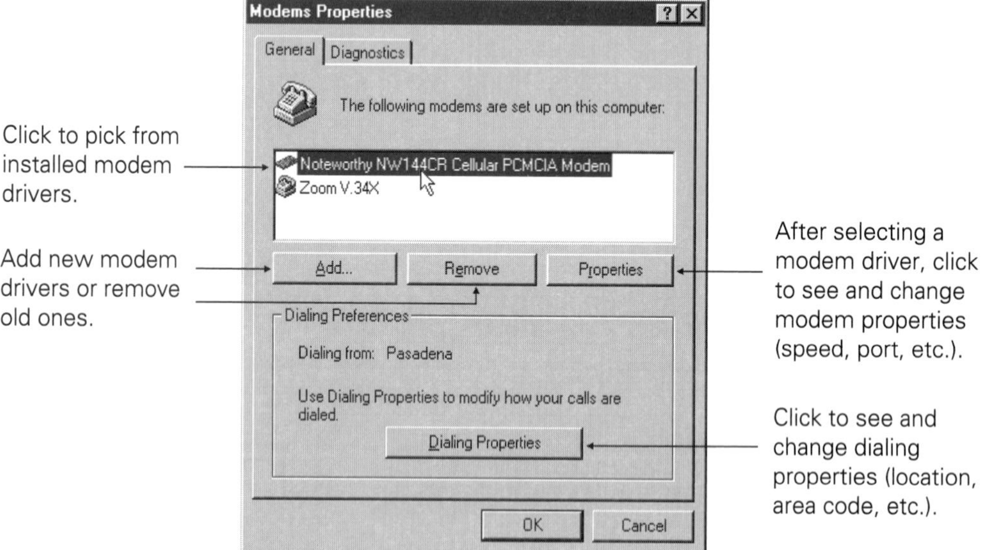

Begin by double-clicking the Modems icon in the control panel. Click the Dialing Properties button. Either name the location or leave the words *Default Location* in the "I am dialing from" box. If you want to create a new location, click the New button. Then make the necessary choices (numbers, if any, needed to reach an outside line; disabling call waiting; etc.). Here are some typical dialing properties for the My Locations tab:

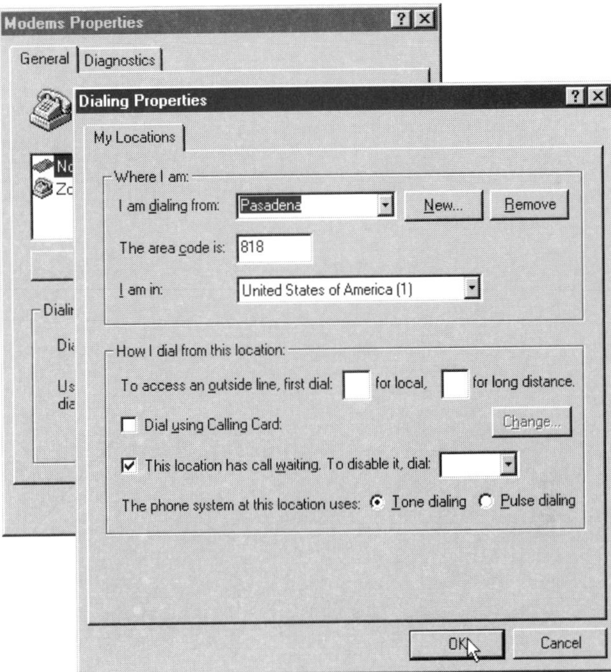

If you plan to use a calling card for your long-distance calls, place a checkmark in the "Dial using Calling Card" box, then click the Change button to set up the card parameters.

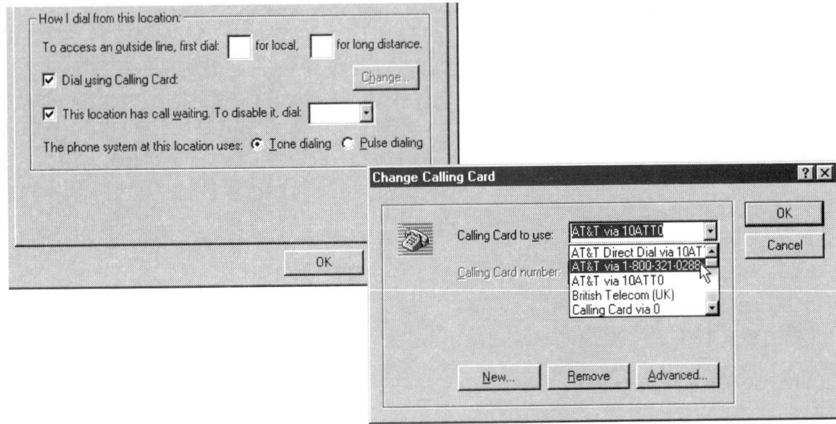

Set up additional locations as necessary. Finally, choose the location where you and your computer are currently located and then click OK.

EXPERT ADVICE

I take my laptop to clients' offices. Even though many are in Los Angeles, their settings (area codes, outside line access numbers, etc.) are unique. I set up numerous locations, one named after each client. Don't just think in terms of cities when creating locations—think situations, as well.

Seeing and Changing Modem Settings

Although Windows does most of the modem setup for you, if you are knowledgeable about such things, you can change the master modem settings used by TAPI-savvy programs. And, when working with older software, you'll need to change settings for each program. Let's look at the TAPI settings first.

CAUTION

If you are unfamiliar with modem minutiae like data bits, parity checking, handshaking methods, etc., be sure to get knowledgeable help when changing those settings. In the vast majority of cases, they are fine just the way Windows originally sets them.

Seeing and Changing TAPI Settings

To see—and possibly change—the modem settings used by all your TAPI-compatible programs, visit the Modems Properties window and pick the installed modem of interest.

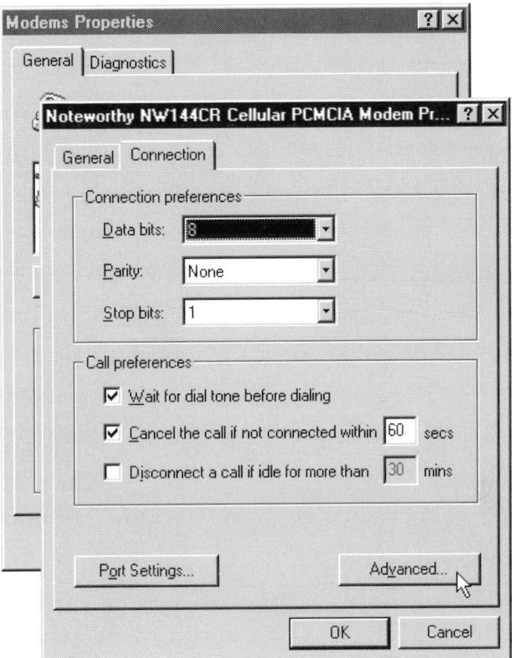

Double-click the Modems icon in the control panel and click the General tab in the Modem Properties dialog box if necessary to bring it foremost. Choose the modem of interest if more than one is installed, and click the small Properties button (not the Dialing Properties button) in the Modem Properties dialog box. Review the settings (COM port number, etc.), and make any necessary changes in the General and Connection tabs for the modem you are checking (the Noteworthy NW144CR in our example).

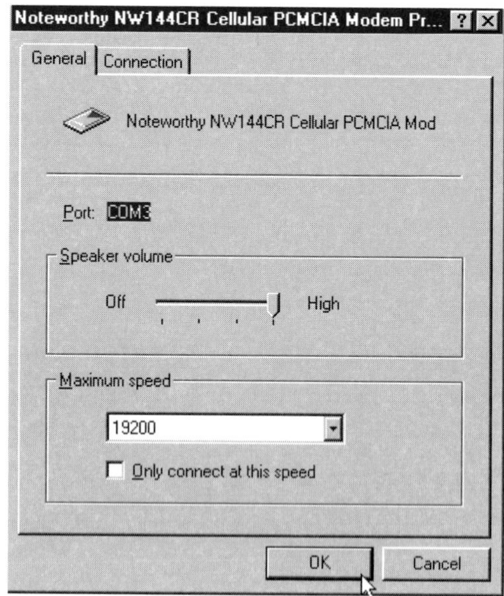

Access the Port Settings and Advanced Port settings by clicking General. Click OK. Click Close to save any changes.

Telling TAPI-Savvy Programs About Your Modem

Once you've installed a modem and specified your location settings, you must tell your communications software about the modem. If you are using TAPI-savvy programs (like Microsoft HyperTerminal), all you need do is pick the modem from a modem settings window as shown here:

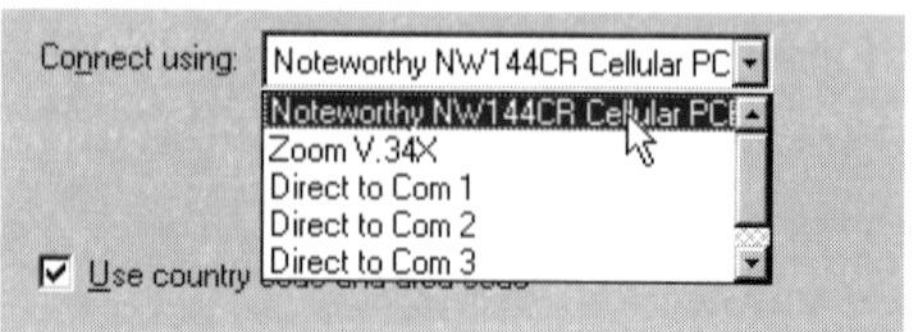

The communications program and Windows 95 (thanks to TAPI) will take care of things like the COM port number, modem setup strings, etc.

Telling Non-TAPI Programs About Your Modem

If you are using older, non-TAPI-ready software, you may still need to visit the modem setup boxes within some or all of your non-TAPI programs and pick settings appropriate for your modem. Most communications programs provide lists of modem models from which you choose. For example, Figure 12.1 shows a modem setup dialog box from a non-TAPI America Online program.

Check the documentation that came with your older software to learn how to specify the modem settings.

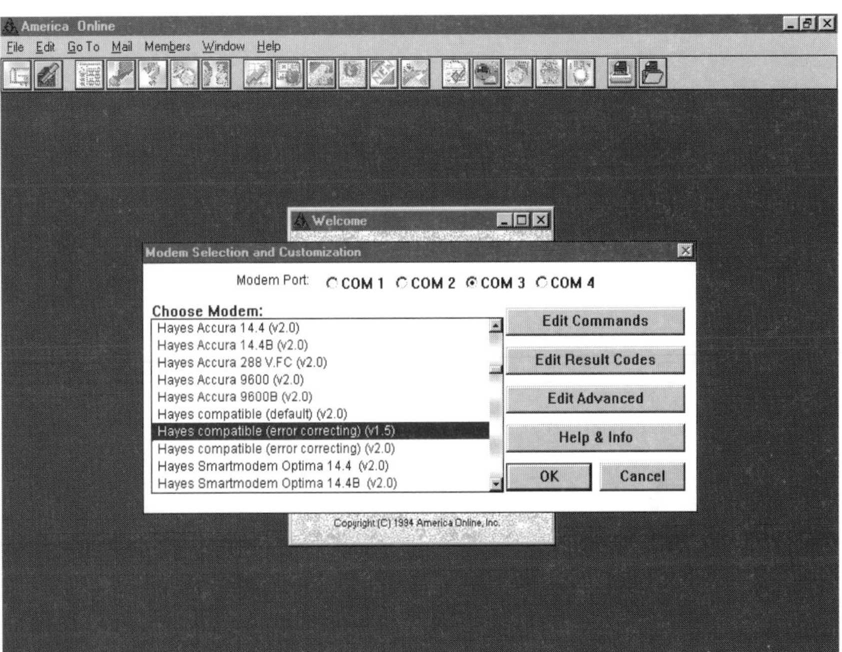

Figure 12.1 A sample modem setup screen

The Internet and Other Dial-Up Services

Modems have done for this century what railroads did for its predecessor. Your modem-equipped computer can transport your brain to any part of the globe in a flash. You can make friends, aggravate enemies, enjoy art, be overwhelmed by other people's bad taste, get free stuff, spend obscene amounts of money, learn the truth, and be badly misinformed all in the same evening. While the "free" Internet is the glamorous place to play, you can have just as much fun (and maybe more) on the "pay" services like America Online and CompuServe. This book can't begin to show you all the ins and outs. Entire bookstore aisles of guidebooks can't do that. But you should be aware that Windows 95 can make it easier to get wired. Here's an overview.

The Internet

The Internet is a worldwide collection of computers all interconnected using common networking standards and naming schemes. You can send mail to many of the computers on the Net, and they can send mail to you. You can "browse" the contents of many of these machines, download (obtain) files from them, and much more. If you so choose, you can let others on the Net browse the files on your machine.

Before you can do any of this, you'll need to connect your computer to the Internet, either via your computer's Ethernet or other network adapter, or via modem, or an ISDN device. If you are in a large or technically bullish organization, you might already have Internet access available via your network. If so, you just need to install the appropriate Windows 95 networking protocols and bindings to begin an Internet connection. (Contact your support people to find out if this is true, and what is involved in getting you up and running.)

You also can connect to the Internet via modem or an ISDN device by contracting with an Internet provider. This is called a *dial-up* connection. Although handy, dial-up connections are frequently slower than direct Internet connections, so if you have a choice, use your network hookup rather than a modem or ISDN line.

If you must use a modem or ISDN device, you'll need an Internet service provider. You'll use your modem or ISDN device to dial the provider, and the provider will hook you up to the Internet. In addition to the hundreds of mom-and-pop providers springing up (and the giants like Sprint and MCI), the folks at CompuServe, America Online, and Prodigy are all providing "gateway Internet services."

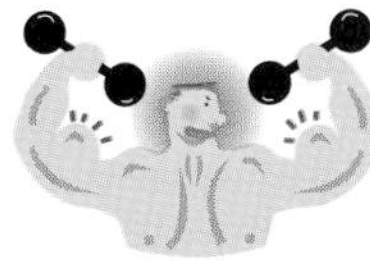

DEFINITION

Internet Service Providers (ISP): *Large and small telecommunications service providers in your area who offer dial-up access to Internet services.*

Once you connect to the Net, you'll require additional software to do useful work. You'll need "browser software" if you plan to explore other people's machines, for example, and mail software if you plan to exchange E-mail. Some programs like Microsoft Explorer, Netscape, and Mosaic integrate some or all of the necessary tools for browsing, E-mail, file downloading, etc. Figure 12.2 shows what a typical Netscape screen looks like.

Newer browsers take advantage of Windows 95 features and advanced Internet technologies like Microsoft's ActiveX controls, so when shopping for software and Internet service providers, ask if their wares are designed with Windows 95 in mind. To learn more about the Internet and Windows 95, type **Internet** in the Search tab of Windows' Help window, or look up "Internet, connecting to" in the Help index.

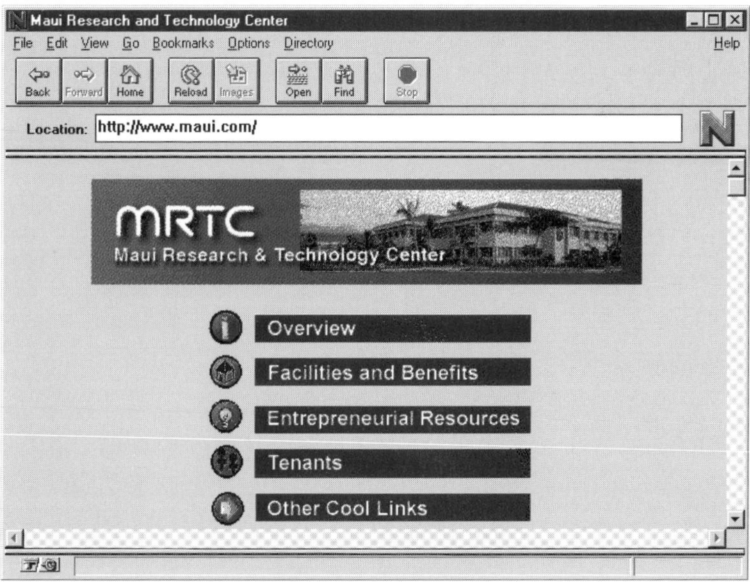

Figure 12.2 A typical Internet browser screen

Setting Up Dial-Up Connections with Windows 95

There are a bewildering number of steps required for setting up Internet services on your computer, and, while you could have someone else do it, most people can and should learn the process. It is also very important to make a file folder containing all of your setup information in case (God forbid) you need to reinstall everything after a computer crash, theft, upgrade, or whatever. Thus forewarned, read on.

Getting an Internet Service Provider Account

Start by exploring ISP options in your neighborhood. The computer sections of local papers often carry ads. Ask around. There are even ISP booths set up in shopping malls and at swap meets now. Look around.

You want a vendor capable of providing PPP support with local access numbers free of any and all toll charges. Remember that just because an ISP is in your area code does not mean that calls to the ISP's lines will be free. Phone companies often charge "unit" fees on calls just across the street if you are in the wrong exchange, or neighborhood. This can add hundreds of dollars to your phone bill each month if you are not careful. (I know this from experience.)

If you plan to use an ISDN device, or very high-speed modem, be sure the ISP supports it. Again, make sure there is a toll-free number for the device(s) you plan to use!

If you plan to set up your own web page, find out if the ISP will host it for you. How much extra will this cost? Some ISPs provide free hosting, others charge hundreds of dollars a month. How much disk space can you have for your page? Are there restrictions on the traffic you may generate with your page?

You want an ISP with a good track record and excellent technical support. Ask current users about their experiences. Be sure you understand the hours of operation of the tech support staff, particularly if you're an early riser or a night owl. Be sure you understand the pricing options and track your billing.

It will probably take a day or two for your service to become available after you sign up. Just because you signed the contract and paid your setup fee does not mean the ISP's computers will let you online. There will be a credit check (perhaps just a call to your credit card company if that's the way you will pay your bill). The ISP will need to do some paperwork, set up your account name, password(s), E-mail box, etc. They will either hand, mail, or fax you a copy of your contract along with a bewildering collection of account information. Here are the typical items you will receive:

- User name
- Password
- Access phone number(s)
- A Host name
- A Domain name
- A Domain Name Server (DNS) server address, and perhaps a secondary address
- An IP address and subnet mask if required
- DNS search order information if required
- A Gateway address or two
- Authentication procedure instructions (Terminal log-on instructions)
- E-mail account name(s) and password(s)
- News settings information

You might get more or fewer items. While you will need some or all of this information to get up and running, fortunately you will not need to know what it all *means*. Make a copy of the sheet(s) listing all of this stuff, and get ready to let Windows 95 walk you through the necessary steps after your account is activated at the ISP's end.

CAUTION

Your ISP might send you a software disk designed to automate the installation process. Before you use it, make a pre-installation call to the ISP's tech support folks. Explain your computer setup (Win 95, modem and ISDN details, desired browser, etc.). Ask if there will be any problems.

Make Sure Your Modem Is Set Up

While you are waiting for the ISP to be ready for you, check to see that your modem or ISDN device is properly installed, or install it. Make sure the settings (speed, etc.) are appropriate for the ISP.

Install the Windows Dial-up Networking Software

Installation steps will vary. Your ISP should provide you with clear instructions for a Windows 95-specific installation. Here's an overview of what to do with or without an installation disk from your ISP, just in case:

1. If the ISP provides an installation disk that you are certain is 100% compatible with Windows 95 and your modem or ISDN device, use it, following any instructions carefully.
2. If you don't get a Windows 95-specific installation disk from your ISP, open Windows Help and click on the Find tab.
3. Type **internet account** and double-click the resulting "Connecting to the Internet using Dial-up Networking" topic.
4. You will be presented with a series of help topics, many of them containing buttons leading you to other steps and possibly Wizards based on your situation.
5. Read each screen very carefully. Follow the steps exactly. If you have questions while installing, call your Internet Service Provider's help line.
6. If you haven't already done so, install a network browser like the Microsoft Internet Explorer or Netscape. Using the information provided by your ISP, set up your mail, news, and other features as necessary.

Places for Busy People on the Net

It's impossible to keep up with the flood of web sites of interest to busy people. But I thought you might enjoy visiting a few of my favorites, so I've listed them here. By the way, for a more current and complete list, please feel free to visit *my* personal page at **http://members.aol.com/rmansfield/index.htm**.

Study Links

Need a snappy quotation for that speech or report introduction? Want to find the meaning of an acronym? Want a free trial of many of the latest electronic encyclopedias and other reference publications? Need a Shakespeare fix? Want to translate something from or to English, French, Japanese, or German? Are the kids asking you about the periodic table? Need a Bible quote? How about finding a city on a map? Well, one web site can do all of that for you. Check out **www.holli.com/hotlist/helpful.html**. As Ralph Waldo Emerson might have said if he were alive today, "This site, well, it's the place for folks ...too busy with the crowded hour to fear to live or die."

FedEx

Want to know if that FedEx package you sent has arrived yet? In a new town and wondering where the closest drop-off site is located? Wonder where you can make a Saturday drop? Need to know what your delivery options are? Visit **www.fedex.com**.

PC Magazine

A timely source of computer information, product reviews and comparisons, technology, new trends, and links to other sites. Worth a visit at **www.pcmag.com**.

Microsoft.com

Microsoft has a ton of useful web sites. Begin your journey at **www.microsoft.com** . This site will give you an overview of the available Microsoft sites along with plenty of hot links, Microsoft news, and more.

The Microsoft Network

Speaking of Microsoft, back in 1995 (or was it '94?), Microsoft launched a brand-new online service with the unfortunate name of *The Microsoft Network* (oft-abbreviated *MSN*). Why they called it that, I'm sure I'll never know. Why not *Microsoft Online* or *Bill's Place* or anything but The Microsoft Network? Anyway, don't confuse MSN with the built-in Windows 95 networking feature called *Microsoft Network* (go figure), which you can use for peer-to-peer connections, in-house file sharing, and the like.

MSN was originally a dial-up service for which you paid a small amount (under $5.00, as I recall, if and when they remembered to bill you). It is now basically a collection of web sites that you will visit automatically after you install the Microsoft Internet Explorer web browser. (You need not use Microsoft's Internet Explorer, either. Netscape and other browses work as well. Visit **http://www.msn.com**.) Whichever way you get there, you'll see a welcome screen like the one in Figure 12.3.

MSN will connect you to a large and growing collection of libraries, interesting people, and services. There are great ways to track your investments, check movie showtimes in your neighborhood, catch up on the entertainment buzz, link with MSNBC (Bill's television network), and so much more. (Sounds a little like a press release, huh?) At any rate, give it a try. Keep an eye out as MSN evolves. There appear to be many interesting new features in the works, some of them free, others probably for a fee.

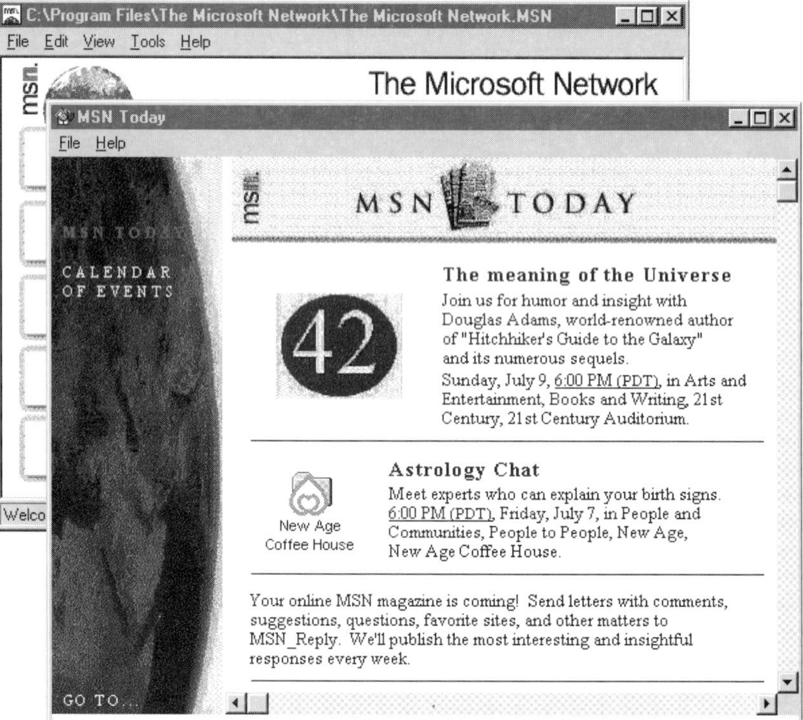

Figure 12.3 A typical Microsoft network screen (yours might look different)

When signing up for an online service, let the vendor know that you have Windows 95. You might get better software.

Commercial Online Services

Your modem probably came with free sign-up kits for the popular commercial sites like CompuServe, America Online, etc. There are entire magazines devoted to the subject of specialized online service vendors hawking everything from Bible study files to...how shall I say this? People who want to get to know you in the biblical sense.

The fancier services like America Online provide software that makes it possible to see photos, have real-time "conversations" with fellow modem addicts, etc. Figure 12.4 shows a typical AOL screen.

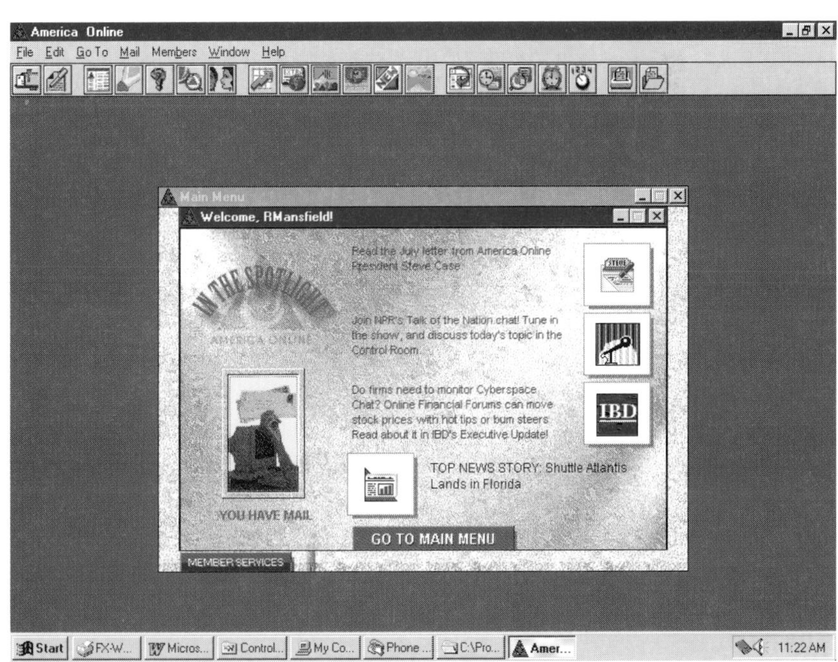

Figure 12.4 Reaching out in style with AOL

An excellent source of free and low-cost BBS listings is that unwieldy, oversized magazine **Computer Shopper.** *Just remember to lift with your knees, not your back!*

Free Bulletin Boards

There are thousands of free and low-cost Bulletin Board Services (often abbreviated BBS). Although many of these are available via the Internet, others you must dial directly via modem. Again, depending upon the service, you'll need either a general-purpose program like Microsoft's HyperTerminal (described next) or specialized software provided by the folks running the BBS.

The Hyperterminal Accessory

HyperTerminal, an accessory shipped with Windows 95, makes it possible for you to dial into BBS sites that do not provide their own specialized communications software. HyperTerminal lets you set up "connection settings files" for the various computers you regularly dial. You can use HyperTerminal to dial other Windows 95 users and exchange files. The program is TAPI-savvy, so it is pretty easy to get the modem set up properly.

To create a new connections setting, follow these steps:

1. Pick HyperTerminal from the Accessories submenu found under the Programs submenu on the Start menu.
2. Double-click the Hypertrm icon in the resulting window.

You can create Shortcut icons for your favorite HyperTerminal settings files and place them on your desktop or in your Start menu.

3. Type a name for the new settings file. (Make the name meaningful.)
4. Scroll to pick an icon to associate with the connection settings, and click OK. When the next dialog box appears, enter the area code for the computer you hope to dial, then type the phone number.

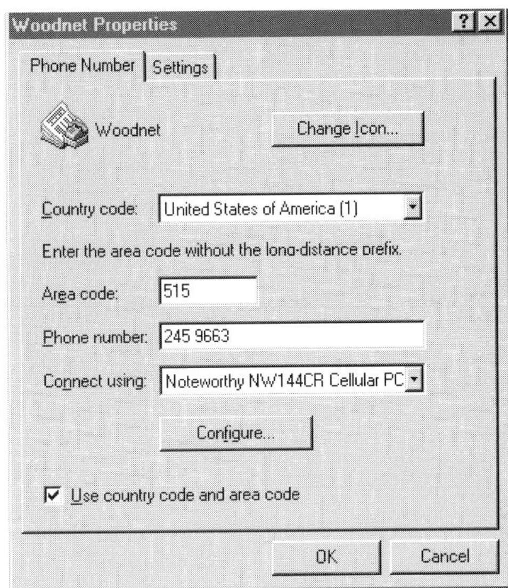

5. Because the Program is TAPI-happy, you can pick a modem from the resulting Connect Using list if you have more than one modem installed on your computer.
6. Click OK.
7. Change your location if that's appropriate (if you are on the road, for instance). Use Save on the File menu to store the settings.
8. To test the setup, click Dial. Do whatever is expected of you to log on at this dial-in location—enter a name and password, make menu choices, etc.

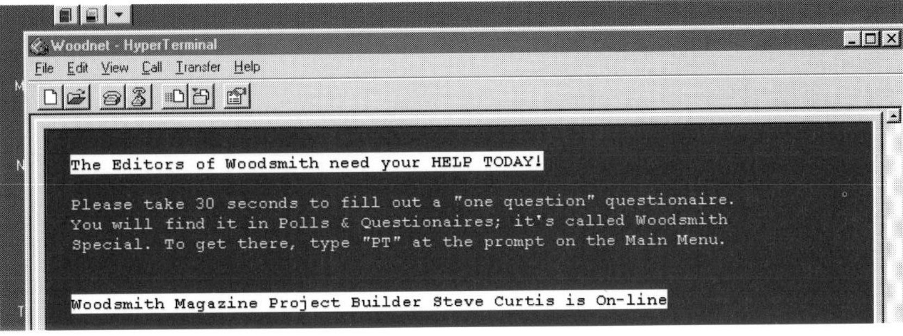

9. When finished, click the Disconnect button to hang up, and then choose Exit to quit HyperTerminal, or use the Open command to pick a different connection, or New to create new settings for a different location.

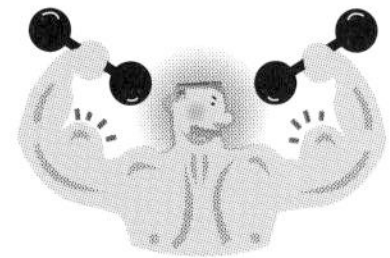

DEFINITION

download: *To retrieve copies of files from a remote computer. (See also* Getting Something for Nothing *and* Viruses.*)*

Downloading Files from a BBS with HyperTerminal

When you are connected to a BBS with HyperTerminal, you can visit the remote computer's file libraries and download files of interest (programs, sound files, etc.). HyperTerminal supports all of the popular file-transfer protocols including 1k Xmodem, Xmodem, Ymodem, Ymodem-G, Zmodem, and Kermit. When possible, use Zmodem. It is easy, reliable, and efficient. The actual downloading methods will vary from BBS to BBS.

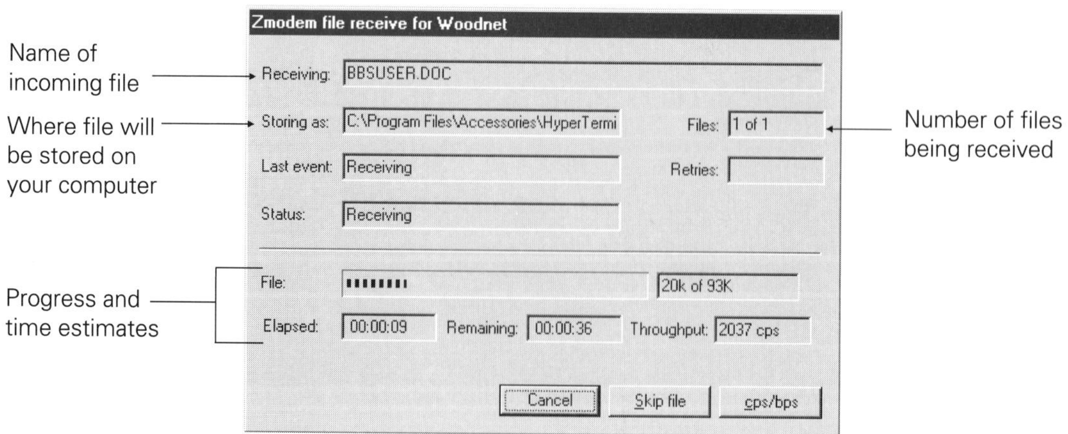

Dialing Into Your Office Network

If you work out of the office, you can use your modem-equipped computer to dial into your network if at least one of your network servers is equipped to accept your calls. You will need compatible modems and communications software on both the remote and the server machines. (Microsoft includes dial-up server software in its separate Microsoft Plus! package.)

Direct Connect

If you have two computers in the same room (or at least within spitting distance), and you want to exchange files between them but do not have network adapters installed, you might want to try the Windows 95 *Direct Connect* feature. It lets you exchange data by using the two computers' serial or parallel ports (connectors). You'll need a proper cable as well.

Direct Connect is not a shortcut you can use to avoid setting up regular network file-sharing services like the ones described in Chapter 11. In fact, you'll need to set up file sharing in order for Direct Connect to work. You'll be able to exchange files only if they reside in shared folders. So, before you start buying serial or parallel cables, and futzing with Direct Connect, consider installing Ethernet network cards, and leave those serial and parallel ports available for the purposes that God intended.

EXPERT ADVICE

If you plan to swap files infrequently, and if the files are small enough to fit on a diskette or two, use floppies rather than Direct Connect. For bigger projects, in the long run you'll be better off setting up a "real" network rather than using Direct Connect.

What You Will Need for a Direct Connection

You will need two Windows 95 computers, each with an available serial or parallel port. *Both* machines must have a serial port available or both must have a parallel port available. (It's no go if one has only an available serial port and the other has only a parallel port.)

If you have parallel ports available on both machines, and if you own the right cable, use the parallel ports rather than serial ports. This enables faster data transfers. To order parallel cables made for this purpose, phone Parallel Technologies at (800) 789-4784.

For serial ports, you want a *null modem cable* or a *regular serial cable* and a separate *null modem adapter.* In case you are asked by a technical salesperson, the goal is to swap the *send* and *receive* data lines via the cabling.

When buying cables, you need to count the number of pins on each connector (a serial cable typically—but not always—has either 25 or 9 pins) and know the *gender* (male or female) of the connectors on both cable ends *and* on the computer's ports. No, I am not making this up. That's the proper terminology; and when you look at a few cables and connectors, you'll figure out why the terms are so...easy to remember. What you want is a cable that properly *mates* (I know, I know) with both computers.

There is a good chance that you can get what you need for serial connections at your local Radio Shack store. Make drawings or tracings of each computer's ports (connectors) before going. Be sure to write down the, umm...sex of each computer's connector. Some computers, particularly portables, use oddball, non-standard plugs and jacks that will make life difficult.

Sometimes, Windows 95's Direct Connect software is not automatically installed by the Windows installer. Both computers require it. So you might need to use the Add/Remove Software feature in the Windows control panel on one or both machines first. To see if the Direct Connect software is installed, look for a Direct Cable Connection option in the Accessories submenu of the Programs choice.

Using Direct Connect

Once you find mates for all of those connectors, and once the Direct Connection software is installed on both machines, you are ready to rock and roll. You begin by running the Direct Connect software on one machine. It displays a Wizard to lead you through the necessary steps:

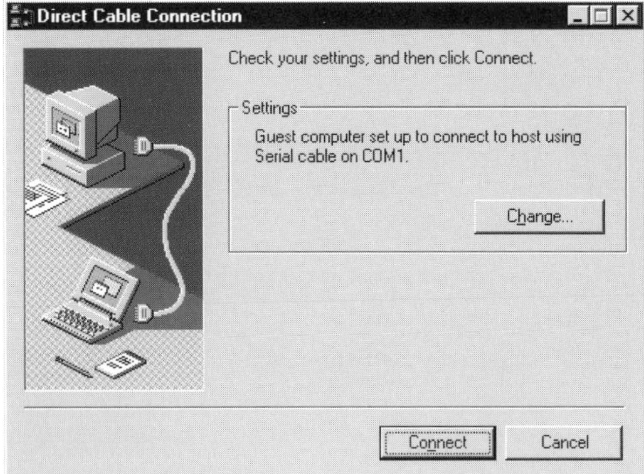

Direct Connect Tips

You will be asked if you want the computer to be a Host or Guest. Make the computer you're working on a Host, and make the other machine a Guest (you can't connect two Hosts or two Guests). Know which port you've used on each machine (COM1, LPT1, etc.). Labels near a computer's connectors should provide you with clues as to which port you're near. Don't guess about which port you're using. The software will prompt you for the name of the port you're hooked into, and if you type in the wrong port name the entire operation will be a bust. Stay the course and keep looking until you know into which port you're plugging that connector.

CAUTION

Although you can't get hurt connecting and disconnecting serial and parallel cables, in rare instances, your computer can. To be safe, power down before plugging and unplugging computer connectors.

Be sure you've enabled the appropriate file sharing on the machine with the resources to be shared so that the guest can "see" and use the desired resources.

Know the *network* names of both computers. You might be asked for one or both names if the Wizard can't connect automatically. Read dialog boxes *carefully* and think about what you are being asked. Once you get connected, you'll see a Host window that will look like disk and folder windows that you've used previously. Use shared resources as you'd expect. (Drag files and folders from one machine to the other, etc.)

Sending and Receiving Fax Messages

If your modem is fax-capable (virtually all contemporary modems are), you can use your computer to send and receive faxes. As is so often the case, you have more than enough options in this regard. Your modem probably came with fax software, some of which is pretty good. (WinFax and WinFax LITE, for example, are both thorough, easy-to-use programs.)

Once you've installed it, you can let this software run in the background where it will answer the fax line whenever it rings, save the incoming fax to disk, and alert you. When you have the time, you can display, print, save, or delete the fax.

You can use this same fax software to prepare and send faxes, and even create a phone book containing fax phone numbers, distribution lists, and so on.

In addition, most fax programs have features that enable your fax-capable modem to behave as though it were a printer. When using these fax printing features, you simply choose the fax modem as the printer, as shown in Figure 12.5. Then you can "print" your Word documents or Excel spreadsheets, or CorelDRAW images and what-all to your fax modem, where they will be sent to the specified recipient(s).

Fancier fax programs also have built-in optical character recognition (OCR) features that turn received faxed documents into text for editing with programs like Word.

Another way to send and receive faxes is to use Microsoft Exchange, discussed next.

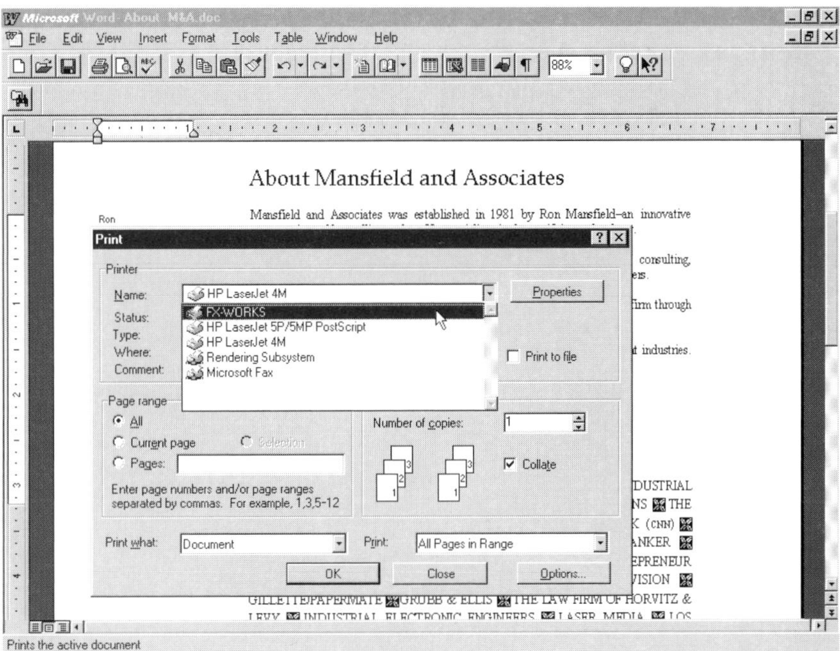

Figure 12.5 With the right fax software, transmitting a Word document can be as easy as printing

Faxing with Microsoft Fax

Once you've properly installed Microsoft Exchange, you should be able to send faxes either from the Inbox (described later in this chapter), or by using the Microsoft Fax choice in any Print dialog box. In order to receive faxes, you'll need to have your computer powered up and your modem set to answer the fax line when fax calls arrive. (If you have non-TAPI software, this older, non-Windows 95-compliant software must not be running.) Received faxes can be viewed from the Exchange Inbox window and printed on your printer. The first step to doing any of this, however, is to be sure your fax properties are properly configured.

EXPERT ADVICE

As always, when shopping for fax programs, give extra points to Windows 95-savvy software. It is likely to be quicker and more robust than olderware.

Setting Fax Properties

If you plan to send and receive faxes, you'll need to have your fax properties in order. Here is the procedure for a typical setup:

1. Double-click the Inbox icon on your desktop to open the Inbox.
2. Choose Services from the Tools menu in the Inbox - Microsoft Exchange window.

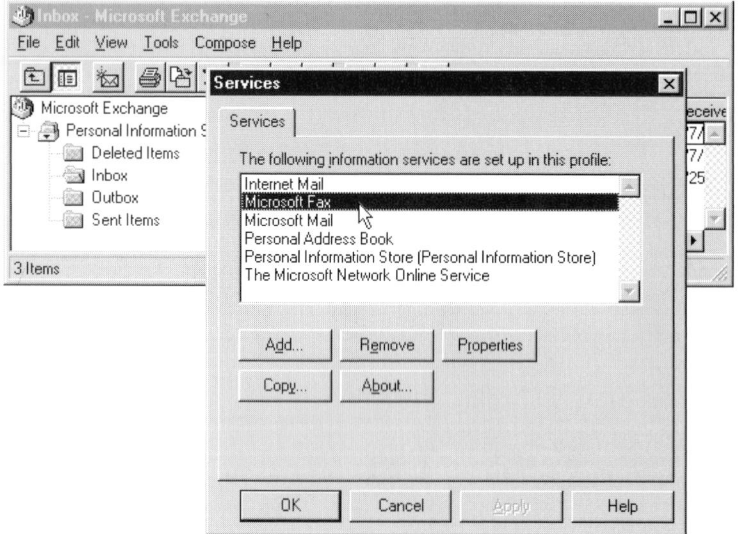

3. Double-click Microsoft Mail in the resulting Services tab (you might need to scroll the list to see this choice).
4. When you see the Microsoft Fax Properties dialog box, shown here, check out all four tabs.

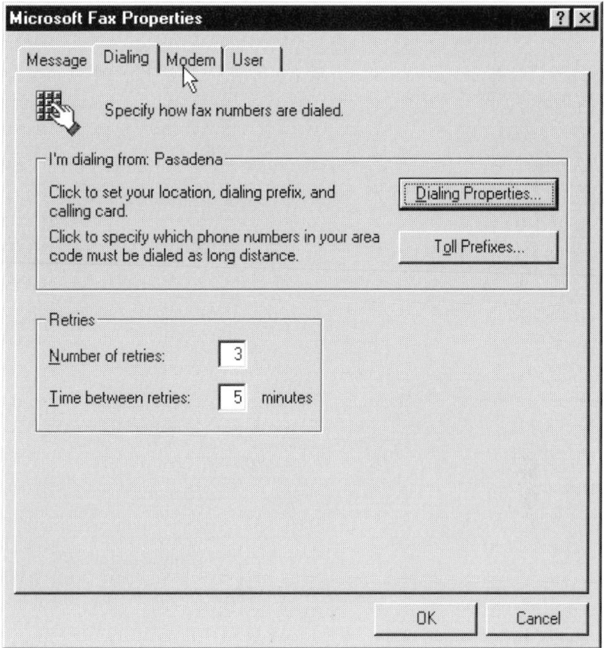

Start by making sure that information on the User tab (your name, phone number, etc.) is correct. Next, check to see that the correct modem has been specified as the Active Fax modem in the Modem tab. Specify the desired number of retries and the time between retries in the Dialing tab. Finally, visit the Message tab to be sure that the Time to end is set to "As soon as possible" if you want fax messages to go out immediately.

5. If you want your modem to answer the phone for incoming faxes, you'll need to visit the Fax Modem Properties dialog box as well. (Notice that this is not the same as the Modem Properties dialog box.) You can reach the Fax Modem Properties dialog box by using the Properties button in the Modem tab of the Microsoft Fax Properties dialog box.

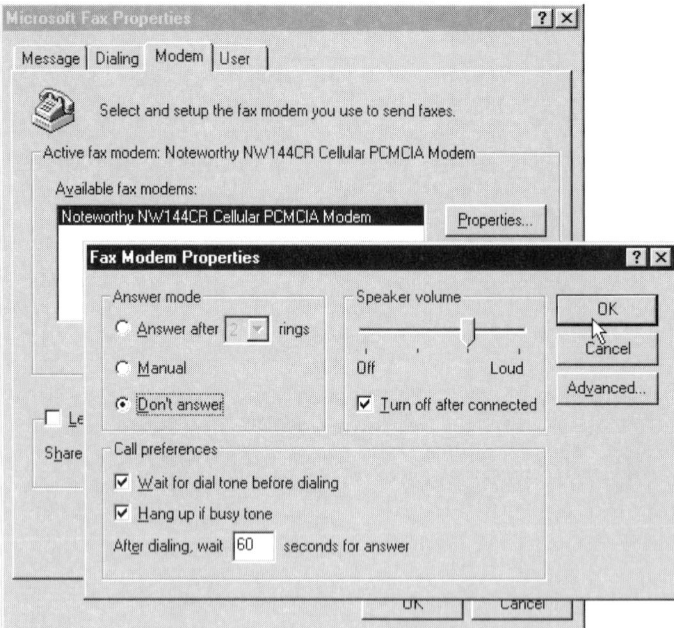

6. Specify the number of rings desired before the modem answers the phone. (Or, choose "Manual" if you want to be in charge of answering, or "Don't answer" if you never want the modem to pick up.)
7. Make any other desired changes, and then click OK to close the Fax Modem Properties dialog box.
8. Click OK again to close the Microsoft Fax Properties dialog box.
9. Click OK yet again to close the Services dialog box.
10. Say a little prayer to the Fax Gods. You should now be ready to send and receive fax messages. Let's find out.

Sending Faxes with Microsoft Fax

Rather than printing out documents on paper and stuffing them into a traditional fax machine, Windows lets you "print" directly to your fax modem so that fax recipients can get nice-looking (up to 300 dpi) faxes without your getting up from that chair. Assuming that Exchange and your modem are properly installed, here are the basic steps:

1. Prepare your document normally. It can be a Word memo, an Excel spreadsheet, time cards, or any document from any application that supports Windows 95 printing.
2. Choose Print from the File menu or use the CTRL-P keyboard shortcut (but not *necessarily* the little Print buttons in so many toolbars these days, since many times, the button will not take you to a Print Dialog box before printing).
3. When you see the Print dialog box, pick Microsoft Fax from the list of printers.

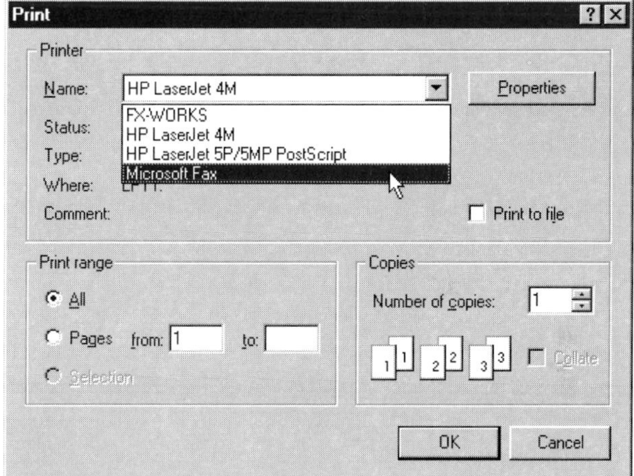

4. To adjust the settings for your faxing tasks (page orientation, resolution, page size, etc.), click the Properties button, make the changes, then click OK to return from the Properties dialog box.
5. Back in the Print dialog box, specify the number of pages you want to print or a page range (all, just page 1, just the current page, etc.).
6. Use the Options button in the Print dialog box to choose additional printing options appropriate to the task (OLE updates, etc.).

7. Click OK in the Print dialog box.
8. Your disk drive will hum for a moment, and you'll see a "Compose New Fax" Wizard:

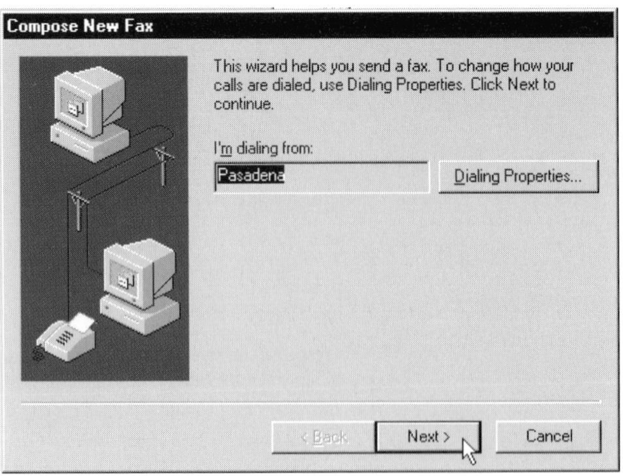

Be patient! You are shipping a lot of tiny little dots over phone lines designed long ago to perform an entirely different task.

9. Specify the "Dialing From" location if the correct location isn't already listed, then click the Next button.
10. When you see the next screen, either enter the name of the recipient and her or his fax machine phone number, or choose a recipient from your Address Book if you've already set one up. (The Address Book is discussed later in this chapter.)
11. If you only need to send the document to one recipient, click Next. Or, to specify multiple recipients at this point, use the Add to List button instead of the Next button. When you have specified all desired recipients, click Next.
12. You will be asked if you want a cover page. Pick one if you do (Confidential, Urgent, etc.), or click No to cut transmission time and minimize paper waste at the other end.
13. Click Next.

14. Enter a subject and optional note for the cover page in the resulting dialog box and click Next.
15. Click Finish to send the fax.
16. You should see the Inbox and a Microsoft Fax Status window. With any luck you'll see the Status window display the phone number being dialed, the progress of the call, the speed of the connection, etc.

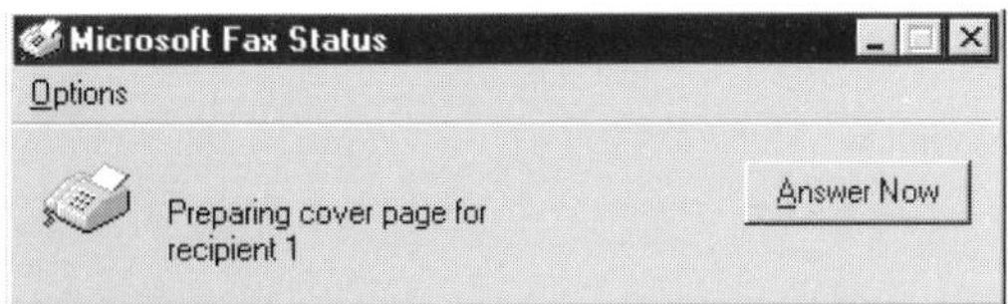

17. Call your partner-in-crime at the receiving end to see if the document arrived satisfactorily. While you are on the phone, why not ask your friend to send you a test fax for the next stop on our pilgrimage: receiving fax messages?

Receiving Faxes with Microsoft Fax

If your computer and modem are powered up, and if you've set the modem to answer, and if the Exchange software is running, Exchange will answer the fax line on the number of rings you have specified. You will get a status report as the fax arrives.

Once it is all in, you will be able to view and print the fax with the Inbox tools described in a moment.

CAUTION

It's easy to quit Exchange instead of minimizing it when cleaning up your desktop. If exchange is not running, your incoming faxes will not be accepted. If you use Exchange as your primary incoming fax system, it's especially important that you check the Taskbar regularly to ensure that Exchange is running.

The Exchange Window

The Exchange window is the focal point of Microsoft Exchange. "In-and-Out-Box" might be a better name for this window, because this is where you check to see if you have new mail as well as where you begin the process of composing new, *outgoing* mail. It is where you read your mail and manage your mail-related files. The Exchange window is also where you view and print fax messages.

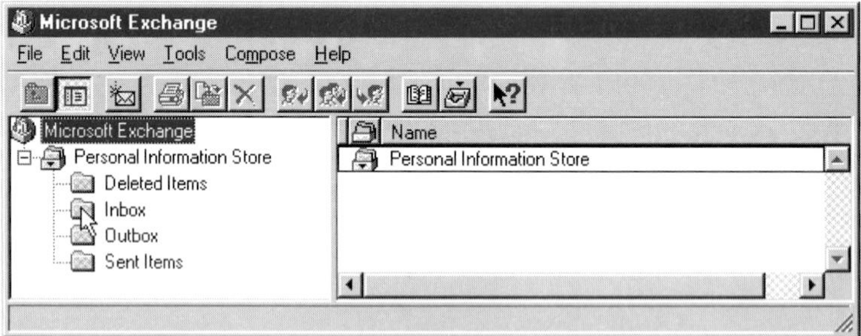

The window normally has two panes with folders in the left pane. (If you don't see folders, use the Folders command on the View menu to display them.) The left pane shows you the available folders for storing your message files. These folders are called *Information Stores.* When you click a folder in the left pane, its contents are displayed in the right pane. You can create very complex arrangements of information stores if you plan to keep lots of old messages and choose to organize them by project, or correspondent, for example. For now, keep things simple, busy person.

Viewing and Printing Faxes and Other Messages

You open the Inbox either by double-clicking the Inbox icon found on your desktop or by clicking on the Inbox folder in the Exchange window. The incoming messages might be from others in your workgroup, or perhaps from CompuServe and MSN users.

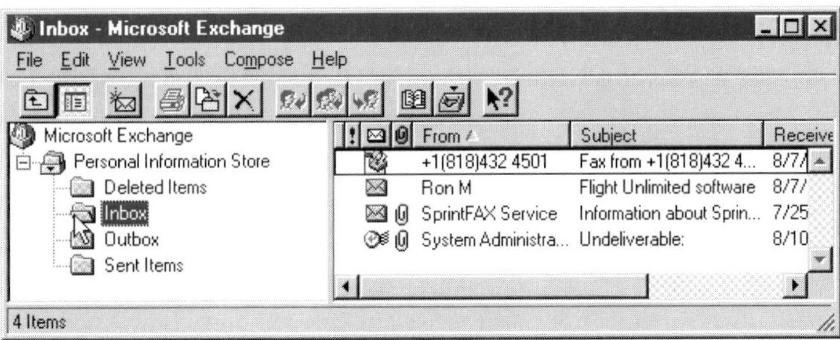

The messages can be just plain text, or text and an attached file, or even fax messages. This is the whole point of Microsoft Exchange—it gives you one place to deal with messages from a variety of sources.

Listings for unread messages are bolder than listings for things you've already read. You can change the size and shape of the Inbox window, and drag column headings to change column widths. As you can see, whenever a message has a file attached to it, you'll see a little paper clip next to the sender's name.

Viewing Messages in Your Inbox

To view an Inbox fax or other message, double-click it in the Inbox list. Exchange will open the message and display it. Scroll, if necessary, to read the whole thing. Figure 12.6 shows a typical message window. Your other Windows skills (like resizing windows, selecting, copying, and pasting) can be employed in the Inbox as well.

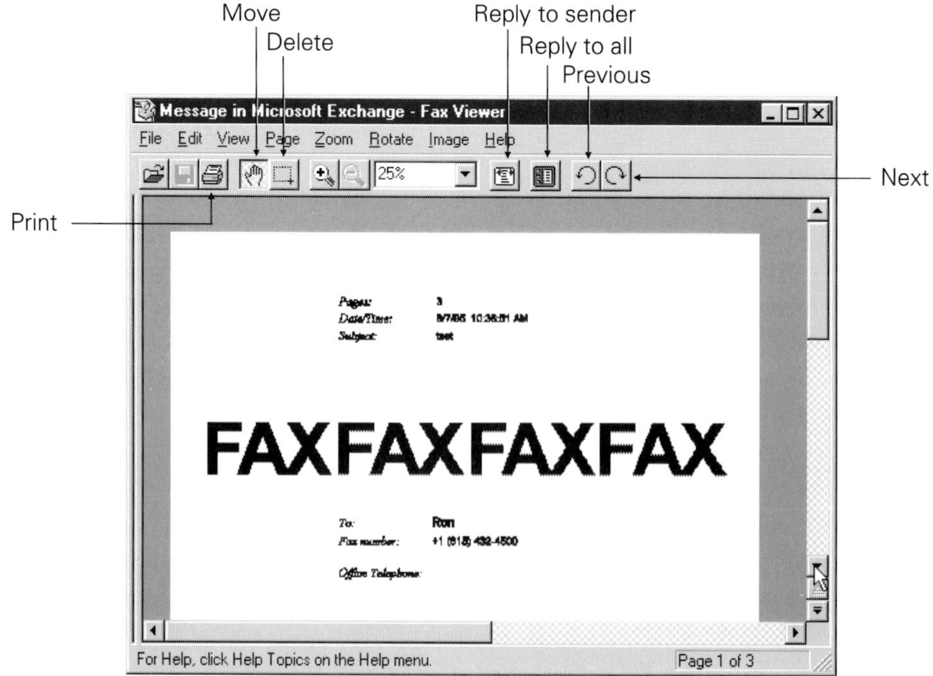

Figure 12.6 A typical Exchange fax message window and its button functions

Using Windows as a Telephone Speed-Dialer

If you plug a phone into the phone jack on modems that have both a line and a phone jack, or if you plug your modem into the same wall socket as your phone, you can use the Windows 95 dialer accessory to "speed-dial" favorite numbers.

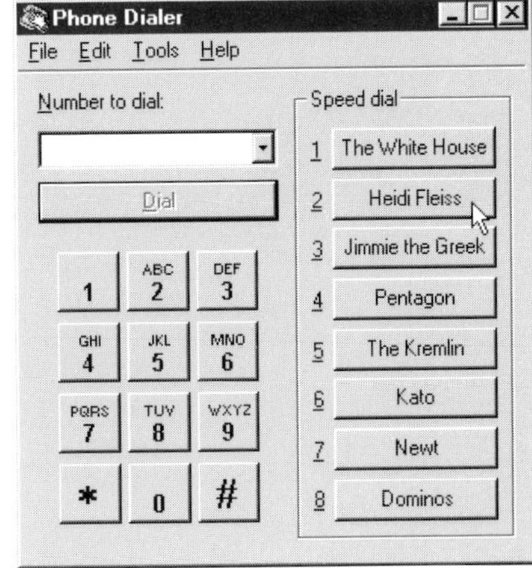

It also supports OLE links to Microsoft Schedule+ contacts lists, so if you have Schedule+, you can automatically dial phone numbers by clicking the little telephone icon in your Schedule+ Contacts screen.

Troubleshooting Modem Connections

Committees design modems, so there's plenty to go wrong. If you've had success using your modem for something in particular, only to have it fail later at the exact same task, ask yourself what's changed.

- Check the phone line. Have the squirrels devoured the wire running from the pole to the building?? (They eat mine at least twice a year.)
- Do some software packages work while others don't? This probably means the modem's okay and you are having a software problem.
- Try turning the modem (and perhaps the computer) off and back on.

The Windows 95 online help system has some built-in modem troubleshooting features. From the Help window's Find tab, type **troubleshooting modem**, and the following Help window will appear. Simply poke the buttons therein.

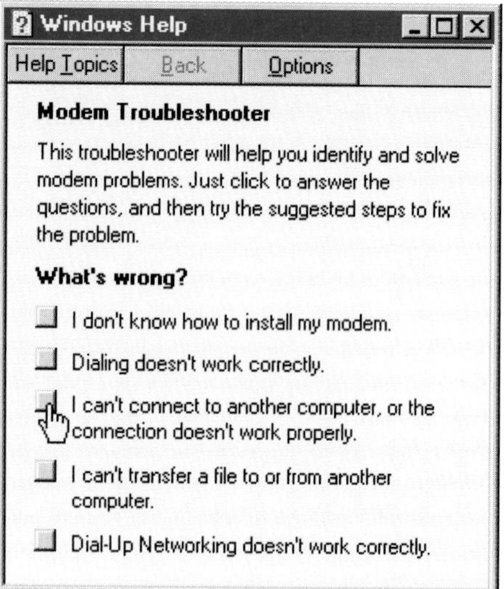

Well, that's a lot of ground in one chapter, huh? If you haven't already done it, set up your modem location information and check the other settings. If you've been putting off getting set up for the Internet, why not get started now? If you are already on the Net check out some of those sites mentioned in this chapter. Or dig out that America Online and CompuServe sign-up software and establish an account or two.

Multimedia is the topic of our final chapter. If you don't now have speakers and a CD-ROM drive for your system, Chapter 13 might get you thinking about a trip to the store.

CHAPTER

13

Multimedia: Sights and Sounds

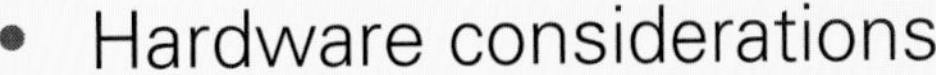

INCLUDES

- Hardware considerations
- Playing music files
- Playing video clips
- MIDI
- Playing music CDs on your computer
- Recording music files
- Sources of multimedia information and files

FAST FORWARD

Find and Play Sounds ➤ pp. 334-335

1. Choose Find on the Start menu.
2. Choose Files or Folders.
3. Type ***.wav** in the Named box.
4. Specify My Computer in the Look In box.
5. Click the Find Now button.
6. Double-click files that appear in the resulting list.

Find and Play Video Clips ➤ p. 336

1. Choose Find on the Start menu.
2. Choose Files or Folders.
3. Type ***.avi** in the Named box.
4. Specify My Computer in the Look In box.
5. Click the Find Now button.
6. Double-click files that appear in the resulting list.

Find and Play MIDI Files ➤ p. 337

1. Choose Find on the Start menu.
2. Choose Files or Folders.
3. Type ***.mid** in the Named box.
4. Specify My Computer in the Look In box.
5. Click the Find Now button.
6. Double-click files that appear in the resulting list.

Play Music CDs ➤ pp. 337-339

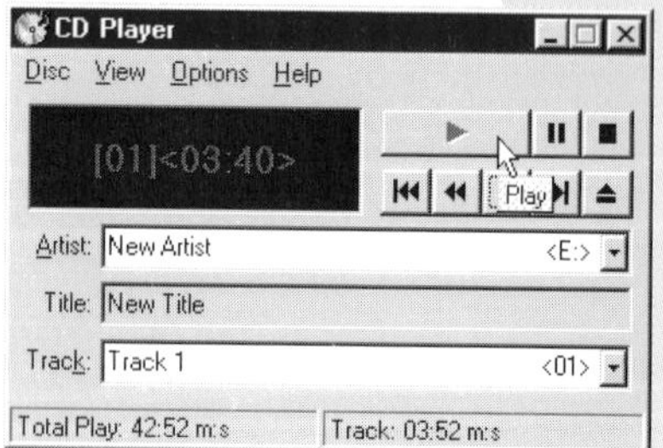

1. Insert a music CD.
2. Windows 95 will display the CD Player accessory and play the music, thanks to AutoPlay.
3. Click the onscreen buttons in the CD Player window to pause, advance, etc.
4. Music continues if you minimize or deactivate the window.
5. Closing (exiting) the Player stops the music.

Record Your Own Audio Files ➤ *p. 339-341*

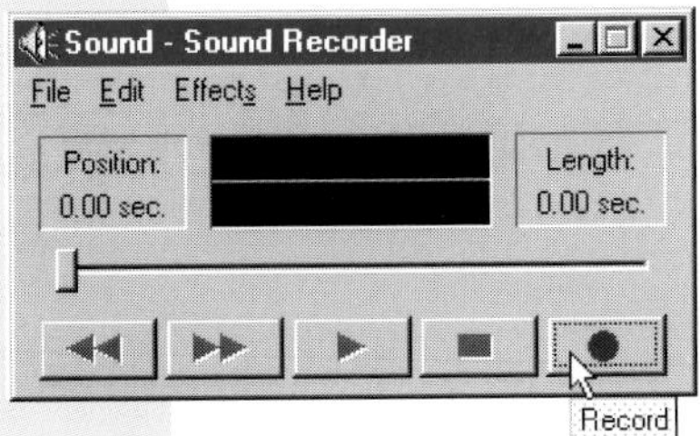

1. Connect an audio source to your computer's audio input (microphone, etc.).
2. Choose Programs from the Start menu.
3. Pick Accessories, then Multimedia.
4. Launch Sound Recorder.
5. Click the round, red Record button.
6. To avoid distortion, level spikes should not touch the black window's edges.
7. Play back and optionally save your recording.

Check Multimedia Settings ➤ *pp. 341-342*

1. Choose Settings from the Start menu.
2. Choose the Control Panel option.
3. Double-click the Multimedia icon.
4. Select the tab(s) of interest.

Place Multimedia Files in Documents ➤ *p. 343*

Drag icons for multimedia files into documents created by most OLE-savvy programs, including Word, PowerPoint, etc. Icons will appear at the insertion points in the documents. Double-clicking will play the multimedia files.

I need your thoughts on this guy

Here's the new announcer we are thinking about using in the commercials. Double click the speaker to hear him. What say?

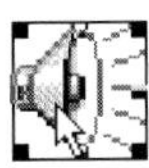

In the past, I've joked that the term multimedia refers to any four-thousand-dollar-and-up collection of mostly inoperative hardware and software attached to cheap-sounding speakers. That's changing. Everything's getting less expensive. Seriously, the stuff's getting more reliable too. Let's check out multimedia and perhaps play a clip or two.

An Overview of Multimedia

As software designers increase their use of multimedia features, you'll see more and more video woven into games, encyclopedias, etc. You'll also hear awesome sounds in games, reference documents, product demos, and so on.

For our purposes, think of *three* multimedia ingredients: audio, video, and MIDI. Even though these three ingredients often work together, we'll explore them separately. If your computer is properly equipped, Windows 95's *audio* multimedia features will let you hear, and perhaps record, nearly lifelike sounds. These sounds are often stored in disk files ending with the extension .wav. (As you will see in a moment, sounds can be stored in other types of files as well.)

Video capabilities will let you see "television-like animation" on your computer's screen. Again, the files that produce these moving pictures can be stored on your hard disk or come to you on CD-ROMs. Frequently, the names of these digital video files end with the extension .avi.

If you have the right hardware and third-party software, you'll be able to capture your own still pictures and full-motion video to disk. There are even products for sale that let you create "video telephones" that (almost, kinda, sorta) work over the Internet.

MIDI features let you, among other things, connect musical instruments like electronic keyboards to your computer. Musicians use MIDI setups to create and document their music. They use MIDI in performances as well. MIDI features also let non-musicians play stored MIDI files on their computers, mimicking a wide array of instruments, turning computers into one-man bands (and one-woman bands). MIDI files typically end in the extension .mid.

Hardware Considerations

Let's start with what you probably already have. Look in the lower-right corner of your Windows screen. Is there a little icon of a speaker there?

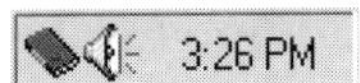

Yes? Good. That means you probably have some kind of Windows 95-compatible audio hardware installed that Windows 95 recognizes. If not, skim this chapter anyway. It might get you jazzed enough to whip out the old checkbook.

At a minimum, you will need a sound card or built-in audio features. Even older 8-bit sound cards like early Sound Blasters will work. Turning to your display, minimally, you'll need a VGA color monitor and display adapter capable of displaying at least 256 colors. To really enjoy multimedia requires a reasonably fast processor (read Pentium or at least a 486DX 50), a 4X-speed or faster CD-ROM drive, local-bus video with 24-bit display electronics, Super VGA (800 × 600), 16-bit color, 32-bit audio, and MIDI (either a card or built into your motherboard), and probably a gold Visa or MasterCard.

AutoPlay

If your computer *is* multimedia capable, you might have experienced a multimedia event when you popped in your Windows 95 installation CD, thanks to a new standard called *AutoPlay.* Windows 95 recognizes CD-ROMs containing AutoPlay instructions for multimedia presentations, and can start them as soon as the CD-ROM is inserted.

To prevent AutoPlay from doing its thing, hold down the SHIFT key when you insert a CD-ROM.

If you have your Windows CD-ROM handy, pop it in the old CD-ROM drive and see if you get a welcome screen and hear music. If you do, that's AutoPlay at work. Click the Video Clips button and double-click the .avi files in the resulting window. Or, to play a killer multimedia-embellished game, click the Hover icon. The Microsoft Expo icon will give you a pretty cool multimedia sales pitch for guess what? More Microsoft toys.

Playing Audio Files

There are plenty of multimedia files on your hard disk even if you don't have a CD-ROM drive yet. Let's round up some and play them by following these steps:

STEP BY STEP Finding and Hearing Audio Files

1. **Choose Find from the Start menu, then choose Files or Folders.**
2. **Type** *.wav **in the Named box.**
3. **Change the Look In choice to My Computer, and be sure there's a checkmark in the Include Subfolders box.**
4. **Click the Find Now button. You should see a list of sound files.**
5. **Double-click the icon of a sound file to play it.**
6. **You should, albeit briefly, see the Sound Recorder box and hear the sound you've chosen.**

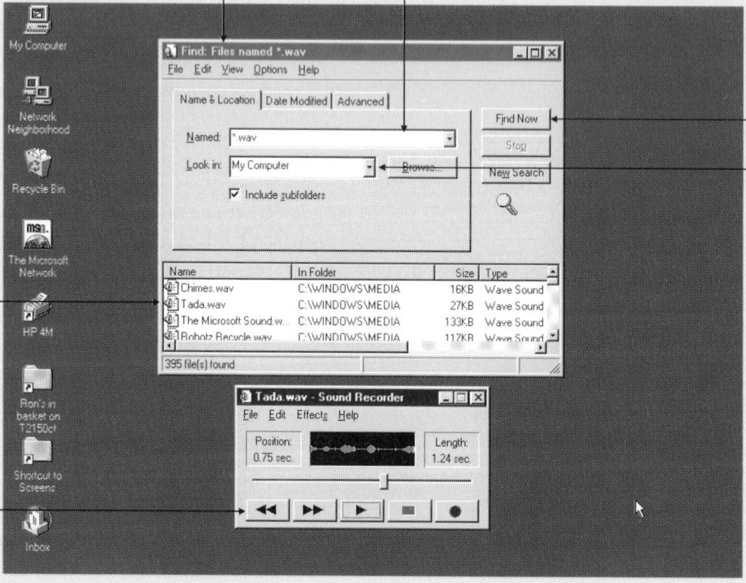

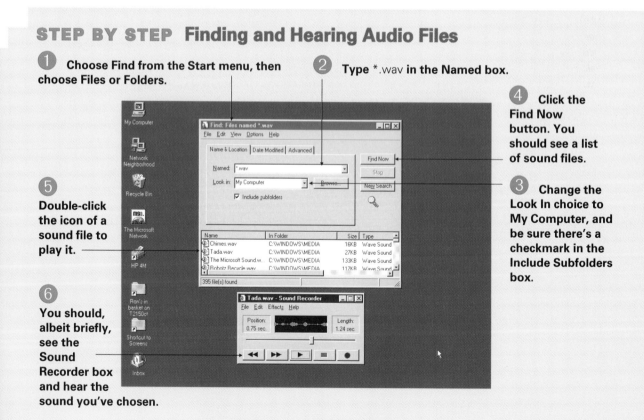

Controlling Volume

There are almost too many ways to control the audio volume of multimedia presentations. Your computer or its external speakers might have regular old volume control knobs. Mine do. These are handy and effective. My favorite software control is the little speaker icon in the Taskbar. Right-clicking it brings up a little volume control slider. Drag it to adjust loudness.

The Multimedia control panel's Audio tab has a sliding volume control that adjusts the overall playback volume of multimedia sounds. (The Multimedia control panel is explored in detail later in this chapter.)

Finally, there is an accessory called Volume Control:

If you have the Windows 95 CD-ROM, be sure to check out the files in the Videos folder (located in the FunStuff folder). My favorite is Welcome3. Goodtime is a close second.

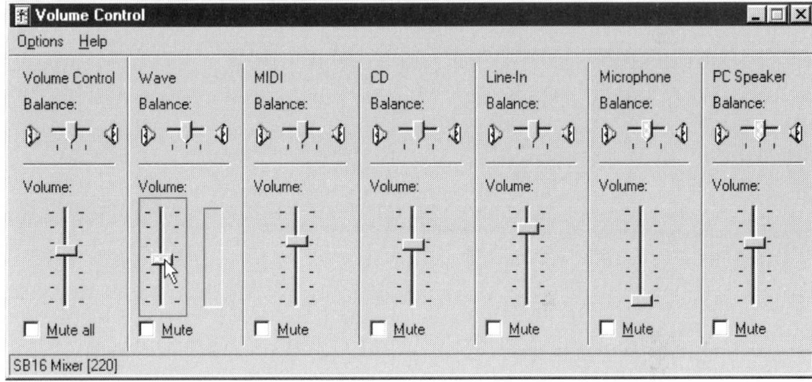

It's an onscreen *mixer* that lets you see and control the levels of most multimedia sounds. Reach the Volume Control from the Start menu by choosing Programs, then Accessories, then Multimedia.

A mixer is an audio device that has multiple sliders to control volume. The actual number of sliders on your mixer will vary based on how many potential sound sources are installed on your computer. When a clip is playing, you'll see a level indicator rise and fall for the sound source. Dragging the associated knob up or down increases and decreases the volume.

Playing Video Clips

To find and play *video* files, use the same basic techniques that you used to locate sounds, but this time look for ".avi" filenames. When you double-click .avi files in the Find list (or elsewhere on your screen), the Multimedia Player plays them. Follow these steps:

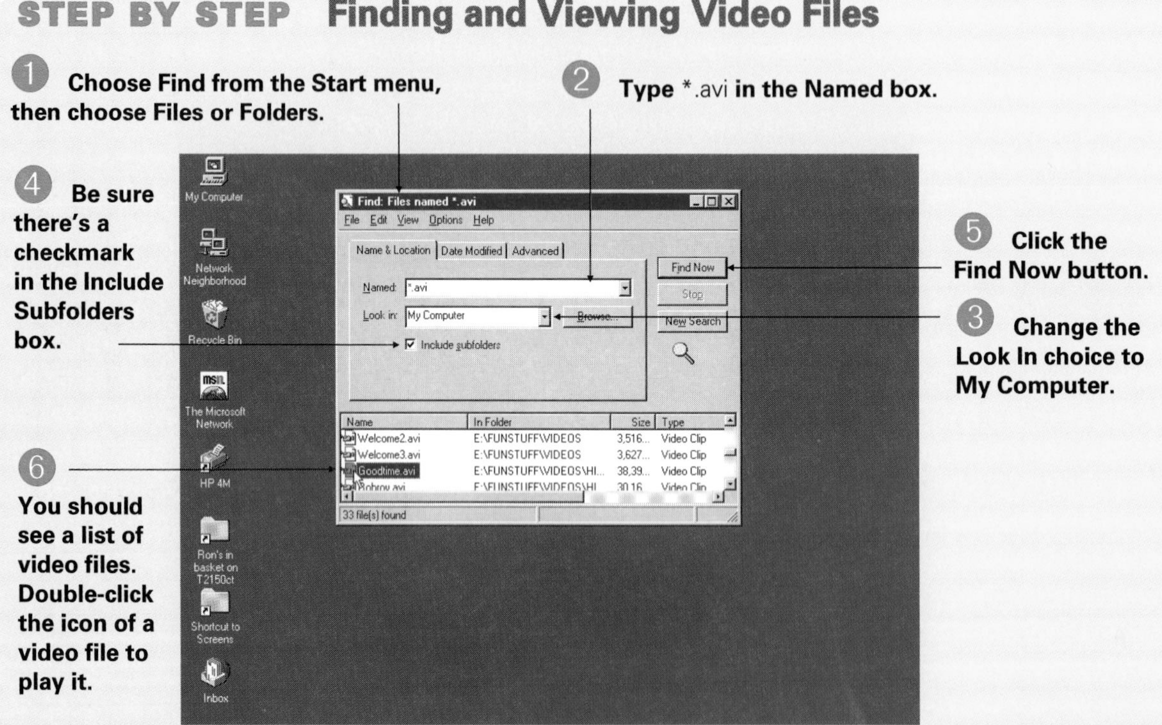

Onscreen Video Size and Quality

You can make the video image fill your screen by visiting the Video tab in the Multimedia control panel (described later in this chapter). The Video tab offers a number of additional image size choices. The results can be grainy and surreal—interesting, but probably not the way you will run most of your video clips.

What's MIDI Anyway?

MIDI is an industry-wide standard for connecting and controlling electronic musical instruments. Like all standards, it is convoluted enough that even the richest and nerdiest musicians can be heard uttering the F word when they use it, but nearly any one of 'em would kill you if you ever tried to take away their MIDI toys. For those of us who are musically challenged, MIDI enables us to play musical creations of others, either on musical instruments that we buy, or through MIDI-capable sound cards in our computers. You can, for example, purchase MIDI files created by famous keyboard artists and play them on your home MIDI keyboard. It's a little like having your favorite piano player over to the house for dinner. (Yeah, right.)

Much (some would argue most) of the free and nearly free MIDI files floating around are crap. (Can I say that in a computer book?) Play as many MIDI files as you can get your hands on and let me know what you think.

EXPERT ADVICE

To find and play MIDI files, use the same basic techniques you used to locate sounds and video, but this time look for the .mid extensions. When you double-click a .mid file in the Find list (or elsewhere on your screen), the Media Player plays it.

Playing Music CDs

Have you ever wanted to turn your computer into the equivalent of a $50 CD player? Well, gadgeteers, keep reading. Most CD-ROM drives will also accept music CDs. Windows 95 comes with a nifty little multimedia accessory called CD Player, shown here, which lets you play music CDs by clicking onscreen buttons that look like the real thing.

You can specify the order in which songs are played, skip the dog cuts, and so on by creating and storing *play lists*. Heck, setting up play lists for your favorite CDs is the perfect way to fritter away a rainy Saturday, huh?

First, some potential gotchas: Either your CD-ROM drive must have a headphone jack (so that you can plug in headphones), or the audio outputs from your CD-ROM drive mechanism must be jumpered (cabled) into your computer's audio electronics. (Although this is often done at the factory, it isn't *always* done.) Alternatively, your CD-ROM drive might have audio jacks that can be connected to amplified speakers or a real stereo. In other words, you need to find a way to get the sound outta the CD-ROM drive and into your ears. Occasionally, the documentation that comes with add-on drives and computers makes the necessary hookup steps perfectly clear, but you might need technical help. The quick way to get started is to just give it a try (perhaps with and without headphones). Here's how:

1. Pop in a music CD (Bonnie Raitt would be my preference).
2. Shut the CD-ROM drive door (by pressing the Eject button or whatever).
3. Watch the screen. You'll see a CD Player window open (that's AutoPlay helpin' ya). The CD Player window's counter will increment, indicating that music's streamin' into somewhere. With luck, it will be streaming into your computer's *speakers*. (Bonnie's complaining that she wants a *real* man as I write this.)
4. Adjust the volume either with your amplified speaker's knobs or with the Volume Control accessory. (You know...in the Multimedia sublevel of the Accessories sublevel of the Programs choice on the Start menu.)

5. Click the CD Player window's onscreen buttons to pause, skip, go back, etc.

   When you *minimize* the CD Player window (or make a different window the active window), the music continues, and the Taskbar button for the CD Player shows you the current track number and incremental track time.
6. To stop the music, click the Stop button, or close the CD Player accessory.
7. To restart the CD Player, either insert a music CD or visit the Multimedia submenu and pick CD Player.
8. To learn more about creating track lists, random play, etc., consult the Help menu in the CD Player window.

CAUTION

I almost forgot the most important part. Music played this way can sometimes sound like ... well, I hate to use the C word again, so let's put it this way: Don't sell that home theater electronics and those B&W 850 speakers 'til you've listened to your CDs on your computer for a while.

Creating Your Own Audio Files

If your computer has audio input jacks for a microphone (and perhaps line inputs for other sources like tape players, etc.), you can use the Sound Recorder accessory to record external sounds to disk. Once you've recorded them, you can play sounds as described earlier, assign them to play automatically at startup or other noteworthy events, or include them in documents. You could, for instance, record your own startup sound that plays when Windows starts, or create a written report in Word or a slide show in PowerPoint and add your own "voice-over" audio narration. Even if your computer does not have audio input jacks, you can combine prerecorded .wav and other sound files to create a new sound file. Check the documentation that came with your computer or add-in sound board. Rummage through the closet. Can you still find the microphone that came with your sound card? You thought you'd never use it, huh?

Look behind the computer to see what the audio input jacks look like. Plug in the microphone or another sound source. Run to Radio Shack for the necessary cables and adapters, if you want to connect some external audio source like your electric guitar amp, or your VCR's Audio Out jacks.

To record you'll need to run the Sound Recorder accessory. Follow these steps.

1. Make sure a microphone or other compatible sound source is plugged into your computer.
2. Choose Programs from the Start menu.
3. Choose Accessories. Select Multimedia and then Sound Recorder.
4. Click the Red (circular) button to begin recording. You should see an audio waveform corresponding to the sound being recorded. Spikes should stay within the top and bottom of the rectangular window, as shown in Figure 13.1.
5. Press the Stop (rectangular) button to stop recording.
6. Choose Save from the File menu to name and save the recorded sound.

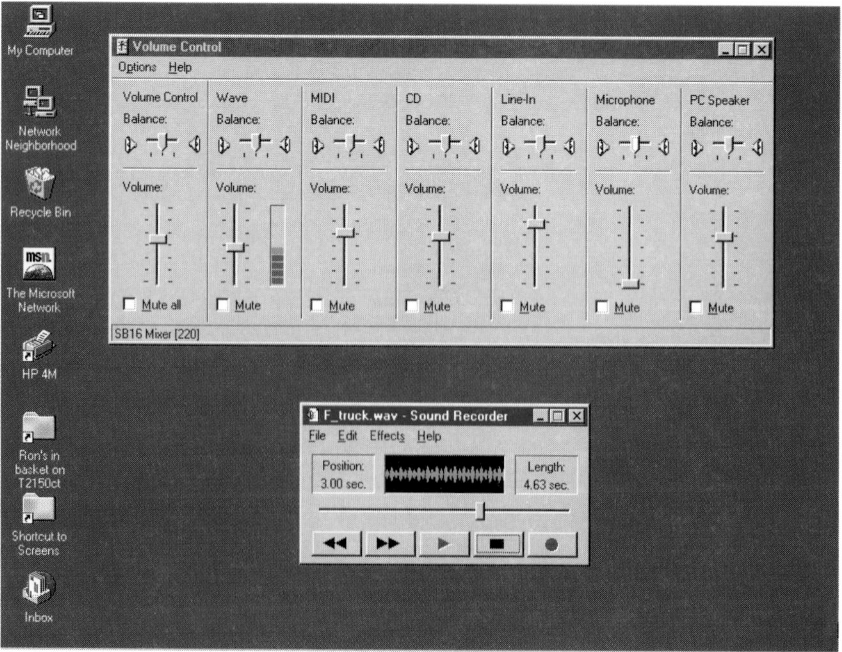

Figure 13.1 The Sound Recorder box shows the audio waveform of the sound being recorded.

If your computer is equipped with fancy audio capabilities, you can use the mixer to combine sounds from multiple sources. All you advanced fritterers should consult the manuals that came with your sound accessories, and get online help for details.

Playing Back Your Sound Files

Use the Sound Recorder accessory to open the sound file (unless you've just recorded a sound, in which case it is ready to be played). Click the Play (right-pointing triangle button) to play back the sound. Drag the slider to start playing mid-sound, if you like.

Sound Editing

Use the Sound Recorder accessory to open the sound file (unless you've just recorded a sound, in which case it is ready to be edited). Use the choices on the Effects menu to add echo, change speed, etc. Play the edited sounds.

Save the changes if you like them; otherwise, answer No when asked if you want to save changes when closing the file or exiting the accessory.

The Multimedia Control Panel

The Multimedia control panel collects most of the salient settings for your audio and video system elements. You can use it to review and adjust your system's audio and video settings.

Pick a multimedia device.

Adjust settings.

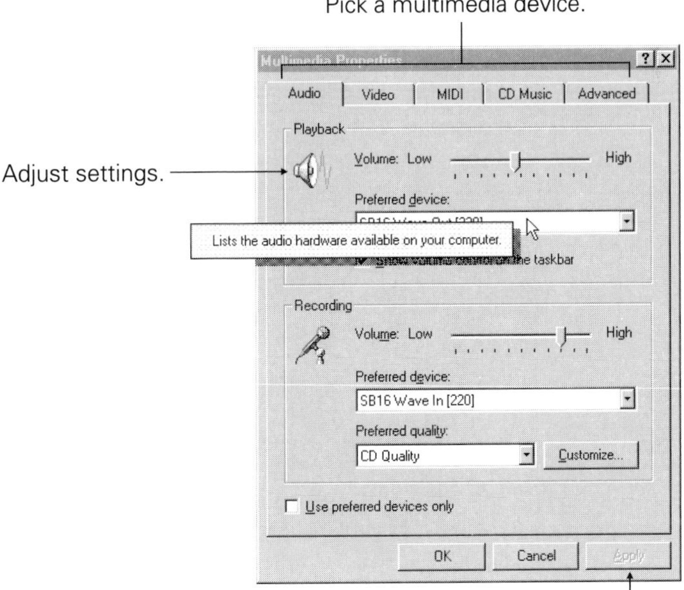

Sometimes you can preview settings changes.

You get to the Multimedia control panel by double-clicking the Multimedia icon in the Control Panel. Click the tab that interests you (Audio, Video, etc.). Use the What's This button to explore the available settings on your computer.

Viewing Artists' Credits and Other Properties

When I really enjoy a specific computer image or sound, it bugs me not to know where it came from or how to reach the artist. Microsoft has added a place to display this information and more. Let's hope it catches on. To see a multimedia file's properties, right-click on the file's icon and choose Properties. The Details tab tells you plenty of interesting things about the Goodtime video, for instance.

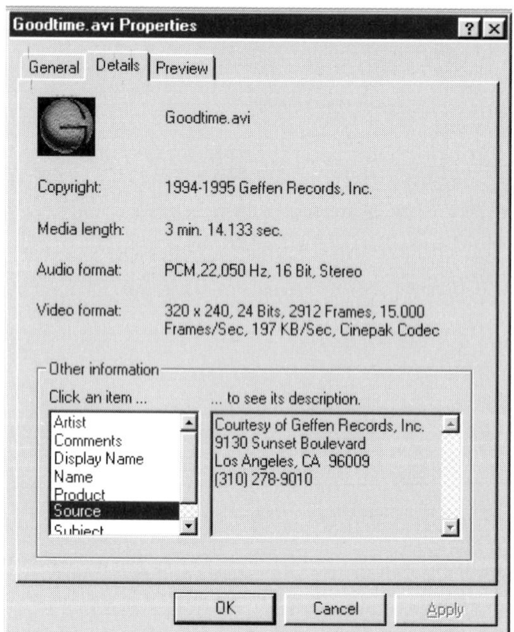

Notice that there's a Preview tab in the Properties dialog box. It plays the video when you click the Play triangle button. Cool!

Placing Multimedia Files in Your Documents

You can drag and drop or copy and paste multimedia files into many programs, including Word, Excel, and PowerPoint. A little speaker icon appears at the point where the multimedia item is pasted. For example, here's a sound file pasted in a Word memo:

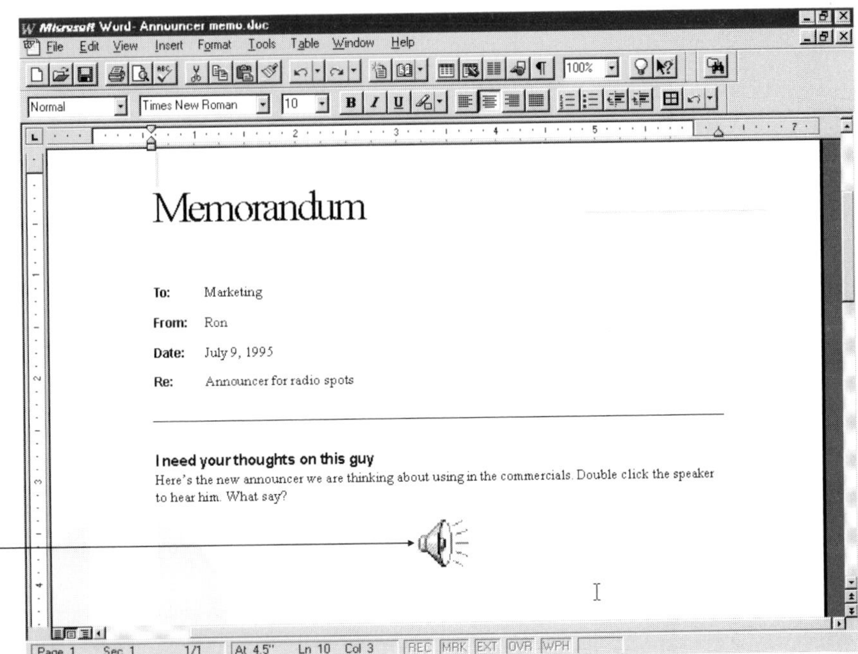

The speaker icon indicates an embedded sound file (double-click to listen).

You can just as easily include video clips in a PowerPoint slide show and have them play automatically when the appropriate slide is shown. Just remember that multimedia inserts can drastically increase the size of your document files.

Sources of Multimedia Files and Tools

There are many, many sources of multimedia files (movie clips, MIDI files, accessories, and utilities) to make your computer more multimedia savvy, etc. Here are a few places to look, just to get you started:

Source	Notes
America Online's Multimedia Zone	This section of AOL's colossal collection features lots of how-to information, tips, techniques, demos, support forums, product reviews, software library, Internet links, and more. Reach it from AOL's start-up "splash" screen, or type **Multimedia** when using AOL's Keyword command.
Multimedia World Magazine section of America Online	Here you can read the current and back issues of Multimedia World Magazine, which mostly explores CD-ROM titles of all sorts (especially multimedia games), hardware and software advancements, and more. Type **Multimedia** when using AOL's Keyword command and choose **Multimedia World Magazine.**
Multimedia Forum (America Online)	The Multimedia forum is another great place to get multimedia tips, files, and much more. Type **Multimedia** when using AOL's Keyword command and choose **PC Multimedia Forum.**
America Online's Music and Sound Forum	A good source of MIDI and other types of sound files, tips, techniques, help, and software, the Music and Sound forum at America online is worth a visit.
CompuServe's MIDI Forums	Speaking of MIDI, check out CompuServe's MIDI forums by typing **MIDI** when using the GO command.
CompuServe's Multi Media section.	Typing the word **multimedia** at CompuServe's GO prompt will display an entry screen with buttons leading to a vast collection of multimedia tips, techniques, sound files, utility programs, and more. Worth a look!
The Internet	The Net is stuffed to overflowing with multimedia-related sites. Here are just a few to get you started: Multimedia Links **http://www.cdmi.com/Lunch/multimedia.html** Index to Multimedia Information Sources **http://viswiz.gmd.de/MultimediaInfo/index.html** Free Multimedia Hyperarchive **http://idoseek.ucr.edu/hyperarchive.html**

This is where our exploration of Windows 95 draws to a close, but of course *your* adventure is really just beginning. Good luck to you!

CAUTION

Index

E

F

L

M

N

O

P

Q

R

S

T

U

V

W

Y

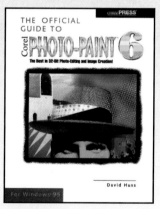

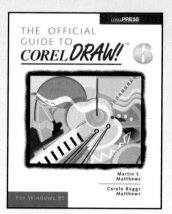

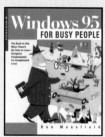